Sin

A THOMISTIC PSYCHOLOGY

STEVEN J. JENSEN

THE CATHOLIC UNIVERSITY OF AMERICA PRESS
Washington, D.C.

Copyright © 2018
The Catholic University of America Press
All rights reserved
The paper used in this publication meets the minimum requirements of
American National Standards for Information Science—Permanence
of Paper for Printed Library Materials, ANSI Z39.48-1984.
∞

Cataloging-in-Publication Data available from the Library of Congress
ISBN 978-0-8132-3033-7

~ For Roy Lepak

> *En soledad vivía,*
> *y en soledad ha puesto ya su nido,*
> *y en soledad la guía*
> *a solas su querido,*
> *también en soledad de amor herido.*
>> Juan de la Cruz

~ In memoriam
James Stromberg
1926–2017

> *A la tarde te examinarán en el amor.*
>> Juan de la Cruz

CONTENTS

Acknowledgments ix

1. The Enigma of an Evil Will — 1
2. The Order of Actions to the Ultimate End — 15
3. The Satisfaction of Desire — 41
4. Venial Sin — 66
5. The First Moral Act — 84
6. The Shared Good — 103
7. Sins of Passion — 124
8. Weakness of Will — 142
9. Sins from an Evil Will — 158
10. Sins of Ignorance — 185
11. Omissions — 194
12. The First Cause of Moral Evil — 212
13. Compatibilism or Libertarianism — 238
14. Free Decision — 260
15. Choose Life — 285

Bibliography 293
Index 301

ACKNOWLEDGMENTS

I would like to thank all those who have helped with this book. Michael Torre, as well as an anonymous reviewer, provided many valuable suggestions. My wife, Christine, whose love supports me in all of my work, supplied careful reading and correction. I would also like to thank Louise A. Mitchell for her fine work in copyediting the manuscript. For the cover art, I am indebted to Barbara Stirling, who first suggested the artwork. The beautiful cover design I owe to Anne Kachergis at Kachergis Book Design, who captured the spirit of sin perfectly. Finally, I would like to thank all those at the Catholic University of America Press who have brought this project to realization, especially John Martino, Trevor Lipscombe, Theresa Walker, and Brian Roach.

Sin

~ CHAPTER I

THE ENIGMA OF AN EVIL WILL

When he was sixteen years old, Saint Augustine joined with fellow adolescents in raiding a pear tree, taking its fruit and throwing it to the pigs. Years later Augustine reflected upon why he did this evil deed.[1] He considers the possibility that in doing evil he was seeking some good, or at least some apparent good. Perhaps he wanted the camaraderie or approval of his friends. Perhaps he wanted a feeling of power over his victim or even over God. Perhaps in some way he wanted to be like God. Augustine also dwells upon another possibility: perhaps he did the evil deed simply because it was evil.

Thomas Aquinas famously (or infamously) rejects this last possibility (as Augustine himself may have), affirming that in all of our choices we always act for some good, however confusedly perceived.[2] It follows that sin, in which we pursue what is in fact evil, must arise from some ignorance of the good. Perhaps from fear that Thomas has conceded too much to Socrates—making evil nothing other than ignorance—many have pulled

---

1. Augustine, *Confessions*, trans. Henry Chadwick (New York: Oxford University Press, 1991), 28–34.
2. See Thomas Aquinas, *Questiones disputate de malo*, q. 3, a. 12, ad s.c. 2; see also Aquinas, *Summa theologiae* I-II, q. 10, a. 2.

back from Aquinas's teaching on sin.[3] By trying to explain sin in terms of pursuit of the good (so the thought goes), Thomas has explained away sin.[4] He has failed to grasp the true essence of evil.

A CATALOGUE OF ERRORS

This supposed error is only the first of many attributed to Aquinas's treatment of sin. Otherwise friendly readers of Thomas find it difficult to accept much of what he says concerning sin. He teaches that the very first moral action of an unbaptized youth must either be an act of ordering himself to God or a mortal sin, that is, a rejection of God. But surely (the objection goes) it is absurd to suppose that a youth, or at least every youth, is so informed at the time of his first moral action as to be contemplating his order to God.[5]

Thomas teaches that those who sin from weakness do not advert, at the moment of choice, to the evil character of the action they choose. Someone who commits adultery under the influence of passion, for example, does not advert to the adulterous character of his action. Not only does Thomas (his detractors insist) thereby explain away sin; he also explains away the true character of weakness, in which a person knowingly perceives the evil of the deed but nevertheless succumbs to temptation.[6]

Thomas teaches that someone can be guilty of a sin of omission even while he sleeps, or even when he has completely forgotten about his obligation. Someone who sleeps through Mass, for instance, can be guilty—as he sleeps—of the failure to go to Mass. Has Aquinas lost sight of the

---

3. Or, at any rate, to a common interpretation of Socrates.

4. See, for instance, Carlos Steel, "Does Evil Have a Cause? Augustine's Perplexity and Thomas's Answer," *Review of Metaphysics* 48 (1994): 265–67, 273; John Langan, "Sins of Malice in the Moral Psychology of Thomas Aquinas," in *The Annual of the Society of Christian Ethics*, ed. D. M. Yeager (Washington, D.C.: Georgetown University Press, 1987), 179–98.

5. See Peter F. Ryan, "Must the Acting Person Have a Single Ultimate End?" *Gregorianum* 82 (2001): 326–39; Germain Grisez, "The True Ultimate End of Human Beings: The Kingdom, Not God Alone," *Theological Studies* 69 (2008): 48–49; Germain Grisez, "Natural Law, God, Religion, and Human Fulfillment," *American Journal of Jurisprudence* 46 (2001): 32–33.

6. See Daniel Guevara, "The Will as Practical Reason and the Problem of Akrasia," *Review of Metaphysics* 62 (2009): 525–50.

fact that sin is a voluntary action, and that what is voluntary requires some act of will?[7]

Thomas teaches that the very first cause of moral evil is a failure to consider the moral rule.[8] A person commits adultery, for instance, because he does not consider the rule that adultery should be avoided. Underlying this doctrine of Thomas is the error at the head of this catalogue of supposed errors. If we always act for some good, and if evil always presupposes some ignorance, then in some way a person who does evil must have set aside his knowledge of the moral rule.[9] However subtle Thomas may be, the objectors insist, he cannot hold the sinner responsible for what he does in ignorance.[10] By focusing upon knowledge and ignorance, Aquinas has left out the central role of the will in the explanation of sin.

Regarding the will, Thomas teaches that the will always follows upon a judgment of reason.[11] He thereby explains away, claim some, the very foundation of morality itself, namely, free will.[12] If the will must always follow the judgment of reason, then in what way is it free? Thomas makes the will simply the obedient servant of reason. His doctrine must fail (so the objection goes) because he does not give to the will the power to reject reason.

The catalogue of errors continues. Thomas teaches that when committing venial sin a person does not reject God, but then neither does he order his action to God.[13] In this regard, the objection claims, Aquinas is inconsistent with himself, for he teaches that in all we do we must order

---

7. See Michael Barnwell, *The Problem of Negligent Omissions: Medieval Action Theories to the Rescue* (Leiden: Brill, 2010), 105–12.

8. Aquinas, *De malo*, q. 1, a. 3.

9. Ibid.; Aquinas, Summa contra Gentiles III, chap. 10, no. 14.

10. See Michael Barnwell, "The Problem with Aquinas's Original Discovery," *American Catholic Philosophical Quarterly* 89 (2015): 277–91; Steel, "Does Evil Have a Cause?"; James F. Keenan, "The Problem with Thomas Aquinas's Concept of Sin," *Heythrop Journal* 35 (1994): 401–403. See also Patrick Lee ("The Relation between Intellect and Will in Free Choice According to Aquinas and Scotus," *The Thomist* 49 [1985]: 336), who presents but does not endorse this objection.

11. Aquinas, *Summa theologiae* I, q. 82, a. 4, ad 3.

12. See Thomas Williams, "The Libertarian Foundations of Scotus's Moral Philosophy," *The Thomist* 62 (1998): 193–215.

13. See Aquinas, *De malo*, q. 7, a. 5; Aquinas, *In Sent.* II, d. 38, q. 1, a. 1, ad 4.

our acts to some ultimate end.[14] It seems, however, that venial sins can have no ultimate end. On the one hand, venial sins are not ordered to God as to an ultimate end, or they would be good actions. On the other hand, they are not ordered to any creature as to an ultimate end, for if they were, then they would become mortal sins. It follows that venial sins have no ultimate end. Aquinas himself, however, insists that every action must have some ultimate end.[15]

A UNIFIED SOLUTION

These difficulties with Aquinas's teaching on sin have a certain unity to them, and their solution will be unified as well. The unity arises from Aquinas's account of the human will. Thomas teaches that the will has a certain nature, and as such it has a necessary object.

> Natural necessity is not repugnant to the will. Indeed, just as the intellect adheres to first principles, so also the will must adhere by necessity to the ultimate end, which is beatitude.... For of necessity that which belongs to a thing naturally and immovably is the foundation and principle of all else, for the nature of the thing is first in everything, and every motion proceeds from something unmovable.[16]

The will, like any other power, has a definite nature with a corresponding definite object.[17] The power of sight has a nature directed to the object of color, while the power of hearing is directed to the object of sounds. Likewise, the will must have a natural object; otherwise, it would be no power at all. Its object is beatitude or the human good. Just as the power of sight, if it is to see anything at all, must see colors, so the will, if it is to seek anything at all, must desire the good.[18] Since we desire the good only if we first are aware of it, it follows that the desires of the will always

---

14. See Ryan, "Must the Acting Person," 349–54; Grisez, "True Ultimate End," 44–46.
15. Aquinas, *Summa theologiae* I-II, q. 1, aa. 4–6.
16. Ibid., I, q. 82, a. 1. "Similiter etiam nec necessitas naturalis repugnat voluntati. Quinimmo necesse est quod, sicut intellectus ex necessitate inhaeret primis principiis, ita voluntas ex necessitate inhaereat ultimo fini, qui est beatitudo.... Oportet enim quod illud quod naturaliter alicui convenit et immobiliter, sit fundamentum et principium omnium aliorum, quia natura rei est primum in unoquoque, et omnis motus procedit ab aliquo immobili."
17. Ibid., I-II, q. 10, a. 1.
18. Ibid., I-II, q. 10, a. 2.

follow upon knowledge.[19] Most precisely, then, the object of the will is the human good as perceived by reason.

Consequently, every act of will must follow upon some judgment of reason, and even free choice is bound by the object presented through reason.[20] Furthermore, if the will must always seek good, then even while sinning, a person must be seeking some good. Whatever good he seeks, however, he cannot seek the true good, or there would be no sin.[21] He can sin, then, only if reason has presented a false good as if it were a true good. Consequently, every sin follows upon some ignorance of the good, and the first cause of moral evil must be some deficiency in the will concerning the awareness of the moral good. One such deficiency is found in sins of weakness, in which a person's passions prevent him from recognizing the sinful character of the action he chooses.[22] Another such deficiency is found in certain sins of omission, in which a person is unaware, at the moment of the sin, that he is failing in his responsibility.[23]

The difficulties concerning venial sin and the first act of the unbaptized youth both concern the ultimate end. Aquinas's teaching concerning the ultimate end, however, is simply a more detailed analysis of the will with its natural object. Everyone naturally desires his overall good, sometimes called the formality of the ultimate end.[24] When he is morally well ordered, a person identifies his overall good with the divine good. As such, in his first moral act, the unbaptized youth must decide whether to find his overall good in God or in some creaturely good.[25]

This choice, between the divine good and some creaturely substitute, is the fundamental choice between good and evil. To choose God is to choose the true good. To choose a creature as an ultimate end is to choose what is only apparently good and what is in fact evil. The essential nature of mortal sin is the rejection of the divine good while pursuing some creaturely good as the ultimate end.[26] Since the ultimate end is singular, there is no

---

19. Ibid., I, q. 80, a. 2.
20. Ibid., I-II, q. 13, a. 6; Aquinas, *De malo*, q. 6.
21. Aquinas, *Summa theologiae* I, q. 48, a. 1, ad 2; Aquinas, *De malo*, q. 1, a. 3.
22. Aquinas, *Summa theologiae* I-II, q. 77, a. 2; Aquinas, *De malo*, q. 3, a. 9.
23. Aquinas, *De malo*, q. 2, a. 1.
24. Aquinas, *Summa theologiae* I-II, q. 1, a. 7.
25. Ibid., I-II, q. 89, a. 6.
26. Aquinas, *De malo*, q. 7, a. 16; Aquinas, *Questiones disputate de caritate*, a. 6.

middle ground: one must be for God or against God, one must choose life or choose death. One must choose the good or choose mortal sin.

Venial sins, however, seem to reside in a no man's land between these two extremes. The person who commits a venial sin does not reject God nor does he set up some creaturely good as his ultimate end (otherwise, he would be sinning mortally). At the same time, he does not direct his sinful behavior to the divine good as to an ultimate end (otherwise, he would not be sinning at all but doing good).

While asking whether gluttony is a mortal sin, Thomas first identifies a mortal sin as an action that is opposed to the love of God. He then proceeds to distinguish mortal and venial sin in the case of gluttony as follows:

> The desire for pleasure can be disordered in two ways. In one way, it may exclude the order of the ultimate end, which happens when a person desires pleasure as the ultimate end. Since it is not possible for one person to have many ultimate ends, this sort of disorder is opposed to charity with regard to the love of God, who ought to be loved as the ultimate end. In another way, the desire can be disordered according to those things that are directed to the end, while saving the order of the ultimate end.[27]

Evidently, then, the difficulty surrounding venial sin—like the other difficulties discussed above—focuses upon the identity of the divine good as the ultimate end. This difficulty also, then, arises from the nature of the will, which has for its object the overall good of the individual. Its resolution, as well, demands a more complete understanding of the will and its ultimate end.

One might attempt to solve some of the above difficulties by dividing the will. On this view, the will does not have a single object but multiple objects, perhaps including the ability to choose evil.[28] Perhaps the will

---

27. Aquinas, *De malo*, q. 14, a. 2: "Concupiscentia enim huius delectabilis potest esse inordinata dupliciter. Uno modo sic quod excludat ordinem finis ultimi; quod contingit quando talem delectationem homo appetit ut finem ultimum, eo quod non est possibile unius hominis esse multos fines ultimos; et talis inordinatio repugnat caritati quantum ad dilectionem Dei, qui debet diligi ut finis ultimus. Alio modo concupiscentia potest esse inordinata secundum ea quae sunt ad finem, salvato ordine finis ultimi."

28. Christopher Toner portrays much of the history of ethics as a divide between those who maintain, like Aquinas, that the will has a unified nature, and those who maintain, like Scotus, that the will is divided. See Christopher Toner, "Angelic Sin in Aquinas and

sometimes seeks good and sometimes evil. Or perhaps the will sometimes seeks the divine good and sometimes its own good. In any event, there is no unifying good that shapes every desire of the will. Only as such, someone might think, can the freedom of the will be defended. Only as such, can the choice for evil be explained; if the will has multiple objects, then ignorance would no longer be needed to explain sin. Only as such, can venial sin be explained; if the will has multiple objects, then venial sin need not be explained in terms of the ultimate end.

Thomas, however, wishes to explain evil while insisting upon the unity of the human will. He wishes to explain evil while insisting that God made us with some nature, that God made us good. As such, he made us with a single good, and evil is simply the failure from this one good.

Can Thomas succeed in his project of explaining evil, or is he doomed to explain evil away? Is he doomed to become another Socrates, for whom (says Thomas) the only evil is ignorance?[29] Such questions underlie the current investigation, which hopes to show that Thomas can succeed. He can remain faithful to a united human nature and yet explain the evil we call sin. The focus of this investigation is upon the psychological aspects of sin, rather than upon what might be called the ontological or metaphysical aspects. The focus will not be upon the nature of adultery or the nature of murder, trying to explain what makes these actions to be evil. Rather, the focus will be upon what leads a person to commit adultery or what leads a person to commit murder. How can a person choose evil when he is made for good?

The true nature of sin is ultimately psychological. Sin is the voluntary rejection of God. In order to understand the nature of sin, then, we must understand that the sinner chooses to abandon the divine good. He does so, teaches Aquinas, because he pursues some other good in place of God. We cannot understand the nature of sin, then, nor the psychological motivation underlying it, if we do not understand the good it replaces. The human good is ultimately found in God. Good human actions are ordered to God; evil actions lack this order, substituting an alien order in its place. Any treatment of sin, then, must first begin with a treatment of the good.

Scotus and the Genesis of Some Central Objections to Contemporary Virtue Ethics," *The Thomist* 69 (2005): 79–125.

29. Aquinas, *Summa theologiae* I-II, q. 77, a. 2.

A SINGLE END

We can understand the unity of the will and of its object more completely by examining our human actions. If Anna drives to the grocery store in order to buy milk, then she orders her act of driving to the end of buying milk. This end is far from a final stopping point. Presumably, she directs the act of buying milk to something further, such as nutrition, which she directs to something further yet, such as staying alive, which she directs to something further.... Anna desires one good for the sake of another good for the sake of yet another good. At some point, however, her desires must come to some final resting point. She cannot go on forever desiring one thing for the sake of another. Ultimately, she must desire something simply for its own sake.

Every action we perform must certainly have some such stopping point. The question is not whether every action has a stopping point; the question is whether all of our actions have one and the same stopping point. Does Anna's act of driving to the grocery store have the same end as her act of studying the natural law? Both actions must have some ultimate end, but must they have the same ultimate end? Following Aristotle, Thomas thinks they must.[30]

Aristotle has been accused of a quantifier shift error. As G. E. M. Anscombe puts it, "There appears to be an illicit transition in Aristotle, from 'all chains must stop somewhere' to 'there is somewhere where all chains must stop.'"[31] In short, Aristotle concludes that everyone, in all that he does, seeks happiness.

Thomas sees no error, perhaps because he knows from experience that our various pursuits are united. The unity of our pursuits is revealed in the unity of our deliberations.[32] At some point, Anna must decide whether to set down her book on the natural law and go eat. Her decision presumes some standard by which she can judge between the diverse goods she pursues. Her life involves a wide variety of goods, and yet she deliberates concerning them all, choosing some goods over others, thus

---

30. Ibid., I-II, q. 1, a. 5.
31. G. E. M. Anscombe, *Intention*, 2nd ed. (Ithaca, N.Y.: Cornell University Press, 1963), 34.
32. Aquinas, *Summa theologiae* I-II, q. 1, a. 4.

putting order into her life. All these diverse goods, then, must fall under a single standard by which they can be compared to one another. This single standard is happiness.

In this sense, happiness refers to nothing more distinct than a general understanding of one's overall good. The idea that everyone pursues happiness is simply that everyone seeks his complete good. Each individual good he seeks, such as knowledge or pleasure, is not a full stopping point beyond which there is no further desire. Rather, each good is sought insofar as it belongs to his overall good. "Necessarily, everything that a man desires, he desires on account of the ultimate end ... Because whatever a man desires he desires under the formality of being good. And if something is not desired as the complete good, which is the ultimate end, then necessarily it is desired as tending into the complete good because the beginning of something is always ordered to its full realization."[33] Only in reference to this complete good can someone ever sort through, in his deliberations, the many goods in his life. Only in reference to this complete good does his life have unity.

Everyone by nature seeks this complete good because the good in general is the natural object of the will. Just as the power of sight has color for its object and the power of hearing has sound for its object, so the will has a natural object, which is nothing other than the overall good of the person. "The principle of voluntary movements must be something naturally willed, which is the good in common, into which the will naturally tends, as does any power into its object."[34] Aquinas sometimes says that the object of the will is the ultimate end, but more often he says that it is the good in general.[35] He does not mean some abstract notion of the good that

---

33. Ibid., I-II, q. 1, a. 6: "Necesse est quod omnia quae homo appetit, appetat propter ultimum finem. Et hoc apparet duplici ratione. Primo quidem, quia quidquid homo appetit, appetit sub ratione boni. Quod quidem si non appetitur ut bonum perfectum, quod est ultimus finis, necesse est ut appetatur ut tendens in bonum perfectum, quia semper inchoatio alicuius ordinatur ad consummationem ipsius."

34. Ibid., I-II, q. 10, a. 1: "Similiter etiam principium motuum voluntariorum oportet esse aliquid naturaliter volitum. Hoc autem est bonum in communi, in quod voluntas naturaliter tendit, sicut etiam quaelibet potentia in suum obiectum."

35. Thomas says that the object of the will is the ultimate end in *De veritate*, q. 6, a. 2; and *Summa theologiae* I-II, q. 1, a. 8, arg. 3. He says that it is the end, the good, or the good in common in several places, including *Summa theologiae* I-II, q. 1, a. 1, ad 2; and I-II, q. 1,

would include the good of trees, beetles, and squirrels. Rather, he means the *human* good in general, or even *my* good in general. "Since everything desires its own perfection, someone desires as an ultimate end that which he desires as his own complete and fulfilling good."[36] We seek not just this or that particular good, such as the good of knowledge or the good of health; rather, we seek our good in general, including both knowledge and health and other goods as well. Each individual good is perceived as good only as belonging to some overall good.[37] This greater good may be rather nondescript: I may not have any clear notion of what this overall good is. I know simply that each good is good insofar as it belongs to me, and that I, being one or a unit, must have some unified good.

This overall good can be called the ultimate end, because an individual directs all his actions and all that he desires to this overall good. It is the final resting place, beyond which there are no further desires. Everything else is desired for the sake of this complete good, but this complete good is desired for nothing further. If there were no such united end, then the individual would not be one; he would be a multitude of desires that happen to reside in one body.

THE CONCRETE REALIZATION OF THE OVERALL GOOD

According to Thomas, the ultimate end is twofold: the *ratio* of the ultimate end and that in which the end is found.[38] The *ratio*, which is often translated "formality" but might be better translated "essence," refers to the completion of the individual, what might be called his overall good. Everyone seeks this ultimate end, for everyone desires his own perfection. Everyone must seek this perfection, however, in concrete realities; some people might expect to find it in wealth, others in pleasure, others in knowledge, and so on. "That in which the ultimate end is found" refers to

---

a. 1. He also sometimes identifies the object of the will as beatitude or happiness, as in *Summa theologiae* I-II, q. 3, a. 4, ad 2; and *Summa contra Gentiles* III, chap. 26, no. 10.

36. Aquinas, *Summa theologiae* I-II, q. 1, a. 5: "Prima est quia, cum unumquodque appetat suam perfectionem, illud appetit aliquis ut ultimum finem, quod appetit, ut bonum perfectum et completivum sui ipsius."

37. Aquinas, *De malo*, q. 7, a. 10, ad 9. Aquinas, *Summa theologiae* I-II, q. 10, a. 1.

38. Aquinas, *Summa theologiae* I-II, q. 1, a. 7; I-II, q. 1, a. 8.

the particular good in which the individual expects to find his completion. As such, we will designate it the "concrete realization" of the ultimate end. In this sense, the ultimate end differs from person to person.

In our deliberations, we typically proceed from a more general consideration to a more precise determination.[39] Someone might begin by seeking the largest diamond in the world; he then discovers that this is realized in the Golden Jubilee diamond, which he now pursues. He has moved from the formality (the largest diamond) to that in which it is found (the Golden Jubilee). Someone might seek a high paying job, and then discover that actuaries get paid well; consequently, he seeks to become an actuary. He has moved from the formality to that in which it is found. This determination can take several steps. Someone might begin seeking an enjoyable evening out; he then determines that a concert would be enjoyable; finally, he determines that the concert at 8 PM at Jones Hall is the most enjoyable concert.

Similarly, we begin by seeking our good. We then realize that our good is found in health, knowledge, friendship, and so on. Next we determine that among these goods, one is highest. We then determine that our highest activity is intellectual activity. Finally, we determine that the highest object of the intellect is God.[40] We have moved from the overall good to the more precise determination, namely, that knowledge of God is our final end.

The difference between the overall good and its determination is not stark.[41] It is not as if the former refers to a mere abstraction and the latter to something entirely concrete. Both refer to a concrete reality at varying

---

39. Michael E. Bratman, *Intentions, Plans, and Practical Reason* (Cambridge, Mass: Harvard University Press, 1987), 17; see also Scott MacDonald, "Ultimate Ends in Practical Reasoning: Aquinas's Aristotelian Moral Psychology and Anscombe's Fallacy," *The Philosophical Review* 100 (1991): 59–60.

40. Aquinas, *Summa theologiae* I-II, q. 3, a. 8.

41. P. De Letter thinks that the overall good, or the formality of the ultimate end, is a mere abstraction, which must be applied to something concrete; as such, it cannot be desired; only the concrete realization can be desired (in so far as it falls under the formality); see P. De Letter, "Venial Sin and Its Final Goal," *The Thomist* 16 (1953): 36, no. 15. Garrigou-Lagrange notes, however, that even the overall good is desired as a concrete reality, although it is known only under a very broad abstract description; see Reginald Garrigou-Lagrange, "La fin ultime du péché veniél," *Revue Thomiste* 29 (1924): 315.

levels of abstraction. "My good" is still a concrete reality, even if all I know about it is that it is my overall perfection. "The vision of God" is still an abstraction from the full detail of the concrete reality; it does not include, for instance, the exact time of its realization.

The term "concrete realization," then, has a definite disadvantage. It implies that the overall good is not concrete, and it implies that the realization is indeed entirely concrete. Both are concrete in reality but abstract in consideration. Nevertheless, the term "concrete realization" is more graceful than "that in which the ultimate end is found," and it does convey the notion of being "more" concrete in consideration.

The will is the power that corresponds to the whole person, and as such it is directed naturally to the overall good of the person.[42] Nevertheless, some people seek this good in pleasure, others in riches, and still others in the knowledge of God.[43] "Every rational mind naturally desires happiness in a universal and indeterminate manner, and concerning this end it cannot fail, but the motion of the will of a creature is not determined in particular to seek happiness in this or that thing."[44]

THE ONE TRUE ULTIMATE END

Up to this point, the modern mind might feel quite comfortable with Aquinas's teaching. Certainly, our desires do seem to be unified, and we do seek some overall good. Furthermore, different people do seek their overall good in different things, whether it be wealth, power, friendship, knowledge, or something else. To each his own, as we say.

On this latter point, however, the modern mind parts company with Aquinas. As we have seen, Thomas acknowledges that different people seek their overall good in different things. Nevertheless, he does not conclude "to each his own." People do seek their overall good in different

---

42. Aquinas, *De veritate*, q. 22, a. 5, ad 3 (Editio Leonina, XXII.3: 624, ll. 238–43): "Intellectus enim etsi habeat inclinationem in aliquid non tamen nominat ipsam inclinationem hominis, sed voluntas ipsam inclinationem hominis nominat. Unde quicquid fit secundum voluntatem fit secundum hominis inclinationem."

43. Aquinas, *Summa theologiae* I-II, q. 1, a. 7.

44. Aquinas, *De veritate*, q. 24, a. 7, ad 6 (Editio Leonina, XXII.3: 698, ll. 214–19): "Felicitatem indeterminate et in universali omnis rationalis mens naturaliter appetit, et circa hoc deficere non potest, sed in particulari non est determinatus motus voluntatis creaturae ad quaerendam felicitatem in hoc vel in illo."

things, but they are often mistaken. Those who pursue wealth as the concrete realization of their ultimate end, for instance, are simply wrong.[45] Wealth will never complete the individual; it will never satisfy his desire for the overall good.

The concrete realization of the overall good is not relativistic, as if each person could decide for himself what is his chief good. Rather, human goods have a natural order to them, such that one stands above all the rest. These many goods exist for the sake of one chief good. Thomas considers and rejects many possible chief goods, such as wealth, pleasure, honor, and so on. Ultimately, he concludes that human beings are made complete only through knowledge, which is the highest of all human goods. More precisely yet, they are made complete through knowledge of God. Indeed, they are made complete through the vision of God offered to us in heaven.[46]

The good human life, then, is not realized in some hodgepodge collection of diverse goods. It is realized most completely in one highest good. All other goods must be directed to this one chief good. As we pursue health, pleasure, friendship, and so on, we must direct all of these goods to the divine good.

Aquinas's teaching on sin may be briefly summed up in terms of the concrete realization of the ultimate end, which is the knowledge of God. Actions are good insofar as they are directed to the true ultimate end; actions are evil insofar as they oppose this true ultimate end, setting up some other good as the chief good.[47] In a well-ordered life, a person loves God above all else. In a sinful life, a person loves some creature above all else, whether it be wealth or pleasure or honor or something else.

Sin is particularly mysterious because the person who pursues a disordered good has some knowledge, at least some dim glimmering, that the good he pursues is not his complete and chief good. The precise interplay of knowledge and ignorance within sin will be the focus of much of this investigation. A person must be ignorant in order to pursue a false good; at the same time, he must have knowledge in order that he might

---

45. Aquinas, *Summa theologiae* I-II, q. 2, a. 1.
46. Ibid., I-II, q. 3, a. 8.
47. See ibid., I-II, q. 73, a. 3, ad 2; I-II, q. 87, a. 4; II-II, q. 20, a. 1; Aquinas, *De malo*, q. 4, a. 2; q. 13, a. 2.

be responsible for his evil choice. Such is the corner into which Thomas is backed on account of his vision of the nature of the will. If the will has the nature of seeking the overall good of the person, then it can pursue some defective good only on account of ignorance. But ignorance takes away the voluntary nature of an action and thereby removes responsibility. A sinner must somehow be aware that he is rejecting the true good, but at the same time he cannot be aware. An evil will is indeed an enigma.

In order to unravel the mystery of sin, we must accomplish three primary tasks. First, we must begin with a clearer understanding of the good and the order of our actions to the ultimate end (chapters 2, 3, 4, 5, and 6). Second, we must examine the ways in which human beings can fail from the ultimate end (chapters 7, 8, 9, 10, and 11). Finally, we must determine in what manner human beings can be responsible for sins, despite the accompanying ignorance (chapters 12, 13, and 14).

The first task—of understanding the order to the ultimate end—will involve five parts. First, we will examine the diverse ways in which we as human beings can order our actions to an end (chapter 2). We will see that Thomas discusses three manners of ordering an action to an end: actual, virtual, and habitual. Second, we will see in what way the ultimate end satisfies or does not satisfy our desires, which will involve an investigation into the relation between inherent goods and the satisfaction of desires (chapters 3). We will discover three different accounts of this relationship, which we will call the assortment view, the aggregate view, and the strong-set view. Third, we will see that a fourth view, which we will call the weak-set view, is necessary to explain venial sins and much of what human beings actually do with their lives (chapter 4). Fourth, we will see that the order of an action to an end can take on another meaning, having less to do with the good to be achieved and more to do with the person to whose good we direct the action (chapter 5). Finally, we will develop this idea through an understanding of the ultimate end as a shared good (chapter 6).

CHAPTER 2

THE ORDER OF ACTIONS TO THE ULTIMATE END

Aquinas's notion of sin includes the idea of the order of an action to an end. Good actions are ordered to the true ultimate end; evil actions are ordered to some false or apparent good as though it were an ultimate end. Any understanding of sin, then, demands some understanding of the manner in which our actions are ordered to an ultimate end. If this point is misunderstood, then the rest of Aquinas's teaching on sin will likewise be misunderstood. Unfortunately, confusion concerning this point is not uncommon.

THE INCOHERENCE OF A SINGLE ULTIMATE END

Some of the criticisms against Thomas are directed at his account of the concrete realization of the ultimate end, that is, the beatific vision.[1]

---

1. See Grisez, "True Ultimate End," 44–53, who provides five arguments, mostly directed at the beatific vision. Two of these arguments (the second and fifth) have been addressed by Brandon Dahm, "Distinguishing Desire and Parts of Happiness: A Response to Germain Grisez," *American Catholic Philosophical Quarterly* 89 (2015): 97–114. The inconsistency of Grisez's own position with Church tradition has been addressed by Ezra Sullivan, "Seek First the Kingdom: A Reply to Germain Grisez's Account of Man's Ultimate End," *Nova et Vetera* (English) 8 (2010): 959–95.

We will address these concerns in the next chapter. Other criticisms, however, are less specific.[2] They do not object to the beatific vision as an ultimate end (or not *merely* to the beatific vision); rather, they object to the very idea that there is some one ultimate end of human life. There seems no reason (so the objection goes) that everyone must settle upon one single ultimate end. Perhaps those of a more fanatical bent will pursue pleasure in everything that they do; others will always pursue power or fame; and the saints of the world might always pursue God. Most people, however, are not so single-minded. They sometimes pursue pleasure, at other times power, and at others friendship.

Even those individuals who seem to have a dominant goal still lead lives with disparate pursuits. Consider a Mafia boss.[3] Suppose he is driven, chiefly, by the pursuit of power. Nevertheless, his diverse pursuits are not inexorably linked to this primary pursuit. Perhaps in a given day, he has competitors killed, casino funds collected, and police officers bribed, all for this single goal of power. But surely he sometimes pursues independent goals. Perhaps he has sexual relations with his consort for the sake of pleasure, or he kills his enemy for the satisfaction of revenge rather than for the sake of power. He might even do some kind deeds.[4] Perhaps he encounters a disturbed elderly woman, who is unable to pay for her bus fare, and in a moment of compassion, he buys her a ticket. It is unrealistic to suppose that the mafioso is unable to do such kind deeds. Even those who lust for power are sometimes touched by compassion for those in need.

Or consider someone on the opposite end of the spectrum from the mafioso, a kind and saintly individual. For this individual, as well, Aquinas's teaching seems unrealistic. Even the saint is not so single-minded that all his pursuits have a single goal. At times, he pursues independent goals.[5] In what Thomas calls a venial sin, for instance, the good individual might pursue some idle pleasure, or he might unreasonably defend his own reputation.

---

2. See Ryan, "Must the Acting Person." See also Grisez, "Natural Law, God, Religion," 30–33.

3. See Ryan, "Must the Acting Person," 339–41.

4. Ibid., 341–48.

5. Ibid., 349–54; Grisez, "True Ultimate End," 44–46

Of course, Thomas was not so unrealistic as to believe that saintly individuals never commit venial sins. He recognized the human weakness consequent on original sin. The question is not whether Thomas himself was realistic; it is whether his teaching concerning a single ultimate end is realistic. Does this teaching allow Thomas—if he is to remain consistent—to accept the possibility of venial sin? Again, Thomas certainly acknowledges that bad people sometimes do good deeds. The question is whether Thomas can do so consistently. Can he teach, at the abstract level, that everyone must order all of his actions to a single ultimate end, while also acknowledging, at the concrete level, that some people with evil ends at times do kind deeds?

As we will see, when Thomas is correctly understood, his teaching concerning a single ultimate end is completely consistent with the haphazard lives that we human beings sometimes lead. To perceive this consistency, however, we must clarify two concepts. Thomas teaches that everyone must order all of his actions to a single ultimate end. An explanation of this teaching demands an understanding of what it means to order an action to an end; it also demands an understanding of the character of the ultimate end.

ORDERS TO AN END: ACTUAL, VIRTUAL, AND HABITUAL

Aquinas's teaching would be very unrealistic indeed if he maintained that everyone, in everything he does, consciously keeps before his mind some ultimate goal.[6] We quite often direct our actions to a goal but do not consciously dwell upon the goal. Initially, for instance, Anna consciously directs her act of driving to her end of getting milk. As she is driving, however, she is not constantly thinking about milk but is thinking about this right turn or that left turn, of this stoplight or that stop sign; in those moments, her action is still ordered to the end of getting milk, but without conscious attention. The direction that she previously (and consciously) gave to her action of driving remains with the action, even when she does not now consciously advert to it. Peter Ryan, in his criticism of Aquinas,

---

6. Portions of the next two sections appeared originally in Steven J. Jensen, "Venial Sin and the Ultimate End," in *Aquinas's Disputed Questions on Evil: A Critical Guide*, ed. M. V. Dougherty (Cambridge: Cambridge University Press, 2016), 75–100.

gives the name "habitual" to this direction without conscious attention.[7] Anna's act of driving is "habitually" ordered to the end of getting milk, even when she is thinking nothing about milk but is focused simply upon the traffic signals and cars around her. As we will see, the terminology will have to be refined for a correct understanding of Aquinas.

Ryan thinks that the distinction between actual and "habitual" direction is insufficient to repair the inadequacies of Aquinas's view. Why? Because, observes Ryan, a "habitual" order presupposes a previous actual order.[8] Realistically, however, we cannot suppose that everyone makes such a prior conscious order of his actions to a single end. Certainly, not everyone recalls making such a conscious direction. Furthermore, many people "engage in various projects for the sake of *diverse* benefits, which they desire without regard to anything else."[9] In short, many people act without a single ultimate end; their desires have multiple stopping points, multiple final ends. The ten-year-old who plays baseball and then studies his homework pursues diverse goods; he has no thought—whether consciously or by some prior consciousness—of some single good to which everything is directed.[10]

Unfortunately, Ryan has not adequately presented the view of Aquinas. Thomas himself does use the term "habitual," but he does not mean by it the same thing as Ryan. For Ryan, a habitual order to an end is an order of an action to an end that remains from some prior conscious ordering. To such an ordering, Thomas does not give the name "habitual"; rather, he calls such directions to an end "virtual." He reserves the word "habitual" for a third kind of order to an end.

What is the difference between these three orders: actual, virtual, and habitual?[11] For an actual order to the end, a person consciously directs his action to some end, as when Anna consciously directs her act of driving to

---

7. Ryan, "Must the Acting Person," 332.
8. Ibid., 334.
9. Ibid.
10. Ibid., 335.
11. For a thorough treatment of this distinction, see Thomas M. Osborne, "The Threefold Referral of Acts to the Ultimate End in Thomas Aquinas and His Commentators," *Angelicum* 85 (2008): 715–36. Edmund Skrzypczak also discusses the relation between these three orders, which he calls intentions; see Skrzypczak, "Actual, Virtual, and Habitual Intention in St. Thomas Aquinas" (Master's thesis; Chicago, Ill.: University of Chicago, 1958).

the end of getting milk. For the virtual order, someone who has previously directed his action to an end, need not always be thinking upon this end in order to maintain the direction to the end. While driving, Anna need not be thinking about the milk; her action will retain, virtually, the order to the end of getting milk.

What, then, does Aquinas mean when he speaks of a "habitual" order to an end? Unlike the other two orders, it sometimes applies to no action at all, and it sometimes applies to actions that are not in fact ordered to the end. Thomas says, for instance, "It is one thing to order into God habitually and another to order virtually. Someone can refer habitually to God when he does nothing and when he does not actually intend anything, as someone who is sleeping. To refer something to God virtually, however, belongs to one who acts for an end, ordering it into God."[12]

Habitual order is best approached through habitual love, where we more readily perceive the concept. To love someone is to seek his good; it is, then, an instance of directing ourselves and our actions to an end, namely, to the good of another.[13] A mother loves her child sometimes in act, sometimes virtually, and sometimes habitually. She loves him in act when she is driving him to school, consciously directing the action to his good. She loves him virtually, when she is driving him to school but is not now thinking upon him, although she has previously directed the act of driving to his good. She loves him habitually throughout the day and even at night while she sleeps. This love remains with her all the time. A mother loves her son while she sleeps, while she reads a novel, and while she exercises. In the first case, she is performing no voluntary human action at all; in the second and third cases, she is performing actions that are not in fact directed to his good, or at least they are only incidentally directed to his good. She still loves her son while performing these actions, even if she has not previously directed these actions to his good. The love she has in these cases is habitual.

What, then, is habitual love? Like virtual love, it does presuppose a

---

12. Aquinas, *De virtutibus*, q. 2, a. 11, ad 3 (*Questiones disputatae*, Mandonnet, vol. 3, 308): "Aliud est habitualiter referre in Deum, et aliud virtualiter. Habitualiter enim refert in Deum et qui nihil agit, nec aliquid actualiter intendit, ut dormiens; sed virtualiter aliquid referre in Deum, est agentis propter finem ordinantis in Deum."

13. Aquinas, *Summa theologiae* I-II, q. 26, a. 4.

previous conscious act of directing oneself and one's actions to an end. Unlike virtual love, it is more an order of the person than of her actions. A habitual order is often incidental in relation to an action.[14] We can say that the mother's act of exercising is ordered to the good of her son, but it is only incidentally so, insofar as it is an action performed by someone who is ordered to his good.[15]

Habitual order has a certain staying power, such that it remains unless it is removed by some opposite action. A habitual order is a kind of plan that a person has set. It might be as simple as a plan to go to the concert tonight at 8 PM, or it might be as grand as a plan to become the CEO of a company within ten years. In any event, it is a decision we make; a course of action upon which we settle. If we have really settled upon it, then we must treat it as if it will come to be. If Kenny plans on going to a concert at 8 PM, for instance, then he cannot agree to do something else at the same time.[16] If we did not fix ourselves to a course of action, then we would become immobilized in making future decisions, for we could not determine what we are going to do at any given future point. By the nature of the case, then, a decision is something that we set in place, not to be removed.

Of course, we can change our minds. If an old friend drops by, Kenny might decide to forgo the concert in favor of a peaceful evening reminiscing upon old times. The point is simply that the decision can be removed only by another decision. It has a permanence that deliberation does not exhibit. Once setting an end, we stick with it, unless we make an act of removing it.[17] Thomas describes the sinner who has not yet developed an ingrained habit of sinning as follows: "The will of the sinner, having

---

14. Ryan claims that a habitual order must be a per se order of an action, which is true for what Ryan means by a habitual order ("Must the Acting Person," 350). Aquinas's virtual order of an action is indeed a per se order of an action, but his habitual order is not.

15. Similarly, a musician builds a house when the carpenter happens to be a musician. See, for instance, Aquinas, *De malo*, q. 1, a. 3, ad 14.

16. For a good treatment of how we form and change plans, see Bratman, *Intentions*. He treats the stability of plans—how they remain unless overturned—under the heading of "commitment" (see esp. 15–18, 30–49, 60–75, 107–10).

17. A possible exception might be negligent omissions (see Barnwell, *Problem of Negligent Omissions*), which may not involve an *explicit* decision to abandon the end. Even in that case, however, it seems that the agent at least decides to risk giving up the end.

abandoned the unchangeable good, adheres to a changeable good as to an end, and the power and inclination of this adhering remains in it until it inheres once again in the unchangeable good as in an end."[18] Or, one might add, until it rejects the changeable good for some other changeable good. We might also add that at least for some ends, the habitual order can cease to be simply because the end ceases to be. If Kenny does indeed go to the concert, then his habitual order toward going to the concert ceases to be because the concert itself has ceased to be and is a thing of the past. Even if Kenny fails to go to the concert (because he gets stuck in traffic), his habitual order still disappears, since he recognizes that the end is no longer attainable.[19]

The relation between habitual order and action is far from clear. We have said that, strictly speaking, habitual order is applied to persons and only secondarily to actions. Certainly, however, habitual orders must have something to do with actions. In relation to the concert, Kenny has a habitual order. This habitual order is itself directed to a certain action, namely, going to the concert. Furthermore, this habitual order guides other actions performed by Kenny. It leads him to buy a ticket, and it prevents

---

18. Aquinas, *De veritate*, q. 24, a. 12 (Editio Leonina, XXII.3: 777, ll. 356–60): "Voluntas tamen peccantis, derelicto incommutabili bono bono commutabili quasi fini adhaesit; et huiusmodi adhaesionis vis et inclinatio in ea manet quousque iterato bono incommutabili quasi fini inhaereat."

19. Habitual orders should not be confused with habits. Although the two have similarities, they also have differences. Most dramatically, habits can be directed to a type of action, as the habit of anger is directed to actions of anger. In contrast, a habitual order must be directed to some particular end, not just to a type of action. An angry person does not, by the fact of his habit of anger, have a habitual order to some end of anger. If he has, in the past, set the goal of getting revenge upon an enemy, then he has a habitual order to this end, but the habit of anger by itself does not provide this order. The supernatural habit of charity may be an exception. In order to have the habit of charity, a person must have directed himself to the divine good as to an ultimate end. For the habit of charity, a direction to a type of action does not suffice.

Perhaps as a consequence of this difference between type and particular end, the two also differ in our manner of attribution. We can attribute a habitual order to actions, even if only incidentally, but we cannot do the same for a habit. We can say that the mother's act of reading the book has a habitual order to the good of her son (because she herself does); we cannot say that the action has a habit of love. Habits belong only to persons, not to actions. Orders belong both to persons and to actions.

him from going to the basketball game, which conflicts with the concert. Ultimately, it seems that our habitual ends structure our daily activities, and our more remote and grand habitual ends structure our whole lives.

Habitual ends, it seems, structure other activities insofar as they become virtual ends for these activities. Kenny's habitual end of going to the concert, for instance, becomes the virtual end of the activity of buying a ticket. The goals that we have set for ourselves inevitably become the goals of other actions, for we achieve the goals we have set by way of activity. If we have really settled upon an end—and this end has thus become habitual—then we will pursue this end by way of actions—and these actions will be virtually ordered to this end. These actions, then, take on a direct relationship to the end. They do so, however, not insofar as they are habitually ordered to the end; rather, they do so insofar as they are—at the same time—virtually ordered to the end. By its nature, then, a habitual end belongs properly to persons, and it belongs only secondarily to actions. At the same time, by its nature a habitual end grows into virtual order, which belongs primarily to actions.

In our discussion of habitual order, we have not been talking about the ultimate end. We have been talking about any and all ends, including getting milk, driving a son to school, and getting a job. If Anna decides in the morning that she will later that day go get milk, and in the meantime she exercises and reads a novel, then she is still ordered to the end of getting milk, even while performing these actions. We can even say that the act of exercising is ordered to getting milk, insofar as the one who exercises is also ordered to getting milk.

When Aquinas says that all the actions of a person in the state of grace are habitually ordered to God as to an ultimate end, he does not mean that the person has previously ordered the action to the ultimate end of God but is not now consciously adverting to this order. Rather, Thomas means that the person has previously ordered *himself* (rather than *this action*) to the ultimate end of God, which order remains through all his actions, unless he changes his mind through mortal sin. Whether he orders this or that action to the divine good, consciously or virtually, is a separate question.

As we have seen, Aquinas claims that we must order all of our actions to the ultimate end. With the threefold distinction of orders, we can now clarify this teaching. Thomas does not claim that we must order all of our actions actually to the ultimate end. Indeed, he claims that it is impossible for us, in this life, consciously to order all of our actions to God.[20] Does he mean to say, then, that we must order all of our actions habitually to the ultimate end? Or does he mean to say that we must order all of our actions virtually to the ultimate end? Those who criticize Aquinas, tend to read him in this latter manner, even if they use the word "habitual" rather than "virtual."

Matters will prove to be more complicated than a simple either/or choice between these two alternatives. Nevertheless, Thomas certainly does seem to make the former of the two claims: when an individual sets some end as an ultimate end (to which all other goods are directed), then *he* has a habitual order to this end, which order can be applied to all that he does. The same might be said of the not-so-ultimate end of getting milk. The habitual order to this end applies to all that Anna does, whether she eats, sleeps, or reads a book, for she herself is ordered to this end. Likewise, if someone directs himself to the ultimate end of pleasure, then all that he does is habitually ordered to this end.

The mafioso who aims chiefly to attain power orders all of his actions to this end only in the sense that he himself is ordered to this end, so that his actions must always be at least incidentally ordered to this end as well. He might well commit adultery with only an eye to pleasure. He does not consciously order the action to power, nor has he previously ordered acts of adultery (or *this* act of adultery) to the end of power. Nevertheless, the act of adultery is directed to this end, although only incidentally. The mafioso might well help out a lady in need, not because he is consciously seeking power through this action (actual order), nor because he has previously ordered this action toward power (virtual order), but simply because he has compassion toward her. Nevertheless, the action is incidentally ordered to the end of power, insofar as the person who performs it is ordered to power (habitual order).

The objection against Aquinas seems to have something else in mind. It supposes that Thomas is claiming that everyone must order all of his actions, at least *virtually*, to a single ultimate end. When a person sets an

---

20. See, for instance, Aquinas, *De virtutibus*, q. 2, a. 11, ad 2.

ultimate end, then he directs all his actions to this end. If someone directs himself to the ultimate end of power, then everything he does, whether eating, reading, helping an old lady across the street, or going to confession, is for the sake of power. This claim is indeed highly implausible, but it is not the view of Aquinas.

What Thomas actually claims, it seems, is rather uncontroversial. Indeed, the term "ultimate" and the term "single" might readily be dropped, with little change to the doctrine. A person must direct all of his actions habitually to whatever ends he sets, however multiple those ends might be and however far removed from ultimate they might be. When Anna sets the goal of buying milk, then everything that she does is habitually ordered to this end, in the trivial sense that her actions belong to her and she herself is directed to this end. At the same time, everything she does is habitually ordered to the end of learning about the natural law, another goal that she has set. One might well wonder, then, why Aquinas would ever bother arguing that we must order all of our actions habitually to a single ultimate end.

In fact, Aquinas's argument does not concern this claim (true though it may be). Rather, he argues that we must order all of our actions *virtually* to a single ultimate end.[21] In short, Thomas seems to be making the point that the objectors, such as Ryan, attribute to him. Matters are not so straightforward, however. We pointed out earlier that the claim of Aquinas is ambiguous in two ways. First, the term "order" is ambiguous between actual, virtual, and habitual. Second, the term "ultimate end" is also ambiguous. Unless this second ambiguity is resolved, we cannot determine the precise meaning of Aquinas's claim.

THE UNITY OF THE ULTIMATE END

When Thomas states that we must order all of our actions virtually to the ultimate end, to which end does he refer? To the overall good or to the concrete realization of it? As we will see, he refers to the overall good. One way to reach this conclusion is disjunctively. If Aquinas must refer to one or the other, and if his teaching clearly rejects the concrete realization, then it remains that he must be referring to the overall good.

---

21. Aquinas, *Summa theologiae* I-II, q. 1, a. 6, ad 3.

A cursory survey of Aquinas (provided below) does indeed reveal a denial of the second disjunct: according to Thomas, at least some actions are not ordered virtually to the concrete realization of the end.

Indeed, it is not difficult to surmise that with regard to the concrete realization, Thomas is in full agreement with the objection that has been laid against him, that is, he thinks that life is full of examples of people who do not order their actions virtually to their single ultimate end, if by "ultimate end" one means the concrete realization of the ultimate end. Venial sin is a case in point, as are the diverse actions, both sinful and good, of those in a state of mortal sin. In the following texts, for instance, Aquinas reveals that those who lack charity, that is, those in a state of mortal sin, need not always direct their actions to their sinful end.

> Within an infidel is found both infidelity and the good of nature. Consequently, when an infidel does some good according to the dictate of reason, not referring it to some evil end, he does not sin.[22]

> The act of someone lacking charity can be of two sorts. First, [some acts of those who lack charity are done] precisely insofar as the person lacks charity, for example, when someone does something ordering it to that through which he lacks charity. Such actions are always evil.... Second, some acts of those who lack charity are not done precisely insofar as they lack charity; rather, the actions are done insofar as the person has some other gift of God, either faith or hope or even the good of nature, which is not entirely eliminated through sin.[23]

The following statement concerning venial sin is unambiguous, although the term "virtual order" is not explicitly used:

> In order for an action to have God or charity as its end it is not necessary to think about God or charity while performing the action. On the other hand, it does

---

22. Aquinas, *Super Epistolam ad Romanos*, chap. 14, l. 3 (Marietti, 213, no. 1141): "Sed in homine infideli cum infidelitate est bonum naturae. Et ideo cum aliquis infidelis ex dictamine rationis aliquod bonum facit, non referendo ad malum finem, non peccat."

23. Aquinas, *Summa theologiae* II-II, q. 23, a. 7, ad 1: "Ad primum ergo dicendum quod actus alicuius caritate carentis potest esse duplex. Unus quidem secundum hoc quod caritate caret, utpote cum facit aliquid in ordine ad id per quod caret caritate. Et talis actus semper est malus.... Alius autem potest esse actus carentis caritate non secundum id quod caritate caret, sed secundum quod habet aliquod aliud donum Dei, vel fidem vel spem, vel etiam naturae bonum, quod non totum per peccatum tollitur, ut supra dictum est."

not suffice for someone to have God or charity as an end only in habit (for then someone would order even venial sins into God, which is false). It is necessary that there be some prior thought upon the end, which is charity or God, and that reason ordered the subsequent actions into this end, so that the rectitude of this ordination is retained in subsequent actions.[24]

Venial sins, then, are not directed virtually to the divine good, although for a person in a state of grace they are directed *habitually* to the divine good, which is (for those in a state of grace) the concrete realization of the ultimate end.

The denial of the disjunct can be perceived in another way. Thomas teaches that an act ordered actually or virtually to an end takes on the moral character of that end. For instance, the person who gives alms for the end of vainglory ultimately does an evil action; his good deed of giving alms takes on the character of the end to which he directs it.[25] If all of our actions were directed virtually to the concrete realization of the ultimate end, then they would take on the moral character of that concrete realization. All acts of those in a state of grace would be acts of charity; all acts of those in a state of mortal sin would be mortal sins. Aquinas clearly thinks otherwise.[26]

These conclusions are in no way perplexing for Aquinas, for his true doctrine states that all actions must be ordered habitually, not virtually, to the concrete realization of the ultimate end. Actions do not take on moral character from a habitual end, for as we have seen, a habitual order is only incidentally an order of an action.[27]

Thomas does teach that we must order all of our actions, at least vir-

---

24. Aquinas, *In Sent.* II, d. 38, q. 1, a. 1, ad 4 (Mandonnet, v. 2, 969): "Ad hoc quod alicujus actionis finis sit Deus vel charitas, non oportet quod agendo illam actionem aliquis de Deo vel charitate cogitet: nec iterum sufficit quod aliquis in habitu tantum Deum et charitatem habeat, quia sic etiam actum venialis peccati aliquis in Deum ordinaret, quod falsum est: sed oportet quod prius fuerit cogitatio de fine, qui est charitas vel Deus, et quod ratio actiones sequentes in hunc finem ordinaverit; ita quod rectitudo illius ordinationis in actionibus sequentibus salvetur." See also ibid., d. 40, q. 1, a. 5, ad 7.

25. See, for instance, Aquinas, *Summa theologiae* I-II, q. 18, aa. 4, 6, and 7.

26. See, for instance, Aquinas, *In Sent.* II, d. 40, q. 1, a. 5; *De malo*, q. 2, a. 5, ad 7; *Summa theologiae* I-II, q. 114, a. 3; II-II, q. 10, a. 4.

27. For the idea that a habitual order does not provide moral character to an action, see Osborne, "Threefold Referral," 732.

tually, to the ultimate end, and he does *not* teach that we must order all of our actions, at least virtually, to the concrete realization. What he does teach, then, becomes evident: we must order all of our actions, at least virtually, to the overall good. At least this conclusion would follow, supposing that Thomas is consistent. But perhaps he is not. Perhaps his argument in fact concerns the concrete realization, but he does not consistently uphold some of its absurd conclusions.

To investigate this possibility, we must examine the text in which Thomas makes the troubling claim. *Summa theologiae, prima secundae,* question 1, concerns the ultimate end. In article 4, Aquinas argues that everyone must have an ultimate end. In article 5, he argues that no one can have multiple ultimate ends. Finally, in article 6, he argues that everyone must desire everything as ordered to this single ultimate end. In the reply to the third objection of this article, Aquinas says that we must order all of our actions, at least virtually, to the ultimate end.

Do these texts give a clear indication of what Thomas means by the ultimate end, whether the overall good or the concrete realization? Unfortunately, the answer is not immediately forthcoming, because Thomas does not make the distinction between the two senses of the ultimate end until the next article, that is, article 7. We must examine the arguments and statements in articles 5 and 6, carefully, then, to determine whether they refer to the overall good or to the concrete realization. We would expect Thomas to remain consistent in texts so closely connected. If article 5 refers to the overall good, then we should expect article 6 as well to refer to the overall good. Conversely, if article 5 refers to the concrete realization, then so should article 6.

We can begin with article 6, in which the crucial claim is made. When Aquinas argues, in article 6, that we must desire everything as ordered to the ultimate end, is he referring to the overall good or to the concrete realization? In that article, Thomas describes the ultimate end as follows: "Whatever a man desires, he desires under the formality of good. If it is not desired as the complete good, which is the ultimate end, then it must be desired as tending into the complete good."[28] Evidently, in this article

28. Aquinas, *Summa theologiae* I-II, q. 1, a. 6: "Quidquid homo appetit, appetit sub ratione boni. Quod quidem si non appetitur ut bonum perfectum, quod est ultimus finis, necesse est ut appetatur ut tendens in bonum perfectum."

Thomas is referring to the overall good, which he sometimes describes as the complete good. Nothing he says later in the article makes any reference to any concrete realization of the overall good.

The question might appear to be settled, since in the very article in which Aquinas claims that we must order all of our actions virtually to the ultimate end, he seems to be referring to the overall good rather than to the concrete realization. Doubt might be cast upon this conclusion, however, if the previous article can be shown to refer to the concrete realization. If, in article 5, Thomas argues that everyone must have a single concrete realization for his ultimate end, then it seems plausible that, in article 6, he is arguing that everyone must desire everything as ordered to this same concrete realization. Peter Ryan and Germain Grisez both make precisely this claim.[29] Article 5, they say, unquestionably refers to a single concrete realization of the ultimate end. It follows that Thomas must think that everyone is bound to order his actions to a single concrete realization of the ultimate end.

Before examining the basis for their interpretation of article 5, it is worth briefly considering another argument presented by Ryan, which suggests that the question is irrelevant, that is, it is irrelevant whether Aquinas refers (in these articles) to the overall good or to the concrete realization. The same conclusion is reached in either event. Why? Because the two ultimate ends cannot be separated. A person cannot desire the formality of the overall good without also desiring some concrete realization. Ryan's evidence for this claim is merely negative: "Nowhere does [Aquinas] suggest that it is possible to pursue perfect happiness except by pursuing something definite that one takes to be perfectly fulfilling."[30]

What Ryan says, no doubt, has some truth. Kim cannot order a pizza

---

29. See Ryan, "Must the Acting Person," 331–33. Besides the arguments addressed in this chapter, Grisez provides two arguments that I will address only in this footnote ("Natural Law, God, Religion," 29–30). First, in the *sed contra* Aquinas refers to "the belly" as the last end of the glutton, which appears to be a concrete realization. What appears in the *sed contra*, however, merely provides an indication of Aquinas's view, not an accepted argument for it. Second, in the body of the article (in the third argument), Thomas refers to the end of the will of the individual. It is far from clear how Grisez thinks that this point establishes his claim.

30. Ryan, "Must the Acting Person," 333.

without ordering some kind of pizza, such as cheese, pepperoni, mushroom, and so on. Kenny cannot buy a car without buying a car of some color, such as blue, gray, white, or red. Nor, it seems, can we have a formality of goodness that is not some concrete kind of good.

Our desires, however, can abstract from the details.[31] Kim can desire pizza without yet having settled on any particular kind of pizza. Kenny can desire a car without caring what color it might be. Ultimately, Kim will have to settle upon some kind of pizza, and Kenny will have to settle upon some color of car. Nevertheless, their desires can begin under an abstract consideration. Indeed, our desires often do. Only through deliberation do we bring our desires to the concrete level. We might begin by desiring food, and then settle upon pizza, and then settle upon pepperoni, and then settle upon a medium pizza, and so on. Nowhere in this process do we desire something abstract; rather, we desire the concrete, for that is where the good is found. What good would food be if it were abstract? Nevertheless, we can desire something concrete, such as food, under an abstract consideration. We can desire food simply as food, with no further details considered.

When it comes to the ultimate end, we never desire some abstract formality. We always desire the end as something concrete. But just as we might desire food simply insofar as it is food, so we might desire the ultimate end under no more concrete consideration than that it is our complete good.[32] Of course, the desire cannot remain at this level of abstraction. Just as Kim must settle upon some kind of pizza, so we must settle upon some more particular realization of the good. In that sense, the overall good cannot be separated from the concrete realization. We can never stop at the overall good. Nevertheless, the two can be separated, for we can start with the overall good and only then move on to the more concrete realization.

Ryan's claim concerning the inseparability of the formality and the concrete realization, then, has only limited truth. We can never stop with the desire for the formality; we must go on to the concrete realization. Nevertheless, the start of our desire can be for something under no more

---

31. Aquinas, *Summa theologiae* I-II, q. 6, a. 6.
32. Scott MacDonald, "Aquinas's Ultimate Ends: A Reply to Grisez," *American Journal of Jurisprudence* 46 (2001): 45–46.

precise consideration than that it is our overall good. We cannot, however, do the opposite. We cannot start desiring some concrete realization unless we have in some manner recognized that concrete realization as falling under our overall good. In that direction the inseparability is complete, which is just to say that we must order all of our actions virtually to our overall good.

Ultimately, then, the desire for the overall good can be separated from the desire for the concrete realization. What Thomas says of the overall good, then, might not always apply to the concrete realization. In particular, he might claim that we must order all of our actions virtually to the overall good; at the same time, he might not make a comparable claim for the concrete realization. Indeed, we have seen that he does not make the comparable claim. In many places, he claims the contrary: we are not bound to order all of our actions virtually to the concrete realization.

The question, then, cannot be dismissed by claiming that the two ends are inseparable. If Aquinas argues, in articles 5 and 6, that we must order all of our actions virtually to the overall good, then it need not follow that we must order all of our actions virtually to the concrete realization. To what Aquinas refers in these two articles—whether it be the overall good or the concrete realization—is of great consequence for understanding his claim. We have seen that article 6 appears to be discussing the overall good. Ryan and Grisez, however, have claimed that article 5 concerns the concrete realization. What basis do they give for their interpretation?

DOES ARTICLE 5 CONCERN THE OVERALL GOOD OR THE CONCRETE REALIZATION?

In a few places in article 5, Thomas appears to be referring to a concrete realization, rather than to the formality of the overall good. He says, for instance, not only that everything desires its own completion (which would be the desire for the overall good) but also that what an individual desires as an ultimate end, he desires as that which completes himself. Aquinas even talks about the impossibility of desiring "two things" as if both were a complete good.[33] Also, in a reply to an objection, Thomas explicitly states that someone can take as an ultimate end an aggregate of

---

33. Grisez, "True Ultimate End," 41.

goods, for example, someone might place his ultimate end in the aggregate of pleasure, rest, the goods of nature, and virtue.[34] Clearly, then, Aquinas thinks that the ultimate end is more than a formality of completion; it includes some concrete realization.

Or is it clear?[35] In article 5, Thomas gives three arguments for the conclusion that an individual must have a single ultimate end. Ryan and Grisez rely upon the first argument and the reply to an objection.[36] Before we turn to this first argument, it is worth looking at the two arguments that Ryan and Grisez overlook. A brief examination reveals that both arguments are irreconcilable with their interpretation of the text.

According to Aquinas's second argument, what first moves the will must be a natural desire, for the first mover of a thing is what is natural to it, just as what first moves the intellect are certain naturally known first principles. Nature itself, however, must be directed to a single end;[37] it follows that the first natural desire of the will, which is its first movement, must be directed to something one or singular. In article 4, however, we have seen that the first mover of the will is the ultimate end; consequently, the ultimate end must be one.

In this argument, to what does Thomas refer? Does he refer to the overall good or to the concrete realization of it? He cannot possibly be referring to the latter, for it is not naturally desired. What is naturally desired by the will is the completion or overall good of the individual. This desire is universal, found in everyone, as would be expected of a natural desire.[38] In this argument, then, Aquinas can be referring only to the overall good.

According to Aquinas's third argument, actions receive their species

---

34. Ryan, "Must the Acting Person," 331.

35. In fact, many authors interpret Thomas as being concerned with the unity of the overall good, not with the concrete realization. See MacDonald, "Aquinas's Ultimate Ends," 39; Fulvio Di Blasi, "Ultimate End, Human Freedom, and Beatitude: A Critique of Germain Grisez," *American Journal of Jurisprudence* 46 (2001): 115; Ralph McInerny, *Aquinas on Human Action: A Theory of Practice* (Washington, D.C.: The Catholic University of America Press, 1992), 30–31; David W. Ardagh, "Aquinas on Happiness: A Defense," *New Scholasticism* 53 (1979): 428–59.

36. Grisez, "True Ultimate End," 41; Ryan, "Must the Acting Person," 331.

37. Aquinas, *Summa theologiae* I-II, q. 9, a. 1, ad 3.

38. Ibid., I-II, q. 1, a. 7.

or characterization from their ends.[39] All human actions, then, must receive their overarching genus (of being a human action) from the ultimate end, for this end is common to all human actions. Since everything desired by the will can be unified under one genus, it follows that the last end must be one.

Once again, we can ask to what does Thomas refer? To the overall good or to the concrete realization of it? And once again, he cannot possibly be referring to the concrete realization. The divine good and pleasure can each be chosen as a concrete realization of the ultimate end, yet as such they give rise to quite distinct species of human actions, good on the one hand and evil on the other. If Aquinas were referring to the concrete realization, there would be no unifying genus for human actions.

Of the three arguments, then, only the first remains to give support to the interpretation of Ryan and Grisez. If they are correct, then in this first argument Aquinas is making a point distinct from the point he makes in the second and third arguments. In the first argument, he would be attempting to show that there must be a single concrete realization; in the second two arguments, he would be attempting to show that there must be a single overall good. Yet nowhere does Thomas indicate any shift in his meaning. He simply asserts that there are three reasons for a single point, namely, that a person cannot have multiple ultimate ends. Should we expect someone as careful as Aquinas to give, in fact, three arguments for two distinct points?

The article begins by saying, "It is impossible for the will of a single man to relate, at the same time, to diverse *things* as toward ultimate ends."[40] I have italicized the word "things" for two reasons. First, because a thing seems better to describe a concrete realization rather than a *ratio* or formality. Second, because the word is not in the Latin (and is not needed) but must be added in the English. Yet the statement, however it is translated, cannot be referring to the concrete realization, at least not exclusively, for this statement is Aquinas's general formulation, which applies to all three subsequent arguments. As we have seen, the second and third arguments refer to the overall good, not to the concrete reali-

---

39. See ibid., I-II, q. 1, a. 3.

40. "Impossibile est quod voluntas unius hominis simul se habeat ad diversa, sicut ad ultimos fines."

zation. Neither, then, can this introductory statement refer exclusively to the concrete realization.

We should be cautious, then, when we turn to the first argument. Like this introductory statement, it will prove, especially in the English, to be ambiguous, open to either interpretation. It might be arguing that each person must have a single concrete realization, but it might also be arguing, in line with the second and third arguments, that each person must aim at the overall good, which is one rather than multiple. English references to "two things" do not preclude this interpretation, no more than references to "diverse things" in the opening statement indicate that Thomas is introducing three arguments concerning the concrete realization, which clearly he is not.

The first argument begins with the following premise: "Everything desires its own completion."[41] What follows is an application of this general principle to human beings. It follows, says Aquinas, that, "someone desires as an ultimate end what (*illud*) he desires as the complete good and as what is fulfilling of him."[42] The argument might be stated briefly: all things desire their completion; therefore, human beings desire their completion.

Thomas proceeds to show that this ultimate end must satisfy all desires. Finally, he reaches the conclusion that the ultimate end must be one: "Consequently, it cannot be the case that the appetite tends into two things (duo) as if both were its complete good."[43] Essentially, Thomas is saying that if we have one thing that completes desire, then there can be nothing else added to it; to add another would imply that the first was not complete. It would be something like saying that in my library I have the complete works of Shakespeare, and I hope to get some more of his works.

Taken by itself, this first argument could refer either to the overall good or to the concrete realization. When placed next to the other two arguments, however, it seems unlikely that it alone should refer to the concrete realization. If its wording pointed exclusively to the concrete realization, then we would have to conclude that Aquinas, without realiz-

---

41. "Unumquodque appetat suam perfectionem."

42. "Illud appetit aliquis ut ultimum finem, quod appetit, ut bonum perfectum et completivum sui ipsius."

43. "Unde non potest esse quod in duo sic tendat appetitus, ac si utrumque sit bonum perfectum ipsius."

ing it himself, is arguing two distinct points in this article. But since the wording of the first argument could well refer to the overall good, there seems no reason to suppose that Aquinas made this blunder.

There remains the reply to the first objection, in which Thomas refers to an aggregate of goods. A single person, the objection argues, can place his happiness in a collection of goods, such as pleasure, wealth, the goods of nature, and virtue. Since an aggregate of goods seems to be a concrete realization, rather than a generic overall good, it seems that this objection is arguing that a single person can have multiple concrete realizations. The objection, then, presumes that Thomas is arguing for a single concrete realization.

How does Aquinas reply to this objection? He does not, in fact, argue that there can be only one concrete realization. To the contrary, he concedes that the concrete realization can be many things, such as pleasure, wealth, the goods of nature, and virtue. He argues, however, that this multiplicity has a certain unity to it. From where does it receive its unity? From the notion of a perfect or complete good. In short, it receives its unity from the overall good: "All those many things were understood, by those who placed their ultimate end in them, under the notion of a single perfect good constituted by these things."[44] In his reply to this objection, then, Aquinas is affirming that the unity of the ultimate end comes from the overall good. He does not go beyond the claim in the body of the article, clearly provided in the second and third arguments, that everyone must order his actions to the overall good.

WHAT DOES IT ALL MEAN?

In article 5, then, Thomas is making a fairly limited claim. He is claiming that our desires are united by some formality, by some overall good. In all that we desire, we desire our complete good, and this desire is for something one or singular, namely, our own completion. Aquinas is making something like what Scott MacDonald calls a conceptual truth.[45]

---

44. Aquinas, *Summa theologiae* I-II, q. 1, a. 5, ad 1: "Omnia illa plura accipiebantur in ratione unius boni perfecti ex his constituti, ab his qui in eis ultimum finem ponebant."

45. MacDonald, "Aquinas's Ultimate Ends," 38. McInerny notes, however, that Aquinas's claim is substantive and is not uncontroversial; see McInerny, *Aquinas on Human Action*, 31; see also Ardagh, "Aquinas on Happiness," 444.

He is filling in Aristotle's argument that everyone pursues happiness. In his three arguments, he shows that Aristotle's conclusion is not erroneous. Everyone does indeed pursue a single ultimate end. Thomas does not make the false claim, which he elsewhere repudiates, that everyone must order all of his actions *virtually* to some one concrete realization. On his view, however, everyone must order himself, and by association his actions as well, *habitually* to some one concrete realization, such as pleasure, money, or friendship with God.

Aquinas's doctrine, then, may be summed up in three statements, one each for the three different orders to an end. First, an action need not be actually ordered to any ultimate end, whether the overall good or the concrete realization. Second, an action (whether good or evil) must be ordered virtually to the overall good, but it need not be ordered virtually to the concrete realization. Third, an action must be ordered habitually to the concrete realization and presumably also to the overall good (although such a "habitual" order amounts to nothing more than having a human nature and a human will, since habitual order is not an order properly of the action but of the person).

The first of these three claims is unproblematic and uncontroversial. What of the next two claims? Are they contrary to common experience, as the objections of Ryan might lead us to believe? Are they internally inconsistent and incoherent?

Let us begin with the third claim, that each person must order all of his actions at least habitually to some ultimate end. We have already observed that if the words "single" and "ultimate" are dropped, then this claim is certainly unproblematic. Any time we set some goal, however far from ultimate, such as the goal to go to a concert in the evening, we are then habitually ordered to that goal, and all that belongs to us, including our actions, is incidentally ordered to that goal as well. What changes when we add the word "ultimate"? Does the claim then become controversial?

If we modify the claim so that it does not refer to everyone, but rather to most people, then it does not seem trivial but neither does it seem controversial. Most people order themselves to some ultimate good. The mafioso seeks power; the libertine seeks pleasure; the committed Christian seeks the divine good; and so on. The claim is not that these individuals order everything they do, at least virtually, to these goals (which is contrary to the second claim of Aquinas mentioned above). Rather, these individuals order *themselves* to these goals, and these goals can be described as ultimate, in the sense that they are the overriding goal around which the individuals order their lives. Other goals remain, but they are subsidiary. When the individual must decide between goals, he decides in favor of his chief good.

Must this overriding goal be "singular" or "one"? Thomas does not say. Or rather, he says that this overriding goal can be an aggregate of goods, unified only insofar as the aggregate is perceived as constituting the overall good of the person. There is no reason, for instance, why the mafioso cannot structure his life around the goal of "power and pleasure." In a sense, this goal is still "one" chief good, insofar as the two goods constitute a whole, which the mafioso perceives as the chief good that structures his life.

This claim of Aquinas, then, is a substantive claim, for it explains how people structure their lives. At the same time, it is not controversial to suppose that most people find some chief good, or set of goods, around which they structure their lives. The claim may well become controversial in the form in which Thomas maintains it, namely, that *everyone* must order their lives around some chief good. The reason for this stronger claim will become evident when we look more carefully at the second claim mentioned above.

In one sense, this second claim is fairly minimal. It maintains only that an individual, in all that he does, seeks his own good (although "his" good can include the good of others, if he is united to them). The unity of this overall good is itself fairly minimal. The individual perceives himself as a unit, so he perceives that whatever completes him is unified just insofar as it does complete himself.

Although minimal, this claim is substantive. It explains, for instance, the unity of an individual's deliberations. When a person is faced with a conflict of goods, he must resolve the conflict and settle upon one over the other. Suppose that the mafioso can now pursue pleasure in an adulterous relationship but that the relationship will ultimately undermine his power. He must decide between these two driving passions of his life. How is he to decide? If both goods belong to his single overall good, then he can judge between them based upon the merits of this one good. He might judge, for instance, that power fulfills him more than does pleasure. The judgment is based upon a single standard: what fulfills me? This fulfillment is nothing other than his overall good.

This settling of conflicts reveals why the overriding good of the third claim will tend in the direction of unity. The mafioso might well pursue an aggregate of power and pleasure combined, but when the two come into conflict, then he must settle upon one over the other. For this reason, perhaps, Aquinas maintains the strong claim that *everyone* must order himself habitually to some chief good. The force behind the second claim tends toward the third claim.

Evidently, then, the second claim—that we must order all of our actions virtually to the overall good—is not trivial. It has substantive implications concerning our deliberations. This claim, however, is controversial, at least in our day. Nevertheless, it can hardly be described as plainly contrary to common experience. Indeed, common experience does reveal a kind of unity to our deliberations. Furthermore, the following everyday experience should not be counted against this claim: when presented with various goods, we often pursue them without questioning how they fit into our overall good. Christine is presented with chocolate, and with no profound deliberations she chooses to eat it. Such everyday experiences reveal only that the order to the overall good is not always actual; it often remains virtual. In the past, Christine has recognized that the pleasure of chocolate belongs to her overall fulfillment, so now she eats the chocolate with little thought.

Within Aquinas's ethical theory, the habitual order to an end and the virtual order to an end play two distinct roles. As we have seen, the virtual order gives character to the action, while the habitual order does not. A venial sin (performed by someone in a state of grace, who has God as his ultimate end), for instance, is not virtually ordered to the divine good. If it were, then the venial sin would itself be a good action, since actions take their moral character from the ends to which they are virtually ordered. Nevertheless, the venial sin is habitually ordered to the divine good, which means simply that the person himself is ordered to the divine good as to his chief good.

Virtual order, then, gives character to actions. In contrast, habitual order gives character to the person himself. The person who is habitually ordered to the divine good is himself good, even if not all of his actions (such as venial sins) are good. The person who has ordered himself primarily to some false good, such as worldly power, is himself evil, even if he sometimes performs good actions, such as helping out a woman in difficulty. As long as a person maintains his habitual order to the divine good, then, he remains fundamentally good, in a state of grace. Only when he rejects this habitual order does he lose grace. This rejection is called a mortal sin, in which the person decides concerning a serious matter, settling for some creature rather than God.

A ten-year-old boy who plays baseball without thinking upon God does not order his action actually to the divine good. Nevertheless, he might be ordering the action virtually to the divine good.[46] If, in the past, he has recognized that good actions are ordered to the divine good, and if he has recognized that playing baseball is good, then he might well be playing baseball with a virtual order to the divine good. There is no reason to suppose that he commits a mortal sin, although he does not think upon God. It is no difficult matter for the boy to recognize that playing baseball, if nothing stands in the way, is a good action and can be ordered virtually to the divine good.

These two roles—the virtual order giving character to action and the habitual order giving character to the person—need not conflict with one another, as Ryan seems to think. A venial sin is not, for Thomas, an inexplicable enigma, in conflict with his teaching that we must order all of our actions to the ultimate end. Venial sins, like all other actions, are ordered virtually to the overall good. Nevertheless, they are not ordered to the divine good, even for those in a state of grace. Or rather, they are ordered only incidentally to the divine good, with a kind of habitual order, insofar as the person himself is ordered to the divine good.

Only by confusing these two roles can Ryan imagine another of his objections against Aquinas. Ryan claims that Aquinas leaves no room for spiritual growth. If everyone in a state of grace did indeed order all of his actions virtually to the divine good, then there might be little room for spiritual growth.[47] As it is, those in a state of grace are themselves ordered

---

46. See MacDonald, "Aquinas's Ultimate Ends," 41–42.
47. Ryan, "Must the Acting Person," 335–36.

habitually to the divine good, but not all of their actions have a virtual order to this good. As such, they often lead disjointed lives; they often pursue a multiplicity of goods, independent of the divine good. They are ready to curb these pursuits when the goods exclude the divine good (else they would commit a mortal sin), but as long as these independent goods do not eliminate the divine good, they are often pleased to pursue them. Eliminating these independent goods—ultimately seeking to subordinate everything virtually to the divine good—is the work of the spiritual life. Indeed, the spiritual life involves eliminating even the attachment to these independent goods. This account of spiritual growth may not be that which Ryan would like to see, but it is a coherent account of spiritual growth nevertheless.

A DIVIDE BETWEEN THE OVERALL GOOD AND ITS CONCRETE REALIZATION

A mystery does remain, or at least a question remains to be answered. The person who commits a venial sin seems to create an unwarranted divide between the overall good and the concrete realization. He directs the venial sin virtually to the overall good, but he does not direct it virtually to the concrete realization.

The divide might be expressed in terms of desire. The overall good, according to Thomas, is supposed to satisfy all desires. Evidently, the same cannot be said for the concrete realization. The person in a state of grace finds his concrete realization in the beatific vision, and yet he commits venial sins. What desire motivates him to commit the sins? Not a desire for the beatific vision, since venial sins are not ordered to the beatific vision (or they have only a habitual order to this end, which is really an order of the person rather than of the action). It follows that the person in a state of grace must have some desires that are not satisfied by the beatific vision, or at least he thinks they are not *when* he commits a venial sin. On the one hand, then, the overall good satisfies all his desires; on the other hand, the concrete realization of the overall good does not satisfy all his desires.

The same divide can be found in the person in a state of mortal sin. The concrete realization of his overall good is some creaturely good. Not everything he does, however, contributes to this creaturely good. At the very least, his good actions are not directed to a creaturely good as to an ultimate end, or they would not be good. What, then, motivates him to do these good actions? Not the concrete realization of his overall good. It follows that he has some desires not satisfied by his concrete realization.

The separation between the overall good and its concrete realization cannot be readily dismissed as insignificant. The concrete realization is supposed to be just that, a concrete realization, that is, it is supposed to be a more particular realization of the overall good. It seems to follow that what applies to the overall good should also apply to the concrete realization. If an isosceles triangle is a particular instance of a triangle, then an isosceles triangle should have all those attributes that belong to triangles more generally. If the concrete realization is a particular instance of the overall good, then it should have all those attributes that belong to the overall good. If the overall good satisfies all desires, then also the concrete realization should satisfy all desires.

But it does not, or at least many people act as if it does not. Aquinas's tidy account of how actions relate to the ultimate end, it seems, relies upon a fundamental logical error. It does not maintain the basic truth that what applies to the universal must also apply to the particular. Any explanation of the psychology of sin must account for this apparent error.

CHAPTER 3

THE SATISFACTION OF DESIRE

We have noted that those who sin often act as if the ultimate end does not satisfy all their desires.[1] The current chapter, however, will concern a more fundamental question surrounding the satisfaction of desires. In what manner does the true ultimate end satisfy all desires? Thomas says that the ultimate end is realized in the vision of God, which does indeed satisfy all desires.[2]

According to Germain Grisez, Aquinas is inconsistent on this point.[3] A careful reading of Aquinas, thinks Grisez, reveals that even the beatific vision leaves some desires unsatisfied. Thomas says that those now in heaven desire to have their bodies back, and he says that those in heaven love not only God and themselves but also those who are with them in heaven, indicating a desire for something beyond their own realization

---

1. Parts of this chapter were originally delivered in a talk titled, "Non nisi te, Domine," presented at the Third International Conference on Thomistic Studies at the University of St. Thomas, Santiago, Chile, July 19–21, 2016.

2. Aquinas, *Summa theologiae* I-II, q. 3, a. 8.

3. Grisez, "True Ultimate End." Grisez gives five arguments to conclude that Aquinas's insistence upon a single ultimate end is deficient. For a reply to the first, which concerns venial sins, see Jensen, "Venial Sin." For a reply to the second and fifth arguments of Grisez, see Dahm, "Distinguishing Desire."

of the beatific vision.⁴ Furthermore, he teaches that the saints in heaven pray for those on earth, but to pray for something implies the desire for something.

These details indicate, thinks Grisez, that the true concrete realization of the overall good does not in fact satisfy all desires, even on Aquinas's own admission.⁵ Aquinas faces another difficulty of consistency in his teaching on Limbo.⁶ Those in Limbo do not have the beatific vision, which alone is supposed to satisfy all desires. Nevertheless, Thomas says that those in Limbo have no unsatisfied desires.⁷

None of these difficulties have anything to do with sin. Neither those in heaven nor those in Limbo commit any sins. Consequently, these difficulties seem to indicate that even apart from sin Aquinas's teaching on the ultimate end is confused and insupportable. Since this teaching underlies his understanding of the very nature of sin, it is little surprise (so the argument contends) that his account of sin should also be confused.

These difficulties might lead someone to suspect that Aquinas's attempt to reduce all desires to a single desire is simply misguided, that is, perhaps the idea that there is one single good to which all other goods must be ordered is mistaken. Is it not more realistic to suppose that there are multiple independent goods? Is it not more realistic to suppose that no single good can satisfy all of our desires, for we all want multiple goods?

According to this objection, Aquinas's teaching concerning the ultimate end is inconsistent with a multiplicity of goods. He teaches that one chief good—the knowledge of God—satisfies all of our desires. All other goods, he maintains, must be directed to this one chief good, or else they cease to be good. If Thomas is correct, then it seems these other goods must be simply instrumental; they cannot be inherently good. If their good depends upon an order to some external object, to the vision of God, then they do not have a good of their own but only the borrowed good arising from some contribution to what is truly good.⁸ In Grisez's

---

4. See Aquinas, *Summa theologiae* I-II, q. 4, a. 5; and I-II, q. 4, a. 8.
5. Grisez, "True Ultimate End," 49–53; Grisez, "Natural Law, God, Religion," 35.
6. Grisez, "True Ultimate End," 47–48.
7. Aquinas, *De malo*, q. 5, a. 3.
8. Grisez, Finnis, and Boyle make some such argument against a unified good; see Germain Grisez, John Finnis, and Joseph M Boyle, "Practical Principles, Moral Truth, and

words, Aquinas's view, "downgrades most of the specifically human goods for which Christians hope."[9] In short, the objection claims that Aquinas makes two inconsistent claims: first, there is a multiplicity of inherent goods; second, all goods are good by order to one chief good, which good satisfies all of our desires.

A response to these concerns demands a better understanding of what it means for something to be an inherent good. Is it possible for diverse inherent goods also to be subordinated to one single good? The investigation begins with a consideration of three distinct conceptions of inherent goods and the relation of these goods to one another. These conceptions provide types or categories; they do not necessarily represent any given author.[10]

THE ASSORTMENT VIEW

The first conception of inherent goods, which we will call the assortment view, gives rise to the objection against Aquinas. Something is good in itself—according to this view—insofar as it is desired for its own sake and not for the sake of anything else. As such, it is a full stopping point. Our desire stops with an inherent good and goes no further. Knowledge is inherently good, for instance, if it is desired for its own sake and not because of anything else.

The point needs clarification, for certainly we sometimes desire knowledge for the sake of other goods. The point is not, then, that inherent goods are never desired for the sake of other goods; clearly, they are. Rather, the point is that inherent goods provide their own justification

---

Ultimate Ends," *American Journal of Jurisprudence* 32 (1987): 110. See also Grisez, "Natural Law, God, Religion," 34–35. Scott MacDonald makes a similar argument in "Ultimate Ends in Practical Reasoning," 49. The same sort of argument is often laid against Aristotle, beginning with W. F. R. Hardie who claims that Aristotle maintains an "exclusive" notion of the final good, rather than an "inclusive" notion (in "The Final Good in Aristotle's Ethics," *Philosophy* 40 [1965]: 277–95). See also Anthony Kenny, *The Aristotelian Ethics: A Study of the Relationship Between the Eudemian and Nicomachean Ethics of Aristotle* (Oxford: Clarendon Press, 1978).

9. Grisez, "Natural Law, God, Religion," 34.

10. Any given author, not having considered the diverse categories, might hold positions reflecting different aspects of multiple views. There is no need to peg a view to certain authors, although Aquinas unquestionably holds the final view.

and have no need of an order to any further good.[11] They might, in particular instances, be directed to some further good, but they remain good even without this further direction.

For this reason, so the argument goes, Thomas cannot allow for a multiplicity of inherent goods. He has only one inherent good, only one stopping point. He has a single chief good to which all other goods must be ordered. His other goods require an order to the chief good, and consequently they are not good in themselves. Thomas, then, has only one inherent good and multiple instrumental goods.

In contrast, the assortment view certainly seems to allow for a multiplicity; it is unclear, however, whether it can allow for a unity within this multiplicity. Each good is independent of the others; in what way, then, can they be united to one another?

Within the assortment view, the unity of goods does not come from the goods themselves but from the person who pursues them. In particular, the unity comes from the single power by which the person pursues the multiplicity of goods, that is, practical reason. Whether the person pursues knowledge, friendship, play, marriage, or any other inherent good, he deliberates concerning the goods and adjudicates their pursuit based upon the single power of practical reason.[12] Because this power may have certain characteristics that apply to all goods, it may turn out that certain rules derive from this unity of practical reason, for instance, perhaps it may never be permissible to attack directly any inherent good.[13] There is no need to dwell upon the details of this unity, except to note that it is pretty weak. In particular, the diverse goods are not united by any good; rather, they are united by some power directing them.

---

11. Grisez, Finnis, and Boyle seem to give some such account of inherent goods, which they call basic goods. They say that for basic goods there is no further reason for action; see Grisez, Finnis, and Boyle, "Practical Principles," 183, 133; see also Grisez, "Natural Law, God, Religion," 5.

12. Grisez, Finnis, and Boyle deny that basic goods must be ordered to one primary basic good, and they attribute any order of basic goods to the directedness of practical knowledge; see Grisez, Finnis, and Boyle, "Practical Principles," 139.

13. See Germain Grisez, *The Way of the Lord Jesus*, vol. 1, *Christian Moral Principles* (Chicago, Ill.: Franciscan Herald Press, 1983), 215–22.

THE AGGREGATE VIEW

The second conception of inherent goods, which we will call the aggregate view, differs from the assortment view, most fundamentally, concerning the unity of the goods. The diverse inherent goods, on this view, are united in a single overarching good, namely, the overall good of the person.[14] Each good, whether it be knowledge, or pleasure, or life, is a good only insofar as it belongs to the good of the whole person. When an individual pursues knowledge, then, he pursues it as part of his overall good. So also when he pursues pleasure or life. Each of these goods is good insofar as it belongs to his overall good.

This initial difference implies another profound difference between the two views. According to the assortment view, a good is inherently good insofar as it is a full stopping point, not requiring an order to anything beyond itself for its goodness. According to the aggregate view, there is only one such full stopping point, namely, the overall good of the individual; all other goods are good only insofar as they are ordered to this one overarching good. Knowledge would not be good, for instance, if it ceased to be ordered to the overall good of the individual; nevertheless, knowledge is considered an inherent good.

On this view, then, what does it mean for something to be good in itself? The subject of the good, which plays a central role in the conception of the unity of the goods, also plays a central role in the notion of something being good in itself. Something is inherently good insofar as it completes the subject. The individual has a capacity to know, so knowledge is an inherent good. Likewise, the individual has the capacity to reproduce, so reproducing is an inherent good. For each diverse capacity, there will be diverse inherent goods.

These inherent goods need not be full stopping points. Indeed, they

---

14. The following authors reflect aspects of this view. Louis Janssens, "Ontic Evil and Moral Evil," *Louvain Studies* 4 (1972): 115–56; Richard A. McCormick, *Ambiguity in Moral Choice* (Milwaukee: Marquette University Press, 1973); Bruno Schüller, "Direct Killing/Indirect Killing," in *Moral Norms an Catholic Tradition*, ed. Charles E. Curran and Richard A. McCormick (New York: Paulist Press, 1979), 137–57. Scott MacDonald also presents (but does not necessarily espouse) this view in "Aquinas's Ultimate Ends," 43-46; MacDonald, "Ultimate Ends in Practical Reasoning."

should not be. Rather, they must all be ordered to the overall completion of the individual. A completion of a part that failed to complete the whole would cease to be good. The act of contemplating the natural law as the house is burning down is not a good act, although it completes part of the individual; ultimately, it undermines the overall good of the individual.

Does it follow that these partial completions are only instrumentally good? Not at all. A merely instrumental good is defined as something that does not of itself complete the individual; rather, it conduces toward something that does complete the individual. Surgery, for instance, is not a completion of any capacity of the individual, but the health it produces is a completion of the individual.

Good in itself, then, refers to something being a completion by its nature and not by something it produces. What completes by its nature, however, need not complete the whole person in each and every instance. Something added on to the nature of a good might oppose the overall good of the person. Contemplating the natural law, by itself, does complete the individual, that is, it has an order to his overall good. When the house is burning down, however, then spending time contemplating the natural law is an obstacle to saving one's life. In this case, the contemplation ceases to be good for the person. Inherently good does not mean always good; it means good from what is within the nature of the thing; it allows for the possibility of becoming evil from what is in addition to the nature.

We can close the consideration of the aggregate view by returning to the question of unity. We have seen that the assortment view unifies diverse goods through the single power of practical reason. The opposite holds for the aggregate view. The power of practical reason is unified through a single overarching good. Practical reason can deliberate concerning knowledge, pleasure, life, reproduction, and so on, making comparisons between these diverse goods and ultimately judging between them. These feats of practical reason are possible only because all the goods are themselves united in the overall good of the individual.[15] What the person pursues in all his pursuits, in all his deliberations, is his overall good. This overarching good serves as a standard by which he can compare other goods. Since the assortment view lacks this unifying

---

15. See Di Blasi, "Ultimate End, Human Freedom," 116–17.

standard, it considers all the diverse goods incommensurable, that is, one good cannot be measured against another.[16]

THE STRONG-SET VIEW

The third view, which we will call a strongly ordered set of goods, or the strong-set view for short, develops this idea of making comparisons, providing a new standard of unity beyond the overall good of the individual. For the aggregate view, no particular good serves to unify the others; rather, only the overall good of the individual—something like an aggregate—serves to unify. In contrast, for the strong-set view, one particular good stands out above the others and provides a kind of unity. If some particular goods are better than others, as the ability to make comparisons seems to imply, then one chief good must be better than all the others. This chief good seems to answer the question, "What is most important to the individual?" Perhaps it is knowledge, perhaps it is pleasure, perhaps it is friendship. This chief good might differ from person to person, but each person must have some good that stands above the others. The concrete realization of the overall good, then, is not merely a collection of individual goods, loosely united by the subject in which they reside; rather, it is the greatest good of the subject.

On this account, then, there is a double unity to the goods. On the one hand, the overall good still provides the primary source of unity, as it did with the aggregate of goods. On the other hand, one particular good stands above the others and provides a further unity. Every pursuit is still a pursuit of the overall good of the individual. Nevertheless, no good remains good if it opposes the pursuit of the chief good. Something belongs to the overall good of the whole person only if it is consistent with the pursuit of the chief good.

Not only does the chief good stand above the rest. In addition, this chief good is the end to which all other goods must be ordered.[17] Other

---

16. Grisez, Finnis, and Boyle assert that basic goods are incommensurable; see Grisez, Finnis, and Boyle, "Practical Principles," 137; see also Grisez, "Natural Law, God, Religion," 15. While they do claim that basic goods are in some manner fulfilling of the person, they deny that there is some overarching fulfillment of the person that guides all pursuits (Grisez, Finnis, and Boyle, "Practical Principles," 133).

17. See McInerny, *Aquinas on Human Action*, 32.

inherent goods, when they lack the order to the chief good, cease to be good. Even if an action does not oppose the chief good, it still might be idle or useless—lacking any good for the individual—if it is not ordered to the chief good.

This idea is simply a development of the notion that first appeared in the aggregate view, namely, that a particular good, in order to be good, must belong to the good of the whole individual. Those things that are good in themselves belong to this overall good by what comes to them from their nature; nevertheless, they might oppose the overall good by something additional, as contemplating the natural law might prove to be an obstacle to life. For the strong-set view, this idea is further developed: no inherent good remains good if it lacks the order to the chief good. Effectively, the strong-set view develops a more precise sense of the overall good. The overall good is realized only in the chief good; all other goods are good only if they have a relation to this chief good.

An analogy may help explain the point. The good of a car is found in transportation, yet there are many secondary goods that enhance and contribute to this chief good. Some of these are more central, such as having doors, and others are more peripheral, such as having air conditioning or a stereo system. Nevertheless, all of these secondary goods are good insofar as they are ordered to the chief good of transportation. In this manner, Aquinas, who holds the strong-set view, envisions the unity of the human good. Just as a car is for transportation, so human beings are for knowledge, most especially for knowledge of God. This chief good must enter into all other goods or they cease to be good.

On this view, the idea of what is good in itself is fundamentally the same as that found in the aggregate view. It adds two things. First, it adds a stronger sense of unity between the multiple inherent goods. According to the aggregate view, diverse goods are united insofar as they belong to the overall good of the individual. According to the strong-set view, the overall good of the individual is identified chiefly with one good, so that all other goods are united by this single good.

Second, the strong-set view adds, beyond the aggregate view, the idea of greater or lesser goods. While all inherent goods complete the individual, some complete the individual more than others. Intellectual knowledge of the truth, for instance, might complete a human being more than does sensible knowledge of physical things. What is more, the individual can be identified most of all with some one capacity and its corresponding completion. If the chief good is pleasure, then the individual is most of all a pleasure-seeking animal. If the chief good is intellectual knowledge, then the person is most of all an intellectual animal. A greater unity of goods implies some greater unifying principle in the person himself.

A MULTIPLICITY OF GOODS?

Thomas clearly maintains some version of the strong-set view, in which the beatific vision is the chief good to which all other goods must be ordered.[18] The assortment view, on the other hand, gives rise to the objection against Aquinas. According to this objection, the strong-set view can allow for only one inherent good, namely, the chief good to which all the others are directed. Only knowledge—or even only the knowledge of God—is inherently good. Health and friends, relaxation and appreciation of beauty, are all good only insofar as they are ordered to this one chief good. They do not have a goodness of their own (so the objection goes), but only the goodness that comes from an order to the chief good. We must now see whether the strong-set view can consistently uphold multiple inherent goods.

The aggregate view can allow that something good in itself can be evil in some concrete situations. To the degree that something completes some capacity, it also completes the whole person. This completion, however, can be evil in some concrete situation because it can become something more; additional features can remove the order to the overall good. Knowledge is good in itself, for instance, because it completes the individual's capacity to know the truth. In concrete situations, however, it can be more than knowledge. When the house is burning down, the act of contemplating the natural law is also an obstacle to saving one's life. An inherent good, then, is good from that which it has in itself, but it can become evil from additions arising in the concrete situation. In such cases, an inherent good becomes only apparently good.[19]

---

18. For a defense of this interpretation of Aquinas, see Beatriz Bossi De Kirchner, "Aquinas as an Interpreter of Aristotle on the End of Human Life," *The Review of Metaphysics* 40 (1986): 41–54; McInerny, *Aquinas on Human Action*, 25–50; Ardagh, "Aquinas on Happiness."

19. See Lee, "Relation between Intellect and Will," 339.

Can the strong-set view take the same approach? It would seem not. According to the strong-set view, a completion is good not simply by what it has in its nature. Something additional is needed, namely, an order to the chief good. When this order is lacking, then the completion ceases to be good. The act of playing a game, for instance, is not good if it lacks the order to the chief good of contemplating God. In other words, the aggregate view can claim that an inherent good, just by what it has in its nature, with nothing additional added on, is good. The strong-set view cannot make the same claim, or so it seems. It seems wrong, however, to call something good in itself, if it is not good by what it has in itself but only by what it has by some addition. According to the strong-set view, then, it appears that nothing is inherently good except the chief good; every other good is something additional to its nature.

The response to this objection depends upon a distinction between two manners in which a good can be ordered to the overall good: consciously and nonconsciously. We have focused upon conscious order, which is actual at first but then can remain as virtual or habitual. As such, these latter two, although not actually conscious at the moment, can fall under the broad category of conscious orders.

The idea of a nonconscious order to the overall good was first introduced by the aggregate view. A completion, by what it has from its nature, belongs to the good of the person. Prior to any conscious desire on the part of the individual, the completion already has an order to the good of the person. Indeed, only through this prior order can the will then desire the inherent good with a conscious desire. In the concrete situation, this nonconscious order can be obviated by various circumstances. By its nature, knowledge of the natural law is a completion of the individual—it has an order to the overall good—but in this concrete situation, when the house is burning down, it also takes on an order opposed to the overall good, which undermines the initial order.

The strong-set view requires that individual goods have a positive order to some particular good, namely, the chief good. What is the nature of this positive order? Is it conscious or nonconscious? Our prior focus might lead us to suppose it must be a conscious order. This supposition, however, would be hasty.

Health is a completion of an individual whether he consciously desires it or not. Furthermore, health is ordered, by itself, not only to the overall good but to the true concrete realization as well. The health of an individual is directed to his good of knowing God. Just as the parts of an automobile are directed to the chief good of transportation, so the individual completions of a human being are directed to his chief good, even apart from his consciously directing them. The various completions of the car are indeed ordered to the overall good of the car. Any part of the car, with its completion, belongs to the car only insofar as it is ordered to the chief purpose.

Similarly, according to the strong-set view, particular capacities, and consequently the goods that complete them, are directed to the purpose of the whole individual. In short, particular goods have an inherent order to the chief good. The imagination, for instance, serves the purpose of presenting images to the intellect, so that the intellect can know the natures hidden therein. The body serves the purpose of having a mind that can have an imagination, and the powers of growth, nourishment, and reproduction, serve the purpose of the body.

This view implies two levels of discovery and consequently two levels of inherent good. We begin by discovering that we have various completions. They are completions of ourselves, and as such they are ordered to our overall completion. With time, we begin to recognize an order within these various completions. Some chief completion provides the reason for all the rest. We now reach a deeper understanding of these individual completions. By their nature, they are for the sake of the chief completion of the whole person.

Any particular good, such as health, can become evil by some opposite order that accrues to it in the concrete situation. Just as knowing the natural law becomes evil when it is an obstacle to escaping fire, so the inherent good of health can take on some detrimental order. In particular, it can take on a detrimental conscious order. If it is desired as a full stopping point, and not insofar as it is ordered to the chief good, then it has a harmful order attached to it. Health, precisely insofar as it is desired as the chief good, ultimately opposes the overall good of the individual. Any individual good (except the chief good) can become evil in this way. In order to avoid this evil, we must consciously desire any particular good as ordered at least virtually to the chief good. Otherwise, the particular good takes on an order unfriendly to the overall good. The good of health can remain good for the person even while he is not consciously directing it to his chief good. It becomes evil only when he consciously directs it to some false good, perhaps by desiring health itself as the false chief good. What is inherently good, then, becomes evil only by some additional contrary order.

The individual can still enjoy health as an inherent good; what he cannot do is enjoy it as if it were the chief good. Thomas says that we can enjoy something "for its own sake" in two ways. In one way, as a final cause; in another way, insofar as it has a form, or nature, that gives delight. In the first way, there is but a single good to be enjoyed for its own sake; in the second way, there can be multiple goods.

When we say that the will enjoys something for its own sake, we may understand it in two ways. In one way, insofar as "for its sake" refers to final cause, and in this manner only the ultimate end may be enjoyed for its own sake. In another way, insofar as "for its sake" refers to formal cause, and in this manner someone can enjoy for its own sake everything that gives delight according to its own form. A sick person, for instance, enjoys health for its own sake, as an end. He enjoys a sweet medicine, however, not as an end but insofar as it has a pleasurable flavor. But he in no way enjoys bitter medicine for its own sake; he takes delight in it only for the sake of something else. It follows that a man ought to enjoy God for his own sake as on account of an ultimate end, but he should enjoy virtuous actions not as an end but because of the inherent good that belongs to them, which is delightful to the virtuous man.[20]

The assortment view recognizes only the first manner in which something can be enjoyable for its own sake. Only a final end can be good in

20. Aquinas, *Summa theologiae* I-II, q. 70, a. 1, ad 2: "Cum dicitur voluntas in aliquo propter se delectari, potest intelligi dupliciter. Uno modo, secundum quod ly propter dicit causam finalem, et sic propter se non delectatur aliquis nisi in ultimo fine. Alio modo, secundum quod designat causam formalem, et sic propter se aliquis potest delectari in omni eo quod delectabile est secundum suam formam. Sicut patet quod infirmus delectatur in sanitate propter se, sicut in fine; in medicina autem suavi, non sicut in fine, sed sicut in habente saporem delectabilem; in medicina autem austera, nullo modo propter se, sed solum propter aliud. Sic igitur dicendum est quod in Deo delectari debet homo propter se, sicut propter ultimum finem, in actibus autem virtuosis, non sicut propter finem, sed propter honestatem quam continent, delectabilem virtuosis."

itself. The aggregate view and the strong-set view, however, allow for both manners in which a thing is good for its own sake.

We have, then, three views of inherent goods. According to the assortment view, an inherent good is a full stopping point for desire. There is no overarching good to which all inherent goods belong, for if there were such a good, then the inherent goods would not be full stopping points; they would be desired on account of something further; they would be desired for the overall good.

Both the aggregate view and the strong-set view share a different notion of an inherent good. An inherent good is not a full stopping point of desire. Rather, it is something that by its nature, and not by what it produces, completes part of the individual. On these views, there is an overarching good, to which all inherent goods must be ordered. The completion of some part is good only because it completes the whole. The good of the whole, then, stands as a good above the rest. On both these views, then, what is inherently good might not be good in some particular situation, because in the concrete it might oppose the overall good.

DOES THE CHIEF GOOD SATISFY ALL DESIRES?

As we turn our attention to desire and the satisfaction of desire, we can see that Aquinas's strong-set view can explain the desire for sin in terms of inherent goods that lack the order to the chief good, or even oppose the order to the chief good. As we have seen, the will by nature desires each inherent good, for each is ordered by itself to the object of the will, which is the overall good. Nevertheless, these inherent goods might prove not to be good. The will, then, has a natural desire for certain objects that can turn out to be evil. The will does not desire them insofar as they are evil; it desires them insofar as they are partial completions. Led on by this natural desire, the person can sin.

Such are the general outlines of a Thomistic psychology of sin. Before the details can be filled in, however, the difficulties surrounding the concrete realization must be addressed. Two difficulties were raised. One concerned inherent goods. It seems that Aquinas cannot present a coherent account of multiple inherent goods, for he claims that all goods must be subordinated to one chief good. This subordination, it seems, makes all other goods to be instrumental.

As we have seen, this objection is based upon a particular notion of an inherent good, namely, that advanced by the assortment view. Thomas holds a different notion of inherent goods, according to which multiple inherent goods must be subordinated to one chief good. They always remain partial completions, but they complete the whole person only with this subordination.

There remains another difficulty, which concerns the satisfaction of desires. Thomas asserts that the overall good satisfies all desires, yet it seems that the concrete realization of the overall good, despite Aquinas's claims to the contrary, does not satisfy all desires. The overall good is realized in the beatific vision, or the face-to-face knowledge of God, which is supposed to satisfy all desires. Nevertheless, individuals in heaven exhibit other desires, for example, they want their bodies back and they want the society of other people.

The result is a rift between the overall good and its concrete realization. The overall good satisfies all desires; its concrete realization does not. This rift, so the objection claims, reveals an inconsistency in Aquinas's view. If the concrete realization is indeed a realization of the overall good, then it should include everything found within the overall good. An isosceles triangle must have whatever triangles have in general; so must the concrete realization of the overall good have whatever the overall good has. But it does not. Thomas is led into this inconsistency (so the objection goes) by his insistence upon a single ultimate end. If he admitted multiple final ends, then he would not have to settle upon some one thing that satisfies all desires. As long as he maintains the unity of the ultimate end, however, either he must deny multiple inherent goods, with their attendant desires, or he must deny the satisfaction of all desires.

THE BEATIFIC VISION AND THE SATISFACTION OF DESIRES

Thomas admits that the blessed in heaven desire to have their bodies back. Does he conclude that they have a desire for some distinct good, beyond the concrete realization of the overall good? It seems not. Rather, he says that the good of the beatific vision can be realized, through a kind of overflowing, in the good of the body. In the reply to the fourth objection, he says:

The separation from the body is said to hold back the soul, so that it does not tend into the vision of the divine essence with its entire being. The soul desires to enjoy God such that its enjoyment overflows into the body, insofar as it is possible. Consequently, when the soul enjoys God without the body its desire rests in that which it has, but at the same time it wishes its body to share what it has.[21]

The blessed in heaven, then, do not have a desire for two distinct goods, the good of the beatific vision and the good of the body. Rather, they have a desire for a single good—the good of the beatific vision—but as realized in diverse ways, as realized in the soul and as realized in the body. The same conclusion may be surmised from the reply to the fifth objection: "The desire of the separated soul is entirely at rest on the part of the thing desired, because it has that which fulfills its desire, but it is not entirely at rest on the part of the one desiring, because the good is not possessed in every way that he wants to possess it. Consequently, when it has the body back, its happiness will increase extensively, but not intensively."[22]

The reply relies upon a distinction between a good thing and the possession of it. The miser wants the good of money, but what he wants about it is to possess it. Similarly, in the beatific vision, the good thing is God himself, but he is possessed most essentially through an activity of the intellect.[23] The reply makes clear that this same good may be possessed through more than the intellect.

Putting the two replies together, it seems that the divine good is possessed essentially by the act of the intellect knowing God, but that this possession can overflow and form a kind of shared possession with the body. Thomas makes a similar point in the following text, which speaks

21. Ibid., I-II, q. 4, a. 5, ad 4: "Separatio a corpore dicitur animam retardare, ne tota intentione tendat in visionem divinae essentiae. Appetit enim anima sic frui Deo, quod etiam ipsa fruitio derivetur ad corpus per redundantiam, sicut est possibile. Et ideo quandiu ipsa fruitur Deo sine corpore, appetitus eius sic quiescit in eo quod habet, quod tamen adhuc ad participationem eius vellet suum corpus pertingere."

22. Ibid., I-II, q. 4, a. 5, ad 5: "Desiderium animae separatae totaliter quiescit ex parte appetibilis, quia scilicet habet id quod suo appetitui sufficit. Sed non totaliter requiescit ex parte appetentis, quia illud bonum non possidet secundum omnem modum quo possidere vellet. Et ideo, corpore resumpto, beatitudo crescit non intensive, sed extensive."

23. Ezra Sullivan indicates that while Grisez acknowledges this distinction between two senses of an end or good, he ultimately confuses them when considering the ultimate end of the beatific vision; see Sullivan, "Seek First the Kingdom," 972–74.

of the enjoyment (or perhaps attainment) of reason being shared with other powers:

> The higher reason, whose object is that which is eternal, which it enjoys, is the principle of enjoyment, so that the soul enjoys by way of the higher reason enjoying. The enjoyment belongs to other powers, or to the essence of the soul, only by a kind of overflow, such that by way of the enjoyment of the higher reason some effect is left in the essence of the soul or in lower powers.[24]

This line of reasoning suggests that, with regard to the concrete realization of the overall good, Aquinas does not see multiplicity and unity as mutually exclusive. The concrete realization of the ultimate end may consist of a single good and yet be possessed through many goods. The single good of God—and even the single possession through the intellect—may be shared in the possession of multiple goods, for example, in the goods of the body or in the good of friendship with others.

This unity in multiplicity is most evident not in the beatific vision but in the imperfect happiness that Aquinas says can be had in this life. Most essentially this happiness consists, as with the perfect happiness of the beatific vision, in an act of the intellect, namely, in the act of understanding the truth of the world around us and of its cause, insofar as we are able.[25] To attain this chief good, many distinct inherent goods are necessary. In order to understand the truth, for instance, we must have images in the imagination, from which we can abstract the natures of things.[26] In order for the imagination to have images, we must first have sensation. In order

---

24. Aquinas, *Quodlibet* 7, q. 2 (Editio Leonina, XXV.1: 16, ll. 28–35): "Superior ratio, cuius obiectum est res eterna, qua fruendum est, est principium fruitionis, quo scilicet anima fruitur; ad alias autem uires, uel ad anime essenciam, fruitio pertingere non potest nisi per quamdam redundanciam: prout scilicet ex illa fruitione superioris rationis aliquis effectus in essencia anime uel in potenciis inferioribus relinquitur."

25. See Aquinas, *Summa theologiae* I-II, q. 3, a. 6. For discussions of imperfect happiness, see McInerny, *Aquinas on Human Action*, 33–45; Anthony J. Celano, "The Concept of Worldly Beatitude in the Writings of Thomas Aquinas," *Journal of the History of Philosophy* 25 (1987): 215–26; Patrick M. Gardner, "Thomas and Dante on the *Duo Ultima Hominis*," *The Thomist* 75 (2011): 415–59; Thomas Joseph White, "Imperfect Happiness and the Final End of Man: Thomas Aquinas and the Paradigm of Nature-Grace Orthodoxy," *The Thomist* 78 (2004): 247–89.

26. Aquinas, *Summa theologiae* I-II, q. 4, a. 5.

to have sensation, we must have bodily organs for sensation; in short, we must have an organic body.

Furthermore, the imperfect intellectual activity of this life is a good achieved only together with others in community. Our individual minds are severely limited, both in their capacity to understand and in the times in which they can understand, which leads to the need for understanding in union with others.[27] In addition, the body brings with it the necessity of death. This last limitation implies the need for reproduction and the good of a family. The limitations of a family imply the need for a yet greater community, the political community. This brief sketch provides an idea of the many inherent goods that enter into the imperfect happiness of this life.

Not every inherent good is needed at every time, nor even is every inherent good needed by every person. The overflow from the chief good to other goods, however, does not require necessity. Louis might enjoy a good meal, even though some lesser meal would have sufficed; the good meal is not necessary for his fulfillment, but it can still share in the intellectual good. Other goods can share in the chief good, then, as long as they have some order to the chief good; that order need not be the order of necessity.

Of course, if other goods oppose the chief good, then they cannot share in it. If Louis eats in excess, then he might fulfill his potential to sense flavors, as well as his potential to take enjoyment in these flavors. The realizations of these potentials are good in some respect, but not truly good for Louis overall, for they are not directed to his chief good.

The human good, then, is possessed through many distinct goods, all united under one chief good and united even under one essential possession.[28] The life of imperfect happiness is realized in this one chief good, insofar as it is possessed in many other goods. The human good is possessed essentially through knowledge, but this possession is shared through friendship, through the body, through reproduction and the family, and so on. The chief good, through its possession, characterizes all the others; it is found within all the others. Where it is not found, the other goods cease to be good.

27. Ibid., I-II, q. 4, a. 8.
28. Di Blasi also argues that the single divine good encompasses the many other goods; see Di Blasi, "Ultimate End, Human Freedom," 129–31.

The perfect happiness of the beatific vision is different. No other good, besides God possessed through intellectual vision, is at any time necessary. As we have noted, for imperfect happiness some of the lesser goods, which share in the essence of happiness, are necessary at least sometimes and at least for some people (although they can still share in happiness, even when necessity is absent). In contrast, in the beatific vision none of the lesser goods ever become necessary. We can have the vision of God without our bodies, and we can attain this vision without the society of human friends (although the friendship with God is necessary).

Thomas speaks of two ways in which diverse inherent goods can be ordered to the chief good. On the one hand, they can contribute to the attainment of the chief good. In this life, for instance, the goods of the body help us to attain knowledge of the world around us and of God. On the other hand, Thomas says that inherent goods can be ordered to the chief good not because they are necessary for its attainment but because through these goods the chief good is "had well."[29] Perhaps we might say they "enhance" the possession of the chief good. He expresses the contrasting relationship of perfections or goods in the following text: "In perfect happiness the whole human being is perfected, but the lower part is perfected through an overflow from the higher. In the imperfect happiness of the present life, in contrast, the perfection of the lower parts leads up to the perfection of the higher."[30]

We can understand the concrete realization as a collection of many goods, then, as long as we recognize that these many goods are all united through a single good. All goods must participate in this one chief good. No good is independent of the chief good. In the following text, Thomas portrays happiness—or the concrete realization of the ultimate end—as a collection of goods pointing to the one perfect operation: "Perfect happiness, such as the angels have, has a collection of all goods through union to the universal source of all good, but it does not need every single particular good. But imperfect happiness requires a collection of goods

---

29. A rendering of the somewhat enigmatic Latin, "bene esse."

30. Aquinas, *Summa theologiae* I-II, q. 3, a. 3, ad 3: "In perfecta beatitudine perficitur totus homo, sed in inferiori parte per redundantiam a superiori. In beatitudine autem imperfecta praesentis vitae, e converso a perfectione inferioris partis proceditur ad perfectionem superioris."

sufficient for the most perfect operation of this life."[31] The concrete realization of the overall good, then, is truly an ordered set; it is many goods all sharing in a single good, which overflows into the others.

Does the beatific vision, then, satisfy all desires? Yes, it does. This good of the beatific vision, however, can be possessed in diverse goods. If it is realized essentially in the good of the intellect, then it can yet be shared with other goods; it can overflow into other powers of the person. The separated soul who possesses the vision of God, then, possesses happiness most essentially, but this possession can be shared and extended. Something of "desire" remains, then, but not a desire for a new good; rather, what remains is a desire that the good already possessed be had in more ways. Brandon Dahm calls such desires, "desires from fulfillment," in contrast to desires from need or deficiency.[32] These desires do not arise from the lack of some good. Rather, they result from the attainment of some good. Once attained, the good may be shared, with other people or with oneself through a diversity of goods.

Aquinas himself distinguishes two different senses of "desire."[33] Properly speaking, desire is for something not yet possessed, and as such it is contrasted to satisfaction or enjoyment, which we take in a good that is possessed. In another sense, however, desire is a kind of overflowing of satisfaction; this desire in the broad sense, says Aquinas, coincides with the possession of the good, rather than its absence. This "desire" refers to an intense satisfaction that excludes repugnance or distaste. In this latter sense, says Thomas, even the angels desire to look upon God. Their satisfaction in God is such that they "want" it to continue, that is, they in no way want it to cease. Similarly, we might say that the blessed in heaven who do not yet have their bodies are satisfied with what they have, such that they have no repugnance to it extending to the body. In contrast, says Aquinas, the satisfaction of bodily pleasures ultimately leads to repugnance, as when someone overeats.

---

31. Ibid., I-II, q. 3, a. 3, ad 2: "Beatitudo perfecta, qualem Angeli habent, habet congregationem omnium bonorum per coniunctionem ad universalem fontem totius boni; non quod indigeat singulis particularibus bonis. Sed in hac beatitudine imperfecta, requiritur congregatio bonorum sufficientium ad perfectissimam operationem huius vitae."

32. Dahm, "Distinguishing Desire," 105.

33. Aquinas, *Summa theologiae* I-II, q. 33, a. 2.

No rift exists, then, between the overall good and the concrete realization of it. Furthermore, the desires of the blessed in heaven for their bodies, for communion with others, and for the fulfillment of their prayers are not inconsistent with Aquinas's notion of happiness. In all such cases, the blessed desire that the good they possess should be shared, either by their bodies or by others. These desires are not inconsistent with the profound fulfillment of the blessed; similarly, God's desire (when he creates) to share his goodness is not inconsistent with his own profound fulfillment. In such cases one could even put the word "desire" in scare quotes, recognizing that the "desire" is not on account of some imperfection that needs completion; rather, it is on account of a perfection that moves to overflow into further perfection.

IMPERFECT HAPPINESS AND THE SATISFACTION OF DESIRES

There remains a difficulty concerning the imperfect happiness of this life, which is supposed to be a concrete realization of the overall good; nevertheless, it does not satisfy all desires, for only the beatific vision brings our desires to rest.[34] At the natural level, then, a divide exists between the overall good and its concrete realization, that is, imperfect happiness. While the overall good satisfies all desires, imperfect happiness does not.

Thomas clearly indicates that the imperfect happiness of this life does not satisfy all desires.[35] After all, says Thomas, "Imperfect happiness does not attain [the true notion of happiness], but shares a certain particular likeness of happiness."[36] By definition, imperfect happiness is an imperfect realization of the overall good.[37]

Most importantly, imperfect happiness does not satisfy the desire to know God. By nature, says Thomas, we desire to know the causes of things and the nature of those causes. When we come to the first cause,

---

34. The ideas in this section may also apply to Grisez's concern about Limbo, since the state of Limbo is in many ways similar to the imperfect happiness in this life.

35. Aquinas, *Summa theologiae* I-II, q. 3, a. 8.

36. Ibid., I-II, q. 3, a. 6: "Oportet autem intelligere perfectam beatitudinem, quae attingit ad veram beatitudinis rationem, beatitudinem autem imperfectam, quae non attingit, sed participat quandam particularem beatitudinis similitudinem."

37. See Celano, "Concept of Worldly Beatitude," 221–24.

which is God, our minds are limited, so that we can attain only minimal understanding of God, mostly an understanding of what he is not.[38] Grace overcomes this limitation, so that those in the beatific vision perceive the very essence of God. For the imperfect happiness of this life, however, the elevation of grace is absent. Imperfect happiness, then, does not satisfy even our most fundamental desire to understand the nature of God. More precisely, imperfect happiness does attain to the *object* of God, but the *possession* of God is incomplete, so that it does not completely fulfill our desire to understand the nature of God. Imperfect happiness, then, aims at the same good as does perfect happiness. The two differ in the possession of that good. If imperfect happiness involves an imperfect possession, then in what way can it be a concrete realization of the overall good, which is supposed to satisfy all desires?

An answer to this difficulty involves a distinction between two different kinds of natural desires in the will.[39] First, we can desire something considered in itself; second, we can desire something in the concrete, as it exists here and now. The sea captain in a storm, for instance, desires to keep his cargo but ultimately chooses to jettison it for the safety of his ship. His desire to keep the cargo, then, is an imperfect kind of desire, perhaps described best as a wish; he desires to keep the cargo considered in itself. When he considers the additional detail that the cargo is a deadly weight in the storm, then he desires to jettison the cargo. His desire to jettison the cargo, then, is a perfect or complete desire, which concerns the cargo as it is here and now, in the concrete.

The desire for something considered in itself can be of two sorts. First, we can abstract from details of the object as it is realized; second, we can consider the object in a way contrary to its realization. In the latter manner, Aristotle says that we can desire—or wish for—immortality. In the strict sense, however, this desire is no desire, for ultimately we can desire only that which is possible.[40]

We can distinguish, then, between three kinds of desire. First, a com-

---

38. Aquinas, *Summa contra Gentiles* III, chap. 39, no. 1.
39. See Aquinas, *Summa theologiae* I-II, q. 6, a. 6. For a consideration of imperfect desires, see Lawrence Feingold, *The Natural Desire to See God According to St. Thomas Aquinas and His Interpreters* (Ave Maria, Fla.: Sapientia Press of Ave Maria University, 2010), 23–25.
40. Aristotle, *Nicomachean Ethics*, bk. 3, chap. 2 1111b22–26.

plete or full-fledged desire seeks the object as it exists. Second, what might be called a simple desire seeks something considered apart from particular details. Third, what might be called a velleity seeks something considered in opposition to particular details.[41] Both the simple desire and the velleity are kinds of incomplete or imperfect desires.

Thomas speaks of a natural desire both for the overall good and for particular goods of particular powers, what we have called particular inherent goods.[42] What sort of natural desire does he mean? According to Thomas, what is good in all respects—that is, the overall good—*must* be desired (at least if there is any act of desire in the will). On the other hand, particular goods, which may be good in some way but fail to be good in another, need not be desired.[43] The desire for the overall good, then, is unqualified. For this good no further consideration will remove the goodness. In contrast, the desire for any particular inherent good seems to be an imperfect desire, a desire for something considered in itself.[44] A person has a natural desire for knowledge; it does not follow that knowledge is good in all and every concrete situation. Considered in itself, knowledge is desirable, but given further consideration it might not be. The desire for knowledge becomes full-fledged only when it can be ordered, in the concrete situation, to the ultimate end, for which the person has a full-fledged desire.

The overall good, as we have seen, does not include the satisfaction of every desire for every particular good. When the house is burning down, Anna must set aside her desire to contemplate the natural law. Although

---

41. See Aquinas, *Summa theologiae* I-II, q. 13, a. 5, ad 1; Aquinas, *De malo*, q. 16, a. 3, ad 9. "Impossible" in these contexts seems to be taken quite loosely, referring to things that are literally possible but not possible to will given one's other commitments. Sometimes, however, Thomas uses the term *velleitas* to refer to any volitional desire for something considered in itself, without adding the conditional aspect; see Aquinas, *Summa theologiae* I, q. 19, a. 6, ad 1.

42. Aquinas, *Summa theologiae* I-II, q. 10, a. 1.

43. Ibid., I-II, q. 10, a. 2.

44. In much the same vein, John R. Bowlin argues that the natural desire for the overall good is a natural *intentio*, while the natural desire for particular goods is a natural *velle* ("Psychology and Theodicy in Aquinas," *Medieval Philosophy and Theology* 7 [1998]: 141–42). Unfortunately, he subsequently fails to draw a distinction in which these natural desires imply necessity (142–43).

she desires this good considered in itself, she recognizes that in the current situation it has become evil, and does not belong to her overall good. The natural desire for understanding, then, is left unsatisfied in this situation.

Nevertheless, the overall good satisfies all desires. It does not satisfy all imperfect desires, which would certainly be impossible under any conception of inherent goods. We cannot at all times be satisfying all of our desires for various goods. These desires, however, are imperfect. In contrast, the desire for the overall good is a perfect desire. When Aquinas says, then, that the overall good satisfies all desires, he is not referring to every desire (or wish) for every good considered in itself.[45]

Does the imperfect happiness of this life leave desires unsatisfied? That depends on what is meant by the word "desire." Does it mean perfect desires or the imperfect desires we call wishes? The desire for the overall good is unqualified, and it is this desire to which Thomas refers when he says that the overall good satisfies desires. Insofar as the concrete realization also satisfies all desires, it must concern a like desire, that is, a complete desire. Aquinas never implies that the overall good or its concrete realization satisfies all imperfect desires. Someone may have an imperfect desire for bodily immortality, which is not satisfied by imperfect happiness. It does not follow that imperfect happiness fails to realize something found in the overall good. No full-fledged desire is left unsatisfied.[46]

With a divine gift, of course, immortality (of the body and not merely of the soul) is indeed possible, so that in heaven we will in fact be immortal. But someone unaware of this gift, such as Aristotle, does not know that immortality (of the body) is possible. As such, he can only *wish* for immortality. His awareness of his own mortality leaves no full-fledged desire left unsatisfied, although it does leave a wish unsatisfied.

A similar point can be made concerning the knowledge of God. By our natural capacities, we cannot attain complete knowledge of God. Indeed, we can attain only very limited knowledge. Since complete knowledge is impossible, we cannot have a full-fledged desire for it; we can only wish for it. Aristotle had a natural desire to understand God completely, but

---

45. Aquinas, *Summa theologiae* I-II, q. 10, a. 1.
46. MacDonald gives a similar account of the satisfaction of desires for the concrete realization; see MacDonald, "Ultimate Ends in Practical Reasoning," 57–58.

he recognized that such understanding was impossible; his desire, then, was a mere wish. If we limit the word "desire" to full-fledged desires, then Aristotle had a natural desire to understand God in the limited way available to him.[47]

Once again, through the divine gift even our natural wishes can be satisfied, for in the beatific vision we come to complete knowledge of God. Someone such as Aristotle, however, who is unaware of the divine gift, cannot truly desire this complete knowledge. The satisfaction of all his desires, then, does not include the satisfaction of his wish for the beatific vision. By nature we are moved only to a completion that is possible, for an impossible completion is no completion at all.[48]

THE PURSUIT OF INDEPENDENT GOODS

This teaching may resolve the apparent conflict between the overall good and its concrete realization; nevertheless, it poses a difficulty for an account of sin. We have natural imperfect desires for various inherent goods. Conceivably, these imperfect desires might lead to a desire for sin. The desire for pleasure, for instance, might lead to the desire for adultery. This desire, however, is not full-fledged, and it will not lead to action unless it becomes full-fledged. The sea captain can desire to keep his cargo, so long as he considers the cargo in itself. Can this imperfect desire become a perfect desire? Not, it seems, when the cargo also happens to be a deadly weight, on account of the storm. When this further consideration is added, the cargo becomes an evil to be avoided.

Likewise, a person might desire adultery just insofar as it is pleasurable, but when the further consideration is added that adultery destroys the chief good, then the desire must be replaced by aversion. An imperfect desire becomes perfect when it is directed to the ultimate end, but the desire for adultery cannot be directed to the ultimate end, at least when the person is aware of the inconsistency between adultery and the chief good. His desire for adultery, then, can become full-fledged only if he is

---

47. See Feingold, *Natural Desire*, 27–46, 261–76. See also White, "Imperfect Happiness."

48. This point also addresses Grisez's third criticism of Aquinas's position. See Grisez, "True Ultimate End," 47–48. Those in Limbo, says Thomas, are unaware of the possibility of the beatific vision (*De malo*, q. 5, a. 3). At most, then, they have unsatisfied wishes.

unaware of the hazard it poses to his chief good. If he is ignorant of the evil of the action, however, then it seems he cannot be held responsible for the sin he commits. Aquinas's teaching on the natural desires of the will, then, seems to preclude the desire for sin.

The reality of sin seems to require some full-fledged desire that is independent of the chief good. Aquinas's strong-set view, however, allows no such independent goods. Sin, then, may involve a rejection of the strong-set view and the substitution of some other notion of inherent goods, perhaps a notion in which diverse goods have much greater independence from one another. Indeed, those in a state of mortal sin typically seem to act upon some notion of loosely connected goods. They seem to pursue a diversity of goods (some of which are in fact evil), which are not all related to some one single good.

This notion of goods independent of some chief good also seems to underlie at least some venial sins. The good desired in venial sin does not replace the chief good—which would make it mortal sin—but the person desires it nevertheless. He must suppose, then, that this good retains its goodness even when disconnected from the chief good.

Evidently, then, both those in a state of grace and those in a state of mortal sin think that the concrete realization at which they aim does not satisfy all their desires. The true concrete realization of the overall good, that is, the beatific vision, may indeed satisfy all desires, but most people, it seems, do not pursue such an overarching good. They pursue a multiplicity of goods. The conception of the good under which they operate will be best uncovered by further examining venial sins.

~⸫ CHAPTER 4

VENIAL SIN

Thomas has been accused of inconsistency in his teaching on venial sin.[1] All actions, he says, must be ordered to the one ultimate end. Venial sins appear to be an exception; they are not ordered to the ultimate end. As we have seen, however, the inconsistency is only apparent. Aquinas consistently teaches that all actions—including venial sins—must be ordered, at least virtually, to the overall good; furthermore, he consistently teaches that all actions—including venial sins—must be ordered, at least habitually, to the concrete realization. The appearance of inconsistency arises from a confusion of the two ultimate ends and of the two orders. If the overall good is not separated from the concrete realization, and if a habitual order to the end is confused with a virtual order, then it seems that venial sins are an impossibility. As long as the two ends and the two orders are kept distinct, the inconsistency disappears.

A STATE OF CONFUSION

Nevertheless, an anomaly remains, not in the thought of Aquinas but in the thought of the one who commits the venial sin, who evidently creates an unwarranted divide between the overall good and the concrete

---

1. Grisez, "True Ultimate End," 44–46; Ryan, "Must the Acting Person," 349–54.

realization.[2] If the concrete realization is indeed a concrete realization of the overall good, then when a person directs an action to the overall good he should likewise direct that action to the concrete realization. If someone seeks to attain the largest diamond in the world, and if he recognizes that the Jubilee diamond is the largest in the world (it is a kind of concrete realization of his goal), then he must seek to attain the Jubilee diamond. He cannot claim that he seeks the largest diamond while having no interest in the Jubilee diamond, which he knows to be the largest.

If the person tours the Tower of London, where the diamond is stored, and he directs this action (actually or virtually) toward attaining the largest diamond in the world, then he must also direct the action (actually or virtually) toward attaining the Jubilee diamond. Whatever he directs toward the end of attaining the largest diamond must be directed toward the end of attaining the Jubilee diamond, for he knows the two are one and the same.

The person (in a state of grace) who commits a venial sin, however, breaks this pattern of consistency. He directs his sin virtually to the overall good, but he does not direct it virtually to the divine good, which he knows to be the concrete realization of the overall good. If the beatific vision is the realization of the overall good—and he knows it—then how can he direct an action virtually to one (the overall good) but not to the other (the concrete realization)? In some sense, it seems, he must not fully recognize that the divine good is indeed the concrete realization of his overall good. At the same time, in some sense he must recognize this truth. How else could he remain in a state of grace, loving God above all else? He who commits a venial sin, then, is clearly in some state of confusion.[3]

Furthermore, he is not alone in his confusion. We have seen that those in a state of mortal sin also fail, at times, to order actions virtually to their conception of the concrete realization.[4] Someone who has set

---

2. Parts of this chapter originally appeared in Jensen, "Venial Sin and the Ultimate End."

3. See Grisez, "Natural Law, God, Religion," 31–32; Grisez, "True Ultimate End," 44–46; Ryan, "Must the Acting Person," 349–55.

4. See Grisez, "Natural Law, God, Religion," 31; Ryan, "Must the Acting Person," 339–48.

pleasure as the concrete realization of his ultimate end, for instance, still might perform actions for other ends, such as for fame or power, quite distinct from his pursuit of pleasure. Indeed, he might perform morally good actions, for instance, he might help someone in need, or he might perform acts of faith and hope. All of these actions are directed habitually to pleasure but not virtually. They are, however, directed virtually to the overall good, as all actions must be. This individual, then, has made an unwarranted divide between his overall good and his concrete realization. His belief that pleasure is the concrete realization of his overall good, then, must be mixed with confusion.

Both those who commit venial sins and those in a state of mortal sin, then, are confused. Both have identified some concrete realization of the overall good, yet both refuse in particular instances to direct their actions virtually to this concrete realization. In order to understand this common state of confusion, we will focus primarily upon venial sins, only later applying what we discover to those in a state of mortal sin.

Thomas does indeed think that venial sin involves confusion. When thinking clearly, a person should order all of his actions virtually to his overall good and to the concrete realization of this overall good. No one, thinks Thomas, can order all of his actions *actually* to the divine good.[5] Often we must be preoccupied with the work before us, and we cannot be thinking upon the divine good. When Anna drives to the grocery store, she cannot possibly keep in mind throughout her drive the goal of getting milk. She must focus upon her driving, which would be hindered if she continued to think about the milk. Likewise, when Kenny is taking a test, he must focus upon the test, and he cannot always be thinking about the divine good. So it is with other actions. We should try to order our actions actually to the divine good as much as possible, but realistically we cannot always do so.

We can, however, order all of our actions virtually to the divine good. We can and we should.[6] Kenny can recognize, before he takes the test, that it is a good action directed to the divine good, so that when he takes the test his action will be ordered virtually to the divine good. Any action

---

5. Aquinas, *Questiones disputatae de caritate*, a. 11, ad 2.
6. Ibid.

that fails to be ordered virtually to the divine good, however, is a venial sin; it is, at the very least, an idle or vain action.[7] The person recognizes that the action does not serve the divine good, yet he chooses it anyway. He thereby falls short of the ideal. When we order ourselves and our actions rightly, then, there is no divide between the overall good and the concrete realization; all our actions are ordered virtually both to the overall good and to the concrete realization of it.

How is it, then, that the person who commits a venial sin severs the overall good from the concrete realization, which he knows to be the divine good? How does the virtual order, which must belong to the overall good, disappear for the concrete realization? The answer to this riddle requires a better understanding of the difference between venial and mortal sins.

THREE KINDS OF ACTION

Both venial sin and mortal sin are, in some manner, evil or disordered actions. They differ, most notably, in their punishment.[8] Mortal sins are deserving of the eternal punishment of hell, while venial sins receive only temporary punishment, in this life or in the next. Aquinas insists, however, that this difference is incidental; the essential difference has to do with the life of grace. Mortal sin destroys the life of grace and the love of God, for it turns one against God and turns toward some creature as toward an ultimate end; in contrast, venial sin leaves the life of God intact, for it does not turn one against God.[9] Mortal sin has two elements, an aversion and a conversion; it turns one away from God and toward a creature. In contrast, venial sin has only the latter element, a conversion toward some creature.[10]

The difference between mortal and venial sin can be clarified through a threefold division of actions and their relation to an end: some actions contribute to the end, others are inconsistent with the end, and still others are neither, that is, they do not contribute to the end but neither are they inconsistent with it. Buying a ticket contributes to going to the concert at

---

7. Aquinas, *In Sent.* II, d. 38, q. 1, a. 1, ad 4; Aquinas, *De malo*, q. 2, a. 5.
8. Aquinas, *De malo*, q. 7, a. 1; Aquinas, *Summa theologiae* I-II, q. 88, a. 1.
9. Aquinas, *De malo*, q. 7, a. 1.
10. Ibid., q. 7, a. 1, ad 3; a. 2, ad 8; a. 10, ad 10.

8 PM; going to the basketball game, which begins at 7 PM, is inconsistent with it; eating at Tony's Restaurant at 5 PM does not contribute to it but neither is it inconsistent with it. In relation to the ultimate end, good actions contribute to the end, mortal sins are inconsistent with it, and venial sins neither contribute to the end nor are they inconsistent with it.

Actions that contribute to an end are good or desirable (insofar as the end itself is desirable). In contrast, actions that are inconsistent with the end are evil or to be avoided. Insofar as Kenny desires to go to the concert, he will also desire to buy a ticket. Insofar as he desires to go to the concert, he will have an aversion to going to the basketball game. Actions of the third category—actions that neither contribute to the end nor are opposed to the end—are characterized neither as good nor as evil (in relation to the end), and the person's desire for the end leads neither to desire nor to aversion. Kenny's desire to go to the concert generates no desire within him to go to Tony's Restaurant at 5 PM; at the same time, it generates no aversion.

If actions that contribute to the end are good (in relation to that end) and actions that are opposed to the end are evil, then what characterization belongs to actions of the third category? They might be described as "possible" actions. Going to Tony's Restaurant is something that Kenny *can* do while still maintaining the end of going to the concert. The word "possible," however, is ambiguous. In relation to the end of going to the concert, even good actions might be described as possible. Kenny can get to the concert by taking the subway or by driving. Both these actions, then, are possible; at the same time, both are good.

More precisely, then, actions of the third category should be described as "merely possible." They do not interfere with the end; neither do they promote the end. These actions, then, are doubly negative; they involve the denial of both of the other categories of actions. What is "possible" in a broad sense has a single negation: it is not opposed to the end. What is "merely possible" adds another negation: it does not contribute to the end.

We have, then, three kinds of actions: good, evil, and merely possible. Each term is used very broadly, in reference to any particular end (and not just the ultimate end). Buying the ticket is good, even if not morally good, insofar as it contributes to the end of going to the concert. Going to the basketball game is evil, even if not morally evil, insofar as it is opposed to going to the concert. Going to Tony's Restaurant before the concert is merely possible in relation to the end of going to the concert, although it might have another designation in relation to some other end, such as the ultimate end.

How do these three kinds of actions relate to the three kinds of orders (habitual, virtual, and actual) discussed earlier? As one might expect, evil actions can be ordered to the end in no way, neither habitually, virtually, nor actually. Going to the basketball game, for instance, cannot be ordered to the end of going to the concert in any way whatsoever.

Merely possible actions can be ordered habitually to the end (concerning which they are merely possible) but they cannot be ordered virtually or actually. Going to Tony's Restaurant can be ordered habitually to the end of going to the concert. Insofar as Kenny plans to go to the concert, he himself is directed to this end, and so are all his actions, unless he changes his mind. Going to the basketball game requires that he change his mind; going to Tony's restaurant does not. The habitual order, then, can remain. Going to Tony's Restaurant, however, in no manner contributes to the end of going to the concert, so Kenny cannot actually direct the action to this end, and if he cannot actually direct it, neither can he virtually direct it.

Finally, good actions must be directed to the end at least virtually. Only if the person is ignorant that the action is good—which means that he *believes* it to be merely possible—can the order remain merely habitual.

We have said that venial sins belong to the third category of actions, those that are merely possible in relation to the end. This identification is not quite accurate. More precisely, they belong to a subcategory of merely possible actions. Venial sins are merely possible actions that undermine the end without destroying the order to the end. If they destroyed the order, then they would belong to the category of mortally evil actions. Instead, they simply undermine or lessen the end, or perhaps more precisely, they pose an impediment to the end. Suppose that going to Tony's Restaurant will give Kenny indigestion, which will diminish his enjoyment of the concert. Going to Tony's Restaurant, then, is still merely possible in relation to the end, although it does reduce the most complete realization of the end.

Merely possible actions, then, may be divided into two categories:

some merely possible actions have no relation whatsoever to the end; other merely possible actions diminish the end but are still merely possible because they neither destroy nor promote the end. For the ultimate end, however, this division is irrelevant, for no action belongs to the first subcategory (those that have no relation whatever to the end). As we have seen, all goods belong to the ultimate end; if they lose the connection to the ultimate end, then they cease to be good. Consequently, an action that does not promote the ultimate end, but at the same time does not destroy the ultimate end, still takes something away from the good; at the very least, it occupies time that could be spent with a good action.

Aquinas clearly places mortal sins in the second category of actions, those that are inconsistent with the end, and he places venial sins in the third, those that are merely possible, although they diminish the good.

> Deliberation can concern an action that is in all ways contrary to the end, so that if it is performed then it is impossible to come to the end; these actions are mortal sins.... Deliberation can also concern that which does not exclude the end but nevertheless the end can be attained better without it, since it impedes progress to the end or disposes to a contrary end; these actions are venial sins, as when someone says an idle word, even after he has recognized that a venial sin disposes him to a mortal sin and is in some manner deficient from the rectitude of justice, which leads to God.[11]

This character of being merely possible also explains why Aquinas says that venial sins are not against the law; rather, they are apart from the law.[12] The law is a directive of reason, ordering to the end.[13] Consequently, those things that destroy the end are to be avoided and can be said to be against the law. Those things that help attain the end can be said to be according to the law. But those things that neither destroy the

---

11. Ibid., *De malo*, q. 7, a. 5 (Editio Leonina, XXIII: 173, ll. 186–98): "Deliberationem acceptatur aliquid quod est omnino contrarium fini, ut eo posito non possit ad finem perueniri; et tunc est peccatum mortale.... Cum uero acceptatur aliquid quod non excludit finem, set tamen sine eo melius ad finem perueniri possit, quia in aliquo retardat a fine, uel disponit ad contrarium finis, tunc est peccatum ueniale: puta, cum aliquis dicit uerbum otiosum, etiam deliberans quod est peccatum ueniale disponens ad mortale, et in aliquo deficiens a rectitudine iustitie, que ducit ad Deum." See also ibid., q. 7, a. 1, ad 22.

12. Ibid., q. 7, a. 1, ad 1.

13. See Aquinas, *Summa theologiae* I-II, q. 90, aa. 1 and 2.

end nor promote the end can be described neither as against the law nor as according to the law. They are, rather, apart from the law.

The character of being merely possible explains one further element of Aquinas's doctrine of venial sins. He teaches that the word "evil" applies unequally to mortal sins and venial sins.[14] Mortal sins are most properly evil, but venial sins are evil only in an analogical sense. Clearly, the second category of actions, those that are opposed to the end, might be described as evil in relation to that end. Less clearly, merely possible actions can be described as evil in relation to the end. Since they do not destroy the end, they are not strictly speaking evil, but then neither are they good, for they do not promote the end.

MERELY POSSIBLE ACTIONS AND THE ULTIMATE END

With the characterization of venial sins provided above, we can now recast the problem they pose. Merely possible actions pose no mystery for ends lesser than the ultimate end, such as the end of going to a concert. It is not surprising that Kenny should want to go to the concert and also that he should want to go to Tony's Restaurant. Kenny's life, after all, has more to it than the concert; it has many goods besides the concert that might entice him to act. The ultimate end, however, poses a special difficulty. By supposition, it is the goal to which we direct all of our actions. Any good that lacks an order to the ultimate end, we have seen, ceases to be good. Such "goods," it seems, can provide no motivation. Yet they must, if a person is indeed to commit a venial sin. When committing a venial sin, a person treats as if desirable—and therefore as if ordered to the ultimate end—that which has no order to the ultimate end.

It would be as if Kenny claimed that the only thing he wanted in life was to go to the concert; when asked why he is going to Tony's Restaurant, he replies that "at least it still allows me to go to the concert." That explains why he does not avoid Tony's Restaurant, but it in no way explains why he is pursuing it.[15] In reality, the dinner at Tony's poses no mystery,

---

14. Aquinas, *De malo*, q. 7, a. 6, ad 1; a. 1, ad 2, ad 7; Aquinas, *Summa theologiae* I-II, q. 78, a. 2, ad 1; I-II, q. 88, a. 1, ad 1.

15. Ryan rightly argues that what is called "negative causality" involved in a venial sin does not explain what positive final causality gives rise to the action; see Ryan, "Must the Acting Person," 353.

for Kenny can recognize that going to Tony's Restaurant is merely possible in relation to his plan to go to the concert, while at the same time perceiving the action as "desirable" in relation to some other end, for example, the end of enjoying food.

In contrast, the ultimate end leaves no alternative. Someone who rightly conceives the ultimate end recognizes that all other goods must be ordered to the divine good, at least virtually. Someone who commits a mortal sin misconceives the ultimate end, denying that all goods must be ordered to the divine good, for he chooses some other good in its place. The person who commits a venial sin fits into neither of these categories. He still maintains the divine good as his ultimate end. Nevertheless, he pursues goods that are not ordered to the divine good, goods that are merely possible in relation to the beatific vision. Somehow, then, he has misperceived the ultimate end without thereby entirely rejecting the ultimate end. The nature of this misperception remains to be explained.

As we have seen, a similar confusion can be found in those in a state of mortal sin. Someone who sets his heart on pleasure above all, for instance, might nevertheless perform good actions, such as helping an old lady across the street. These good actions belong to the third category, those that are merely possible in relation to the end. They do not promote pleasure; nor do they oppose the order to pleasure. What, then, provides the motivation for such actions? If pleasure is really the concrete realization of the overall good, then it seems that it must provide motivation for all of his actions. Since pleasure cannot explain these merely possible actions, such as helping the lady across the street, they remain a mystery.

Both these individuals—those who commit venial sins and those in a state of mortal sin—have a divide between their overall good, to which they order all actions virtually, and the concrete realization of it, to which some actions are not ordered virtually. What belongs to triangles in general must belong to the more particular kind; likewise, what belongs to the ultimate end in general should belong also to its concrete realization. Often, such is not the reality.

The virtual order to the end is not the only attribute belonging to the overall good that shows up missing in the concrete realization. The satisfaction of desires also disappears. As we have seen, the overall good satisfies all desires. So also, should the concrete realization satisfy all desires. Evidently, when we commit venial sins, we think otherwise. For the person who commits deliberate venial sins, it seems that the divine good, which he recognizes to be the concrete realization of the ultimate end, is one independent good among others. He thinks it is possible to satisfy two independent desires—his desire for the beatific vision and his desire for whatever satisfaction he finds in the venial sin.

THE WEAK-SET VIEW

Clearly, the individuals discussed above do not conceive the ultimate end as does Aquinas, as a well-ordered set of subordinated goods (strong-set view). Thomas can maintain a single concrete realization, such as the beatific vision, in union with other goods because these other goods, in order to retain their goodness, must always participate in the chief good. The person who deliberately chooses a venial sin, however, chooses what is merely possible (in relation to the chief good), and what is merely possible neither contributes to the chief good nor participates in the chief good.

At the same time, the person does not seem to conceive his good in the manner of the aggregate view. The person in a state of grace still maintains (habitually) the divine good as his ultimate end, despite his venial sin. The good he pursues, then, is not simply an aggregate of various goods, including the beatific vision, pleasure, reputation, security, and whatever else. The person does pursue multiple goods independently of one another, but the beatific vision has a special place among these goods. It continues to exert a kind of negative influence on the other goods. These goods are pursued only if they remain "possible" (in the broad sense), that is, only if they are consistent with the beatific vision.[16] Otherwise, the person would fall into mortal sin rather than venial sin.

It is also hard to see how he views these goods as an assortment (in the manner of the assortment view). If every good is a full stopping point, then he could not give greater priority to some goods over others. At any rate, any such priority would be arbitrary.

The good pursued, then, is not a simple aggregate but seems to be a kind of ordered set of goods. It is not, however, the strongly ordered set

---

16. As Alan Donagan points out, our intentions include plans, and plans require consistency (*Choice: The Essential Element in Human Action* [New York: Routledge and Kegan Paul, 1987], 101).

that Aquinas envisions. Like the strong-set view, the view of the person committing the venial sin does demand that the pursuit of various goods must in some manner relate to the chief good. The required relation, however, is much weaker than that of Aquinas's strong-set view. What might be called the weak-set view of the overall good requires only a negative relation to the chief good, that is, the pursuit of all other goods must be consistent with the chief good; it must not interfere with the chief good.[17]

As we have seen, for the strong-set view the ultimate end enters into and characterizes the actions ordered to it. The same can be said for the weak-set view. The characterization, however, is negative. For the weak-set view, the ultimate end assures that actions *do not* have a certain character, that is, the character of opposing the ultimate end. The person who commits a deliberate venial sin preserves, in his pursuit of other goods, something of the order to the ultimate end. His action must *not* have a particular order, namely, the order of opposition that excludes the beatific vision. In some manner, then, the beatific vision remains the chief good, even while the person, in his sin, deliberately pursues other goods.

When discussing venial sins we are forced to emphasize this negative aspect of the ultimate end. We should not forget, however, that the ultimate end shapes and structures a person's life. It does so, we have seen, by becoming the virtual end of the actions ordered to it. The person in the state of grace who acts under the weak-set view makes certain that his actions do not oppose the divine good. The ultimate end, however, plays more than this negative role. The person does much in his life to pursue the divine good. It positively shapes and characterizes many of his actions, including prayer, his relations with others, and the work he performs. While discussing venial sins, however, we must emphasize those actions that the ultimate end does not positively shape; even then, it still shapes the actions, but negatively.

Most people in a state of mortal sin also seem to maintain some version of a weak-set view. The person who pursues pleasure as his ultimate goal, for instance, does not pursue an aggregate, in which pleasure is but one good among others. In some manner, pleasure stands above the other

---

17. In this manner Di Blasi portrays the ten-year-old boy playing baseball just so long as it does not conflict with heaven; see Di Blasi, "Ultimate End, Human Freedom," 120.

goods. Pleasure exerts at least a kind of negative influence upon other goods: the other goods cannot destroy his pursuit of pleasure, even if they do not positively contribute to it. Other goods must be "possible" in relation to pleasure. If he pursues an aggregate, then, it is not a pure aggregate; it is an aggregate with some primary or chief good.

Recall that the assortment view makes no comparison between particular inherent goods, for there is no overall good by which they can be measured against one another. Each is a final stopping point, so each provides an independent standard. In contrast, the aggregate view allows for comparisons between goods, since all goods must be ordered to the overall good of the whole person. The weak-set view develops this idea of making comparisons, but does not take it so far as does the strong-set view.

In our daily pursuit of various inherent goods, we come to recognize that they often conflict with one another. The pursuit of pleasure might interfere with the pursuit of knowledge, and the pursuit of security might interfere with the pursuit of friendship. In order to resolve these disputes, we must prioritize between the goods, recognizing some as better than others. In this manner, the weak-set view—like the strong-set view—comes to recognize one chief good that stands above the others.

Nevertheless, the two views differ concerning the precise role of this chief good. For a strongly ordered set of goods, other goods must be positively ordered to the chief good; otherwise, they cease to be good. For a weakly ordered set of goods, the other goods need not be positively ordered to the chief good. Nevertheless, the other goods must retain a kind of "negative" order, that is, they cannot exclude the chief good. Otherwise, they themselves cease to be good within the ordered set. In short, other goods must be at least possible, in the broad sense, in relation to the chief good. Again, we should emphasize that the ultimate end, even for the weak-set view, often does positively characterize many actions in a person's life.

Within the weak-set view, diverse goods are not so unified as are goods within the strong-set view. Both these views share the unity found within the aggregate view, according to which all goods are good only insofar as they belong to the overall good of the person. The strong-set view adds another unity, namely, all particular goods must be unified by a chief particular good, which is the concrete realization of the overall good. The weak-set view also adds another unity, although it is a minimal unity. While all particular goods of an individual are good insofar as they belong to his overall good, they are not all equally good. Among the many competing goods, he settles upon one that most of all fulfills him. The other goods must relate at least minimally to this one chief good. They must, so to speak, stay out of its way. At many times, of course, the unity goes beyond this bare minimum. The person who pursues wealth as his ultimate end, for instance, typically orders many other goods toward this one chief good. Sometimes, however, these other goods are not positively ordered to the chief good, but they must always retain the negative order. In this manner, it is still the ultimate end.

These two views—the strong-set view and the weak-set view—also differ with regard to the satisfaction of desires. For the strong-set view, a single good satisfies all desires; all other goods are good, and provide satisfaction, only insofar as they partake of this one chief good. In contrast, within the weak-set view, no single good satisfies all desires. All goods complete the individual to some degree or other. The individual must settle upon one good that fulfills him most of all, but even this chief good does not complete him entirely. As such, it still leaves other desires for other goods.

The person who commits a deliberate venial sin, for instance, thinks that the beatific vision, which is his chief good, still leaves unsatisfied his desires for reputation, pleasure, or whatever. Although he has settled upon the beatific vision as his chief good, he leaves open other independent desires, that is, they are independent of his desire for the chief good, although not independent of the desire for the overall good. He ceases to desire these independent goods (with a full-fledged desire) when they conflict with the chief good.

The strong-set view and the weak-set view, then, do not share the exact same vision of the chief good. For the strong-set view, all other goods must participate in the chief good, so that the chief good can be said to satisfy all desires. For the weak-set view, other goods can remain independent of the chief good, providing their own independent satisfaction of desires.

How do these diverse visions of the chief good relate to what we have called the concrete realization of the overall good? For the strong-set view, there is simple identity: the chief good simply is the concrete realization of the overall good. For the weak-set view, matters are more ambiguous. In one way, the chief good seems to be the concrete realization, for this good is pursued above all others and it constrains the pursuit of every other good; furthermore, it shapes much of his life. In another way, the chief good seems to be an aggregate of goods, although an ordered aggregate.

In the last chapter, we saw that even Thomas was willing to characterize happiness as a collection of goods, as long as we recognized that the goods are collected into a single good, since all partake of the chief good. All the more, the concrete realization for the weak-set view might be characterized as a collection of goods, but a collection only loosely connected together. The diverse goods cannot be said to be a single good, except insofar as all belong to the overall good of the person.

THE UNDERLYING NOTION OF THE HUMAN PERSON

The vision of a weakly ordered set of goods can be more fully understood by considering the notion that the person has of himself, as a human being, that underlies his conception of the good. Indeed, each of the four views of inherent goods can be better understood by perceiving it as associated with a conception of the human person.

For the assortment view, just as the goods themselves are independent and disconnected, so the person is a collection of disconnected capacities. These capacities do happen to belong to a single subject, but the subject himself has no overarching good that unites the capacities. By itself, "human nature is indeterminate."[18] The subject himself finds unity only through one power that directs the others, namely, practical reason. Most essentially, then, the human person is a practical reasoner.

The aggregate view supposes that the human person is a collection of unrelated capacities that are united because the subject as a whole has a good. The goods that fulfill the individual capacities, then, are part of an overarching good, to which all the others must be directed.

According to the strong-set view, the person is not a collection of unrelated capacities. Rather, he is one chief capacity with other secondary and *related* capacities. Just as a car is for the sake of transportation, and all

---

18. Grisez, "True Ultimate End," 59.

of its attributes may be explained as in some way necessary for transportation or as enhancing that transportation, so a human being is for the sake of knowing God, and all of his other powers are explained in terms of this one chief power. The completion of any singular power is a partial completion of the individual, but it becomes a completion of the whole person only if it is ordered to the realization of the chief power. This chief power gives rise to all the others, so that they make sense only in relation to this central power. For the strong-set view, then, the human person is himself a strong unity. He is nothing haphazard, but is cohesively ordered like a well-designed machine. This unity is reflected in the following passage:

All other human operations seem to be ordered to the end of contemplating truth. For a certain soundness of body is necessary for the completion of contemplation, for which reason all those products necessary for life are manufactured. Contemplation also requires rest from the disturbances of the passions, which is achieved through the moral virtues and through prudence. Contemplation requires freedom from external disturbances as well, to which the whole structure of civil life is ordered. When rightly considered, then, every human office serves the contemplation of the truth.[19]

What of a weakly ordered set of goods? What notion of the human person underlies it? Like the aggregate view, it supposes that the human person is a collection of unrelated capacities, united only through the good of the whole subject. Although these capacities are unrelated, nevertheless, an order of priority can be found between them. Some capacities are more central to the person than others, and the person ultimately identifies himself most of all with one chief capacity, which completes the individual more than any other. Most essentially, the individual is this one chief capacity, with other secondary and *unrelated* capacities added on. The person is not a cohesive whole, but something of a hodgepodge.

---

19. Aquinas, *Summa contra Gentiles* III, chap. 37, no. 7 (Editio Leonina, XIIII: 93, ll. a6–b5): "Ad hanc etiam omnes aliae humanae operationes ordinari videntur sicut ad finem. Ad perfectionem enim contemplationis requiritur incolumitas corporis, ad quam ordinantur artificialia omnia quae sunt necessaria ad vitam. Requiritur etiam quies a perturbationibus passionum, ad quam pervenitur per virtutes morales et per prudentiam; et quies ab exterioribus perturbationibus, ad quam ordinatur totum regimen vitae civilis. Ut sic, si recte considerentur, omnia humana officia servire videantur contemplantibus veritatem."

He is one thing, with other secondary things tacked on. The individual, for instance, might identify himself as someone who can know God, or as someone who can experience pleasure, but he will also have other capacities with their own independent completions.

On this vision, the human person has two distinct unities that do not line up with one another. On the one hand, the person as a whole has an overarching good, that is, an overall good. On the other hand, the person has one central or chief good, with which he most of all identifies. For the strong-set view, these two unities are themselves united. The overall good is entirely realized in the chief good. For the weak-set view, on the other hand, these two unities do not coincide. The central good does not in fact fully realize the overall good. Rather, the overall good has nothing that completely realizes it, although it is (on this view) largely realized in the chief good.

It is little wonder, then, that the individual cannot find anything that completely realizes the conditions of the overall good. He conceives himself as lacking the unity necessary for any such realization. We should not expect an accidental collection of capacities to have some good that would happen to complete all of these capacities. At most, some central capacity might be completed, leaving the other capacities to be completed at some times and not at other times.

This vision of the human person as an assorted collection of capacities, one of which is primarily identified with the person, is so commonplace in the modern age that any other conception appears foreign. Especially the strong-set view, with the notion of the person underlying it, appears laughably romantic. How could our capacities be so united that they are all directed to one operation? We are, after all, nothing but an accident of the universe. How could an accident exhibit such fine unity?

To complete the modern notion of the human being, we need note only that the central capacity is a matter of choice. An individual does not discover that he happens to have some central capacity. Rather, he discovers multiple capacities, and he settles upon one as most central to his identity. He might later switch this identity for some other. What most completes him, what is most central to his identity, depends upon his desires. The strength of his desires determines his identity.

In contrast to this modern view, the strong-set view relies upon discovery, not choice. A person must discover the purpose of each of the capacities, so that he can recognize how they relate to the purpose of the whole person. Only as such, can he identify the one true good of the person. Thomas himself gives a model of this analysis.[20] He notes that the purpose of a human being must be found in his most excellent capacity, which he eventually identifies with the intellect. Next he notes that the acts of the intellect themselves are directed to discovering the truth and the causes of things. This end can be achieved, and rest attained, only when the very first cause is reached and understood. Since this first cause is God, it follows that the human purpose is ultimately found in knowledge of God. For this end we are most elegantly designed, and all of our diverse capacities can be accounted for through this end.

AN IMPERFECT CONCRETE REALIZATION

For the weakly ordered set of goods, then, the individual supposes that nothing can fully realize his overall good. Some chief good, however, does complete what is most central to him, and this he sets as the concrete realization of his overall good; it is what best meets the conditions. It is the best he can manage, given this imperfect world in which he finds his rather haphazard self. Because he has secondary goods attached to the central good, he sometimes pursues the secondary goods, under the condition that they do not eliminate his central good, that is, under the condition that they remain possible in relation to the central good.[21]

His order to the chief good as an end remains habitually, but he does not always direct his pursuits toward it virtually. In one way he is united, insofar as he seeks, in all of his pursuits, his overall good. In another way he is divided, insofar as he seeks many goods unrelated to one another, except negatively (in that none of these pursuits must eliminate his chief good). He is an enigma, a collection of capacities. Is it any wonder that his pursuits are also an enigma? Of course, much of his life remains well ordered, and the disorder appears only on occasion. Indeed, the disorder might remain mostly in his dispositions, showing itself only in moments of weakness.

20. Aquinas, *Summa theologiae* I-II, q. 3, a. 8.
21. Fulvio Di Blasi recognizes that most human beings pursue goods only loosely connected with their concrete realization; see Di Blasi, "Ultimate End, Human Freedom," 114.

The same kind of order can be found in a person in a state of mortal sin. He pursues some chief good, such as pleasure, as that which most essentially completes himself; he is most essentially a pleasure seeking animal. Nevertheless, he is other things besides, things that are added on, in a disconnected fashion. As such, he can pursue his reputation, power, wealth, and goods such as companionship with others. He will not let these get in the way of his central pursuit, but he will pursue them when they are possible in relation to his chief good. He always maintains a habitual order to his chief good, but he does not order everything virtually to this good. Many things will be positively ordered, much of the time, to his chief good, but he retains the liberty to pursue goods independent of the chief good, because his diverse capacities, with their corresponding goods, have no inherent order to one another.

This disconnected pursuit of disconnected goods is possible only insofar as he has settled upon a second best. The ideal of some good that would entirely complete himself is, to him, nothing but an ideal. Reality demands that he pursue his overall good in one chief good that does not in fact completely fulfill him. At times he has disconnected pursuits, in which he seeks his overall good in other secondary goods. These goods, however, remain secondary, always subject to the condition that they not interfere with his chief good.

Those who commit deliberate venial sins, then, do indeed create a rift between their overall good and the concrete realization of it. The same can be said for those in a state of mortal sin who nevertheless perform disconnected actions, even good actions. The separation between the overall good and its concrete realization depends upon a misunderstanding of the human person. Given this misunderstanding, the concrete realization does not in fact satisfy all desires. Consequently, some goods can be pursued disconnected from the concrete realization. Or rather, they are pursued with only the tenuous and accidental connection of a habitual order to the concrete realization. This order is an order of the person himself—of what the person most centrally is. It need apply to his actions or pursuits only secondarily, not as a proper order belonging to them.

CHAPTER 5

THE FIRST MORAL ACT

To the modern mind, one of the more distasteful doctrines of Thomas concerns the first moral act of an unbaptized youth.[1] This first moral act, so says Aquinas, must be a choice for or against God.[2] As such, either it will usher in grace and remove original sin, or it will be a mortal sin. This first act can in no way be a venial sin. When the youth reaches the age of discretion, he begins to reflect upon himself, and then he must decide whether or not to order himself to God. If he decides not to order himself to God, then he sins mortally. Although Thomas explicitly discusses an unbaptized youth, his teaching may plausibly be extended (as we will see) to every youth when he reaches the age of discretion.

THREE DIFFICULTIES

This doctrine is unpalatable to the modern mind for several reasons. First, none of us, or at least very few of us, remembers making such a decision. Thomas does not specify the age of the youth, so perhaps the age falls before the memory of most people. Elsewhere, Thomas discusses the story related by Saint Gregory of a five-year-old child who committed

---

1. The doctrine has troubled Thomist commentators well before the modern age.
2. Aquinas, *Summa theologiae* I-II, q. 89, a. 6.

blasphemy and was taken to hell.³ Thomas argues that such a boy could indeed consent to mortal sin, although he sets the age of making decisions for one's present concerns a little higher, at seven. For at least some youths, then, the age of reason comes at some point before five, which does indeed strain the memory of most people. Furthermore, as Maritain suggests, the child may be working with ideas that are ill-defined and consequently hard to retain.⁴

Even supposing this first difficulty can be brushed aside, other difficulties remain. Thomas lived in an age when most children, whether Christian, Jewish, or Muslim, were taught early in life that God exists, that God created them, that God created the whole world, and that God is to be loved above all else. We now live in an age in which many children are taught little or nothing of God. What are we to say about these children? We should not expect them, at such an early age, to conclude to the existence of God on their own. Thomas himself says that knowledge of God takes much time and work, time and work surely not available to a five-year-old.⁵ In no way, then, can these children, who have no notion of God, make a first act in which they decide for or against God.

The Thomistic tradition has attempted to address this second concern by allowing a substitute for God.⁶ Some youths, perhaps, do not reflect upon God but upon the noble good. Everyone has some notion of such a good, even a five-year-old; and it is to this good that he must decide whether or not to direct himself. This decision is not entirely disconnected from God, for God is brought into the picture by implication. By ordering oneself to the noble good, one implicitly orders oneself to God, who is in fact the true noble good.

Even should we accept this modification of Aquinas's view, thereby forestalling the second objection, a third difficulty awaits this doctrine of Aquinas. It is simply unrealistic to suppose that five-year-olds occupy themselves with such weighty decisions when they first come to make a moral choice. A child is concerned more with questions about whether to take this piece of candy from his sister, or whether to hit his sister, or

---

3. Aquinas, *In Sent.* IV, d. 27, q. 2, a. 2, ad 2.
4. Jacques Maritain, *The Range of Reason* (New York: Scribners, 1952), 67.
5. Aquinas, *Summa theologiae* I, q. 1, a. 1; Aquinas, *Summa contra Gentiles* I, chap. 4.
6. See Maritain, *Range of Reason*, 69–71.

whether to lie to his sister, or whether to cheat at a game. It is a rare youth indeed who focuses his attention upon his relation to God, or even who focuses his attention upon the noble good. The first moral decisions of youths are more trivial than Thomas suggests. They are, as Maritain says, "a bit of straw, a trifle," more the matter for venial sins than for mortal sins.[7]

For these three reasons, then, Aquinas's doctrine concerning the first moral act of a youth is rather unpalatable. We might be inclined to marginalize it as an odd teaching that can be set aside with little effect upon the rest of his moral teaching, much as his teaching that fire goes up and earth goes down can be set aside while retaining unaffected much of his natural philosophy and metaphysics.

This option, however, appears unavailable. This doctrine touches upon the ultimate end, which is the first matter—says Thomas—that falls in our deliberations. We must first pursue the overall good, then the concrete realization, and then more specific goods. Our deliberations proceed backwards from the end to the more particular means. The ultimate end, then, must be the first thing that we decide upon. Thomas identifies this ultimate end with God, but if the youth is unable to perceive this identity, we may suppose that he can at least recognize that the ultimate end should be identified with some noble good. Our first decision, then, must concern the question of how we will relate to the noble good that is the concrete realization of our ultimate end. This necessity applies, as suggested above, not only to the unbaptized youth, but to every youth. If this teaching is set aside, then the whole edifice of the ultimate end begins to crumble.

Is there some way, then, to defend Aquinas's view against the modern objections? Let us begin by considering what Thomas himself says on the matter.

AQUINAS'S TEACHING ON THE FIRST MORAL ACT

Thomas begins by saying that there is no sin in a youth before he reaches the age when he has discretion.[8] If he does anything that by its

---

7. Ibid., 67.
8. Aquinas, *Summa theologiae* I-II, q. 89, a. 6.

nature would be a sin, either mortal or venial, he is excused from it. This excuse, however, no longer applies once the youth begins to use reason. Aquinas does not explain what he means by the use of reason. Presumably, he does not mean simply forming syllogisms of some sort or other. Very young children exhibit this capacity. By this criterion, the children Aquinas excuses for performing objectively mortal sins would necessarily be very young indeed, too young to do much that would count as objectively mortal. Perhaps Aquinas, then, refers to the forming of practical syllogisms? Again, this minimal use of reason seems unlikely, for it also can be found in very young children, who can rationally decide whether to eat a marshmallow or to wait and receive an additional marshmallow. "The use of reason," then, seems to refer to some very specific use of reason, perhaps the use of moral reason.

When this use of reason arises, Thomas says that, "The first thing that occurs to the person is to deliberate about himself. If he orders himself to the required end, then original sin will be removed by grace. If he does not order himself to the required end, then insofar as he is at the age capable of discretion, he sins mortally, because he does not do what is in him to do."[9] These are the only two possibilities. Venial sin is thereby excluded.

Evidently, a moral norm directs the youth to some required end. What this end is, however, Thomas does not say. The reply to the third objection seems to fill this lacuna. In addition, it provides further insights into the deliberation of the youth and explicitly identifies the moral norm directing to the end:

The youth who has the use of reason cannot be free from the sin of omission mentioned above unless he turns himself to God as soon as he is able. For the first thing that occurs to a person having discretion is to think upon himself, to which he orders other things as toward an end, since the end is prior in intention. Consequently, at this time he is obliged by the affirmative divine precept, in which the Lord says (in Zech. 1), "Turn to me ... and I will turn to you."[10]

---

9. Ibid., I-II, q. 89, a. 6: "Sed primum quod tunc homini cogitandum occurrit, est deliberare de seipso. Et si quidem seipsum ordinaverit ad debitum finem, per gratiam consequetur remissionem originalis peccati. Si vero non ordinet seipsum ad debitum finem, secundum quod in illa aetate est capax discretionis, peccabit mortaliter, non faciens quod in se est."

10. Ibid., ad 3: "Puer incipiens habere usum rationis ... a peccato omissionis praedictae

God, then, is the required end to which the youth must direct himself. At the same time, the youth himself is a kind of end to which he directs other things. Since the end is the first thing that enters deliberation, his deliberations first begin to focus upon himself, which is the end. His deliberations reveal that he must direct himself toward some other end, which is God.

CAJETAN'S INTERPRETATION

A typical reading of this text is represented through the commentary of Cajetan, who uses a distinction, made elsewhere by Aquinas, between the love of concupiscence and the love of friendship.[11] With concupiscence, we love some good; while with love of friendship, we love the person for whom it is good.[12] If Helena desires health for Max, then she loves health with concupiscence, and she loves Max with friendship love. The two are not distinct acts of love, but two aspects of a single love; Helena loves—in a single act of love—both health, as a good to be attained, and Max, as the person for whom it is to be attained.

The term "friendship" should not be taken literally, as involving an intimate and mutual love that we have for another person, for we can have friendship love for ourselves and even for strangers. Essentially, the love of friendship refers to the love that we have for a person. If Helena desires

---

non liberatur, nisi quam cito potest, se convertat ad Deum. Primum enim quod occurrit homini discretionem habenti est quod de seipso cogitet, ad quem alia ordinet sicut ad finem, finis enim est prior in intentione. Et ideo hoc est tempus pro quo obligatur ex Dei praecepto affirmativo, quo dominus dicit, convertimini ad me, et ego convertar ad vos, Zachariae I."

11. Thomas De Vio Cajetan, *Commentaria in Summam Theologicam S. Thomas Aquinatis* (Rome: Editori di San Tommaso, 1892), 938–39.

12. Aquinas, *Summa theologiae* I-II, q. 26, a. 4. For a thorough examination of this distinction see G. Mansini, "*Duplex Amor* and the Structure of Love in Aquinas," in *Thomistica*, ed. E. Manning (Leuven: Peeters, 1995). Mansini notes that Aquinas has expressed the distinction in diverse ways throughout his career. Nevertheless, the fundamental meaning of the distinction remains the same throughout his career. Mansini also notes that the distinction can be used in more general and in more particular ways. In the current discussion, we are using it in the most general way: the love of friendship does not refer exclusively to the love of others but to the love of whatever person—even ourselves—for whom we will the good; the love of concupiscence does not refer exclusively to a self-interested desire but to the love for some good, even when that good is desired for another person.

health for herself, then she loves herself with "love of friendship." If she desires health for a sick stranger, then she loves the stranger with "love of friendship." The love of friendship, then, implies that we seek a good for the sake of some person, whether that person be ourselves, an intimate friend, or a stranger.

In order to avoid confusion, I will adopt a different terminology. For love of concupiscence, I will speak of "want." Helena, for instance, "wants" health (whether for herself or for someone else). For the love of friendship, I will speak simply of "love," since this English word is often used with the narrower meaning, by which it refers to the love of some person. Helena, for instance, loves the stranger for whom she wants health. She does not have friendship with him, but she does love him.

Cajetan introduces the distinction in reference to a self-directed love. He is trying to explain in what sense the youth himself is the end that enters first in his deliberations. Thomas says that the youth directs other things to himself. He does so, says Cajetan, not as a good that he wants but as a person that he loves. The youth certainly does not treat himself as the good to be attained; rather, he is the subject who attains the good. When the youth begins to deliberate concerning himself, says Cajetan, he then considers to what end he must direct himself, that is, he begins to deliberate over what good he should want above all.[13]

This text of Aquinas, then, reveals a fundamental ambiguity surrounding the word "end." It might refer to the end wanted, that is, the end to be attained; it might also refer to the subject for whom the good is willed, that is, the person who is loved. According to Cajetan, Aquinas uses the word in both senses. The youth begins deliberating about the person loved—which is himself—and he proceeds to deliberate about the end to be attained. This latter end is the required end (so says Cajetan) of which Thomas speaks, to which the youth must direct himself.

In the reply to the third objection, Thomas identifies this end as God, but Cajetan introduces the idea, mentioned above, that the person need not direct himself explicitly to God. It suffices if he directs himself to the noble good, which is to direct himself to God in a vague and indiscrimi-

---

13. Maritain also seems to give this interpretation, in which the child directs himself to God as to a good to be attained, although Maritain himself does not make the distinction between the love of concupiscence and love of friendship (*Range of Reason*, 68).

nate manner. Others have expressed this notion in terms of an "implicit" order to God. Someone who directs himself to the noble good, not yet having a clear idea that this noble good is realized most fully in God, still directs himself to God implicitly.

Lawrence Dewan has criticized Cajetan's interpretation on this point. He thinks that even the youth can have a clear enough notion of God, so that he is obliged to order himself to God explicitly.[14] This knowledge of God is not the philosophical knowledge attained through proofs, which is gained only after much training and many years of hard work. Rather, the youth gains a kind of knowledge of God open to everyone, a recognition that the world—and his very self—needs some kind of maker.[15]

In short, Dewan is not troubled by the second objection above, concerning those children who have not been taught about God. Even these children, thinks Dewan, can attain sufficient knowledge of God, so that they can direct themselves to him. St. Paul says that the unbelieving pagans have no excuse for their sin, for from the visible things around them they can know the invisible God (Rom 1:19–20). Their knowledge concerning God may indeed be rather confused. They likely will not know his many attributes, such as his omnipotence, omniscience, eternity, and so on. Still, they do recognize the need for some maker, some cause of the order around us.

Neither Dewan nor Cajetan, then, finds the second objection problematic. According to Dewan, the youth may have sufficient knowledge of God, even if very limited knowledge of God, by which he can direct himself explicitly to God. According to Cajetan, the youth may explicitly direct himself to the noble good, thereby implicitly directing himself to God, whom he may or may not know.

Cajetan also thinks that his teaching concerning the noble good can address the first concern—that we do not remember this first moral act. We do not remember explicitly turning to God, Cajetan says, because we turn to a good only vaguely understood. Can Cajetan address the third difficulty, the worry that youths are concerned with much more mundane

---

14. Lawrence Dewan, "Natural Law in the First Act of Freedom: Maritain Revisited," in *Wisdom, Law, and Virtue: Essays in Thomistic Ethics* (Bronx, N.Y.: Fordham University Press, 2007), 239–41.

15. Aquinas, *Summa contra Gentiles* III, chap. 38, no. 1.

matters than God, matters more the subject of venial sin than mortal? Perhaps. He might claim that when deciding whether to take a piece of candy from his sister, the youth must first settle upon the noble good.

GOD AS THE OBJECT OF LOVE (AS OPPOSED TO WANT)

Lawrence Dewan provides a fundamentally different interpretation of Thomas.[16] On Cajetan's reading, the youth directs himself to God (or the noble good) as toward some good to be attained. But Cajetan himself has pointed out two ways in which something might be directed to an end: the goods that we seek can be ends, but also the person for whom we seek them can be described as an end. The statement that the youth must direct himself to God as to an end, then, has two possible meanings. On the one hand, perhaps he must direct himself to God as to the good to be attained, that is, as to the concrete realization of his ultimate end. On the other hand, perhaps he must direct himself to God as the person to be loved; perhaps the youth must will his own good not simply for himself but also for God. Cajetan suggests the first possibility. Dewan suggests the second. Thomas himself makes clear that God is our end in both ways.[17] He does not make clear, however, to which way he refers when speaking of the first moral act of the youth. Dewan thinks that Aquinas refers to God as the end of love. The point can be understood by examining a natural love that we have for God.

It is well known that Thomas says we must love God above all else—with the love of friendship—through the supernatural love of charity. What is less known is his teaching concerning a *natural* love for God. He teaches that all things—not only human beings and angels—have a natural love for God greater even than the natural love they have for themselves.[18] Dogs and cats, trees and rocks, all love God above all else. Of course, the word "love" must be used in an extended sense when applied to nonrational creatures.[19]

---

16. See Dewan, "Natural Law in the First Act of Freedom." Dewan attributes his interpretation to Cajetan. It seems, however, that Cajetan is better interpreted as presenting a contrasting interpretation of Aquinas.

17. Aquinas, *Summa theologiae* I-II, q. 3, a. 10; II-II, q. 23, a. 1.

18. See, for example, ibid., I, q. 60, a. 5; I-II, q. 109, a. 3; II-II, q. 26, a. 3.

19. Aquinas's teaching on a natural love for God has generated an extensive literature,

Throughout his career, Aquinas's argument has two premises that lead logically to his conclusion.[20] In the first premise, Thomas states that a common or shared good takes priority over the good of the individual. He provides examples, both from nature and from human affairs, that refer to a kind of part/whole relationship, in which the part exists for the sake of the whole. The hand, for instance, naturally exposes itself to a blow, without deliberation, in order to protect the head. Likewise, a citizen sacrifices his life for the good of the whole community.

In the second premise, Thomas identifies God as the shared good for all of creation. From these two premises, it follows that all creatures will love (and not merely want) God above all else. In his discussion of the love of angels, Aquinas concludes the argument as follows:

> The universal good is God himself, and under this good is contained the good of angels, of human beings, and of every creature, since every creature, according to its essence, naturally belongs to God. Consequently, angels and human beings love God, with a natural love, more than they love themselves. If they were to love themselves naturally more than they love God, it would follow that natural love would be perverse.[21]

Dewan thinks that the first moral act of the youth concerns this love for God above all else. When the youth begins to reflect upon himself, he does not consider whether he must direct himself to God as to a good

---

beginning with Pierre Rousselot, *Pour l'histoire du problème de l'amour au moyen age* (Munster: Aschendorffsche Buchhandlung, 1908). Other contributors to the discussion include M. R. Gagnebet, "L'amour naturel de Dieu chez saint Thomas et ses contemporains," *Revue Thomiste* 48 (1948): 394–446; Gregory Stevens, "The Disinterested Love of God According to Saint Thomas and Some of His Modern Interpreters," *The Thomist* 16 (1953): 307–33, 497–541; David M. Gallagher, "Thomas Aquinas on Self-Love as the Basis for Love of Others," *Acta Philosophica* 8 (1999): 23–44; Thomas M. Osborne, *Love of Self and Love of God in Thirteenth-Century Ethics* (Notre Dame, Ind.: University of Notre Dame Press, 2005).

20. On this point, Osborne provides one of the clearest treatments of Aquinas's view; see Osborne, *Love of Self*, 69–112; see also Ezra Sullivan, "Natural Self-Transcending Love According to Thomas Aquinas," *Nova et Vetera* (English) 12 (2014): 913–46.

21. Aquinas, *Summa theologiae* I, q. 60, a. 5: "Quia igitur bonum universale est ipse Deus, et sub hoc bono continetur etiam Angelus et homo et omnis creatura, quia omnis creatura naturaliter, secundum id quod est, Dei est; sequitur quod naturali dilectione etiam Angelus et homo plus et principalius diligat Deum quam seipsum. Alioquin, si naturaliter plus seipsum diligeret quam Deum, sequeretur quod naturalis dilectio esset perversa."

to be possessed; rather, he considers whether he must direct himself to God as the subject of the good. He currently directs goods to himself, as Thomas says, but now he must consider whether all of these goods, and his very self, belong to God as to a shared good, a good that goes beyond himself and resides principally in God.[22]

Dewan raises a difficult objection to this interpretation.[23] Thomas claims that every human being naturally loves God above himself, but the unbaptized youth must *decide* whether to love God above himself. If the love is natural, however, then how can it be a matter of choice? Indeed, if the love of God above all else is a natural love, then mortal sin seems impossible not only for the unbaptized youth but for anyone. Thomas does think that intellectual creatures can fail in love for God. The demons and sinful human beings can love themselves above God, and they can even hate God. Are they, then, opposing their natural love?

As Dewan points out, Aquinas addresses this difficulty when discussing the natural love found in angels.[24] He also addresses it while discussing the hatred of God.[25] All human beings have a natural love of God, insofar as he is the shared good of their own good. At the same time, some human beings (or some angels) can have a hatred toward God, insofar as God is the cause of some evil to them, such as punishment or restrictions upon their behavior (through the moral law). In one way, then, they love God; and in another way they hate God. For those who hate God, however, the hatred wins out.

A similar difficulty arises for the natural love that one angel has for another.[26] They naturally love one another because they share in the good of nature; at the same time, bad angels have a hatred toward good angels, because they are separated from these angels at the level of glory.[27] Na-

---

22. Dewan thinks that the youth does not yet direct any goods to himself but immediately begins thinking upon God as the subject of the good ("Natural Law in the First Act of Freedom," 233–34). It is hard to reconcile this interpretation with the reply to the third objection, in which Aquinas presents the youth as directing other goods to himself.
23. Ibid., 239, 241.
24. Aquinas, *Summa theologiae* I, q. 60, a. 5, ad 5.
25. Ibid., II-II, q. 34, a. 1.
26. Ibid., I, q. 60, a. 4.
27. Ibid., I, q. 60, a. 4, ad 3.

ture provides a union, and with this union comes a natural love; another feature, such as separation in grace, provides a division, and with it comes a hatred. Between these two—both found within the bad angels—it seems that the latter dominates.

It is unclear, however, how natural love can be overridden. If the love is natural, then how can it be obscured by some other love? These cases of tension between two desires might well remind us of the sea captain in the storm, who desires both to keep his cargo and to jettison it.[28] This tension is possible because his desires are imperfect; they are desires for things considered in themselves. The tension is resolved by moving to full-fledged desire. The captain ultimately decides to jettison his cargo, thereby moving this desire (but not the desire to keep the cargo) from imperfect to perfect.

We have seen that most of our natural desires (except for our desire for the overall good) are imperfect desires. Anna has a natural desire to contemplate the truth, but this natural desire is not full-fledged. When the house is burning down, she sets this desire aside. In this case, Anna's natural desire for contemplation remains at the level of imperfect desire; it does not move to become perfect desire, a move that occurs not through nature but through deliberation.

This example concerns a natural want for goods, that is, a natural desire to attain the good of knowledge. It stands to reason that the natural love for persons will likewise be an imperfect love.[29] The natural love of one angel for another is an imperfect love; likewise, our natural love for God above all else is also an imperfect love. The move to complete or full-fledged love requires deliberation. It is this move, on Dewan's interpretation, upon which the youth first deliberates when reaching the age of reason.

The youth has a natural—but imperfect—love for God above all else. He also has a natural love for himself. He must now decide whether to love God above all else with a perfect love. An affirmative precept urges him to turn to God, but he still might ignore this precept. He might love his own separate good—with a full-fledged love—more than his good as

---

28. See ibid., I-II, q. 6, a. 6.
29. See Sullivan, "Natural Self-Transcending Love," 935.

shared with God. In short, his natural love for God does not force his hand; he must still decide whether to order himself to God; he must still decide whether to love God above all else with a perfect love. As it turns out, due to original sin, he cannot make this act of love apart from the healing that comes from grace, a grace that God is willing to provide (as Thomas thinks) even for the unbaptized youth.[30]

The text concerning the unbaptized youth can readily bear Dewan's interpretation as well as Cajetan's interpretation. In the body of the article, Thomas says that the youth must direct himself to the required end, but he in no way indicates whether this end concerns the want for some good to be attained or the love of some person. In the reply to the third objection, he identifies the youth himself as an end concerning the subject loved (in the youth's self love), and he identifies God as the end to which the youth must direct himself, but once again he fails to indicate whether God is an end as a good to be attained or as a person to be loved.

If the text itself bears either interpretation, then is there some way to determine between the two? Are there some other texts, perhaps, that might settle the matter? Unfortunately, other texts are ambiguous as well. One of the more helpful texts is found in the *Questiones Disputatae de veritate*, a text that seems to support the combination of both interpretations. To order oneself to God is *both* to direct oneself to him as a good to be attained *and* to direct oneself to him as the subject for whom one desires the good. Thomas says, "The human mind in some manner touches God by knowing him and loving him. Consequently, for adults, who are able to know and love God, some use of free judgment is required, by which they know and love God. And this [use of free judgment] is the turning to God of which Zechariah speaks."[31]

Turning to God involves both knowing him and loving him. Knowing God seems to apply to what we have called want, since God is attained by knowing him. Loving God seems to apply to what we have called love. Aquinas is discussing the justification of sinners, which justification in

---

30. Aquinas, *Summa theologiae* I-II, q. 109, a. 3.

31. Aquinas, *De veritate*, q. 28, a. 3 (Editio Leonina, XXII.3: 828, ll. 225–31): "Mens autem humana aliquo modo tangit Deum, eum cognoscendo vel amando; unde et in adultis, qui possunt Deum cognoscere et amare, requiritur aliquis usus liberi arbitrii, quo Deum cognoscant et ament: et ista est conversio ad Deum, de qua dicitur Zach."

fact requires the love of charity. Most likely, then, by love (*amare*) Thomas refers to love for God as a person rather than wanting him as a good.

In short, the texts of Aquinas do not settle the matter.[32] The required end to which the youth must direct himself is certainly God, but in what manner God is an end is left indeterminate. Indeed, three possibilities present themselves: Thomas might be referring to an end of a good wanted, to the end of a person loved, or to both.

THE FIRST MORAL ACT AND LOVE FOR GOD AS A PERSON

We are trying to understand the first moral act of an unbaptized youth. We have seen that he must decide whether or not to direct himself to God as to an end. We have also seen that God might be an end in multiple ways, either as a good to be attained or as a person for whom the good is desired. Given what Thomas says concerning the natural love of God above all else, we can conclude that the youth must come to recognize that his good belongs not only to himself but also to God. His good is not a solitary good; it is not simply his own. As the youth reflects upon himself as the end of his various actions, he comes to recognize that his good is not solely his good but belongs to a greater good. He must decide, then, whether he will really direct himself—with a full-fledged desire—to this greater whole. Should he seek his good as simply his own, or should he seek it as belonging to God? The latter possibility is the choice of directing himself to God as to an end.

If he has a full understanding of his own good, then he will recognize that God is his end in two ways. First, God is the good that he must attain by way of contemplation; second, God is the greater good to which his own good belongs and to which his good must be directed as to a person loved.

With regard to the first end, we might well use Cajetan's interpretive tool: it suffices if the youth direct himself to the noble good, vaguely

---

32. The only other text that provides help also seems to allow for both interpretations. In the *Summa theologiae*, Thomas says, "Any movement of the will into God can be called a conversion to him" (I, q. 62, a. 2, ad 3: "Quilibet motus voluntatis in Deum, potest dici conversio in ipsum"). He proceeds to include the movement of will by which we merit beatitude, which is a movement of love rather than want.

conceived. Recognizing that God himself is the chief good to be attained might well be a conclusion reached after much investigation. The youth who has not learned about God might well have only a vague notion of a noble good, not recognizing that this noble good is realized in God.

What about the second end, in which the youth directs himself to God as a person to be loved? Must he have explicit knowledge of God for this act? I suspect that Dewan is correct: the youth can—in Aquinas's mind—recognize that his existence and his good require a cause and that his own good belongs to this cause. Aquinas probably thought, then, that the youth must direct himself explicitly to some concept of God as a maker, however ill-conceived that concept might be. Thomas himself presents some such vague notion of a higher being as elemental to the natural law: "Natural reason informs man that he is subject to someone higher, because of the defect which he perceives in himself, for which he needs to be helped and directed by some higher being. And whatever that higher being is, it is that which everyone calls God."[33]

Someone still might argue that the end of love does not require, strictly speaking, even these vague notions of the divine good. What is most essential to the first moral act is the recognition of a shared good to which one's own good belongs. As the youth contemplates taking a candy from his sister, he begins to recognize—thinking upon himself—that his own good is limited and that the complete realization of his good is not found simply in himself; it is found together with others, including his sister. Will he submit himself to this greater good? Or will he continue to pursue his own good just as his own? Such is the decision that now looms large in his mind. Where is God in this decision? "God" is simply the shared or greater good.

This interpretation concerning the youth reveals a subtle meaning for the "age of discretion." We might suppose that the age of discretion is simply the age at which the child begins recognizing the relation between means and end. His very first deliberation, then, follows upon the age of discretion, for there could be no deliberation without a recognition of means and ends. Familiarity with children, however, reveals that they

---

33. Ibid., II-II, q. 85, a. 1: "Naturalis ratio dictat homini quod alicui superiori subdatur, propter defectus quos in seipso sentit, in quibus ab aliquo superiori eget adiuvari et dirigi. Et quidquid illud sit, hoc est quod apud omnes dicitur Deus."

exhibit signs of making practical syllogisms at a very early age. The age is so young that we would not be inclined to suppose they have yet reached the age of discretion.

Dewan's interpretation allows another meaning for the "age of discretion," although Dewan himself does not advert to it. The age of discretion is the age at which a child recognizes that his good belongs to others. He recognizes that the good to which he should direct himself is not simply his own; it is a shared good. The first moral act ensues because the youth must now choose between a solitary good and a shared good. All prior decisions were simply a matter of carrying out his own personal interest. The age of discretion, then, is not the age of deliberation but the age of moral deliberation.[34]

Aquinas's words imply that the age of discretion follows upon previous reasoning. At the age of discretion, the youth reflects upon himself as the end to which other goods are directed. If the age of discretion is the age at which the child first begins to recognize how one good can be ordered to another, then it seems that the child could not reflect upon himself as the end to which other goods are directed, for he would not yet have had experience of ordering goods to himself. In contrast, if the age of discretion is the age at which a child recognizes his own good as belonging to others, then Aquinas's words pose no difficulty.

THE THREE OBJECTIONS REVISITED

As we have seen, the text of Aquinas is unclear: he never specifies the character of the required end to which the youth must direct himself. Is God the end as a good to be attained? Or is he the end as the subject for whom one seeks the good? Following Dewan, we have developed the latter possibility. It remains to see how this possibility might handle the three objections raised at the beginning of this chapter. The first objection suggested that Thomas is unrealistic because few people, if any, remember this decision of directing themselves to God. The second objection suggested that many youths do not know God, so they could not possibly make this decision. And the third objection suggested that young children

---

34. Maritain presents this discretion as a recognition of the *moral* good (*Range of Reason*, 67).

do not typically occupy themselves with such momentous decisions; they are more often concerned with less significant matters, those proper to venial sins.

The response to the first objection depends upon many factors. How young is an individual when he makes this decision? How clearly has he formulated the terms involved, such as "God," "the noble good," "a shared good," and so on? Finally, how strong is the individual's memory? Clearly, the earlier the decision is made, the less likely it will be remembered. Likewise, the more vaguely the terms are understood, the less likely the decision will be remembered. And finally, the weaker a particular individual's memory, the less likely he will remember the decision. If the decision is made at an early age, and if the terms involved are rather ill-defined, then it is unsurprising that few have a clear memory of making this first moral choice.

Even when the memory of this decision is lacking, it seems plausible that some such decision must have been made. At some point an individual begins to recognize that his good is not solitary. He must then decide whether to submit his good to some greater good, seeking his own good not only for his own sake but also for the sake of others.

To a large extent we have already addressed the second concern. Perhaps the youth does explicitly direct himself to God, since he has an inchoate notion of some maker, and he recognizes that his good belongs to whoever made him. On the other hand, we suggested another possibility. Perhaps the youth does not explicitly conceive the shared good as God. His decision is simply whether to pursue his good alone or to pursue his good as belonging to some greater good. He may not understand that this greater good is in fact the divine good. If the decision of the youth is interpreted in this latter manner, then the existence of this decision, and its importance, is easy to see. Even modern ethical theories, whether utilitarian or deontological, might concede that some such decision must be made at the point when the individual recognizes the importance of the good of others.

We have suggested, however, that Thomas himself may well have thought that this latter possibility does not suffice. The youth does not simply reflect upon some shared good; he reflects upon God as the good to which he as an individual belongs. His conception of God may be fairly minimal—he views God simply as some cause, especially as the cause of his own good—but it is a conception of "God" in some sense. On this reading, the general conception of a shared good does not suffice. The youth reflects upon the shared good because he reflects upon his own good as caused, that is, as not arising from himself alone.

This reading, which is probably more in line with Aquinas's own thought, does not make unreasonable demands upon the mind of the youth. None of his reflections need be particularly distinct. He may have very little notion of what this cause might be like, except that it is indeed a cause of his good. Or, if he has been well trained, he may have a much more complete notion of what this cause is like.

The third objection claims that when young children reach the age of discretion they will typically be faced with decisions concerning minor matters rather than with the serious matter of mortal sin. As we have suggested, however, the age of discretion may be precisely the age at which the youth begins to recognize that his own good is not solitary, an age demanding a very weighty decision indeed. Prior to discretion, then, the youth is always seeking his own good and simply his own good. He makes practical decisions, but they are always decisions about how best to achieve his own personal good. Such a state is not strictly speaking "egoistic," for the youth has not yet conceived of a good beyond his own to which he must direct his own good. Before the age of discretion, then, when a boy decides whether to take a piece of candy from his sister, he simply weighs the pros and cons for his own good, including the pleasure of the candy, the possible reaction of his parents, and so on. He does not exclude his sister's good; he simply has not yet conceived his sister's good as part of the good that he himself must pursue.

Perhaps at some point—perhaps when he considers taking a piece of candy from his sister—he begins to recognize that his own good is limited and can be fully realized only together with others, together with "God," and yes, together with his sister. The decision to take the candy now acquires new magnitude. It becomes a decision of what to do with his own good. Should he pursue it as belonging to some greater good, which includes the good of his sister, or should he pursue it just as his own? The youth must first settle this matter before he settles the matter of the candy, for the question of his good determines how he will judge the question of the candy. The decision to keep his good solitary, not submitting it to some greater good, is no small matter. It is no matter for venial sin. It is the very question of who he is in relation to others.

In short, the first decision of the unbaptized youth does not concern some trivial matter. Rather, a trivial matter might serve as the occasion of deeper reflection, of a reflection that leads the child to think about his role in relation to the good of others. As Dewan says, we should not suppose that the child blows some trivial matter out of proportion, making a minor matter, which carries the weight only of a venial sin, into a major matter, of mortal importance.[35] Rather, the child truly does deliberate concerning a matter of great importance. It is a matter that he must settle before making any further decision, for it sets the standard he must use in subsequent decision making.

If the youth should decide to submit his own good to the greater good, he then, and only then, must yet settle the question of the candy. If he chooses not to take the candy, his choice may depend in part upon the shared good to which he has now submitted himself; it will no longer be a question simply of personal consequences. If he chooses to take the candy, then his choice might well be a venial sin. It is a venial sin, however, that has followed upon a more momentous decision, in which he chose the true good.

THE ULTIMATE END RECONSIDERED

Whatever be the fate of the first moral decision of the youth, the topics discussed in this chapter have far reaching implications for the pursuit of the ultimate end. The discussion in the preceding chapters proceeded on the assumption—incorrect, as it turns out—that when Thomas discusses ordering actions to an end, he is referring merely to an end of a good to be attained, the beatific vision or some such thing. In fact, he often refers to the end of God as a person for whom the good is desired. A sin is a mortal sin not simply because it fails in the want of God as a good to be attained; rather, it fails in the love of God as a person. A sin is venial when it is merely possible—that is, it does not oppose the end but neither does it contribute to the end—with regard to the end of the love of God

---

35. Dewan, "Natural Law in the First Act of Freedom," 226.

as a subject of the good. In a mortal sin, an individual decides that he will no longer direct himself, with love, to the divine good.

One might well wonder whether the discussion in the preceding chapters can be aptly transferred from the domain of a good to be attained to the domain of an end of love, that is, to the domain of a person being loved as a subject of the good. When we discussed actual, virtual, and habitual order, for instance, we focused upon ends to be attained. Do the same three orders apply to the love for a person? Our understanding of the psychology of sin, it seems, demands a clear understanding of the ultimate end, which demands further reflection upon what it means to love someone as a subject of the good.

CHAPTER 6

THE SHARED GOOD

Whatever be the fate of the youth, reflection upon his dilemma has uncovered an undisputed truth of far-reaching consequences. Thomas teaches that we must order ourselves to God as to an end in two ways, both as an end to be attained and as the subject for whom the good is willed. The discussion so far has focused upon the former, but it is by no means clear that it should have. Indeed, there is every reason to suppose that, instead, it should have focused on the latter. After all, sin is most opposed to charity, which loves God as the subject for whom we will the good.

Mortal sin opposes the order to the divine good. We now see, however, that the statement is ambiguous. Mortal sin might be opposed to God as an end to be attained, or it might be opposed to loving God as the person for whom we seek the good. Sins will often oppose God in both ways, but mortal sin is most essentially opposed to God as the object of love, not as the object of want. When Aquinas says, then, that we must order all of our actions virtually to the divine good, he is not referring simply to the attainment of the beatific vision. Rather, he is referring to the divine good as it belongs to God himself. We must order our actions to God not simply as a good to be attained; we must order them to God most essentially as the subject of the good, as the one for whom we desire the good. Venial sin fails in this order, although it retains the habitual order to God as to the person for whom we will the good. Mortal sin destroys even the habitual order.

The discussion so far, then, has rested upon a faulty premise. It has supposed that the order—actual, virtual, and habitual—that must belong to our good actions and that is lacking in sinful actions is an order to an end to be attained. In fact, it is an order of love; it is an order to another person as the subject of the good. We well might wonder, then, what relevance the preceding discussion has to our topic.

FROM GOODS TO PERSONS

The preceding discussion will prove to be far from irrelevant. For one thing, the entire discussion concerning the order of actions can be readily transferred from the realm of goods to the realm of persons. For another thing, the two ends—the end to be attained and the person for whom it is desired—will prove to be intimately related, so much so that it will become difficult to pry them apart.

Consider the first point. The three orders of actions were first introduced with the example of a mother's love for her son, in which she loves her son by willing his good for him. She orders herself, then, both to a good and to a person. Indeed, every order must always include both ends, for as we have seen, the want for goods and the love for a person are not two separate acts; they are two elements of a single love. We cannot have one without the other. When a mother directs herself to the good of her son, she does not direct herself to some good abstracted from the person for whom it is good; nor does she direct herself to some person apart from his good.

We have been led, then, to the second point: the two ends are intimately connected. The two are united by the very nature of the good, which is always the good of some subject. Knowledge is not good as some separate existence, but insofar as it is the perfection of a being with a mind. Health is not good by some independent quality of its own, but insofar as it completes a living being. It is incoherent, then, to want the good without loving the subject for whom it is good. Wanting the good in itself—apart from the subject for whom it is good—is to want no good at all; it is the desire for what could be good, if it were possessed by some subject.

Wanting and loving are connected in another manner, less obvious but more important to our concerns. The kinds of goods that someone desires for himself constrain the love of persons that he can have for others. If someone hates stamp collecting, for instance, then he cannot love a person based upon stamp collecting. This constraint becomes important for sin because someone who sets up a worldly good as his ultimate end, such as pleasure, will then be unable to love God above all else. In short, certain ends to be attained are inconsistent with a love of certain persons. Consequently, the previous discussion concerning diverse concrete realizations, which are ends to be attained, has direct bearing upon the question of ordering oneself to God as a person to be loved.

Unfortunately, this connection between ends to be attained and the love of persons as an end is far from obvious. Why cannot someone seek pleasure as his ultimate end and at the same time love God? The answer to this question is tied to the notion of a shared good, that is, a good that is possessed together.[1] We have already seen that Thomas explains the love of God above all else in terms of a shared good. Creatures have a natural love for God above all else because their good belongs to the divine good. The good is not solitary but shared.

Thomas makes the point in a slightly different manner when discussing the love of one angel for another, or the love of one human being for another.[2] A person always loves that which is one with himself in some good. One angel naturally loves another angel, for instance, because they share the good of being intellectual creatures. One cellist loves another cellist because they share the good of playing the cello. Someone who hates the cello will not love a cellist, at least not insofar as she is a cellist.

For the good of a single individual we find three elements: (1) a good thing, (2) a subject for whom it is good, (3) and the possession of the good, which unites the first two elements. Knowledge of the truth, for instance, is good, but it is good only for particular kinds of subjects, namely, those that can know the truth. This good is realized when the subject actually comes to know the truth, so that now he possesses the good. The same three elements can be found in a shared good. What differs is that the

---

1. For an insightful discussion of the shared good, see Charles de Koninck, *De la primauté du bien commun contre les personnalistes* (Montreal: Fides, 1943).

2. Aquinas, *Summa theologiae* I, q. 60, a. 4.

subject is no longer a solitary individual but a union of multiple individuals; as a result, the possession also differs, for it is shared by many individuals.

The point can be illustrated through a simple shared good, such as the good of playing symphonic music by the members of an orchestra. An individual cellist or an individual violinist cannot, by herself, play symphonic music. Only by uniting with others can she attain the good. She can attain to part of the good—playing her own piece within the whole symphony—but she is inadequate to attain the whole good. The good of playing symphonic music, then, is not the good of a single individual but a shared good. Furthermore, it can be possessed only through a shared activity. The shared activity, however, demands that the members become a united cause of their activity. The shared good of symphonic music, then, demands a shared possession, which demands a united subject of the good, namely, the orchestra.

Similar points can be said of soldiers fighting a battle together. A single soldier can fight only part of a battle. He is inadequate to attain the end by himself, so he unites with others in order that together they might possess the end. Likewise, the members of a soccer team, or of any other sport team, must unite to attain a shared good by way of some shared activity. Even two chess players, although opponents, attain the end of playing chess not singly but only together.

In these cases, the good surpasses the capacity of the individual; only a union of several individuals is adequate to attain the end. Just as several individuals must unite in order to lift a heavy object, so several individuals must unite in order to play symphonic music, to fight a battle, or to play a game. Ultimately, the union supplies for an inadequacy of the individual.

In other cases, individuals share a good even though it does not, by itself, seem to surpass their capacities. Two people watch a movie together, although each is able to watch it separately. Two people interested in horses spend hours discussing horses, thereby sharing the good, although each could separately attain the good by thinking about horses on his own. Two fly fishers go fishing together, sharing with one another the good they enjoy, although each could fish on his own.

In these cases the individual can attain the good on his own, but he wishes to attain it together with another, as if the good is possessed better when possessed together. Although the person can possess the object on his own, his possession is limited. On his own, the moviegoer will be able to appreciate many details of the movie, but his appreciation is increased through union with his friend, perhaps especially by discussing the movie afterwards. The individuals interested in horses can, on their own, attain knowledge of horses, but this knowledge is limited in many ways. They do not know everything about horses, nor can they always be thinking about horses. These inadequacies are supplied through a united possession, for example, by sharing the good through discussion.

We have, then, two cases in which a good is shared through possession. First, a good might exceed the capacity of an individual, so that he can attain it only through a shared possession. Second, a good might be attained at an individual level, but it can be attained more completely through shared possession. For both cases, the individuals unite to form some greater whole, of which each is a member. This point is most obvious for the first case. The members of the orchestra form the greater whole of the orchestra, and similarly for the soccer players. The point is less obvious for the second case. Do the two moviegoers unite into some greater whole of which each is a member? What of the two horse lovers? Although the union is not as obvious in these cases, nevertheless Thomas says that our love always involves some union.

Union relates to love in three ways. One union is the cause of love. For the love of oneself, this union is substantial union, while for the love of others, it is a union of likeness, as was said. A second union is essentially the love itself, which is the union according to the bond of affection, and which is likened to a substantial union insofar as the lover relates to the beloved, in the love of friendship, as to himself, while in the love of concupiscence [which we have called "want"], he relates to the beloved object as something belonging to himself. A third union is the effect of love, and this is the real union, which the lover seeks from the one loved. This union must be adjusted to the love itself, as when Aristotle, in the *Politics*, commenting upon Aristophanes's claim that lovers desire to become one, says that from such a union one or the other would be corrupted; consequently, they seek a union that is fitting and becoming, for example, that they might live together, discuss together, and be united in other such things.[3]

3. Ibid., I-II, q. 28, a. 1, ad 2: "Unio tripliciter se habet ad amorem. Quaedam enim unio

The third union mentioned by Aquinas seems to be nothing other than the united possession itself, which typically occurs through some united activity. That united activity presupposes the first union, in which each person is a kind of member of some greater whole. The two fly fishers say it is "we" who are doing something, as do the two moviegoers. They perceive themselves not as two entirely separate individuals, but as two individuals united in some activity, which activity is ultimately directed to the possession of the good.

Whenever there is a shared good, then, there is a shared possession, and whenever there is a shared possession, there is a union of individuals. In some cases, the individuals unite to possess a good that they cannot attain individually. In other cases, the individuals unite to possess a good that they can attain individually; nevertheless, the good is possessed better together with others.

In both cases, what a person seeks for himself, he also seeks for the one he loves. The two moviegoers seek the good of enjoying a movie, and the members of the orchestra seek the good of playing music. The personal goods of each individual do differ from one another, as the part that the cellist plays is different from the part that the violinist plays, but they have a similarity in proportion to the shared good.

We can now see that the end an individual sets for himself will have far-reaching consequences for the persons he can love as ends. Such is the nature of the good that it is always the good of someone. Such is the nature of love, then, that it always must seek the good of a person. For someone to love God, he must will the good of God for God. Such is the nature of the love of another person, however, that it always involves some shared good. The love of God, then, implies that the divine good is in some manner

---

est causa amoris. Et haec quidem est unio substantialis, quantum ad amorem quo quis amat seipsum, quantum vero ad amorem quo quis amat alia, est unio similitudinis, ut dictum est. Quaedam vero unio est essentialiter ipse amor. Et haec est unio secundum coaptationem affectus. Quae quidem assimilatur unioni substantiali, inquantum amans se habet ad amatum, in amore quidem amicitiae, ut ad seipsum; in amore autem concupiscentiae, ut ad aliquid sui. Quaedam vero unio est effectus amoris. Et haec est unio realis, quam amans quaerit de re amata. Et haec quidem unio est secundum convenientiam amoris, ut enim philosophus refert, II Politic., Aristophanes dixit quod amantes desiderarent ex ambobus fieri unum, sed quia ex hoc accideret aut ambos aut alterum corrumpi, quaerunt unionem quae convenit et decet; ut scilicet simul conversentur, et simul colloquantur, et in aliis huiusmodi coniungantur."

shared; it must be the good not only of God himself but also of the person who loves God. This shared good is found in the concrete realization of the beatific vision, which is a kind of sharing in the very life of God.

It follows that a person who rejects the beatific vision for himself, choosing some other good in its place, also rejects the love of God, for he rejects the good that he shares with God. For this reason, when Dewan attempts to understand the reasoning behind the sinful choice (of the unbaptized youth), he suggests some false good, such as pleasure.[4] Dewan claims that the youth must order himself to God with a love of a person, yet he explains the rejection of this order in terms of the want for false goods.

For two reasons, then, the previous discussion concerning the end to be attained still bears upon our problem. First, what has been said concerning the order of actions to the end attained can readily be transferred to the order of actions to a person loved as an end. Second, the order to a person cannot be separated from an order to the end to be attained. In our actions, we always direct ourselves to both ends. More particularly, in our actions for the good of others, we always direct our actions to some good in the other that is shared by ourselves.

INHERENT GOODS AND LOVE FOR PERSONS

The tight connection between the end to be attained and the end realized in a person indicates that the four views of goods discussed earlier will bear upon the love of a person. Of greatest interest, for our concerns, will be the difference between the weak-set view and the strong-set view. Both the weak-set and the strong-set views recognize the good as the good of some subject. Both recognize, as well, that the individual seeks his overall good first of all. Both views, also, can be led to the notion of a shared good, in which the good is possessed by several individuals united together. The two views differ, however, in their perception of the overall good. Consequently, they will also differ in their perception of love, for we have seen that there is a tight link between the goods that one pursues for oneself and the goods that one pursues for others.

For the strong-set view, all goods are united under a single good. The beatific vision, for instance, makes all other goods to be good for the

---

4. Dewan, "Natural Law in the First Act of Freedom," 236.

whole person. The pursuit of any inherent good must also include the pursuit of the chief good. In contrast, for the weak-set view, diverse goods are not so intimately connected. Different inherent goods can be pursued independently of a unifying good. The only necessary restraint is that they must not interfere with the chief good.

The consequence, at the level of the love for a person, will be a similar unity for the strong-set view and a similar independence for the weak-set view. For the strong-set view, one love will unite every love, just as one good unites all other goods. In contrast, the weak-set view will allow independent loves, just as it allows multiple independent goods, one not directed to the other, except negatively.

On both views, diverse loves will be possible, since there are diverse inherent goods. Love for another person, for instance, could be based upon the love of horses, upon fly fishing, or upon an interest in World War II. Where there are diverse goods that can be shared, there will be diverse unions giving rise to diverse loves.

The two views do not differ in this diversity, any more than they differ in recognizing a diversity of inherent goods. Rather, the two differ in how the diverse loves relate to one another. The strong-set view will unite all of these loves under a single overarching love, just as it unites all goods in an order to a single chief good. In contrast, the weak-set view will leave these loves open to the possibility of independence, in which one is not directed to another but stands on its own.

The strong-set view must unite every love because it unites every good. Since love for others is always based upon some shared good, when those shared goods are united, so also will be the love. Suppose that Anna loves Giuseppe on account of two shared goods: they both love horses, and they both can partake in the beatific vision. If she abides by the strong-set view, then the good of horses must be subordinated to the good of the beatific vision. Consequently, her love for Giuseppe as one who loves horses will be subordinated to her love for Giuseppe as one capable of the beatific vision. She thinks that the good of horses ceases to be good when not subordinated to the beatific vision. If Giuseppe would cease to love the beatific vision but would continue to love horses, Anna would refuse to separate the two goods. She would refuse to desire the good of horses for Giuseppe while omitting to desire the beatific vision for him. Her love for him could continue only insofar as she would continue to desire the beatific vision for Giuseppe.

On the other hand, suppose that Max loves money for himself as his chief good. He does not perceive it as a shared good that can serve as the basis of love for others. If he holds a strong-set view, then all other goods must be positively ordered to this chief, self-interested good. No room for love for anyone else would remain, for any good he shares with others would ultimately be directed to his private good. But suppose (what is more likely) that he holds a weak-set view. Then other goods can be independent of his chief self-interested good of money. Based upon these other goods, he might develop a love for other persons. Perhaps he plays tennis with Cordelia and truly seeks this good not only as his own but also as a good possessed together with Cordelia. This possibility remains open just so long as the good of tennis remains independent of the good of money, which he wills only for himself.

It follows that someone in a state of mortal sin can still have a particular love for others. The mafioso can help the old lady across the street, and not simply because he wishes to get something back for himself. He can truly will the good of helping her for her own sake. Ultimately, every love for others must be negatively subordinated to his chief good. If that chief good is selfish—if it is not a shared good but a good simply for himself— then he will always set aside any love when it proves an obstacle to his chief, selfish good. Nevertheless, as long as there is no conflict, he can maintain both a selfish good as his highest good and other shared goods as independent of (but lesser than) this highest good. With regard to these shared goods, he can have a love for other persons. Ultimately, this love will be inadequate, since he does not seek the true chief good of the other person; he does not seek the divine good for him. He seeks only some lesser good. Still, he does seek it precisely as a good shared with another. An individual who lives by the weak-set view, then, can still have a limited love for others.

Digging marginally below the surface of this discussion, and the discussion of the preceding chapter, we find the topic—much discussed as of late—of pagan virtue.[5] Can someone have virtue without grace? What

---

5. See, for instance, Thomas M. Osborne, "Perfect and Imperfect Virtues in Aquinas," *The Thomist* 71 (2007): 39–64; Brian J. Shanley, "Aquinas on Pagan Virtue," *The Thomist* 63 (1999): 553–77; Angela McKay Knobel, "Aquinas and the Pagan Virtues," *International*

has been said concerning love for others within the weak-set view indicates that even someone in a state of mortal sin could retain some virtue. This minimal admission, however, is not disputed. The question concerns whether, apart from grace, an individual can have only isolated virtues or whether he might have virtue unified by a cohesive vision of the moral life. Lacking a cohesive moral life, the isolated virtues will often fail, because they are not ordered to a single unifying end. This cohesive vision, we have seen, comes with the strong-set view. Can someone without grace, then, seek God above all else, thereby unifying all of his good inclinations? Or must he pursue some other end as his chief good, yet maintain isolated virtues because he operates on the weak-set view?

The discussion of the unbaptized youth does not answer the question. Thomas says that if the youth orders himself to God, then original sin is removed by means of grace.[6] Thomas does not envision ordering oneself to God apart from grace. Indeed, Thomas argues that consequent upon original sin, we cannot love God above all else unless we are given grace.[7] Our discussion has revealed, however, the manner in which someone without grace might have at least imperfect virtue.

LOVE AND THE SATISFACTION OF DESIRES

The unity—within the strong-set view—of all love under a single overarching love has further implications for a topic that has occupied much of our time, namely, the satisfaction of desires. The ultimate end, says Aquinas, satisfies all desires; nevertheless, the attainment of the ultimate end still might leave some desires unsatisfied. This apparent contradiction arises, in the weak-set view, on account of a misperception of the ultimate end. The individual still perceives some goods as independent of the chief good.

Even when the ultimate end is correctly perceived—in the strong-set view—the apparent contradiction remains. Those in heaven still desire, for instance, to have their bodies back. The apparent contradiction is resolved, we suggested, by recognizing that the possession of the chief good can be realized in other goods. We have now seen, however, that God is

---

Philosophical Quarterly 51 (2011): 339–54; David Decosimo, *Ethics as a Work of Charity* (Stanford, Calif.: Stanford University Press, 2016).

6. Aquinas, *Summa theologiae* I-II, q. 89, a. 6.
7. Ibid., I-II, q. 109, a. 3.

our end in multiple ways, both as a good to be attained and as the subject of the good. The previous discussion concerning the satisfaction of desire focused upon wanting goods. Does the introduction of the love for a person affect the earlier conclusion?

The two cases mentioned by Aquinas of objects desired by those who have attained the beatific vision—the desire that the body share in the beatific vision and the desire for the society of others who share the beatific vision—seem to be cases of the love for the subject of the good (rather than the want to attain goods). This point is clearest for the latter desire. The desire for the society of others is precisely the desire to share the good of the beatific vision with others. The prayer of the saints for those on earth, with its implied desire, also arises from a wish to share the good with others. The case of the body is less clear, but Thomas himself is clear enough on the matter. When discussing the objects of charity, he includes the body as an object of love and not just of the want for goods.[8]

Every unfulfilled "desire" of those in heaven, then, is a realization of the love we have for the subject of the good. Consequently, we might well suspect that the previously given resolution of the apparent contradiction was inadequate. We suggested that the single good of the beatific vision can be realized in other goods; it can be realized, for instance, in the goods of the body. This response, however, says nothing of love for a subject. What implications might this love have upon the question of the satisfaction of desires?

Brandon Dahm claims that love does not arise, most essentially, from a lack of some good; rather, it arises from the full possession of some good.[9] God chooses to create, for instance, out of love. He himself lacks no good, and yet he has a kind of "desire," realized in the act of creating. Thomas states that the only reason God could have for creating is not that he desires to attain some good but because he wishes to share the good he already has.[10] We do not want to say that God has some unsatisfied desire; nevertheless, he has a kind of love that leads him to create.

The same conclusion, thinks Dahm, applies to the "desires" of those in heaven. They do not desire to attain any additional goods, for they have

8. Ibid., II-II, q. 25, aa. 5 and 12.
9. Dahm, "Distinguishing Desire," 105–13.
10. Aquinas, *Summa contra Gentiles* III, chap. 18, no. 5.

the complete good themselves; rather, they desire to share the good that they themselves already possess. They desire to share the beatific vision with others, and they desire to share it with their bodies. Their desires, then, do not arise from any lack of satisfaction on their part; rather, their desires arise from an overflowing of satisfaction.

Divine love, no doubt, arises from no defect on God's part. We have suggested, however, that for human beings, love often does arise from some defect in the person. Several individuals cannot attain a good on their own, for instance, so they unite in love in order that they might attain it together. In no way, however, is there some good that God can attain only together with others. He fully possesses the one true good.

We want to avoid saying that God's creation adds something to his good. There is no new good found in creation that is not already present in God. The entire good of creation is simply an extension or sharing in the divine good. Furthermore, it is an extension that does not add anything of goodness. All that is found in creation is simply the divine good, realized in diverse ways. Nothing is added. The same good is simply possessed by more people.

This manner of speaking—as is always the case with God—stretches our minds. We readily suppose that where there is some extension there is also some addition. We readily suppose that where there is some wish, there is a lack of some good. To the contrary, God wishes to create, but he lacks nothing; and no good is added by his creation. One and the same good is simply shared. God creates not because he lacks any good but because he has all good.

Similarly, those in heaven lack no good, but they can share the good they have with others. This sharing is "better," although no good is gained. It is better on account of love, not on account of the want to attain goods. It is better because one and the same good is realized in diverse ways; it is possessed by diverse individuals. As Dahm argues, then, Aquinas is not saying that the beatific vision leaves some desire unsatisfied; rather, he is saying that the complete satisfaction of desires—the complete attainment of the good—overflows into a wish for this same good to be had by others. To claim otherwise forces one to conclude that God himself is lacking in the good.

THE ORDER TO A PERSON

As we have seen, a person must order himself to some chief good that stands above the others. The parallel order found in the domain of love is open to two misunderstandings. First, someone might suppose that the order to another person ultimately comes back to oneself in a kind of self-interested love. Second, someone might suppose that the order of love goes out to another person in an entirely "altruistic" manner. We will consider each mistake in turn.

Shared goods can be interpreted in an entirely egoistic manner. Several thieves band together in order to attain an end they cannot achieve on their own, such as robbing a bank, but the diverse individuals unite with others solely for the sake of the personal profit that they might gain. The individuals each seek a good that he possesses individually (such as money), and they unite for the sake of some common means; together they form the kind of agent that can produce the goods that each desires singly.

A truly shared good is different. The members enter an association for reasons beyond self-interest. The members of the orchestra, for instance, may truly desire that their fellow members share in the good of playing symphonic music. In this case, the members unite not simply for a common means but in order that the good itself might be possessed together through some common activity. The fly fishers want the activity of fishing, and they want it together. The fishing does not simply produce some other good that each wants for himself (such as food); rather, they want the fishing itself, and they want it together.

We have, then, two kinds of shared goods: first, a means can be shared; second, the good itself can be shared.[11] When the means are shared, the end might be possessed singly, as with the thieves, and then the shared good involves nothing other than egoistic desire. In contrast, we are suggesting that when the end is shared, then the individuals go beyond the desire for their own singular good and they seek the good of others.

Thomas expresses these ideas in terms of two manners that someone can love a shared good.

---

11. See De Koninck, *De la primauté du bien commun*, 17–18.

The good of society may be loved in two ways. In one way, so that it may be had for oneself, in another way so that it might be preserved. To love the good of society so that it might be had and possessed by oneself does not make someone politically good, for even the tyrant loves the good of society so that it might be subject to himself, which is to love oneself more than society, for one desires this good for oneself, not for society. But to love the good of society so that it might be preserved and defended is to love society truly, and it makes someone politically good, insofar as someone, in order to preserve and increase the good of the state, exposes himself to mortal danger and denies his own private good.[12]

It might be suggested that even in the latter case, when the end itself is shared, the desires of the individuals still remain egoistic, never going beyond the desire for their own individual goods. The objection points out that in both the cases discussed above—both when the members seek some end that they cannot attain individually and when they seek better to possess some end that they could possess individually—the individuals unite on account of some deficiency. The orchestra members cannot attain the good by themselves, so they unite in order to attain it. The moviegoers can attain the end singly, but their possession is somewhat deficient, in that the good can be possessed better together. In both cases, then, it seems that the individuals unite in order to overcome some personal deficiency. In these cases, then, it seems that the motive is ultimately self-interested.

The hidden premise to this objection supposes that any attempt to overcome a personal deficiency is motivated by self-interest. Certainly, the members have something to gain. The fact that something is gained seems to imply self-interest.

This appearance, however, is dispelled when we recognize the manner

---

12. Aquinas, *De virtutibus*, q. 2, a. 2 (*Questiones disputatae*, Mandonnet vol. 3, 275): "Amare autem bonum alicuius civitatis contingit dupliciter: uno modo ut habeatur; alio modo ut conservetur. Amare autem bonum alicuius civitatis ut habeatur et possideatur, non facit bonum politicum; quia sic etiam aliquis tyrannus amat bonum alicuius civitatis ut ei dominetur: quod est amare seipsum magis quam civitatem; sibi enim ipsi hoc bonum concupiscit, non civitati. Sed amare bonum civitatis ut conservetur et defendatur, hoc est vere amare civitatem; quod bonum politicum facit: in tantum quod aliqui propter bonum civitatis conservandum vel ampliandum, se periculis mortis exponant et negligant privatum bonum."

in which the something is gained. What is gained is not gained individually. What the cellist possesses through membership in the orchestra, for instance, she does not possess by herself. She possesses it only together with others. The good that she gains she does not desire simply as her own, for it is not simply her own. Rather, she desires a good of "ours." As Thomas Osborne points out, the individual pursues a good that is greater than his own but includes his own within it.[13]

The point is even clearer for the other sort of union, in which the individuals seek a more perfect possession. Ultimately, this more perfect possession is more perfect only insofar as it is a united possession. The individual by himself gains nothing. What he gains, he gains only in union with another. He gains a good possessed together, which is not simply his good; it is a good for "us." As Charles de Koninck says, "The good is perfect precisely insofar as it can be shared."[14]

In short, seeking to overcome a deficiency need not be self-interested. What is deficient, in both cases, is the possession of the good. The deficiency is overcome, however, through a united possession. What is gained, then, is not gained as an individual. It is gained by the whole, by the united members together. An individual overcomes his deficiency by seeking to possess a good not as his own—which would be egoistic—but as possessed together with others.

The egoistic argument, then, presumes that individuals either seek their own individual good or they seek a good distinct from their own, that is, the good of others. It ignores a third possibility: individuals might seek a good that is their own but is not merely their own. They might seek a good insofar as it belongs to themselves and to others, that is, insofar as it belongs to them as united with others. As de Koninck notes, this argument debases the individual because it denies him the capacity to share in a good greater than his own singular good.[15] In some manner, we can grant that the individual does not get entirely outside of his good, as long as "his" good is understood as more than his singular individual good, even as family members are "my" brothers and sisters. It does not

13. Osborne, *Love of Self*, 92.
14. De Koninck, *De la primauté du bien commun*, 8: "La communicabilité est de la raison même de sa perfection."
15. Ibid., 31.

follow that he acts egoistically. He does indeed pursue the good of others, for he pursues "our" good.

The discussion has led us to the second point mentioned above. Love for others is not egoistic, but neither is it entirely "altruistic." Altruistic love, as the term is used here, refers to the love of another person as entirely disconnected from oneself, as entirely independent of one's own good. As such, altruistic love is not the same as the love we have been discussing, which seeks a shared good, not an isolated individual good.

Aquinas's account of the natural love found in the will excludes the possibility of altruistic love. By nature we desire our own perfection, that is, our overall good. All other desires must be founded upon this first natural desire. Someone might argue that egoism follows of necessity from this view. All love must be based upon natural love, and all natural love must be founded upon the desire for one's own perfection. It seems to follow that all love is merely self-seeking.

This argument, however, rests upon too narrow a notion of "one's own good." It supposes that "one's own good" is a solitary good; it ignores the possibility that "one's own good" might be a shared good. It ignores the possibility that one's completion might be found partly outside oneself. The completion of the cellist is not found simply in herself; it is found in the whole orchestra, through a shared activity. Consequently, the cellist, who desires her own good, need not desire an egoistic good. Her own good is not simply her own. Likewise, human beings, who naturally desire their overall good, need not desire an egoistic good. Their overall good may prove to be a shared good. They may be completed not simply in themselves but only together with others.[16]

We have seen that the unbaptized youth does not begin by recognizing that his good is shared. Rather, he first begins seeking many goods for himself, thereby treating himself as the end. This priority of seeking a personal or private good arises from the awareness of the individual, who first becomes aware of himself (as a person) and then others, and who first becomes aware of his own good and then the good of others. Initially, then, an individual seeks his overall good as realized simply in himself. It does not follow that his love is egoistic, for egoism implies the

---

16. See Osborne, *Love of Self,* 92–93.

love of oneself in opposition to the love of others. There is no opposition here. The individual has not yet considered the good of others. He has not yet perceived that his good might be shared with others. The pursuit of his own individual good becomes egoistic only after he perceives—but rejects—the shared good.

When he recognizes that his good belongs not only to himself but also to others, then he must make a choice. Will he order himself and his good to the others, seeking a shared good; or will he reject their share in the good, seeking only his private good? As we have seen, he has a natural but imperfect love for those with whom he shares a good. He must now decide whether to love this shared good with a perfect love. In short, when he recognizes that his good belongs not only to himself, he is faced with the choice of the unbaptized youth.

At the heart of every love for a shared good (and not just the first such love) lies such a decision. At the heart of love lies a decision to direct oneself and one's good to another.[17] The cellist must seek her own good not simply as her own; she must desire it as part of a united possession, which belongs to many. Her good, then, must be directed to the good of others. If she seeks her good solely as her good, then she becomes like a thief. As Thomas expresses the matter,

The good of any part may be considered in proportion to its whole, so that as Augustine says in book 3 of the *Confessions*, "every part that does not conform to its whole is reprehensible." Since any man is a part of society, it is impossible that a man can be good unless he is well proportioned to the common good, nor can the whole persist well unless its parts are proportioned to it.[18]

The choice at the heart of love may be seen as answering the following question: for whom is the good willed? Is it simply for myself, or is it for myself as united with others? Is my good solely my perfection, or is it the

---

17. Going out to one's friend is called ecstasy by Aquinas; see *Summa theologiae* I-II, q. 28, a. 3.
18. Ibid., I-II,, 92, 1, ad 3: "Bonitas cuiuslibet partis consideratur in proportione ad suum totum, unde et Augustinus dicit, in III Confess., quod turpis omnis pars est quae suo toti non congruit. Cum igitur quilibet homo sit pars civitatis, impossibile est quod aliquis homo sit bonus, nisi sit bene proportionatus bono communi, nec totum potest bene consistere nisi ex partibus sibi proportionatis."

perfection of another subject, to which I relate as a part? To order myself and my good to another is to pursue my good as belonging to the other. If this pursuit is absent, then so is love for others. Any subsequent union becomes like a union of thieves. The first act of love, then, must always be an ordering of oneself to the other as to a subject of the good, which is to order oneself to another as to an end.

The act of ordering oneself to another is an act of submitting oneself as a part. Within love, however, an individual is not what might be called a merely productive part; rather, he is what might be called a possessing part. He does not simply produce some good separate from his own good. Rather, he comes to possess a good, which he orders to others, as possessed together with himself. The cellist does not simply produce music as a product distinct from herself; she *plays* music, and she plays symphonic music insofar as she is united to others. She is ordered to the whole by being a part of the whole, thereby partially possessing the good. Every part has a role to play within the whole. Within a love for others, one's role is most fundamentally to possess the good. Aquinas makes the distinction as follows:

Whenever some things are ordered to an end, those among them that are unable to obtain the end through themselves must be ordered to those that do accomplish the end, which are ordered into the end for their own sakes. For example, the end of an army is victory, which the soldiers accomplish through their own act by fighting. Within the army, only the soldiers are sought for their own sakes; everyone else is given other duties, such as caring for the horses or preparing the weapons, and are sought for the sake of the soldiers. Since the ultimate end of the universe, namely, God, is attained in himself only by intellectual natures, insofar as they know him and love him, it follows that intellectual natures alone are sought in the universe for their own sakes, while all others are sought for the sake of them.[19]

19. Aquinas, *Summa contra Gentiles* III, chap. 112, no. 3 (Editio Leonina, XIIII: 356, ll. a32–47): "Quandocumque sunt aliqua ordinata ad finem aliquem, si qua inter illa ad finem pertingere non possunt per seipsa, oportet ea ordinari ad illa quae finem consequuntur, quae propter se ordinantur in finem: sicut finis exercitus est victoria, quam milites consequuntur per proprium actum pugnando, qui soli propter se in exercitu quaeruntur; omnes autem alii, ad alia officia deputati, puta ad custodiendum equos, ad parandum arma, propter milites in exercitu quaeruntur. Constat autem ex praemissis finem ultimum universi

The first act of ordering oneself to the whole must remain throughout the union of love; otherwise, the love ceases. The order need not always be actual, which would surely be impossible. It suffices if it remains habitual. Once the person has directed himself to the shared good, then he remains so directed unless he changes his mind. He can reverse his decision, choosing to seek his own good simply as a private good, excluding the good of the others. He might do so because the order to the others demands something he does not wish to give. He then "sins" against the love by omission. On the other hand, he might reject the order to the good of the others because he seeks some good inconsistent with it. He then "sins" against the love by transgression.

A FUNDAMENTAL CHOICE

The choice that the unbaptized youth faces, then, is the choice of everyone entering into a union of love. He must decide whether he will treat his good as belonging to some greater good. He must decide whether his good is solitary or whether it is shared. He must decide whether to find his completion simply in his private good or in something beyond himself, in the completion of a union of individuals. To choose the shared good is simply to choose to order himself to another—to some united whole—as to an end.

The fundamental choice in the moral life—the first choice that the youth must make—concerns the greatest shared good of all. It concerns not just this or that particular good; rather, it concerns the overall good of the person. Is this good a singular good or a shared good? In particular, is it to be shared with God? Does the good of the individual belong to the divine good or does it not?[20] Each person must make this choice. To choose in accord with the shared divine good is to choose what is truly good; to choose one's good as separate and individual is to choose evil. The choice for the ultimate end, then, is not simply a choice for some good. It is a choice for or against a *shared* good.

Deum esse, quem sola intellectualis natura consequitur in seipso, eum scilicet cognoscendo et amando, ut ex dictis patet. Sola igitur intellectualis natura est propter se quaesita in universo, alia autem omnia propter ipsam."

20. Gregory Froelich argues that the ultimate end must always be a shared good ("Ultimate End and Common Good," *The Thomist* 57 [1993]: 609–19).

In the future when we refer to the divine good, we will mean the *shared* divine good. When actions are called good or bad in relation to the ultimate end, they are called good or bad in relation to the shared divine good. If adultery is evil, for instance, it is not evil simply because it is opposed to knowledge of God but because it is opposed to the shared knowledge of God. Likewise, if murder is evil in relation to the ultimate end, it is not simply because it is opposed to knowledge of God but because it is opposed to the shared knowledge of God.

WHAT LIES AHEAD

We have reached a break in our study of the psychology of sin. Up to this point we have focused primarily upon different ways in which we as human beings order our actions to ends, and in particular we have focused upon diverse ways in which we order our actions to the ultimate end. This focus has been demanded by the nature of sin, in which we turn away from the true ultimate end and direct ourselves to some false ultimate end. We have seen that the ideal, exemplified in the strong-set view, demands that we order all of our actions, at least virtually, to the ultimate end. This ultimate end is not simply the overall good; it is the concrete realization of that overall good. Indeed, this concrete realization is not simply a good to be attained; it is a shared good, which therefore implies an order to others—chiefly to God—as to a subject with whom we share the good.

We have also seen, however, that few live up to this ideal. Most people have some chief good around which they structure their lives, but in their daily affairs they often pursue other goods independently, quite apart from their order to this chief good. The only requirement placed upon these various pursuits is that they not oppose the chief good. People, then, do not direct all of their actions virtually to their chief good. Rather, they often direct them merely habitually to the chief good.

This habitual order to the chief good, we have seen, suffices to avoid mortal sin, although a virtual order is needed to avoid venial sin. Even when sin is avoided, the desire for independent goods—restrained only by the negative condition of retaining the divine good—opens the door to sin. These goods are desired as if good even when they lack the order to the divine good.

These considerations have prepared the way for a more detailed consideration of how we pass through the open door, moving from the mere temptation to sin to the choice and execution of sin. The character of this study, then, will cease to focus so exclusively upon the ultimate end and our order to it. It will begin to focus upon how we are led into sin. Thomas himself discusses three internal causes of sin: ignorance, passion, and an evil will. These three causes will provide the focus of the next four chapters. An additional chapter will address the enigma of omissions, which pose a special difficulty because in omissions we are not necessarily relating to some false good; it suffices if we fail to be led into the true good.

The study will then consider, in the subsequent three chapters, some more general problems concerning sin: what is the very first internal cause of sin, and what is the kind of freedom by which we can be held responsible for sin. The final chapter will reflect back upon what has been discovered.

↯ CHAPTER 7

SINS OF PASSION

Perhaps the most discussed mystery surrounding sin concerns what is called weakness, in which a person acts against his best judgment.[1] Christine, for instance, has judged that she should not eat another piece of chocolate; nevertheless, she proceeds to eat one, perhaps even eating several pieces of chocolate. Weakness poses a problem given the widely accepted premise that people choose in accord with their best judgment. If Christine judges that she should not eat the chocolate, and if human beings, Christine included, choose according to their judgment, then Christine should choose to avoid the chocolate. Yet, she eats it.

If human beings had the kind of freedom by which they could choose in opposition to their judgments, then weakness would pose no mystery. Such voluntarism, however, seems inexplicable, nor is it advocated by Aquinas, who places the root of weakness not in some independence of the will, but in the breakdown in the judgment upon which the person

[1]. Portions of the material in this chapter appeared in Jensen, "The Error of the Passions," *The Thomist* 73 (2009): 349–79. For other treatments of Aquinas on weakness, see Bonnie Kent, "Transitory Vice: Thomas Aquinas on Incontinence," *Journal of the History of Philosophy* 27 (1989): 199–223; Denis J. M. Bradley, "Thomas Aquinas on Weakness of Will," in *Weakness of Will from Plato to the Present*, ed. Tobias Hoffmann (Washington, D.C.: The Catholic University of America Press, 2008), 82–114; Joseph Caulfield, "Practical Ignorance in Moral Actions," *Laval théologique et philosophique* 7 (1951): 103–12.

acts. Thomas is not alone in this regard. Distinguishing different senses in which an agent can make a judgment is a typical approach to resolving the mystery of weakness.

Weakness does not account for every sin. Only a subset of sins—perhaps a small subset—arise from weakness. Aquinas identifies two other internal causes of sin, namely, ignorance and an evil will. Weakness occurs only when a person (1) judges well—or at least would judge well, if he took the time to judge—concerning what is good and to be done, and (2) intends to do what is good, but (3) ultimately acts against his judgment. Sometimes, the person does not meet the first condition, for on account of ignorance he judges poorly. Sometimes the person does not meet the second condition, for he sets out to do evil.

When examining Aquinas's account of weakness, we must avoid confusing it with modern notions of weakness, which almost certainly do not coincide with that of Aquinas, who identifies sins of weakness with sins of passion, that is, sins that arise from some emotional desire, probably from a strong and pressing emotional desire.[2] Christine, for instance, eats chocolates because of her strong emotional desire for sweets. The contemporary use of "weakness" is almost certainly broader. It includes sins of passion but more besides.[3] In the present chapter, we will focus upon sins of passion; we will examine some other uses of "weakness" in subsequent chapters.

A BRIEF STATEMENT OF AQUINAS'S ACCOUNT OF SINS OF PASSION

A sin of passion meets the three conditions listed above: (1) with his reason, the person judges what is good; (2) he intends to do what is good; but (3) he ultimately acts against his judgment. What goes wrong, thinks

---

2. Aquinas, *Summa theologiae* I-II, q. 77, a. 3.

3. Daniel Guevara, for instance, discusses cases of "aggressive akrasia" ("The Will as Practical Reason," 34). Sometimes his descriptions of such cases seem, to me at least, to be highly improbable, suggesting that no such kind of weakness exists. Insofar as his cases have plausibility, however, it seems likely that they would not belong to what Aquinas classifies as weakness. Likewise, Donald Davidson claims that, at least sometimes, the weak person full well realizes that he chooses the lesser good, a clarity that Aquinas finds only in sins from an evil will ("How Is Weakness of Will Possible?" in *Essays on Actions and Events* [Oxford: Clarendon Press, 1980], 26).

Thomas, is that the passions supply an alternate and opposing judgment to that of reason, and the person acts according to the judgment of the passions rather than according to the judgment of reason.[4] Thomas provides a simplified example of the two strains of reasoning.

The Argument of Reason	The Argument of the Passions
Adultery is to be avoided.	
This action is pleasurable.	Pleasure is to be pursued.
This action is to be avoided.	This action is to be pursued.

At the moment of choice, the weak person uses the argument of the passions. In what way, then, can we say that he meets the first condition above, that with his reason he judges what is good? He cannot be thinking both arguments at the same time, which reach contradictory conclusions. Ultimately, the weak person does not use the argument of reason; rather, he reaches the judgment of the passions. It seems to follow that he meets neither the first nor the third condition of weakness. He fails in the first, for he does not judge correctly; he fails in the third, for he in fact does act according to his judgment, which is nothing other than the judgment of the passions.

Thomas, however, allows that the person can have both arguments, although in different ways. He distinguishes two ways in which an individual can "know" or "judge" something: either actually or habitually. The person knows actually when he is now thinking on the matter. The person knows habitually what he knows with a habit of knowledge (not to be confused with the habitual order, discussed above). An individual knows, for instance, that the square of four is sixteen, but he need not always be thinking of it. He knows it even while he sleeps, or when he is reading a book. The person can use this habitual knowledge when he wants, at which point he begins to think or know actually.

At the moment of choice the weak person judges actually according to the argument of the passions. Nevertheless, he holds the argument of reason—or at least parts of it—by habit. The person acts against what he *habitually* knows to be best, although at the moment of choice he is not thinking upon it.

---

4. The following account is drawn from Aquinas, *Summa theologiae* I-II, q. 77, a. 2; and Aquinas, *De malo*, q. 3, a. 9.

This brief description of Aquinas's solution to the problem of weakness needs to be filled in. From where does the argument of the passions arise? In what precise way does it differ from the argument of reason? In what way is it faulty? We will seek to answer these questions by seeing in what way Thomas might address the criticisms laid against his view by Donald Davidson.

DONALD DAVIDSON'S CRITICISMS

Donald Davidson has criticized Aquinas's explanation of weakness on several counts.[5] First, Thomas is forced to deny what seems to be a true premise, namely, the major premise of the argument of the passions (such as, "Pleasure is to be pursued").[6] Both the argument of reason and the argument of the passions are valid, yet they reach contrary conclusions that cannot both be true. Since the passions reach the incorrect conclusion, it follows that the argument of the passions must have a false premise. It seems difficult, at least in most cases, to deny the minor premise, for instance, that this action of adultery is physically pleasurable. It remains, thinks Davidson, that the false premise must be the major premise, that pleasure is to be pursued. But do we really want to deny this premise? Is it never reasonable to pursue pleasure?

This criticism leads to a second: Thomas, it seems, cannot allow for real moral conflict. Everything is black and white. All the truth falls on the side of reason; the side of the passions is completely in error.[7]

Davidson criticizes Aquinas on a third point as well: Thomas leaves nothing by which the weak person can sort between the two arguments. There is no "will" by which the person can choose between them.[8] Rather, reason and the passions battle it out; the passions win; and the person acts upon the judgment of the passions. How, then, is the person responsible for his weak action, which is just the upshot of the victory of the passions?

We will address the first two criticisms of Davidson in the current chapter. The third criticism we will leave for the next chapter, which con-

5. Davidson, "How Is Weakness of Will Possible?"
6. Ibid., 34.
7. Ibid.
8. Ibid., 33–34.

cerns weakness of will (rather than simply sins of passion). According to the first criticism, Thomas must identify a true premise as false. According to the second, Thomas cannot allow for moral ambiguity or moral conflict. As we will see, Davidson misidentifies the error of the passions. He supposes that the major premise is false; in fact, Aquinas focuses all his attention upon the minor premise. It will turn out, then, that Thomas grants some truth to the major premise. This very admission, however, is an admission of moral conflict or ambiguity, at least as Davidson perceives it. In what follows, then, we will try to show in what way the minor premise of the passions is false and in what way the major premise is true.

THE TRUTH OF THE MAJOR PREMISE OF THE PASSIONS

Thomas does suppose, as Davidson claims, that the passions err in their judgment, but he does not identify the source of the error with the major premise. He says very little about the major premise, except that it is suggested by the passions.[9] Indeed, his entire account of weakness dwells upon the minor premise. The weak person is led into error precisely because the passions focus his attention on the minor premise, which states that the action is pleasurable.[10]

This focus of Aquinas suggests that the error is found in the minor premise. If the passions did provide a false major premise, then this role of the passions—rather than the role of fixating the mind upon the minor premise—would be the primary cause of sins of passion. As it is, Aquinas barely mentions that the passions play some role in providing the major premise. Furthermore, he seems to concede, with Davidson, that this major premise has a true meaning. Thomas acknowledges that pleasures of the senses, considered as such, do not oppose reason.[11] "Sensible and

---

9. Aquinas, *Summa theologiae* I-II, q. 77, a. 2, ad 4.

10. See, for instance, Aquinas, *De malo*, q. 3, a. 9, ad 7; Aquinas, *Summa theologiae* I-II, q. 77, a. 2.

11. Daniel Westberg notes that acting for pleasure is not irrational (*Right Practical Reason: Aristotle, Action, and Prudence in Aquinas* [Oxford: Clarendon Press, 1994], 207), and it is sometimes good to use the major premise of the passions (208). Grisez, Finnis, and Boyle do not include pleasure as a basic good, but they grant that pleasure can provide motivation, although they do not consider it rational motivation; see Grisez, Finnis, and Boyle, "Practical Principles," 104–5.

bodily goods, considered in their species, are not opposed to reason; rather, they serve reason, as an instrument that reason uses to attain its own end. They are opposed to reason chiefly insofar as the sensitive appetite tends into them apart from the measure of reason."[12] Evidently, then, the error of the passions lies in the minor premise, that is, in the statement, "This action is pleasurable."[13]

If the major premise is true, then Davidson's second criticism misses the mark. Pleasure does indeed provide a reason for pursuing something, and consequently Thomas can allow for "moral conflict," that is, he can allow some truth on the side that ultimately leads to error. This possibility is obscured by Aquinas's example of adultery, which is in fact black and white.

The case of Christine eating chocolate is not so black and white. Eating chocolate is not always wrong, and pleasure provides a legitimate reason to eat chocolate. Perhaps pleasure should not be the sole reason for eating chocolate, but it certainly can provide a reason, and perhaps a deciding reason. If the choice is between a piece of chocolate and a piece of caramel (both having been offered by the host, whom it would be rude to refuse), perhaps the decision will come down, not unreasonably, to which of the two Christine considers more pleasurable. Reason, then, might well use the major premise of the passions, urging the pursuit of what is pleasurable.

But now suppose that Christine considers taking a second piece. She recognizes that the pleasure makes the chocolate worth pursuing. At the same time, she recognizes that refusing the candy is no longer rude. Indeed, it may now be rude to take another piece of chocolate, since few pieces remain for the other guests. Previously, the pleasure of the choco-

12. Aquinas, *Summa theologiae* II-II, q. 141, a. 3: "Nam bona sensibilia et corporalia, secundum suam speciem considerata, non repugnant rationi, sed magis serviunt ei, sicut instrumenta quibus ratio utitur ad consecutionem proprii finis. Repugnant autem ei praecipue secundum quod appetitus sensitivus in ea tendit non secundum modum rationis."

13. Bradley affirms that for Aquinas the error of weakness always concerns the minor premise ("Thomas Aquinas on Weakness," 95); see also Caulfield, "Practical Ignorance," 106–7. Kent ("Transitory Vice") seeks to show that Aquinas thought (in opposition to Aristotle) that the incontinent erred in the judgment of the universal, although she acknowledges that Aquinas emphasizes the error in the particular. Kent implies that the error of the major premise is the same as that made in a sin from an evil will, only it is held temporarily by the weak person (214–16).

late was a supporting reason, alongside the desire to be polite. Now, the pleasure of the chocolate becomes the sole reason in favor of taking it. Nevertheless, Christine's passions focus her attention upon the pleasure of the candy, drawing her mind to the minor premise of the passions. She reaches the conclusion that she should pursue the chocolate, and she takes another piece. Her error lies not in the major premise, which she had correctly used in her prior reasoning; rather, it lies in the minor premise. As will become evident below, however, the minor premise will prove more complex than this simplified example reveals.

RESTRICTED CONSIDERATIONS

As we have seen, Davidson says that (for Aquinas) all the truth is on the side of reason and that the passions have nothing to offer. On this point, however, we have seen, Davidson is incorrect. But Davidson has another reason for supposing that Thomas cannot allow for moral conflict. The structure of Aquinas's two arguments, thinks Davidson, do not allow for the combination of pros and cons. Even if both sides have some truth, they cannot be joined into a united judgment.[14]

Why does Davidson suppose that Aquinas cannot allow the combination of "conflicting" true premises? Because all of Aquinas's propositions—premises and conclusions—are categorical; as such they cannot be combined. Suppose that Christine uses the following two lines of reasoning:

The Argument of Reason	The Argument of the Passions
Eating unhealthy foods is to be avoided.	Pleasure is to be pursued.
This is an act of eating unhealthy foods.	This action is pleasurable.
This action is to be avoided.	This action is to be pursued.

The two major premises cannot be combined into a premise that encapsulates the insights of both, such as, "Eating unhealthy foods that are pleasurable should be avoided." After all, if the major premise is a universal categorical proposition (that is, a proposition without qualifiers or conditions), then all pleasure should be pursued; the premise can never be incorporated into a statement about some pleasure that should be avoided.

---

14. Davidson, "How Is Weakness of Will Possible?" 34.

In his own account of weakness, Davidson gets around this difficulty by making his propositions prima facie statements rather than categorical.[15]

The Major Premise of Reason
Prima facie, acts of eating unhealthy foods should be avoided.

The Major Premise of the Passions
Prima facie, pleasure should be pursued.

Will or conscience, then, might combine the evidence of reason and of the passions into the following all-things-considered major premise, which Davidson also calls the judgment of conscience:

The Major Premise of Conscience
Prima facie, acts of eating pleasurable unhealthy foods should be avoided.

The problem with the weak-willed person, on Davidson's view, is that he uses the partial evidence of the passions rather than the more comprehensive evidence of conscience. According to Davidson, this approach is unavailable to Aquinas. He can provide no overall judgment, for he cannot combine the evidence of universal categorical propositions.[16]

Thomas would be surprised that he is unable to provide an overall judgment. Indeed, he seems to think that the judgment of reason itself is a kind of overall judgment. Reason can and does consider multiple aspects of an action, both good and bad.[17] In the *De malo*, Thomas suggests that reason considers various good and bad features of an action, even saying that an action can be good for giving pleasure. When the will is moved according to reason, however, Aquinas says that it is moved according to

---

15. Ibid., 38. My presentations of Davidson's propositions are greatly simplified. I have modified them to appear more like Aquinas's. In a similar fashion, Paul Grice and Judith Baker substitute a simple positive statement for Davidson's comparative ("Davidson on 'Weakness of the Will,'" in *Essays on Davidson: Actions and Events*, ed. Bruce Vermazen and Merrill B. Hintikka [Oxford: Clarendon Press, 1985], 38), and incur no objection from Davidson ("Davidson Responds: Intention and Action/Event and Cause," in *Essays on Davidson: Actions and Events*, ed. Bruce Vermazen and Merrill B. Hintikka [Oxford: Clarendon Press, 1985]).

16. Davidson, "How Is Weakness of Will Possible?" 33–35.

17. Thomas says that we sometimes choose an action based on how it is best at bringing about many things (*Summa theologiae* I-II, q. 12, a. 3). An example of reasoning involving the weighing of benefits and evils is found in ibid., II-II, q. 125, a. 1.

the condition that has greater weight. In other words, the judgment of reason is not one-sided; rather, it is a judgment of what aspects of an act are most important: "The will may be inclined to that which has more to offer in one respect than in another ... insofar as one aspect has greater weight; then the will is moved according to reason, for example, when a man prefers that which is useful for health over that which is useful to pleasure."[18] Furthermore, Thomas says elsewhere that the prudent person considers all the relevant circumstances, judging how one consideration might be overshadowed by others.

Since prudence concerns singular actions, in which many factors come together, it sometimes happens that something considered in itself might be good and fitting for the end, but from some additional feature it becomes evil or inappropriate for the end. When considered in itself, for instance, giving signs of love to someone seems to be an appropriate means of fostering love in his heart, but if he happens to be proud, or if he suspects flattery, then it will no longer be fitting for the end. Therefore, prudence demands careful consideration, involving a comparison between that which is ordered to the end and any additional aspects of an action.[19]

The judgment of reason, then, is not simply one-sided. It is a comprehensive judgment that best corresponds with Davidson's judgments of conscience.

Davidson claims that Aquinas cannot allow for this comprehensive judgment because his premises are universal categorical propositions, which cannot be combined. But perhaps Davidson has mischaracterized

---

18. Aquinas, *De malo*, q. 6 (Editio Leonina, XXIII: 150, ll. 450–56): "Et quod uoluntas feratur in id quod sibi offertur, magis secundum hanc particularem conditionem quam secundum aliam, potest contingere tripliciter. Vno quidem modo in quantum una preponderat,et tunc mouetur uoluntas secundum rationem: puta cum homo preeligit id quod est utile sanitati ei quod est utile uoluptati."

19. Aquinas, *Summa theologiae* II-II, q. 49, a. 7: "Quia prudentia, sicut dictum est, est circa singularia operabilia, in quibus multa concurrunt, contingit aliquid secundum se consideratum esse bonum et conveniens fini, quod tamen ex aliquibus concurrentibus redditur vel malum vel non opportunum ad finem. Sicut ostendere signa amoris alicui, secundum se consideratum, videtur esse conveniens ad alliciendum eius animum ad amorem, sed si contingat in animo illius superbia vel suspicio adulationis, non erit hoc conveniens ad finem. Et ideo necessaria est circumspectio ad prudentiam, ut scilicet homo id quod ordinatur in finem comparet etiam cum his quae circumstant."

Aquinas's major premises. Perhaps they are not, or at least not always, universal categorical propositions. Indeed, it might be absurd to suppose that they are. As G. E. M. Anscombe has pointed out, only a madman would assent to a universal major premise of the form "All pleasure is to be pursued," or "All nutritional food should be eaten."[20] Neither of these precepts can be fulfilled, since there are many mutually exclusive pleasures, and many nutritional foods that could not be eaten simultaneously. The universal precept to pursue pleasure is not followed even by the intemperate person; he is not apt to pursue pleasurable adultery, for instance, if it is likely to get him killed.

The major premise of the passions, then, is not necessarily universally quantified; it does not read, "*All* pleasure is to be pursued."[21] Thomas himself says that the principles of practical reasoning are not necessary, or they have only a conditional necessity: "The final decision or judgment of reason concerning what is to be done is in the realm of contingent things, which can be done by us. In such affairs, conclusions do not follow of necessity, with an absolute necessity, from necessary principles, but only from those that are necessary conditionally, for example, if he runs, then he moves."[22] The premises, then, are in some manner conditional, perhaps like Davidson's prima facie judgments. Aquinas also says that in our deliberations we consider things under various aspects: "Every particular good thing may be considered under the aspect of being good and under the aspect of the lack of good, which has the notion of evil, and in this respect everything may be considered as worthy of choice or as something to be avoided."[23]

---

20. Anscombe, *Intention*, 61.

21. In *De malo*, q. 6, Thomas uses the quantifier "all," in "All pleasures should be pursued," the quantifier is absent in the *Summa theologiae* (I-II, q. 77, a. 2, ad 4). Given Anscombe's arguments about the absurdity of the universally quantified major premise, and given other things that (we will see) Aquinas says concerning the inquiry of deliberation, it seems fair to say that Aquinas would not intend the universal quantifier to be taken literally, for even the immoderate person does not pursue *all* pleasures available. He judges that some are to be avoided, perhaps because avoiding them will afford greater pleasures in the future.

22. Aquinas, *Summa theologiae* I-II, q. 13, a. 6, ad 2: "Ad secundum dicendum quod sententia sive iudicium rationis de rebus agendis est circa contingentia, quae a nobis fieri possunt, in quibus conclusiones non ex necessitate sequuntur ex principiis necessariis absoluta necessitate, sed necessariis solum ex conditione, ut, si currit, movetur."

23. Ibid., I-II, q. 13, a. 6: "Et rursum in omnibus particularibus bonis potest considerare

The propositions, then, might look as follows. "Insofar as an act is eating unhealthy foods, it should be avoided" or, "Insofar as an act is pleasurable, it should be pursued." These two propositions might easily be combined into the following: "Insofar as an action is eating unhealthy foods and is also pleasurable, it should be avoided." This manner of putting things does not seem that different from Davidson's prima facie judgments. Davidson himself uses the terminology "in a certain respect" and "insofar as" to express prima facie judgments.[24]

The same point might be put differently, in terms of a distinction we have already seen. Thomas says that we can desire something considered in itself or as considered in the concrete. The ship captain, for instance, desires to keep his cargo considered in itself but not considered in the concrete. His deliberations might include the following propositions: "Considered in itself, cargo should be kept," and "Considered in itself, a deadly weight should be jettisoned." These propositions might then be combined into another: "Considered in itself, cargo that is also a deadly weight should be jettisoned." Since these propositions restrict considerations to some particular features (perhaps a combination of features), we will call them "restricted considerations."

In this manner, a wide variety of things might enter deliberation. Someone deciding whether to buy a house might consider location, cost, size, need of repair, appearance, and so on. His deliberations might include multiple restricted considerations, for example, "Considered according to its location, the house should be pursued," or "Considered according to its size, the house should be avoided." These individual judgments might be combined into an extensive (but still restrictive) statement, such as, "Considered insofar as it is in this location, of this cost, of this size, of this need of repair, of this appearance, and so on, the house should be bought." Combined judgments of these sorts might well parallel what Davidson calls all-things-considered judgments.

---

rationem boni alicuius, et defectum alicuius boni, quod habet rationem mali, et secundum hoc, potest unumquodque huiusmodi bonorum apprehendere ut eligibile, vel fugibile."

24. Donald Davidson, "Intention," in *Essays on Actions and Events*, 98.

"AND NOTHING ELSE"

Davidson rightly points out that these restricted considerations—or his prima facie propositions—do not reach a categorical conclusion, at least not by a simple categorical minor premise. Consider the following argument of the sea captain:

Major premise:	Considered in itself, cargo that is a deadly weight should be jettisoned.
Minor premise:	This cargo is a deadly weight.

What conclusion should he reach? It is a mistake to suppose that he should conclude that, "This cargo should be jettisoned." Rather, he should conclude that, "Considered insofar as it is a deadly weight, this cargo should be jettisoned." Such a conditional judgment, notes Davidson, will hardly move someone to act. We choose actions, not actions under a consideration. We can *want* things considered abstractly; we can *choose* only what is actual. Full-fledged desire demands a categorical proposition. In Davidson's terminology, it requires an "all-out" or *sans phrase* judgment, which states that an action should be done *tout court*, categorically and without qualification.[25]

How are these judgments reached? Davidson provides no explanation.[26] Some vehicle must move an agent from a prima facie premise to an all-out conclusion. The only available vehicle appears to be the minor premise. If it is to play this role, however, then the minor premise must be more than it first appears. We have seen that the major premise is not usually a simple universal categorical proposition but rather a restricted consideration. Likewise, we will discover that the minor premise must be more than Aquinas's simplified examples suggest.

We can consider an action abstracted from particular conditions, for example, we can consider an act of eating unhealthy foods just as such, abstracting from whether the action is pleasant, rude, and so on. The problem with these abstract considerations is that no action exists as such, that is, no action exists just with the particular conditions under

---

25. Davidson, "How Is Weakness of Will Possible?" 40; Davidson, "Davidson Responds," 197.
26. Davidson, "How Is Weakness of Will Possible?" 42.

consideration; actions always have other features, which are left out of the abstract consideration. But what if there were such an action? What if there were an action that was simply and only an act of eating unhealthy food. Then it seems that a categorical conclusion could be reached. The practical syllogism would look as follows:

> Insofar as an action is eating unhealthy food, it should be avoided.
> This is an action of eating unhealthy food and nothing else.
> ───
> This action should be avoided.

In effect, the "and nothing else" clause—added to the minor premise—takes the abstract character of the major premise and says that for this particular action nothing is being abstracted. The restricted consideration turns out, for this action, not to be restricted. In this manner, the minor premise can become a vehicle to move from a restricted consideration to an all-out conclusion. Unfortunately, it becomes this vehicle only at great expense, for it also becomes obviously false. There is no action that is simply an act of eating unhealthy foods with no other features applying to it.

A further modification makes the minor premise at least less obviously false. The "and nothing else" clause need not exclude every additional feature of the action; it need exclude only features that have some bearing upon the practical value of the action. The premise, then, might be modified as follows: "This action is an act of eating unhealthy foods and nothing else about it has any practical implications." Even this modified premise is still false, for we cannot exhaustively list, or even consider, all of the practical features of an action. Nevertheless, it seems to be closer to the truth, because the "and nothing else" clause excludes fewer items; it excludes from the action only items of practical import.

We might reduce the number of items excluded by increasing the number that are included within the restricted consideration. Rather than considering simply that eating the food is unhealthy, we might consider whether it is pleasurable, polite, and so on.[27] The corresponding

---

27. Michael Barnwell claims that the proposition with the term "fornication" cannot be similarly "complexified" (Barnwell's term; "Aquinas's Two Different Accounts of Akrasia," *American Catholic Philosophical Quarterly* 84 [2010]: 56). He ignores some simple possibilities, for example, "Pleasurable adultery should be avoided." The addition does not change the ultimate judgment with regard to pursuit or avoidance, but it does provide a complex term.

minor premise, when modified appropriately, might look as follows: "This action is an act of eating food that is unhealthy, pleasurable, polite... and (practically) nothing else." The more things included within the ellipsis, the fewer things will be excluded by the "and nothing else" clause. Conceivably, the premise might actually become true. Realistically, however, an individual will usually be unable to fill in enough information. Even when the statement happens to be true, the individual might be unable to determine its truth, since he is not sure whether he has indeed included all the features of practical importance. As Alan Donagan notes, all the things that are considered within an "all things considered judgment" are not all the things that are.[28]

We should note an exception to this uncertainty. Thomas thinks that for absolute negative prohibitions, we can indeed know that we have considered everything of practical importance. If the person knows that an action is adultery, for instance, then nothing else need be considered to determine that it should be avoided. Nothing else will have any practical importance bearing upon whether the action should be pursued. These cases, however, are limited cases, and they do not reflect many of our day-to-day judgments.[29] Unfortunately, Thomas used just such a limited case for his example of weakness, thereby obscuring the fact that the judgment of reason might consider multiple features of an action.

With a few exceptions, then, the minor premise, when modified to include an "and (practically) nothing else" clause, falls short of the truth. At the very least, the individual is left uncertain concerning the truth of the minor premise. This uncertainty arises from the complexity of what might count as practically relevant. As we have seen, the ultimate test of practicality is the final end. Some actions (good actions) are ordered to the final end; other actions (mortal sins) are opposed to the final end; and yet other actions (venial sins) lack an order to the final end but neither are they opposed to it. A feature of an action has practical implications, then, insofar as it bears upon the direction of the action concerning the final end.

28. Donagan, *Choice*, 149.

29. Even when the major premise should be a universally quantified negative proposition, it might not be considered as such. Aquinas says that necessary means are not always considered as necessary. See *Summa theologiae* I, q. 82, a. 2.

Some features by themselves might make the action to be opposed to the final end. That this woman is another man's wife, for instance, is a feature that makes the sexual act to be a mortal sin. Other features are less definitive. They might make the action, considered in itself, to be ordered to the final end, leaving open the possibility that some other feature might take away this order. Still other features will have no bearing at all upon the order of the action to the end, and these features are practically irrelevant.

To make matters more complicated, a feature that is relevant for one action might be irrelevant for another, and vice versa. For the act of sexual intercourse, it is relevant that the woman is married to another man. For the act of courteously opening a door, this feature is usually irrelevant. Given these multiple features and given the complex manner in which they relate to the ultimate end, it becomes clear that often a person will not be able to determine with complete certainty whether all things of practical importance have been considered.

Typically, then, the modified minor premise, which includes the "and (practically) nothing else" clause, will be underdetermined by the evidence, that is, the person will be unable to determine with certainty that it is true.[30] Nevertheless, the individual can still judge that the proposition is true.[31] A scientist does not have absolute evidence that black holes exist, or that a black hole exists at the center of our galaxy; nevertheless, he might affirm the truth of these propositions because he is satisfied with the evidence available. Similarly, someone might judge the minor premise to be true because his evidence is satisfactory, although not conclusive. In this manner, we can reach Davidson's all-out judgments. The argument might look as follows:

---

30. MacDonald makes a similar point ("Practical Reasoning and Reasons-Explanations: Aquinas's Account of Reason's Role in Action," in *Aquinas's Moral Theory: Essays in Honor of Norman Kretzmann*, ed. Scott MacDonald and Eleonore Stump [Ithaca, N.Y.: Cornell University Press, 1998], 154).

31. MacDonald argues that the agent need not positively judge that there is nothing else to be considered concerning the action; it suffices that the agent does not think that something further needs to be considered ("Practical Reasoning," 157).

Fully Practical Syllogism
Considered in itself, an action that is unhealthy, pleasurable, polite ... should be avoided.
This action is unhealthy, pleasurable, polite ... and practically nothing else.

This action should be avoided.

The practical "and nothing else" clause found in the minor premise means that the abstraction found in the major premise is not in fact an abstraction for this particular action. The truth of the minor premise is granted by satisfactory but not conclusive evidence. We readily recognize, for instance, that the shape of a piece of candy rarely has practical implications. Nevertheless, we cannot absolutely exclude the shape from our practical considerations. Its exclusion, then, is a judgment call based upon extensive experience of the practical irrelevance of shape.

ILL-CONSIDERATION

The minor premise is rarely affirmed with conclusive evidence. Still, it does not follow that just any evidence will suffice. The person must have some satisfactory evidence that allows him to add the "and nothing else" clause. If Christine considers only that the chocolate is pleasurable, then she would be hasty in adding on "and practically nothing else." She would still be hasty if she includes only one other feature—for instance, that it is not rude to eat the chocolate. She would have considered too few features of the action. Thomas calls this deficiency of practical reasoning "ill-consideration."[32] The person does not consider all that he should. He is led to action—reaching an all-out conclusion—before he has considered all that is relevant.

Strong emotional desire might push someone in the direction of ill-consideration. Our passions focus our attention upon some features of an action and not upon others. The person tempted by adultery, for instance, focuses upon the pleasure of the action. His desires urge him to make a choice while focusing upon this feature of the action, and his passions might even hinder him from thinking clearly about other aspects of

---

32. Aquinas, *Summa theologiae* II-II, q. 53, a. 4. Bonnie Kent identifies sins of weakness as instances of negligence ("Aquinas and Weakness of Will," *Philosophy and Phenomenological Research* 75 [2007]: 85–86).

the action. Similarly, someone who is afraid has difficulty concentrating upon objects outside his fear, and he imagines every sound or movement to be a threat.

Aquinas discusses three ways in which the passions might cloud our reasoning.[33] First, they might distract our attention from that which deserves consideration. Second, they might pull reason toward a conclusion opposed to reason. Third, the bodily state of strong passion might hinder the mind from clear reasoning, even as being tired hinders clear thinking. The man facing the decision concerning adultery might have his reasoning clouded in some or in all of these ways. If he chooses under the influence of such passions, he sins from weakness, and he also sins from ill-consideration, an ill-consideration caused by his passions. His reasoning has two strains, only one of which comes to actual fruition.

The Argument of Reason	The Argument of the Passions
Major: Considered in itself, an action that is adultery, pleasurable, ... should be avoided.	Major: Considered in itself, an action that is pleasurable should be pursued.
Minor: This action is adultery, pleasurable, ... and (practically) nothing else.	Minor: This action is pleasurable and (practically) nothing else.
Conclusion: This action should be avoided.	Conclusion: This action should be pursued.

The weak person affirms the minor premise of the passions because his emotions focus his attention upon pleasure, making him think that nothing else matters.[34] The person errs, as Thomas suggests, in the minor premise. The premise that the action is pleasurable is certainly true, and from this true premise follows this true (but practically impotent) conclusion: "Considered just as pleasurable, this action should be pursued." But the person does not in fact use this true premise. Rather, he uses the

---

33. Aquinas, *Summa theologiae* I-II, q. 77, a. 2; I-II, q. 33, a. 3.

34. Barnwell supposes that if the argument of reason includes extra terms (unhealthy, rude, and so on), then the argument of the passions must include corresponding additional terms ("Aquinas's Two Different Accounts," 58). He ignores the possibility that the error of weakness is precisely the failure to consider the various terms.

following false premise: "The action is pleasurable and practically nothing else." From this false premise follows a false conclusion and an evil action.

PASSIONS, WEAKNESS, AND THE WILL

Davidson's first two objections against Aquinas, then, miss the mark. He accuses Aquinas of denying a true premise, namely, the major premise of the passions. It turns out, however, that Aquinas affirms the truth of this major premise and denies the truth of the minor premise. Davidson also accuses Aquinas of being unable to consider multiple facets of a situation, both its pros and cons, because Aquinas uses simple categorical propositions in the major premise. It turns out, however, that the major premise of a practical syllogism is more subtle. It is a restricted consideration that can include many aspects of an action.

In the end, Aquinas's account of sins of passion is not that different from Davidson's account of weakness. For both Davidson and Aquinas, the person has two lines of argument, one that is complete and provides an "all things considered" judgment, and another that is incomplete, including only a limited subset of the evidence available. For both, the weak person acts based upon the limited evidence.[35]

Davidson's third objection remains. He claims that Aquinas leaves no room for a "will" to decide between the two lines of argument. Rather, the passions simply defeat reason and the person is left to act upon the argument of the passions. In the next chapter, we will see that this objection also misses the mark. The will does indeed have a role to play in sins of passion.

35. Davidson, "How Is Weakness of Will Possible?" 40.

CHAPTER 8

WEAKNESS OF WILL

Contemporary discussions of weakness focus upon weakness of will, a notion that Aquinas rarely uses. Thomas does speak of weakness, but he refers to weakness of the soul, for a soul is weak when the passions dominate reason, which should be the stronger part.[1] Concerning Aquinas's treatment of weakness, Davidson makes a stronger claim: not only does Aquinas fail to speak of weakness of will; he fails to allow the will any role in sins of weakness.[2] Rather, reason and the passions battle it out; the passions win, and the person acts. In this scenario, the agent does not seem to be responsible for his action, which results from whichever side—reason or the passions—happens to win out.[3]

Bonnie Kent grants that the will plays some role in sins of passion, but she raises another issue.[4] Does something called "weakness" in the

1. See, for instance, Aquinas, *Summa theologiae* I-II, q. 77, a. 3; I-II, q. 88, a. 1. See also Bradley, "Thomas Aquinas on Weakness," 87.

2. Davidson, "How Is Weakness of Will Possible?" 35.

3. Donagan agrees with this criticism (*Choice*, 144). Bonnie Kent and Ashley Dressel, on the other hand, affirm that for Aquinas choice plays a central role in sins of passion ("Weakness and Willful Wrongdoing in Aquinas's *De malo*," in *Aquinas's Disputed Questions on Evil: A Critical Guide*, ed. M. V. Dougherty [Cambridge: Cambridge University Press, 2016], 38–39).

4. See Kent, "Aquinas and Weakness."

will play a causal role for sins of passion? She thinks not. Such "weakness of will" would indeed leave the person a victim of his dispositions, so that Davidson's accusation would prove correct: the individual would not be responsible for his action; rather, his weakness would be responsible. Aquinas's account, according to Kent, grants responsibility to the agent by admitting a role for the will but excluding a role for "weakness of will."

In this chapter, then, we will focus upon the responsibility of the weak person for his sin. We will first determine what role the will plays in sins of passion and how the person ends up being responsible for his sin. We will then turn our attention to "weakness of will."

THE WILL AND THE MINOR PREMISE

Contrary to Davidson's depiction, Thomas does not think that the weak person is determined by a battle between reason and the passions.[5] His faulty reasoning does not force him to act. "It is within the power of the will either to consent to those things into which his passions incline him or not to consent, and to this extent our appetite is said to be under our control. Nevertheless, the very consent or dissent of the will is hindered by the passions in the manner described above."[6] A few articles later Thomas indicates that the passions might sometimes overcome reason entirely, in which case Aquinas concurs with Davidson: the person is not responsible for his action. "Sometimes passion is so strong that it entirely removes the use of reason, for example, in those who go insane on account of love or anger.... Then the action becomes entirely involuntary and so the person is entirely excused from sin."[7] Such cases do not give rise to sins of passion, for they give rise to no sin at all. Thomas proceeds, however, to say that, "Sometimes the passion is not so strong that it en-

---

5. Portions of the next two sections appeared originally in Jensen, "Error of the Passions."

6. Aquinas, *Summa theologiae* I-II, q. 77, a. 3, ad 3: "In potestate quidem voluntatis est assentire vel non assentire his in quae passio inclinat, et pro tanto dicitur noster appetitus sub nobis esse. Sed tamen ipse assensus vel dissensus voluntatis impeditur per passionem, modo praedicto."

7. Ibid., I-II, q. 77, a. 7: "Passio quandoque quidem est tanta quod totaliter aufert usum rationis, sicut patet in his qui propter amorem vel iram insaniunt.... Actus omnino redditur involuntarius, et per consequens totaliter a peccato excusatur." See also Aquinas, *De malo*, q. 3, a. 10.

tirely takes away the use of reason, and then reason is able to drive out the passion, by diverting attention to some other thoughts, or at least to hinder its effect."[8] He makes a similar point when discussing incontinence. "In the incontinent man, concupiscence of the flesh overcomes the spirit not by necessity but on account of a certain negligence of the spirit in failing to resist firmly."[9] Putting the texts together, we can conclude that (outside of cases of temporary insanity) the will need not consent to the judgment of the passions, and once this judgment has been rejected, reason can sometimes return with its own judgment.[10] As Thomas says,[11]

Reason is bound because the attention of the mind is forcefully directed upon an act of the sensitive appetite, so that reason fails to consider in particular that which it knows habitually in the universal. But to apply the attention to something or not to apply it is in the power of the will, so it is within the power of the will to release reason from being bound. Consequently, the act committed on account of the binding of reason proceeds ultimately from the will, so that the person is not excused from blame.[12]

---

8. Aquinas, *Summa theologiae* I-II, q. 77, a. 7: "Quandoque vero passio non est tanta quod totaliter intercipiat usum rationis. Et tunc ratio potest passionem excludere, divertendo ad alias cogitationes; vel impedire ne suum consequatur effectum."

9. Ibid., II-II, q. 156, a. 1, ad 3: "Concupiscentia carnis in eo qui est incontinens, superat spiritum non ex necessitate, sed per quandam negligentiam spiritus non resistentis fortiter." See also ibid., II-II, q. 156, a. 2, ad 2.

10. Bowlin asserts, with no argument, that for Aquinas weakness is simply a matter of conflicting judgments, and that the will simply follows the judgments ("Psychology," 150–51). He does not address the texts quoted above. In contrast, Bradley ("Thomas Aquinas on Weakness," 102–4) and Kent ("Transitory Vice," 207) both emphasize that the will must ultimately choose or consent.

11. Jeffrey Hause, who wishes to argue for the role of reason—at the expense of the will—ignores this passage ("Thomas Aquinas and the Voluntarists," *Medieval Philosophy and Theology* 6 [1997]: 179).

12. Aquinas, *De malo*, q. 3, a. 10 (Editio Leonina, XXIII: 89, ll. 62–72): "Ratio ligatur ex hoc quod intentio anime applicatur uehementer ad actum appetitus sensitiui, unde auertitur a considerando in particulari id quod habitualiter in uniuersali cognoscit. Applicare autem intentionem ad aliquid uel non applicare in potestate uoluntatis existit, unde in potestate uoluntatis est quod ligamen rationis excludat. Actus igitur commissus qui ex tali ligamine procedit est uoluntarius, unde non excusatur a culpa etiam mortali."

Since the "and nothing else" clause renders the judgment "all-out" or completely practical, resulting in action, we might infer that the will is the final arbiter of this crucial clause. Until the will consents, the judgment remains tentative. All things have been considered—and nothing further remains to be considered—only when the will is satisfied. No doubt, reason can play a role, for we sometimes do cast about with our minds, checking to make sure that we have taken into account all the relevant considerations. We can judge with our reason, then, that we have in fact considered all the practically relevant factors. Even after reason has passed this judgment, however, the will must still intervene, moving to final assent.

According to Aquinas, when the evidence does not determine the case, then reason, left to its own devices, reaches doubt, suspicion, or opinion: doubt, if the evidence leaves the question entirely in the air; suspicion, if the evidence leans slightly in favor of one conclusion over another; or opinion, if the evidence leans strongly in favor of one conclusion over another. These judgments do not lead to "belief," which involves a firm assent to the truth of a proposition. At most, they lead to "thinking," as when someone *"thinks* that everything has been considered," without decidedly *believing* that everything has been considered.

Some acts of the intellect involve an unformed thought, apart from a firm assent. Either they incline to neither side, as happens in someone who doubts, or they incline to one side more than the other but by some slight evidence, as happens in one who suspects, or they adhere to one side but with fear that the other side might still be correct, which happens in one who opines. In contrast, the act of "believing" clings firmly to one side, in which the one who believes is like the person with scientific knowledge or with the grasp of principles; at the same time, his knowledge is not perfect by way of plain vision, in which respect he is like the one who doubts, suspects, or opines.[13]

---

13. Aquinas, *Summa theologiae* II-II, q. 2, a. 1: "Quidam vero actus intellectus habent quidem cogitationem informem absque firma assensione, sive in neutram partem declinent, sicut accidit dubitanti; sive in unam partem magis declinent sed tenentur aliquo levi signo, sicut accidit suspicanti; sive uni parti adhaereant, tamen cum formidine alterius, quod accidit opinanti. Sed actus iste qui est credere habet firmam adhaesionem ad unam partem, in quo convenit credens cum sciente et intelligente, et tamen eius cognitio non est perfecta per manifestam visionem, in quo convenit cum dubitante, suspicante et opinante."

Prior to "belief," then, reason can reach only a tentative judgment. How does reason move from suspicion or opinion to belief? Thomas answers this question in a reply to an objection. "The intellect of the person who believes is determined to one side against another not by way of reason but by way of the will. Consequently, assent means, in this case, an act of the intellect insofar as it is determined to one side by the will."[14] When the evidence is not sufficient, the will must step in to push reason to the final act of assent.[15] The final "and nothing else" judgment, then, becomes complete only through the will. Without the consent of the will, the conclusion reached is not all-out, so action does not follow. Deliberation continues and—except in cases of temporary insanity—the person's reason might yet drive out the judgment of the passions. The precise manner in which the will interacts with reason in order to reach the "and nothing else" minor premise will be discussed later, when we examine free will.

WEAKNESS AND IGNORANCE

Bringing the will into play, however, does not necessarily make the person morally responsible for his action. When a person acts in ignorance, we do not blame him for his action. If someone takes an item, thinking that it is his own when in fact it belongs to another person, then he is not responsible for the consequent "theft." His will is involved, for he does choose to take the item; nevertheless, he does not have moral responsibility for the action.

The weak person appears to be in precisely this situation. He chooses to act under the judgment of the passions, so that his action does arise from his will. Nevertheless, he acts in ignorance. He is not aware of the sinful character of his action.[16] If he commits adultery, for instance, he

---

14. Aquinas, *Summa theologiae* II-II, q. 2, a. 1, ad 3: "Intellectus credentis determinatur ad unum non per rationem, sed per voluntatem. Et ideo assensus hic accipitur pro actu intellectus secundum quod a voluntate determinatur ad unum." See also ibid., I-II, q. 17, a. 6; Aquinas, *De virtutibus*, 1, 7.

15. Gallagher also emphasizes the importance of the will for reaching practical judgments that would otherwise be tentative ("Free Choice and Free Judgment in Thomas Aquinas," *Archiv für Geschichte der Philosophie* 76 [1994]: 248–49).

16. Thomas D. Stegman incorrectly states that the one who sins from weakness fully realizes that what he is doing is bad for himself ("Saint Thomas Aquinas and the Problem of Akrasia," *Modern Schoolman* 66 [1989]: 120). Terrence M. Penner distinguishes between

knows only that the action is pleasurable, and he is ignorant of the adulterous character of the action.

Consider what the person knows at the moment of choice. He knows that, considered in itself, pleasure should be pursued; he also knows that this action is pleasurable. More importantly, consider what he does not know. He is unaware, at the moment of choice, that the action he chooses is an act of adultery. The passions have driven this knowledge from his mind. He knows it, but only habitually. If he were to think upon this fact actually, recognizing that the action is not only pleasurable but also adulterous, then he would conclude under the judgment of reason, and he would not sin.

An odd feature of Aquinas's account of weakness, then, is that the person does not know that his action is a sin, or rather, he knows it only habitually.[17] Thomas, following Aristotle, even compares the weak person to a drunken man who recites philosophical truths without understanding them.[18] So also the weak person might say to himself that he should not be doing what he is doing, but he does not understand what he says.

Some clarification may soften this teaching. The person is not aware at the moment of choice. Nevertheless, he might well be aware immediately preceding the choice. He might make the argument of reason, concluding that he should avoid the action, but the next moment his passions push this judgment from his mind.[19] He might even go back and forth between the two judgments in a kind of struggle. As we have seen, the struggle would not be over the major premise as if he is wondering whether it is better to avoid adultery or to pursue pleasure. Rather, the struggle is at the concrete level of the minor premise. He says, as his passions drag

---

synchronic akrasia and diachronic akrasia ("Plato and Davidson: Parts of the Soul and Weakness of Will," *Canadian Journal of Philosophy* 16 [1990]: 35–74). In the former, one chooses contrary to what one believes is best at the very moment of choice; in the latter, one chooses contrary to what one believes in general (but not right now) to be best. Thomas certainly advances diachronic akrasia, while Davidson probably adopts synchronic akrasia.

17. Bradley is much concerned to show that Aquinas does not endorse a kind of "open-eyed akrasia" ("Thomas Aquinas on Weakness").

18. Aquinas, *Summa theologiae* I-II, q. 77, a. 2, ad 5.

19. Kent makes the point that the weak person may at some point reach the conclusion of reason ("Transitory Vice," 221–22). See also Barnwell, "Aquinas's Two Different Accounts," 64–65.

his attention to the pleasure of the action, "This act is pleasurable," and at the next moment he says, "This act is adultery."

Following Aristotle, Thomas distinguishes between two cases of sinning from passion.[20] First, someone might make the judgment of reason but fail to stick by it when his passions overpower him. Second, someone might be propelled to act on account of his passions before he even makes the inquiry of reason. The first is said to be weak, but the second is said to be impulsive. Both fit the general description of "weakness" given above, and both involve some weakness of the soul, but in the former the person holds weakly to his judgment while in the latter he never makes the judgment of reason. Only the one who holds weakly to his judgment vacillates between reason and the passions. The impulsive person never even considers reason.

However we may soften Aquinas's doctrine concerning the ignorance—or ignoring—of the weak person, it remains that at the moment of choice the person who sins from passion is not actually aware that he commits a sin. It seems to follow that the person is not responsible for his sin. If he does not know that the act is adultery, if he does not even know that he should not be doing it, then how is he responsible?

Thomas does not directly address this difficulty, at least not when he is discussing sins of passion. It seems, however, that what he says elsewhere might be applied to this problem. At times, says Thomas, the sinner is like a carpenter who makes a cut without his straight edge; he is to blame for the resulting crooked cut precisely because he should have used his ruler.[21] Similarly, the weak person chooses an action without his straight edge, that is, without the judgment of reason; he is to blame for the consequent evil action because he should have thought about his action more; he should have realized that there were more things worth considering. He acts under a kind of blindness but it is a voluntary blindness—voluntarily judging that the action is nothing more than pleasurable—and so he is to blame for his evil action.[22]

20. Aquinas, *Summa theologiae* II-II, q. 156, a. 1.
21. Aquinas, *De malo*, q. 1, a. 3.
22. Aquinas's sin of weakness, then, does not include what Daniel Guevara calls "aggressive akrasia," in which one chooses with clear-headed understanding that one should not choose it; see Guevara, "The Will as Practical Reason." Guevara's description seems

In other words, the weak person may not be fully aware that the action he performs is adultery; he may be unaware (at the moment) that he should not be doing it. Nevertheless, he is responsible for his action. Why? Because he could have been aware, but he chose to go ahead and act without making the further considerations by which he might become aware.[23] This brief statement of Aquinas's position leaves many unanswered questions that wait to be addressed at a later time, most fully when we examine the first deficient cause of moral evil (in chapter 12).

BONNIE KENT AND WEAKNESS OF WILL

The contemporary discussion concerning weakness typically speaks of weakness of *will*. In contrast, Aquinas typically speaks of the weakness of the soul, insofar as the passions undermine the ruling element of reason.[24] Nevertheless, we have seen that, for Aquinas, the will plays an integral part in sins of passion. Reason and the passions do indeed battle it out, but the winner is triumphant only with the consent of the will. Is it fair to say, then, that weakness of will does in fact underlie sins of passion?

Bonnie Kent thinks not.[25] Aquinas, she says, has little use for the notion of weakness of will, and he certainly does not think that it is a cause of sins. Thomas never uses weakness as an explanation for behavior. Christine chooses to eat the chocolates not because she has weakness of will, or even because she is weak. Rather, "weak" describes a certain kind of sin, not a certain kind of cause. Concerning muscles, we can say that they are too weak to lift a certain object; concerning the will, however, we cannot say that it is too weak for self-control. Indeed, if someone were

---

to approach malice (or sins from an evil will) more than weakness, for the person who sins from malice sins clear-headedly. Perhaps contemporary usage of "weakness" includes such actions. If so, then we need not fault Aquinas's account of weakness; we need recognize only a different usage of terminology. We might argue whether Aquinas's usage or Guevara's is more appropriate to the reality.

23. Gavin Colvert, when addressing the problem of culpability for sins of passion, emphasizes the importance of the ignorance consequent upon the passion remaining voluntary ("Aquinas on Raising Cain: Vice, Incontinence and Responsibility," *Proceedings of the American Catholic Philosophical Association* 71 [1997]: 203–20). See also Bradley, "Thomas Aquinas on Weakness," 98, 102–4; Stegman, "Saint Thomas Aquinas," 123–25.

24. Aquinas, *Summa theologiae* I-II, q. 77, a. 3; Aquinas, *De malo*, q. 3, a. 9.

25. Kent, "Aquinas and Weakness."

too weak for self-control, then he would not sin at all, for he could not be responsible for his sin.

It is tempting, however, to see in Aquinas's teaching concerning continence and incontinence a doctrine concerning weakness of will. After all, Thomas does say that continence and incontinence reside in the will.[26] For both, the person's reason remains intact, and for both, the passions are disordered. What distinguishes them is the will, for with the will the person chooses to side either with reason (for continence) or with the passions (for incontinence). Furthermore, Thomas describes continence as a habit or disposition.[27] Since dispositions can be stronger or weaker, one might conclude that Aquinas is referring to some strength of the will.

Kent rejects this argument as well.[28] There are, she thinks, too many differences between continence and incontinence. The difference upon which she lays the greatest emphasis concerns the relation to the will. Continence is rightly said to belong to the will, but the same cannot be said of incontinence. Kent uses Aquinas's distinction between an action arising from choice (*ex electione*) and an action arising while choosing (*eligens*). To arise from choice is to arise from the set disposition of the will; in contrast, to arise while choosing is simply to arise from an act of choice.[29]

Sins of passion (in contrast to sins of an evil will, which are to be treated in the next chapter) are said to arise while choosing.[30] In other words,

---

26. Aquinas, *Summa theologiae* II-II, q. 155, a. 3.
27. Ibid., II-II, q. 155, a. 1, s.c.; perhaps also II-II, q. 155, a. 3.
28. Kent, "Aquinas and Weakness," 75–78.
29. Kent goes so far as to conclude that the impulsive person need not make a choice. First, she incorrectly asserts that deliberation is necessary for choice. In fact, deliberation is needed only for those matters that are uncertain (Aquinas, *Summa theologiae* I-II, q. 14, a. 4). What choice requires is not deliberation but judgment (ibid., I-II, q. 13, a. 1, ad 2). Second, from the fact that the impulsive person does not make the deliberation of reason, she concludes that the impulsive person makes no deliberation at all. This conclusion does not follow. He does, in fact, make the syllogism of the passions, and only as such can he move to act at all. It seems, then, that even the impulsive person makes a choice, that is, he acts *eligens*. Indeed, when discussing sins of weakness, Thomas explicitly says that, "in any virtuous or sinful act there must be a quasi-syllogistic deduction." (Aquinas, *De malo*, q. 3, a. 9, ad 7: "Necesse est quod in quolibet actu virtutis vel peccati sit quaedam deductio quasi syllogistica.") Only for sins of omission, in which no action is performed, can this deduction be missing.
30. Aquinas, *De malo*, q. 3, a. 12, ad 11.

the person does not have a set disposition, in his will, toward the sinful action, or at the very least the set disposition is not what prompts him to sin. Rather, his passions prompt him to sin. With the disposition of his will, he is inclined to the true good and to the argument of reason. Nevertheless, he does sin while choosing, because as we have seen, it is ultimately up to him, through his will, whether to follow the passions or not.

The continent person has a set disposition of the will toward the true good, and when he acts continently he acts from this disposition, that is, he acts *ex electione*. The incontinent person, on the other hand, still retains the disposition toward the true good; otherwise, he would not be incontinent but wicked. Nevertheless, when he acts incontinently, he acts contrary to his disposition. At most, then, he must be acting *eligens*.

Kent concludes that continence is in accord with the disposition of the will, while incontinence is contrary to it. Since incontinence is opposed to the disposition of the will, it cannot belong to the will. She also thinks that the term "disposition" is rightly applied to continence but not to incontinence.[31] Thomas describes continence as a *habitus*, which Kent translates as a disposition, while he describes incontinence as a *dispositio* (for which Kent provides no translation); a *dispositio* may be lost much more readily than a *habitus*.

WHAT WEAKNESS OF WILL MIGHT BE

Kent makes many valid points. Indeed, she adequately undermines the view she wishes to oppose, according to which the will of the continent person has something called self-control, while the weak person lacks this thing called self-control, so that his will has the opposite disposition called "weakness." Both self-control and weakness, on this view, are causes of our actions—and evidently efficient causes.

Such weakness, claims Kent, can never explain sin.[32] Someone might be too weak to lift one hundred pounds, such that he can never lift one hundred pounds; likewise, someone who is too weak to control himself never will control himself. He cannot be held responsible for any defect

---

31. Kent, "Aquinas and Weakness," 77–78. Later, however, she describes weakness in terms of being "more prone" (90) to do some wrong action, which seems to be the description of a disposition.

32. Ibid., 68–69.

in his resulting action, over which he had no control. On the other hand, we might say that somebody is weak because he can lift fifty pounds but only with great effort. The parallel for the will would mean that someone can control himself with great effort. Once again, this weakness fails to explain sin, for the incontinent person still has the disposition to choose what is good, even if that takes great effort. This weakness, then, will not lead to sin but to good actions done with great effort.

Might there be some other account of weakness of the will, however, that can explain sins of passion? Kent correctly notes that the continent person acts according to his disposition, which is for the good of reason, while the incontinent person acts against his disposition, which is also for the good of reason.[33] If they share the same disposition, then how do they differ? It seems plausible that they might differ in the strength of this disposition. Perhaps the disposition to the good of reason in the incontinent person is weaker, so that it more readily gives way to passions when they arise.

We form dispositions by repeatedly choosing in a certain way.[34] The more often we choose some good, the stronger becomes our disposition to it. No necessity follows upon this disposition, so that Kent rightly notes that anyone can sin from passion, including the continent and the virtuous.[35] The strong disposition of the virtuous person toward the true good does not determine him to this good; he may still choose against it. Conversely, the weak disposition of the incontinent person is no guarantee that he will sin from passion; he can still resist his passions.

Still, the disposition does play some causal role in our actions. As the disposition toward some good increases, two things follow. First, the desire for the good becomes stronger; second, choosing in accord with the disposition becomes easier. The stronger his disposition toward the good of reason, then, the more a person will desire this good and the easier he will find it to choose in accord with it. Siding with the passions will become less likely as the disposition to the true good becomes stronger.

The impact of this strength of disposition is reflected in the behavior of the virtuous person, the continent person, and the incontinent person.

33. Ibid., 78.
34. Aquinas, *Summa theologiae* I-II, q. 52, a. 3.
35. Kent, "Aquinas and Weakness," 72, 82, and 88.

The virtuous person may indeed sin from passion, but his firm disposition (in the will) to the good of reason—as well as his generally ordered passions—makes such a sin highly unlikely. The continent person's disposition to the true good is not so firm as that of the virtuous; consequently, he does not find it as easy to choose in accord with reason. Still, his disposition is fairly strong, so that he typically sides with reason against the passions. Finally, the incontinent person's disposition to the true good is less firm, so that when his passions entice him to some false good, he struggles to choose in accord with reason; he finds it fairly easy to side with the passions.

To some extent, the strength of a disposition is comparative, that is, two dispositions can be compared to one another as being greater or lesser. The person tempted to commit adultery has two dispositions in his will. With one, he is inclined to the true good of reason; with the other, he is inclined to sensible pleasure as an independent good. For the virtuous, continent, and incontinent, the strength of the former disposition is greater; only the wicked person has a comparatively stronger disposition to seek the good of pleasure apart from reason.

Both the continent and the incontinent have these two dispositions—one toward the good of reason and one toward an independent sensible good—and for both, the stronger disposition is that toward the good of reason. The two may differ, however, in the comparative strengths of the two dispositions. For the incontinent, his disposition to the true good might be marginally stronger than his disposition to disordered pleasure. For the continent, his disposition to the true good might be significantly stronger than his disposition to disordered pleasure.

When the incontinent person falls and sins according to his passion, then his disposition to disordered pleasure grows stronger, as does any disposition through repeated choice. When this disordered disposition grows, however, the comparative strength toward the true good becomes weaker. The stronger becomes his disordered disposition, the easier it is to side with his passions. In contrast, as the continent person repeatedly chooses with reason, the comparative strength of his good disposition increases, and it becomes easier to side with reason.

HOW WEAKNESS OF WILL CAN BE A CAUSE OF SIN

Part of Kent's difficulty is that she conceives weakness as a cause of the person's actions, and she supposes that a cause is some kind of efficient cause. The upshot seems to be that the weak person always gives way to his passions while the strong person never does, a conclusion that Kent rightly criticizes.[36] Kent fails to recognize, however, that some efficient causes are perfective while others are only dispositive.[37] Weakness, it turns out, will act as a dispositive cause, and indirectly as a final cause.

When reason presents a good to the will, the will responds with a love or desire for that good, typically with an imperfect desire. The strength of this desire depends upon the strength of the will's dispositions. By analogy, we might compare it to the capacity of dry and wet wood to receive the form of fire. The dryer the wood, the more it is disposed to receive fire. Likewise, the greater the disposition of the will, the more it is disposed to receive the good. Someone who has formed a disposition toward the good of bodily pleasure is more likely to receive this good—desiring it in his will—when it is presented to him.

As we will see more clearly in the next chapter, the strength of the desires in the will affect our deliberations concerning the major premise. Within the major premise, we have seen, diverse good and bad features of an action come together. These diverse "pros and cons" must be compared to one another, and one tool that we use for the comparison is the strength of our desires in the will.[38]

Christine must weigh various factors, such as the pleasure of the chocolate, the unhealthy character of the chocolate, the disapproval of onlookers, the desires of others for the chocolate, and so on. She can evaluate these factors objectively, but she can also weigh them according to her own desires.[39] The pleasure of the chocolate may take precedence over its

---

36. At one point Kent criticizes the view that weakness plays some causal role by noting that while the weak person's capacity for self-control might be lower than the norm, it is never the "sufficient cause of it" ("Aquinas and Weakness," 80). Certainly, she must be correct on this point.

37. See Thomas Aquinas, *In Duodecim libros Metaphysicorum Aristotelis expositio* (Taurini-Rome: Marietti, 1950), bk. 5, lect. 2, nos. 766–67.

38. See Aquinas, *De malo*, q. 6.

39. See ibid., q. 6.

unhealthy character simply because her desire for the pleasure is greater than her desire for health.

The final judgment reached—either by objective standards or by the strength of desires (imperfect desires) or by some combination of both—will itself have a certain strength to it. If the pros vastly outweigh the cons, then Christine may conclude that she should eat the chocolate with little regret. On the other hand, if the pros outweigh the cons only marginally, then she may conclude that she should eat the chocolate, but with strong reservations. Indeed, she might waver, changing her mind, since but a little bit on the other side will tip the balance. Thomas describes this failure to stick by one's judgment as follows: "When the soul completely commands itself to will, then it immediately wills, but in some cases it commands but does not will, because it does not command completely. An incomplete command arises because the mind is moved by diverse reasons to command or not to command, so that it fluctuates between the two and does not command completely."[40]

Now the weak person (as described above) is more likely to be in this ambivalent condition, at least if he consults his desires. His disposition toward the true good is stronger, but only slightly stronger, than his disposition to disordered pleasures (or some other false good). Consequently, his imperfect desires following upon the thought of the true good are stronger, but only slightly stronger, than his imperfect desires following upon the thought of the disordered pleasures. When he evaluates the situation in terms of these imperfect desires, he is more apt to fluctuate between the two. In contrast, if the continent person consults his desires, he finds that his desire for the true good is much stronger than his desire for the disordered pleasures, so that he reaches a judgment more firmly.

Reason presents goods to the will; as such, reason presents an object that serves as a final cause for the will. It turns out that this final cause, as presented by reason, can be modified by the desires of the will itself. The desires do not create goods or evils, pros or cons, but the desires do

---

40. Aquinas, *Summa theologiae* I-II, q. 17, a. 5, ad 1: "Animus, quando perfecte imperat sibi ut velit, tunc iam vult, sed quod aliquando imperet et non velit, hoc contingit ex hoc quod non perfecte imperat. Imperfectum autem imperium contingit ex hoc, quod ratio ex diversis partibus movetur ad imperandum vel non imperandum, unde fluctuat inter duo, et non perfecte imperat."

influence the weight that is placed on various goods or evils. And since the strength of the imperfect desires are themselves influenced by the dispositions in the will, it follows that the dispositions of the will end up affecting the manner in which the compound final cause (pleasure and health and rudeness and …) is presented to the will. Indirectly, then, the strength or weakness of the will plays a part in the final cause that acts upon the will.

Before we apply these ideas to some examples, recall four states in which we might find an individual: he might be virtuous, continent, incontinent, or vicious (we will use the word "vicious" in the Aristotelian sense, meaning "having a vice"). The first three have in common a right desire for the true good, such that they retain the aim of reason. They differ not in this desire, but in the opposition that arises to this desire. The desires of the virtuous person are all in order (or as much so as our imperfect state allows), such that his passions do not oppose the true good that he desires. In contrast, both the continent person and the incontinent person have opposing desires in the passions. In their will, for instance, they desire the true good of sexual chastity, but with their emotional desires they are inclined to various disordered pleasures. These two differ from one another in their response to these disordered desires. The continent person usually sides with reason against the emotions; the incontinent person often sides with the emotions against reason. The vicious person differs from all three of the others because the desire in his will is fundamentally disordered. He does not desire the true good and fail in this desire; rather, from the beginning he aims at the false good.

Let us consider, then, a continent individual and an incontinent individual. The continent person is not virtuous, so she still has a disposition toward the good of pleasure as a good independent of the chief good, but because she is continent, these dispositions are weak in comparison to her dispositions toward the chief good itself. When she evaluates "pleasurable adultery" she is somewhat inclined to the pleasurable aspect, but she is far more repulsed by the evil of adultery. She finds it easy, then, to stick by her judgment that, "Pleasurable adultery should be avoided."

The incontinent person also has a disposition toward pleasure as an independent good, and while this disposition is weaker than his disposition toward the chief good (or else he would be intemperate rather than incontinent), it is comparatively not that much weaker. Consequently, when he reaches the judgment of reason that "Pleasurable adultery should be avoided," he is inclined to waver. Overall, he judges the evil of adultery to be greater than the good of pleasure, but not dramatically greater. Might it come out differently, he wonders, if he reconsidered? Ultimately, he finds it difficult to hold firmly to his judgment of reason. In addition, as the judgment of the passions repeatedly urges itself, he has a stronger disposition (than that of the continent person) to receive the good it dangles before him, namely, the good of pleasure as an independent good. Just as the dry wood is more disposed to receive the fire, so he is more disposed to receive the independent good of pleasure. The comparative weakness of his disposition to the true good, then, makes it more likely that he will not stand by the judgment of reason and that he will cave in to the judgment of the passions. This weakness—like incontinence itself—can concern one area but not another. A person might be weak with regard to bodily pleasures, for instance, but strong with regard to facing dangers.

Weakness of will, then, does not act as a perfective efficient cause. Rather, it acts as a dispositive cause and indirectly as a final cause. Because of his disposition, the incontinent person has a stronger desire toward the disordered good, and he finds it easier to choose in accord with this disposition. Furthermore, his stronger desires to the disordered good affect his judgment of reason concerning the good to be pursued. He still judges in accord with reason, since his disposition to the true good is stronger than his disordered disposition. Nevertheless, the judgment itself is less clear. The good of reason is judged greater, but perhaps marginally so. Since the judgment is questionable, the person is less likely to stand by it.

~ CHAPTER 9

SINS FROM AN EVIL WILL

Sins from an evil will provide a strong contrast to sins of passion.[1] As we have seen, sins of passion involve an emotional desire that clouds reason's perception of particular details, focusing attention upon desirable features and directing it away from the disordered features of the action. In contrast, sins from an evil will do not arise from passion but from the

---

1. Discussions of sins from evil will are fairly sparse in the current literature. See Gregory M. Reichberg, "Beyond Privation: Moral Evil in Aquinas's *De Malo*," *Review of Metaphysics* 55 (2002): 777–84; Kent and Dressel, "Weakness and Willful Wrongdoing"; Colleen McCluskey, "Willful Wrongdoing: Thomas Aquinas on *certa malitia*," *Studies in the History of Ethics* 6 (2005): 1–54; Colleen McCluskey, "Thomas Aquinas and the Epistemology of Moral Wrongdoing," in *Handlung und Wissenschaft: die Epistemologie der praktischen Wissenschaften im 13. und 14. Jahrhundert (Action and Science: The Epistemology of the Practical Sciences in the 13th and 14th Centuries)*, ed. Matthias Lutz-Bachmann and Alexander Fidora (Berlin: Akademie Verlag, 2008); Colleen McCluskey, *Thomas Aquinas on Moral Wrongdoing* (Cambridge, UK: Cambridge University Press, 2017), 116–47; Terence Irwin, "Vice and Reason," *Journal of Ethics* 5 (2001): 73–97; Caulfield, "Practical Ignorance," 112–22; and Langan, "Sins of Malice." Following the advice of Kent ("Weakness and Willful Wrongdoing," 44) and McCluskey ("Willful Wrongdoing," 2; McCluskey, "Thomas Aquinas and the Epistemology of Moral Wrongdoing," 112), I have avoided the standard translation of *malitia*, usually rendered "malice." The word "malice" certainly implies an evil will, but seems too strong and restrictive for what Aquinas means by *malitia*.

will itself.[2] Indeed, the passions need not arise at all; if they do, they are often consequent upon some prior desire of the will. The two sins differ not only in their affective origin; they differ also in the awareness of the one sinning. Sins of passion involve an ignorance (or ignoring), at the moment of choice, concerning the evil of the action. In contrast, the person who sins from an evil will acts with full knowledge of the evil he chooses.[3] The two sins also differ in their aftermath. Once the passion has subsided, the person who sins from passion regrets his act. In contrast, the person who sins from an evil will is pleased with what he has done; repentance is unlikely, almost impossible apart from grace.[4]

A DISORDERED WILL

The will of the person who sins from passion fundamentally desires the true human good, at least prior to the sin. He pursues the correct concrete realization of his overall good. As such, he recognizes the evil of adultery and other sinful behavior. He not only recognizes it intellectually; he has an aversion to it in his will. In contrast, the will of the person who sins from an evil will fundamentally desires some disordered good.[5] He sets his heart upon a false concrete realization of the ultimate end. As such, he is attracted to some evils as if they were good.

The person who sins from passion has a clouded perception of particular details. In contrast, the person who sins from an evil will remains aware, in the concrete, of the disordered features of his action.[6] Nevertheless, he has a more profound confusion than the person who sins from passion. While he perceives the disordered features of the actions, he confusedly supposes that the action is nevertheless worth pursuing.[7] The person who sins from passion recognizes that adultery is not worth pursuing, no matter how pleasurable it might be, but he fails to keep his attention upon the adulterous character of the action he performs. The person who sins from an evil will thinks that adultery is worth pursuing.

2. Aquinas, *De malo*, q. 3, a. 12, c. and ad 5.
3. Ibid., q. 3, a. 12; Aquinas, *Summa theologiae* I-II, q. 78, a. 1.
4. Aquinas, *Summa theologiae* I-II, q. 78, a. 4.
5. Ibid., I-II, q. 78, a. 1; I-II, q. 78, a. 4.
6. Ibid., II-II, q. 156, a. 3, ad 1.
7. Aquinas, *De malo*, q. 3, a. 12; Aquinas, *Summa theologiae* I-II, q. 78, a. 1.

He may even set out to pursue it apart from any initial encouragement from the passions.

The misperception that adultery is worth pursuing arises from disordered desires in the will. In particular, it arises from the disordered *strength* of the person's desires. This skewed priority, desiring lesser goods more, is a characteristic mark of a sin from an evil will. Thomas begins his discussion of sins from an evil will with the recognition of the natural desire for the good.[8] He then notes, however, that the desires of the person with an evil will are corrupted in their strength or intensity.

The will is disordered when it loves a greater good less. It follows that a person chooses to suffer the loss of the good loved less in order that he might attain the good loved more, just as a man might endure the amputation of a limb, even knowingly, in order to preserve his life, which he loves more. In this manner, when someone with a disordered will loves some worldly good, such as wealth or pleasure, more than he loves the order of reason, the order of the divine law, or the love of God, or something of this sort, it follows that he wills to suffer the loss of spiritual goods so that he might attain a worldly good. Since evil is nothing other than the lack of some good, someone knowingly wills a spiritual evil (which is evil simply speaking), through which the spiritual good is lost, so that he might attain a worldly good. Consequently, the person is said to sin from a firm desire for evil, or with evil intent, as if he knowingly chooses evil.[9]

As we have seen, Thomas maintains a strong-set view of the good, in which some goods are greater than others. His account of a disordered will requires this priority (his account makes no sense from the perspec-

---

8. Aquinas, *Summa theologiae* I-II, q. 78, a. 1.

9. Ibid., I-II, q. 78, a. 1: "Est autem voluntas inordinata, quando minus bonum magis amat. Consequens autem est ut aliquis eligat pati detrimentum in bono minus amato, ad hoc quod potiatur bono magis amato, sicut cum homo vult pati abscissionem membri etiam scienter, ut conservet vitam, quam magis amat. Et per hunc modum, quando aliqua inordinata voluntas aliquod bonum temporale plus amat, puta divitias vel voluptatem, quam ordinem rationis vel legis divinae, vel caritatem Dei, vel aliquid huiusmodi; sequitur quod velit dispendium pati in aliquo spiritualium bonorum, ut potiatur aliquo temporali bono. Nihil autem est aliud malum quam privatio alicuius boni. Et secundum hoc aliquis scienter vult aliquod malum spirituale, quod est malum simpliciter, per quod bonum spirituale privatur, ut bono temporali potiatur. Unde dicitur ex certa malitia, vel ex industria peccare, quasi scienter malum eligens."

tive of the assortment view or the aggregate view, in which diverse particular goods cannot be compared with one another). The person with an evil habit does not desire evil itself, which is impossible, but he desires the greater good too little. Consequently, he wills evil—the loss of the greater good—in order that he might have a lesser good (which he desires more).

The person who undergoes the amputation can truly recognize that the loss of a limb is evil and to be avoided; he can even recognize that it is, in general, to be avoided by himself. In a similar fashion, the person with a lustful habit perceives that adultery should be avoided, since through adultery he loses something he recognizes to be good, namely, the divine good, for which he has a natural love. But just as the person undergoing the amputation recognizes that death is to be avoided more than the loss of a limb, so the person with an evil will supposes that the loss of pleasure, which he desires more than the divine good, is a greater evil than the loss of the divine good. All other things being equal, then, he would prefer to avoid adultery, which removes from him a desirable good.[10] But all things are not equal. Avoiding adultery means the loss of pleasure, a loss that he feels more keenly than the loss of the divine good. He prefers to gain the pleasure of adultery by way of the loss of the divine good. His disordered desires—by which he loves pleasure more than the divine good—give rise to a clear-sighted choice for what he knows to be evil.

What he does not know, however, is the degree to which it is evil. The person undergoing the amputation knows that the loss of a limb is evil, but he also knows that it is less evil than the loss of life. The person who sins from an evil will knows that the loss of the divine good (by way of adultery) is evil, but he supposes—incorrectly—that it is less evil than the loss of pleasure.[11] Thomas expresses the matter succinctly: "Some-

---

10. See Kent and Dressel, "Weakness and Willful Wrongdoing," 47–48; and Caulfield, "Practical Ignorance," 115–16. McCluskey, on the other hand, fails to recognize the reluctance of the person who sins from an evil will ("Willful Wrongdoing," 10).

11. McCluskey is not clear on this point ("Thomas Aquinas and the Epistemology of Moral Wrongdoing," 115; McCluskey, "Willful Wrongdoing," 18–19, 39). She seems to think that the agent does not know that he should pursue the greater good; in fact, he does not know which good is greater. At various points she seems to think that a sin from an evil will is simply the pursuit of a lesser good at the expense of a greater (rather than the pursuit of an evil on account of a stronger desire for some false good); she even gives the example of eating an unhealthy breakfast when a healthier one is available (*Thomas Aquinas on Moral*

times ignorance excludes the knowledge by which someone knows that this evil should not be endured in order to attain that good. Nevertheless, he knows simply speaking that this [action] is evil. In this manner, he who sins from deliberate evil is said to ignore."[12]

Ultimately, then, he is more confused than the person who sins from passion.[13] The weak person knows that the divine good is to be preferred to pleasure, so he knows that pleasurable adultery should be avoided; what he does not know (or he knows only in habit) is that the action he now chooses is in fact an act of adultery. In contrast, the vicious person knows that what he chooses is adultery, and he knows that adultery is evil; what he does not know is that pleasurable adultery is to be avoided; given his skewed desires, it seems worth pursuing.

THE ERROR OF AN EVIL WILL

The error of reasoning for a sin from an evil will, then, is not found in the concrete level of the minor premise. Rather, it is found in the major premise. The practical syllogism of someone who sins from an evil will looks as follows:

> Argument of the Evil Will
> Considered in itself, pleasurable adultery is to be pursued.
> This action is pleasurable adultery and nothing else.
> ___
> This action is to be pursued.

In contrast, the weak person can never affirm this faulty major premise. He keeps the argument of reason in mind but simply fails to posit the "and nothing else" clause.

Wrongdoing, 131, 135); Langan makes a similar mistake ("Sins of Malice," 185). Rather, a sin from an evil will is a sin that initiates with the will itself. The person does so because he desires some *false* good more than the avoidance of evil. It does not follow that every time someone chooses a lesser good he does evil (and certainly not as arising from an evil will).

12. Aquinas, *Summa theologiae* I-II, q. 78, a. 1, ad 1: "Quandoque autem excludit scientiam qua aliquis scit hoc malum non sustinendum esse propter consecutionem illius boni, scit tamen simpliciter hoc esse malum, et sic dicitur ignorare qui ex certa malitia peccat."

13. Caulfield, "Practical Ignorance," 118–19.

Argument of Reason for the Weak Person
Considered in itself, pleasurable adultery is to be avoided.
This action is pleasurable adultery.
_____
Considered in itself, this action is to be avoided.

The person who sins from passion, then, will always conclude to avoidance as long as he keeps adultery in the minor premise; only when adultery is excluded from his attention, through the force of his passions, can he choose to pursue the action. In contrast, the person who sins from an evil will can pursue the action even while he focuses upon its being adultery, as long as he also recognizes that it is pleasurable. He does retain something of the argument of reason, for, leaving pleasure aside, he recognizes that adultery is to be avoided.

Argument of Reason for the Person with Vice
Considered in itself, adultery is to be avoided.
This action is adultery.
_____
Considered in itself, this action is to be avoided.

When the consideration of pleasure is added, however, this syllogism becomes irrelevant. While adultery, considered in itself, is to be avoided, pleasurable adultery is to be pursued, leading to the following syllogism:

Restrictive Judgment of Vice
Considered in itself, pleasurable adultery is to be pursued.
This action is pleasurable adultery.
_____
Considered in itself, this action is to be pursued.

The error of reasoning, then, arises only from a comparative judgment. Weighing the evil of adultery against the good of pleasure, the vicious person reaches a faulty judgment. The weight he gives to the divine good, as opposed to the good of pleasure, depends upon the desires of his will. He desires both, for both are inherent goods for which the will has a natural inclination. What is askew is the strength of his desires. He desires pleasure more than he desires the divine good.

The two judgments involve restrictive considerations, so the corresponding desires are imperfect desires. The person considers the loss of the divine good, and he has an imperfect aversion for it; he then considers pleasure in itself, and he has an imperfect desire for it. Between these two desires, however, there is a difference of strength, so that when the person considers the two in conjunction, then the greater desire wins out. Toward pleasurable adultery (considered in itself), he has desire rather than aversion. Of course, further considerations might tip the balance in the other direction. If the jealous husband is likely to discover the liaison, then the prospect of revenge might lead to aversion. Considered in itself, pleasurable adultery linked to vengeance is undesirable. The error of the vicious person, however, is found in the comparison between the divine good and the good of his vice, such as pleasure.

How does the vicious person come to desire pleasure more than the divine good? He does not begin having disordered desires. Rather, he forms his evil habit through repeated actions. He repeatedly chooses pleasure in opposition to the divine good, and his desire for pleasure (as a good independent of the divine good) increases. From where do these repeated choices arise? Evidently, through some other source of sin, such as passion or ignorance.

With each repeated sinful choice, the disposition in the will increases toward disordered pleasure, that is, pleasure opposed to the divine good. Eventually, it increases to the point at which it exceeds the desire for the divine good. At that point, and not prior to it, the individual can sin from an evil will; he can sin with full knowledge that what he chooses is indeed adultery. He has a clear vision of what he chooses; at the same time, he now has a greater ignorance, for he is no longer aware that the divine good is to be desired more than pleasure.[14]

CONFUSION OVER IDENTITY

This profound confusion rests upon another confusion to which Aquinas does not explicitly advert when discussing sins of an evil will. The person is confused concerning his identity. He supposes that he is someone for whom the end of sensible pleasure is greater than the end of the divine good. Thomas discusses this kind of confusion when examining the manner in which a person can hate himself.

[A person can hate himself] on the part of the person himself to whom he wills the good. Everything is most of all that which is primary in it, just as the state

---

14. Aquinas, *Summa theologiae* II-II, q. 156, a. 3, ad 1.

is said to do that which the king does, as if the king is the whole state. Clearly, a human being is chiefly the mind of the human being, but some people judge themselves to be chiefly a bodily and sensing animal. Consequently, they love themselves according to that which they judge themselves to be but they hate that which they truly are, insofar as they will what is contrary to reason.[15]

He develops these ideas when discussing the manner in which a sinner loves himself:

> Everyone loves that which he judges himself to be, but a man is said to be something in two ways. First, someone is said to be what he is according to his substance and nature, and in this manner everyone judges himself to be that which he in fact is, namely, composed of body and soul. In this manner, every human being, whether good or evil, loves himself, insofar as he loves the preservation of his own being.
>
> In a second way, someone is said to be something according to that which is primary within him, just as the ruler of a state is said to be the state, such that what the ruler does the state is said to do. In this manner, not everyone judges himself to be that which he is. What is principal in a human being is his rational mind, while secondarily he has the nature of a bodily and sensing animal.... A good person judges his rational nature to be primary within himself, so that he judges himself to be that which he truly is. An evil person, however, judges his bodily and animal nature to be primary within himself, so that he does not correctly know himself and he does not truly love himself, but he loves that which he thinks himself to be.[16]

---

15. Ibid., I-II, q. 29, a. 4: "Alio modo, ex parte sui ipsius, cui vult bonum. Unumquodque enim maxime est id quod est principalius in ipso, unde civitas dicitur facere quod rex facit, quasi rex sit tota civitas. Manifestum est ergo quod homo maxime est mens hominis. Contingit autem quod aliqui aestimant se esse maxime illud quod sunt secundum naturam corporalem et sensitivam. Unde amant se secundum id quod aestimant se esse, sed odiunt id quod vere sunt, dum volunt contraria rationi."

16. Ibid., II-II, q. 25, a. 7: "Quod enim aliquis amet id quod seipsum esse aestimat, hoc commune est omnibus. Homo autem dicitur esse aliquid dupliciter. Uno modo, secundum suam substantiam et naturam. Et secundum hoc omnes aestimant bonum commune se esse id quod sunt, scilicet ex anima et corpore compositos. Et sic etiam omnes homines, boni et mali, diligunt seipsos, inquantum diligunt sui ipsorum conservationem. Alio modo dicitur esse homo aliquid secundum principalitatem, sicut princeps civitatis dicitur esse civitas; unde quod principes faciunt, dicitur civitas facere. Sic autem non omnes aestimant se esse id quod sunt. Principale enim in homine est mens rationalis, secundarium autem

The vicious person's love of pleasurable adultery, then, rests upon his identification with his nature as a sensing animal.

This confusion over identity follows from the very nature of the good, for as we have seen, the good is the completion of some subject. The good of the hammer is to pound, the good of the pen is to write, and the good of a doctor is to facilitate healing. Different subjects have different goods. If the subject is primarily a rational nature and only secondarily a sensing animal, then pleasurable adultery will be an evil, not a good. But if the subject is primarily bodily and animal by nature, and only secondarily rational, then pleasurable adultery will be a good.

The subject for whom the good is willed can be built into practical syllogisms with an additional "by" phrase:

Argument of Reason
Considered in itself, pleasurable adultery is to be avoided by someone who is primarily rational.
This action is pleasurable adultery.

Considered in itself, this action is to be avoided by someone who is primarily rational.

Argument of an Evil Will
Considered in itself, pleasurable adultery is to be pursued by someone who is primarily a sensing animal.
This action is pleasurable adultery.

Considered in itself, this action is to be pursued by someone who is primarily a sensing animal.

Just as stated, both of these arguments can be equally recognized by both a good person and a wicked person. The person of evil will can recognize that someone who is primarily rational should avoid pleasurable adultery; what he denies is that he is himself primarily rational. Likewise, the good person can recognize that if someone were primarily a sensing animal, then he should pursue pleasurable adultery; what he denies is that

---

est natura sensitiva et corporalis.... Boni autem aestimant principale in seipsis rationalem naturam, sive interiorem hominem, unde secundum hoc aestimant se esse quod sunt. Mali autem aestimant principale in seipsis naturam sensitivam et corporalem, scilicet exteriorem hominem. Unde non recte cognoscentes seipsos, non vere diligunt seipsos, sed diligunt id quod seipsos esse reputant."

he himself is primarily a sensing animal. Similarly, the following argument can be admitted by someone who has no interest in stamps:

> Argument of a Stamp Collector
> Rare stamps ought to be purchased by a stamp collector.
> The Penny Black stamp is a rare stamp.
> ___
> The Penny Black stamp ought to be purchased by a stamp collector.

Just as stated, then, these arguments are not practical, for they do not necessarily apply to the person reasoning. To become practical another sort of argument is needed, in which the person identifies himself with the subject of the "by" phrase. The virtuous person, for instance, might reason as follows:

> Argument of Reason concerning the Agent
> Considered in itself, pleasurable adultery is to be avoided by someone who is primarily rational.
> I am someone who is primarily rational.
> ___
> Considered in itself, pleasurable adultery is to be avoided by me.

He then completes his reasoning with the following syllogism.[17]

> Argument of Reason concerning the Action
> Considered in itself, pleasurable adultery is to be avoided by me.
> This action is pleasurable adultery.
> ___
> Considered in itself, this action is to be avoided by me.

The vicious person fails to posit the minor premise in the argument concerning the agent, for he does not identify himself as primarily rational. It turns out, then, that the vicious person, like the weak person, fails in a minor premise. The failures, however, occur in distinct syllogisms. The syllogism of the wicked person looks something like the following (we should note that "a sensing animal" does not imply that pleasure is the only good belonging to this part of the person; possessions, reputation, revenge, and so on, can also be included):

---

17. Bradley also provides these two syllogisms ("Thomas Aquinas on Weakness," 91).

Argument of Vice concerning the Agent
Considered in itself, pleasurable adultery is to be pursued by
   someone who is primarily a sensing animal.
I am someone who is primarily a sensing animal.

Considered in itself, pleasurable adultery should be pursued by me.

The need to identify oneself as the subject of the good is expressed in passing by Aristotle. Like Aquinas, Aristotle explains the deficiency of the weak person in terms of a failure to posit some singular concrete feature of the act in question. He notes, however, that the major premise contains two universal terms; as such, two singular propositions are needed.[18] The major premise reads as follows:

Dry food is good for every man.

The two universal terms to which Aristotle refers are "dry food" and "man." The two singular premises, then, are (1) I am a man, and (2) this is dry food. From the first, the person may conclude that "Dry food is good for me," and then from the second he may conclude that, "This is good for me." The weak person does not reach this final conclusion because he fails to posit the singular proposition, "This is dry food." Evidently, he successfully posits the singular proposition, "I am a man."

We can drop the obscure example of dry food and modify the premises slightly to generate the following two syllogisms:

Practical Syllogisms concerning the Agent
Pleasurable adultery is to be avoided by every human being.
I am a human being.

Pleasurable adultery is to be avoided by me.

Practical Syllogisms concerning the Action
Pleasurable adultery is to be avoided by me.
This is pleasurable adultery.

This is to be avoided by me.

The vicious person fails to posit that he is a human being. In one sense, of course, he cannot fail to recognize that he is a human being. Everyone, says Thomas, recognizes that he is composed of body and soul, that is,

18. Aristotle, *Nicomachean Ethics*, bk. 7, chap. 3, 1147a4–6.

he can identify himself as a subject that is like others who are identified as human. The failure, notes Thomas, comes in identifying that which is primary within oneself. If a human being is someone who is primarily rational, then the vicious person fails to recognize that he is a human being.

The source of this confusion is the disordered desires of his will.[19] When we examined sins of passion, we saw that the sinner fails to posit the minor premise of reason because his passions focus attention upon another minor premise. Now it appears that for sins from an evil will the sinner also fails to posit a minor premise, although of a different syllogism. He does not acknowledge that he is chiefly someone with the capacity of reason; he conceives himself, instead, as someone who chiefly has the capacity of sensible pleasure (or some such good).[20] The weak person fails in the minor premise on account of passion; correspondingly, the vicious person fails in the minor premise on account of the desires of his will.

In particular, the vicious person is misled by the strength of his desires, by the priority he places on various goods. Consequently, the vicious person fails to posit the minor premise because he has failed in prioritizing the goods. He has set pleasure, or some such good, above the divine good. This disordered priority has arisen only after repeated evil choices.

THAT PART OF US TO WHICH WE ARE MOST ATTACHED

The origin of this confusion (concerning what the person is primarily) needs further explaining. Why should the person reach a judgment based upon the strength of his desires? After all, Aquinas himself argues for the chief human good not based upon the strength of desires; rather, he argues for it based upon the importance of various capacities: the intellect is the highest capacity and knowing the first cause is the highest activity of this highest capacity. According to the strong-set view, then, the primary character of a human being is not determined by strength of desires; it is determined by the importance of capacities.

The strength of desire is secondary. We do not determine our principal element based upon desire. To the contrary, once we determine our

---

19. Caulfield, "Practical Ignorance," 93.
20. McCluskey says that the vicious person "has become the sort of agent for whom defective goods are seen as naturally suitable for choice" ("Thomas Aquinas and the Epistemology of Moral Wrongdoing," 117).

principal element, then our desire should follow. We have a greater desire for that which is more principal within us. The strength of someone's desires should not precede the determination of what he is; rather, the determination of what a person is, or of what he is primarily, should precede desire.

The vicious person, then, seems to engage in an inversion of reasoning.[21] According to the proper order of reasoning, the person must determine three points in the following order: (1) who or what he is predominantly; (2) what is chiefly good for him; (3) what goods should be desired more than other goods. As Aquinas presents it, we first determine that we are predominantly a reasoning being; then we recognize that understanding the truth is our chief good; then we desire to understand the truth more than we desire other goods. The vicious person begins with the third step, reasons to the first step, and concludes to the second step. He recognizes that he desires pleasure above the divine good; he then judges that he is chiefly a being with a sensitive appetite; finally, he concludes that pleasure is his chief good.

In his treatment of free choice in the *De malo*, Thomas addresses these two approaches of determining the greater good (adding another as well, which we will omit):

> The will is led into that which is presented to it more according to one aspect than according to another in three possible ways. First, insofar as one feature does indeed have greater weight, and then the will is moved according to reason, for example, if someone should prefer that which is useful to his health over that which is useful for pleasure.... Third, the will might be led by a disposition in the person, for as the Philosopher says, "As a person is disposed, so the end seems to him." Thus, the will of someone who is angry is moved to something different than the will of someone who is calm, for the same object does not agree with both of them, just as food is perceived differently by a healthy person and a sick person.[22]

---

21. Terence Irwin notes the different approaches of the virtuous and the vicious ("Vice and Reason," 81–89). The virtuous person seeks what is fine because it is fine; the vicious person seeks what he finds appealing.

22. Aquinas, *De malo*, q. 6 (Editio Leonina, XXIII: 150, ll. 450–56, 461–67): "Et quod uoluntas feratur in id quod sibi offertur, magis secundum hanc particularem conditionem quam secundum aliam, potest contingere tripliciter. Vno quidem modo in quantum una preponderat, et tunc mouetur uoluntas secundum rationem: puta cum homo preeligit id

A person might take two different approaches, then, when determining which goods are better and to be pursued. On the one hand, he might consult what really is better; on the other hand, he might consult his desires. The vicious person, it seems, uses the second approach, which approach becomes faulty because his desires are themselves disordered.

As we examine the manner in which we might prefer one good as better than another, it will be helpful to consider what Thomas says about greater or lesser love for other human beings. This degree of love can be of two different sorts.[23] First, we can will for one person a greater good than we will for another person. Second, we can love one person more intensely than we love another person. Why? Because we are more connected with him.

Sam, for instance, desires that the king rule well, which is a greater good than he desires for the gardener, for whom he desires that she does a good job of gardening. It turns out, however, that the gardener is Sam's sister for whom he has a stronger love than he has for the king. Which of the two does he love more? In one sense, the king, for he desires a greater good for the king. In another sense, his sister, for he desires the good more intensely for his sister. I suspect that we are inclined to refer to greater or lesser love more in the latter sense than in the former.

The two different senses of greater or lesser love need not coincide. The greater love that Sam has for the king—because he wishes him a greater good—need not overflow into a greater intensity of love. For the king, he wills the good of a king; for the gardener, he wills the good of a gardener. The intensity of love does not follow upon the greatness of the good willed. It does not depend upon the role (king or gardener) the person plays within the shared good but upon how close the person (his sister) is to the agent.

A parallel may be drawn with love of self. We have a greater or lesser love for some part of ourselves in two ways, either based upon the good we

---

quod est utile sanitati ei quod est utile uoluptati.... Tertio uero modo contingit ex dispositione hominis: quia secundum Philosophum 'qualis unusquisque est, talis finis uidetur ei'; unde aliter mouetur ad aliquid uoluntas irati et uoluntas quieti, quia non idem est conueniens utrique, sicut etiam aliter acceptatur cibus a sano et egro."

23. Aquinas, *Summa theologiae* II-II, q. 26, a. 4, ad 1; II-II, q. 26, a. 6; II-II, q. 26, a. 7; II-II, q. 26, a. 9; II-II, q. 26, a. 11; II-II, q. 26, a. 12.

desire for that part or based upon the intensity of our desire. For the rational part, for instance, we desire the good of reason, which is a greater good than the good of pleasure or the good of reputation, which goods we desire for our sensing or animal part. The vicious person, however, might feel most attached to his sensing part, so that he loves that good more intensely.

In the person with well-ordered desires, the two coincide, such that the part that has the greater good is also the part with which the person identifies most intimately. The good of reason is the greater good, and the virtuous person feels most attached to his rational part. The vicious person, however, has distorted dispositions with consequent distorted desires. That part of himself to which he feels closest is not the part that has the greater good. Someone who sins from an evil will places more weight upon the good being "his own" than he places upon the nature of the good itself. What matters is that the good is his, that he is attached to it. As such, he is driven by pride, placing more importance upon himself than upon the good. This pride is most complete when the person desires what in fact is truly good—the good of reason—but he desires it simply because it is his own.

A very clear-sighted vicious person might even acknowledge that he does not desire the best good but the good to which he is most attached.[24] He might admit that the goods of reason are in themselves greater goods; nevertheless, for him what is most important is pleasure or money or some such thing.[25] More often, however, the vicious person will be apt to deny the primacy of reason, judging the greater good based upon that part to which he is most attached. This erroneous judgment, however, arises from the desires of his will. He begins, at least, recognizing that the goods of reason are greater, for they are the goods of his most central part. At the same time, he recognizes that he himself is most attached to some other part, such as his nature as a sensing animal. He then begins searching for arguments in favor of his preferences. In short, he wants ignorance and error, and he will find pseudo-arguments to delude himself into this ignorance. At some level, however, he remains aware of his self-delusion.

Even after engaging in such intellectual dishonesty, the person still

24. See Caulfield, "Practical Ignorance," 118.
25. McCluskey suggests that agents are sometimes willing to admit they are choosing the lesser good ("Willful Wrongdoing," 39).

might suffer regret over his particular predilections. His natural dispositions, with the consequent natural love, cannot be removed. They can only be buried deeper and deeper under his acquired distorted dispositions. Since they remain, it follows that the (imperfect) love of the true good will sometimes arise, and the person can regret that his own desires lead him astray. As Aristotle says, a person can regret that he has acquired a taste for such disordered pleasures.[26] His regret might also follow upon the consequences that his vicious actions have upon other desires. His gambling, for instance, might prevent him from acquiring possessions. His various disordered desires vie with one another, the satisfaction of one causing the regret over the loss of another.

More fundamentally, the vicious person can recognize that he need not be as he is. He can recognize diverse goods for his nature, including the goods of reason. He can recognize, in moments of honesty, that the greatest goods are those of reason. At the same time, however, he recognizes that he himself is most attached to other goods. Consequent upon each of these recognitions is an imperfect desire in his will. While imperfectly desiring the goods of reason, he can regret that he is so attached to bodily goods.[27]

Such regret is not likely to lead to repentance. The person who sins from weakness repents when the passion subsides. His strongest desire in the will is for the true good. He is led away from this true good only because of the pressing passion that focuses his attention upon some desirable feature of an action. When the passion subsides, the desire for the true good returns. In contrast, for the vicious person, the strongest desire of the will is not for the true good but for some false good. While he can still desire the true good, and consequently have regret, this desire does not lead to repentance, for it is outweighed by his other desires. Regret is idle; repentance takes action.

---

26. Aristotle, *Nicomachean Ethics*, bk. 9, chap. 4, 1166b24. For a discussion of the meaning behind these statements of Aristotle concerning vice, see Thomas C. Brickhouse, "Does Aristotle Have a Consistent Account of Vice?" *Review of Metaphysics* 57 (2003): 3–23; Jozef Müller, "Aristotle on Vice," *British Journal for the History of Philosophy* 23 (2015): 459–77; David Roochnik, "Aristotle's Account of the Vicious: A Forgivable Inconsistency," *History of Philosophy Quarterly* 24 (2007): 207–20; Irwin, "Vice and Reason," 90–91.

27. See Kent and Dressel, "Weakness and Willful Wrongdoing," 47.

SINS OF THE HEART

At the natural level, the move from incontinence to vice does not happen through a single sin of passion. Rather, through repeated sins the individual develops a habit, which habit eventually becomes stronger than his desire for the true good.[28] A typical pathway for developing an evil habit is through what may be called sins of the heart.[29] A person who pursues the true chief good has an abhorrence for adultery. Nevertheless, he might be put in a situation of extreme temptation, and he might succumb under the force of passion. What is more likely, however, is that he will have first succumbed to the temptation in lesser ways, through sins of the heart. The ninth and tenth commandments refer to such sins, as does Christ's proscription against committing adultery in the heart. Such sins are found simply in the desire for evil, without necessarily issuing in overt evil behavior.

To understand how such sins of the heart might pave the road to vice, we must first understand more clearly their sinful nature. It seems particularly harsh to say that every evil desire is a sin; after all, we cannot always control our desires. In fact, Thomas does not teach that every evil desire is a sin. He distinguishes between those desires that precede a judgment of reason and those desires that are consequent upon a judgment of reason.[30] We are responsible for our emotional desires only insofar as they are within our control, and they are within our control through the guidance of reason.[31]

---

28. Langan ignores the possibility that vice develops from sins of passion ("Sins of Malice," 185). He thereby thinks that the development of vice must arise from previous sins from an evil will, which would indeed make the evil habit inexplicable, as Langan seems to think.

29. This suggestion is made by Kent and Dressel ("Weakness and Willful Wrongdoing," 41–44). In contrast, McCluskey seems to attribute the development of an evil habit to a succession of sins of ignorance ("Willful Wrongdoing," 118–19).

30. See, for example, Aquinas, *Summa theologiae* I-II, q. 77, a. 1; I, q. 95, a. 2; I-II, q. 10, a. 3; I-II, q. 24, a. 3, c. and ad 1 and ad 3; I-II, q. 44, a. 2; I-II, q. 77, a. 6, c. and ad 2; Aquinas, *De malo*, q. 3, a. 11. For an excellent treatment of the distinction, see Giuseppe Butera, "On Reason's Control of the Passions in Aquinas's Theory of Temperance," *Medieval Studies* 68 (2006): 133–60.

31. For a thorough treatment of diverse ways in which we might be responsible for our

Consider two individuals presented with a pornographic image. For both individuals, sexual desire arises spontaneously, with no choice or judgment spurring it on. After the desire arises, however, the two individuals take opposite courses. The first averts his eyes and begins to focus upon other matters. His inappropriate desire subsides. The second encourages the desire, taking pleasure in the image; perhaps he even fantasizes. What happens prior to judgment is the same for both individuals. What follows upon judgment is contrary in the two cases. In the second case, the evil desire itself becomes a sin, for it is voluntary.

We can add a third case. This person does not encourage his desires but neither does he take active measures against them, so his desires remain. Even such desires, thinks Thomas, can become sinful, because they are voluntary through a certain failure to act, which failure was itself voluntary.[32]

We must be careful with this third case, however, because even with his best efforts a person may not be able to control his desires. Despite trying to focus upon other matters, the sexual desire might remain.[33] Such persistent desires are not sinful, because they remain in opposition to the will of the person. In such cases, says Thomas, the person can at least retain control of his actions, that is, he need not act out on his desires.[34] Aquinas distinguishes, therefore, between the control of reason, which modifies our emotions, and the control of the will, which determines our actions, often despite our emotions.

A thorough treatment of sinful desires gets more complicated yet. Sometimes, the initial desire itself might be sinful, because it might be voluntary through previous choices. Suppose that the second individual considered above repeatedly indulges his fantasies. In the long run, this repetition increases his sexual desires. Now when he is presented with a pornographic image, he spontaneously has a stronger desire. Although he has not chosen this desire at this moment, it is voluntary through his

---

emotions, see Claudia Eisen Murphy, "Aquinas on Our Responsibility for Our Emotions," *Medieval Philosophy and Theology* 8 (1999): 163–205.

32. Aquinas, *Summa theologiae* I-II, q. 24, a. 1. Kent and Dressel emphasize such cases ("Weakness and Willful Wrongdoing," 43).

33. Aquinas, *Summa theologiae* I, q. 81, a. 3, ad 2; I-II, q. 17, a. 7.

34. Ibid., I-II, q. 81, a. 3.

previous choices.[35] Had he not indulged his passions previously, he would not now have such a strong desire. Culpability for such desires, no doubt, is not so great as when the desire is directly chosen.

We will focus on the second case, for it most clearly might pave the way for vice. Sins of the heart, of course, might themselves arise from an evil will. A person with vice might choose to fantasize. Such cases do not pave the way for vice but presuppose vice. Our concern, then, is with a weak person who commits sins of the heart not from vice but from passion. If he repeatedly commits such sins, he begins to form a vice, which will then more likely spill out into sins of deeds.

Sins of the heart done from weakness must follow the pattern of other sins of weakness. The person must maintain the true major premise, but his passions focus his attention away from the evil of the action and toward some particular good. His reasoning might look as follows:

> Argument of Reason for Sins of the Heart
> Considered in itself, (voluntarily) desiring another man's wife ought to be avoided.
> This is an instance of (voluntarily) desiring another man's wife.
> ---
> Considered in itself, this ought to be avoided.
>
> Argument of the Passions for Sins of the Heart
> Considered in itself, sexual pleasure ought to be (voluntarily) desired.
> This is an instance of desiring sexual pleasure.
> ---
> Considered in itself, this ought to be (voluntarily) desired.

The reasoning differs from cases considered earlier in what is proscribed or prescribed. Formerly, it was action that was prohibited or recommended; now, it is desire. It differs also in that the desire is already occurring. The present desire, however, is not yet voluntary, so what is proscribed or prescribed is different (at least in number) from the present desire. In the end, the person posits the "and nothing else" clause, which then leads to action, that is, he dwells upon his desire.

Such dwelling upon desire can occur in a wide variety of domains, including inappropriate sexual desire, inappropriate desire for other people's possessions, envy of others' goods, sorrow over the burden of one's work,

---

35. Ibid., I-II, q. 77, a. 7.

anger at being slighted by others, and longing for the praise of others. As an individual begins to dwell upon his desires, he more and more begins to play with them, thereby extending them. More and more he increases his disposition to the evil object. Eventually, he is willing to pursue the object with more than desire; he acts out on his desires.

Actions such as serious theft are not likely to arise out of weakness. For one thing, the passion for material possessions is typically not strong enough to focus the attention forcefully away from the evil of the action. For another thing, such actions often involve long-term planning. These actions, then, are more likely to be sins of an evil will. The habit of an evil will, however, must arise from previous sinful actions. It might well arise from sins of the heart, as well as from instances of venial sins involving theft. By repeatedly dwelling upon his desire for possessions, and imagining how happy they will make him, he is led to acts of fraud or theft.

AN EVIL WILL WITHOUT AN EVIL HABIT?

We have been discussing sins arising from an evil will, and we have focused upon the sins of a vicious person, that is, a person who has developed some vice, such that he desires a false good more than he desires the true good. It would be a mistake, however, to identify a sin arising from an evil will as the same thing as a sin arising from some evil habit. In fact, sins arising from vice are only one kind of sin arising from an evil will.[36] Thomas mentions another kind, which does not depend upon an evil habit.

Someone sins from a firm desire for evil only when the will itself is moved to evil, which can happen in two ways. In one way, because the person has a corrupt disposition inclining him to evil, for on account of that disposition some evil becomes as if fitting and similar to the person. Into this evil, by reason of the fittingness, the will tends as if into a good....

In a second way, it happens that the will of itself tends into an evil by the removal of that which prohibits, for example, if someone is prohibited from sinning not because the sin is displeasing to him of itself but because of the hope of eternal life or because of the fear of hell, then when the hope is removed through

---

36. This point is noted by Kent and Dressel ("Weakness and Willful Wrongdoing," 44–54) and McCluskey ("Willful Wrongdoing," 13–15; "Thomas Aquinas and the Epistemology of Moral Wrongdoing," 117–18).

despair, or when fear is removed through presumption, it follows that he sins from a firm desire for evil, as if set loose from the harness.[37]

In the parallel text of the *De malo*, Thomas adds (to despair and presumption) "[the loss of] other gifts of the Holy Spirit, by which a person is restrained from sinning."[38]

What are we to make of these sins of an evil will that are not sins of an evil habit? Thomas provides little description of them. One natural source of confusion is that such sins always involve at least two sins, the initial sin of despair or presumption and then the consequent sin flowing from the desires set loose from the harness. One might easily mistake the first sin (of despair or presumption) for the sin from an evil will; in fact, it is the second sin that counts as a sin from an evil will.[39]

In what way do these sins (which we will call sins from despair, for short) arise from an evil will? As Thomas portrays it, the person has a desire, in his will, for the sin. This desire, however, is restrained by another desire, by the hope of heaven or the fear of hell. When the hope or the fear is removed, then the desire is set loose. In the end, the person does act from an evil desire of his will.

When Aquinas mentions hope and despair, fear and presumption, he is referring to the theological virtue of hope and to servile fear. The person hopes to attain the beatific vision, and he fears the punishment of hell.[40] Hope refers to the striving toward some good that poses a difficulty, and

---

37. Aquinas, *Summa theologiae* I-II, q. 78, a. 3: "Sed tunc solum ex certa malitia aliquis peccat, quando ipsa voluntas ex seipsa movetur ad malum. Quod potest contingere dupliciter. Uno quidem modo, per hoc quod homo habet aliquam dispositionem corruptam inclinantem ad malum, ita quod secundum illam dispositionem fit homini quasi conveniens et simile aliquod malum, et in hoc, ratione convenientiae, tendit voluntas quasi in bonum.... Alio modo contingit quod voluntas per se tendit in aliquod malum, per remotionem alicuius prohibentis. Puta si aliquis prohibeatur peccare non quia peccatum ei secundum se displiceat, sed propter spem vitae aeternae vel propter timorem Gehennae; remota spe per desperationem, vel timore per praesumptionem, sequitur quod ex certa malitia, quasi absque freno, peccet." See also Aquinas, *De malo*, q. 3, a. 14.

38. Aquinas, *De malo*, q. 3, a. 14 (Editio Leonina, XXIII: 98, ll. 230–32): "et alia huiusmodi dona Spiritus Sancti quibus homo retrahitur a peccato."

39. Kent and Dressel seem to make this mistake; see "Weakness and Willful Wrongdoing," 51–53.

40. See Aquinas, *Summa theologiae* II-II, q. 17, a. 2; and II-II, q. 19, a. 2.

fear refers to the avoidance of some evil that is difficult to avoid.[41] The beatific vision is difficult to attain because the person is sinful and desires that which is inconsistent with the beatific vision. Hell is difficult to avoid because sin is so alluring and upon sin follows the punishment of hell. Despair removes hope because the person now judges that the difficulty is too great; it cannot be overcome and the divine good is unattainable.[42] Presumption removes fear because the person now judges that hell is easy to avoid, for he will not go to hell even if he sins.[43] Presumption is itself of two possible kinds: the person believes there is no difficulty either through confidence in his own powers or through overconfidence in God. Thomas has in mind the latter presumption. The person does not fear hell because he has confidence that God will not condemn him to hell even though he sins.

There are a couple of ways to interpret what is going on. Before the sin of despair or presumption, the person is either in a state of grace, loving God above all else, or he is in a state of mortal sin. The latter is possible because someone can still have hope even without loving God above all else.[44] He hopes to attain the beatific vision for himself, without desiring it as a good shared with God.

If we suppose that the person is not in a state of grace, then it is perplexing why Thomas considers these sins any different from the first category of sins that arise from an evil will, namely, those sins that arise from vice. The person is not much different from the lecherous man who is restrained from adultery on account of fear of the vengeful husband. Of course, in the case of theological hope and servile fear, the person is restrained by some true good or some true evil. Conceivably, the same might also be said of the fear of the vengeful husband. Is not death a true evil? Furthermore, the person (in a state of mortal sin) who hopes for the beatific vision or fears hell does not pursue these goals insofar as they are shared goods; he pursues them only for himself. Ultimately, then, it seems little different from the case of vice restrained by some other self-interested desire.[45]

41. Ibid., I-II, q. 40, a. 1; I-II, q. 41, a. 2.
42. Ibid., II-II, q. 20, a. 4.
43. Ibid., II-II, q. 21, a. 1.
44. Ibid., II-II, q. 17, a. 8.
45. As McCluskey notes, the sin still arises from a disordered preference in the will ("Thomas Aquinas and the Epistemology of Moral Wrongdoing," 118).

More likely, then, Aquinas is considering a case of somebody who is in a state of grace but then despairs. Presumably, this person has a strong desire for some independent good. Nevertheless, his strong desire is not strictly speaking a vice, for ultimately the person loves God above all, since he has charity. Perhaps on a natural level, this independent good would be his greatest good, but grace elevates him, giving him an inclination to the divine good above all else. Upon the loss of grace, consequent upon the despair or presumption, the evil desire is set loose, now becoming his strongest.

The problem with this interpretation is that despair or presumption plays the role of any mortal sin, for from any such sin the loss of grace would follow. From one mortal sin, the desire for other sins would be set loose from restraint. There would be no reason for Aquinas to pick out hope and fear as particular restraints that are lost.

SINS ARISING FROM DESPAIR

I wish to consider a third interpretation, going beyond Aquinas's explicit teaching. I will approach the problem from a natural analog, ignoring the fact that Thomas is speaking of theological hope or fear.[46] Consider someone in the following state. He desires the true good above all. Nevertheless, he maintains the weak-set view, at least in his desires, that is, he desires some goods that do not fit within the true good. Indeed, he sometimes desires goods (with an imperfect desire) that are in opposition to the true good. Although he has such disordered desires, they do not master him, that is, they are lesser desires than his desire for the true good. Consequently, he does not choose the independent goods in opposition to the true good. Rather, he forgoes the independent goods, although he desires them, because he wants the true good most of all. Finally, this individual has hope of attaining the true good, for he recognizes that the true good is difficult to attain, in part because it involves resisting his temptations.

So long as this individual keeps his hope, then he cannot make the following syllogism of vice, which presupposes an evil habit stronger than the desire for the true good.

---

46. For an interesting discussion of despair, see Rebecca Konyndyk DeYoung, "The Roots of Despair," *Res Philosophica* 92 (2015): 829–54.

Argument of a Vicious Habit concerning the Agent
Considered in itself, pleasurable adultery is to be pursued by someone who is primarily a body or a sensing animal.
I am someone who is primarily a body or a sensing animal.
_____
Considered in itself, pleasurable adultery should be pursued by me.

The person who sins from despair does not use this syllogism. He does not posit the false minor premise, because he still identifies himself mostly as someone who is ordered to the divine good. As such, he reaches the conclusion that pleasurable adultery should be avoided. If he is to commit a sin from an evil will, then somehow he must reach the false conclusion: "Considered in itself, pleasurable adultery should be pursued by me." In some manner despair must lead to this conclusion. But how?

Recall the distinction between imperfect desire and perfect desire. We have imperfect desire for that which we consider in itself, in abstraction from the final order to the ultimate end. We also have imperfect desire for that which we consider to be impossible, even as we might desire bodily immortality. Prior to despair, the person has full-fledged desire for the true chief good, while he has an imperfect desire for the sinful good that is opposed to the chief good. I wish to suggest that when the person despairs of the true good, these desires are reversed: the individual has an imperfect desire for the true good and comes to have a perfect desire for the disordered good.

How does despair effect this reversal? We can have perfect desire only for that which we think possible. Under the influence of despair, the individual comes to perceive the true good as impossible. Consequently, he settles for what he knows to be a lesser good, but what he considers to be at least a possible good.

A man who is sorely tempted by adultery might resist the temptation because he has a greater desire for the shared intellectual good. As the temptation grows in strength, however, he begins to think that it is unassailable; it is impossible to resist, so that the opposed chief good is impossible to attain. He can no longer hope for the chief good, which he now deems to be impossible in the face of his temptation, so he abandons his full-fledged desire for the chief good. With this desire out of the way, no obstacle remains to his desire for adultery.

His reasoning might be portrayed as follows:

The Argument of Despair concerning the Agent
Considered in itself, pleasurable adultery is to be pursued by someone for whom sensible pleasure is the chief good.
I am someone for whom sensible pleasure is the chief possible good.
_____
Considered in itself, pleasurable adultery is to be pursued by me.

Insofar as he considers the ordering of his capacities, he recognizes that the divine good is indeed the chief good. Even the strength of his imperfect desires supports this ordering, for he desires the chief good—imperfectly—more than he desires pleasure. Ultimately, however, he thinks that the greatest good, which is the divine good, is an impossible good. The force of his temptation makes it impossible to attain. He settles upon the greatest possible good, a good that he desires less. He would wish to have the divine good, if he could, but he cannot (or so he believes).

The person who sins from despair posits the minor premise only on account of another sin, that is, the sin of despair. Wearied by the overwhelming difficulties of the true good, he concludes that this good cannot be attained. The sin of despair might itself be a sin of ignorance, passion, or possibly vice. In any event, the consequent sin (of adultery or whatever) is a sin from an evil will. It does arise from the will of the sinner, for he has a disposition in his will to seek the disordered good as independent of the chief good.

COMPULSIVE BEHAVIOR

Thomas classifies sins consequent upon despair as sins from an evil will, but as we have portrayed them, they share many features with sins of weakness, such that they might be mistakenly classified as sins of weakness.[47] First, the sin is often triggered by passion, for the person often despairs on account of the strength of some passion. Second, the person often wants to do what is right but is tempted to do what is wrong. Indeed, he initially resists the temptation, and gives in to it only consequent upon despair, when it seems impossible to resist the overwhelming passion. Third, these sins are often followed by repentance. After the sin, the passion subsides (having been temporarily appeased), and then the

---

47. For which reason it seems plausible that Guevara's cases of "aggressive akrasia" might often belong to these sins of an evil will ("The Will as Practical Reason").

attainment of the true good no longer seems so difficult. Hope returns and the true good returns to its place as the highest *attainable* good.

Compulsive behavior can sometimes be a cycle of such sins. The compulsive person wishes to avoid the undesirable behavior, and he sets himself to do so. He may have some limited success, but as his desires for the behavior mount, he begins to fall into despair. He thinks that he can no longer resist the temptation, and as such he does not resist the temptation. After giving in, the passion is diminished and the compulsive person regains his hope of overcoming his temptation.

Compulsive behavior is a pattern of behavior exhibiting at least two disorders. First, the person has a disordered desire for some good (or a disordered aversion for some evil). It is not so disordered as to be classified as a vice, for the person still desires most of all to resist this disordered desire. Second, the person has a disorder with regard to despair. He has a patterned behavior of falling into despair. This disorder, as well, may not classify as vice, but may be simply a pattern of weakness (that is, incontinence).

The first disorder is often aggravated by yet another: an inability to manage sorrow well; in modern terms, the person has poor stress management. Aristotle notes that people often seek to escape from sorrow by seeking some pleasure as a distraction.[48] A repeated pattern of such escape makes an individual unable to face sorrow, so that he will habitually flee to some comfort.

The healing of compulsive behavior, then, requires that all disorders be addressed. Focusing upon the disordered desire while ignoring the disordered despair is fruitless. Successful approaches have recommended setting small goals, for which despair is less likely. For the compulsive masturbator, for instance, it is not wise to say, "I will never masturbate again in my life." Rather, it is better to say, "I will not masturbate today." The first approach sets a much too difficult task, and the greater the difficulty the more likely is despair. By repeated success at small goals, the person gains confidence in his ability to overcome difficulties. Hope is encouraged rather than despair. Hope is also encouraged by focusing upon successes, however small, rather than focusing upon failures.

---

48. Aristotle, *Nicomachean Ethics*, bk. 7, chap. 14, 1154b13–14.

On top of the disordered desire and the disorder of despair, the compulsive person may also exhibit a disordered overconfidence. Ironically, despite his weakness, he nevertheless thinks himself capable of managing the situation. Consequently, twelve-step treatments lay emphasis upon one's weakness, even insisting that one is never healed but always recovering. These programs also emphasize the need to rely upon some higher power rather than upon oneself.

Compulsive behavior is parallel to the foregoing analysis of sins from despair in another way as well. The person continues to desire the true good, and he has a repugnance for the evil action. He recognizes, at least to some extent, the true chief good; he recognizes that the action to which he is tempted is not in his own best interest. In the end, he fails to pursue what he knows to be good, and he pursues the hated compulsive behavior, but only because he thinks his temptation impossible to resist. In short, the compulsive person retains an ideal good that he wishes he could have. The wish does not move to full-fledged desire on account of despair.

~† CHAPTER 10

SINS OF IGNORANCE

Compared with sins of weakness and sins of malice, sins of ignorance will prove relatively unproblematic. At first appearance, a sin of ignorance seems to be an oxymoron. After all, ignorance takes away responsibility, so that if a "sin" arises from ignorance, then it would seem to be no sin at all, since the person would not be responsible for it. Thomas concedes this point for certain cases but not for all. In two ways, he thinks, a person can still be responsible for a sin he commits from ignorance.[1] First, the person can be aware of the sinfulness of the action, but some other ignorance leads him to commit the sin he otherwise would not. Second, the person is not aware of the sinfulness of the action, but he is in some manner responsible for his own ignorance.

IGNORANCE THAT REMOVES WHAT PROHIBITS

In the first case, the person still remains aware that the action is sinful; consequently, he is responsible for the sin. If the person is aware that the action is sinful, then how does ignorance come into play? The person is ignorant of some other feature of the action that would have prevented him from acting. A thief, for instance, might break into a house, which he knows to be sinful, but he would have refrained from the action if he

---

1. Aquinas, *Summa theologiae* I-II, q. 76, a. 3; Aquinas, *De malo*, q. 3, a. 6.

had known that the owner was present with a gun. His ignorance (that the owner has a gun) causes him to sin.

This example provides a model for all sins of ignorance, in that the ignorance is a cause because the missing knowledge, were it present, would have prevented the sin.[2] Thomas says it is a kind of accidental cause that involves removing that which prohibits some effect. If a person opens the blinds of a house, thereby letting in the sunlight, then he lights up the house by way of removing that which prohibited the light. Such accidental causes presuppose another direct cause, for example, the sun. In the case of the thief, the direct cause is his desire to steal, which would be impeded by the knowledge that the owner has a gun. The removal of the knowledge, then, causes the sin.

Aquinas gives another case in which the individual is aware that the action is sinful. In this case, the action has multiple sinful aspects to it; the person is aware of some of these but not others.[3] Were he aware of all of them, then he would not sin, but he is willing to sin as long as the action has a limited sinful character. Thomas gives the example of Oedipus, who is willing to strike and kill a man, but if he had known that the man was his father, then he would not have been willing to kill his father. The action has a sinful character simply because it is killing a man, but it has an additional sinful character insofar as it is killing one's father. Oedipus is willing to do the former, but not the latter, so that his ignorance concerning his father causes the sin.

The second way in which ignorance can cause sin involves ignorance of the sinful nature of the action itself. In what way, then, can the individual be responsible for the sin? Thomas says that the person must be responsible for the ignorance itself. Suppose, for instance, that a hunter is on private property, which requires permission in order for him to hunt. He himself is unsure whether or not the property is private. Nevertheless, he continues to hunt in his ignorance. He is responsible for hunting illegally, even though he is ignorant that he is doing so. Why is he responsible? Because his ignorance is not without blame. He could have tried to discover the nature of the property on which he was hunting, but he chose not to.

---

2. Aquinas, *Summa theologiae* I-II, q. 76, a. 1; Aquinas, *De malo*, q. 3, a. 6.
3. See Aquinas, *Summa theologiae* I-II, q. 76, a. 3.

This second kind of sin from ignorance, then, involves a kind of voluntary ignorance. Understanding the nature of this sin, then, will require a better understanding of voluntary ignorance.

We can better understand voluntary ignorance by first considering two possible ways in which Thomas thinks ignorance is not voluntary.[4] First of all, it might be what he calls "invincible," that is, the person is unable to overcome his ignorance. If the person has no way to find out the sinful character of his action, then he is not responsible for his ignorance and neither is he responsible for the subsequent sin. In our own day and age, we are probably more sensitive to ways in which ignorance can be "invincible," even when it is strictly possible to acquire the knowledge. Cultural environments might make it "practically" impossible to perceive certain truths, although the capacity and even the opportunity may be strictly speaking present.

Even when a person can overcome his ignorance, he still might not be responsible for the ignorance, for he might have no moral responsibility to acquire the knowledge. Suppose, for instance, that Brett gives directions to some strangers, telling them to go over an unstable bridge, but Brett is ignorant of the state of the bridge. If Brett knew that the bridge were unstable, then certainly he would not give the directions he does. His ignorance, then, does cause his action.[5] But is his ignorance voluntary? Suppose further that he could overcome his ignorance; he could take the time to go test the bridge himself. Nevertheless, he has no reason to suspect that the bridge is unstable; furthermore, he has no responsibility to determine the stability of the bridges in the area; that responsibility belongs to some public official. Although he could discover the state of the bridge, he has no moral responsibility to do so. His ignorance is vincible (it may be overcome), but nevertheless it is not voluntary. For ignorance to be voluntary, two conditions must be met: the knowledge must be something we are *able* to attain, and the knowledge must be something we *should* attain.[6] In this case, the knowledge does not meet the second condition.

4. Ibid., I-II, q. 76, a. 2; Aquinas, *De malo*, q. 3, a. 7.
5. The example is taken from Stephen L. Brock, "Realistic Practical Truth," *Doctor Communis* (2008): 69.
6. See Aquinas, *Summa theologiae* I-II, q. 6, a. 3.

Aquinas notes that ignorance can be either at the universal level or at the particular level.[7] In other words, the person can have ignorance concerning the major premise of a practical syllogism or concerning the minor premise of a practical syllogism. The person might be ignorant that adultery is a sin, or he might be ignorant that this action is adultery. The examples given above have focused upon the second possibility.

Sins arising from ignorance of the universal, since they concern the moral law, must all involve cases in which the person does not know the sinful character of his action (although, possibly, he might know one sinful feature of an action but not another). Furthermore, one of the excuses for ignorance does not apply to these cases. Everyone, says Thomas, has a responsibility to know the moral law.[8] As such, only invincible ignorance can excuse from ignorance concerning the universal.

In two ways, then, a "sinful" action done on account of ignorance is not in fact a sin. In both cases the person is not responsible for his ignorance; either he could not overcome the ignorance, or he had no obligation to overcome it. Only these two cases of ignorance, which Aquinas calls "antecedent" ignorance (antecedent to the act of will), excuse from sin.[9]

Nevertheless, sometimes ignorance associated with a sin will not give rise to a sin of ignorance. Suppose that the hunter is ignorant that he is on private property. He considers investigating to determine whether he is allowed to hunt, but he decides not to bother because, he thinks, he would just as soon continue hunting even if it is private property; the knowledge might prove to be a nuisance, making him feel uncomfortable. In this case, the ignorance is certainly voluntary. The hunter could find out, and he is obliged to find out. Still, the ignorance does not give rise to a sin of ignorance. Why not? Because the ignorance itself is not the cause of the sin.[10] As we have seen, ignorance causes sin only if the knowledge would have prevented the sin. In this case, the hunter would have sinned even with the knowledge.

Aquinas calls this ignorance "affected," and associates it with sins of

---

7. Aquinas, *De malo*, q. 3, a. 6; Aquinas, *Summa theologiae* I-II, q. 76, a. 1.

8. Aquinas, *De malo*, q. 3, a. 7; Aquinas, *Summa theologiae* I-II, q. 76, a. 2.

9. Aquinas, *Summa theologiae* I-II, q. 6, a. 8; Aquinas, *De malo*, q. 3, a. 8. See Caulfield, "Practical Ignorance," 97–98.

10. Aquinas, *Summa theologiae* I-II, q. 76, a. 3.

an evil will, since the person would have sinned from his evil will with or without the ignorance.[11] Aquinas also calls this ignorance directly voluntary, or directly willed, which he contrasts with indirectly voluntary ignorance: "Ignorance is voluntary either directly or indirectly. Ignorance is directly voluntary when someone deliberately wills not to know something, so that he might more freely sin. Ignorance is indirectly voluntary when on account of work or some other occupation someone neglects to learn that through which he might be restrained from sinning."[12]

The hunter might *want* to be ignorant, as portrayed above, and then he has directly voluntary ignorance. On the other hand, he might truly want to know whether or not he is on private property, but he does not want to know badly enough. He prefers something else to the effort required to gain the knowledge. Perhaps he thinks it rather a hassle to find out; it is much easier simply to continue hunting. In that case, his ignorance arises from negligence. Such indirectly voluntary ignorance is what Aquinas has in mind for sins of ignorance.

A person, then, might be responsible for a sin he performs even though he is ignorant that it is a sin. This responsibility, however, presupposes a prior sin, namely, a failure to inform himself of important features of the action. When the person is aware of the sinful character of his action (as with the thief who is ignorant of the presence of the armed owner), then no such prior sin of negligence is necessary. Even when the person is ignorant of the sinful character of his action, the sin might not depend upon a prior negligence, for the individual might directly will to be ignorant. In that case, his ignorance does not in fact cause the sin, so his failure to inform himself is not presupposed to the sin.

In these sins of ignorance, then, the person does not want to sin; nevertheless, he performs a sinful action, ignorant that it is sinful. His responsibility depends upon a prior negligence, in which he failed to inform himself, not because he wanted to be ignorant. Rather, he found the act

---

11. Aquinas, *De malo*, q. 3, a. 8, ad 1 and 5.
12. Aquinas, *Summa theologiae* I-II, q. 76, a. 3: "Ipsa ignorantia est voluntaria, vel directe, sicut cum aliquis studiose vult nescire aliqua, ut liberius peccet; vel indirecte, sicut cum aliquis propter laborem, vel propter alias occupationes, negligit addiscere id per quod a peccato retraheretur." See also ibid., I-II, q. 6, a. 8. Aquinas, *De malo*, q. 3, a. 8, adds a third way.

of informing himself bothersome in some way or other. It was too much work, or it interfered with his entertainment, or some such thing.

Sin is ready at hand, then, not only because our passions lead us astray and not only because despair leads us to settle for a lesser good. Sin is ready at hand because we do not wish to do the work needed to discover our moral obligation. We prefer entertainment to moral rectitude. Entertainment is easy and passive, while discovering our moral obligations might prove to be something of a nuisance. If we forget the need to inform ourselves, we risk slipping further into sin.

EVERY SIN INVOLVES SOME IGNORANCE

We have seen that in sins of weakness the person fails to recognize the proper minor premise, while in sins from an evil will the person fails to recognize the proper major premise. We might conclude, then, that these sins are also sins of ignorance. After all, Thomas cites favorably the maxim "Those who do evil are always ignorant";[13] and he says, "Since the will concerns the good, or at least the appearance of good, the will is never moved into evil unless that which is not good in some way appears to have the character of good. Consequently, the will never tends into evil apart from some ignorance or error of reason."[14] Every defective action, it seems, must in some way arise from defective knowledge.[15] It seems to follow that every sin is a sin of ignorance. Two reasons, however, suggest otherwise.

First, for the most part Thomas treats the three kinds of sin—sins of ignorance, sins of passion, and sins from an evil will—as mutually exclusive. If an action is a sin from an evil will, then it cannot also be a sin of ignorance, even if the person has some ignorance. The person with affected ignorance, for instance, sins from an evil will. The ignorance is itself not a cause of the sin, but concomitant with the sin.

Second, we can distinguish between ignorance and ignoring, a distinc-

---

13. Aquinas, *De malo*, q. 3, a. 8.

14. Aquinas, *Summa theologiae* I-II, q. 77, a. 2: "Quia cum voluntas sit boni vel apparentis boni, nunquam voluntas in malum moveretur, nisi id quod non est bonum, aliqualiter rationi bonum appareret, et propter hoc voluntas nunquam in malum tenderet, nisi cum aliqua ignorantia vel errore rationis." See also Aquinas, *In Sent.* II, d. 5, q. 1, a. 1; Aquinas, *In Sent.* II, d. 24, q. 3, a. 3, ad 1; Aquinas, *De veritate*, q. 22, a. 6; Aquinas, *Summa theologiae* I-II, q. 58, a. 2.

15. For a thorough treatment of this idea, see Caulfield, "Practical Ignorance," 69–96.

tion that follows upon Aquinas's distinction between habitual and actual knowledge.[16] Recall that the person who sins from weakness can have knowledge habitually but he does not use it in act. He can be aware, in habit, that this action is adultery, but under the pressure of the passions he focuses simply upon the pleasure and ignores the adulterous character of the action. His habitual knowledge is not used actually in his practical reasoning. In this case, is the person ignorant of the adulterous character of the action? Or rather, does he ignore the adulterous character of the action? We seem more inclined to the latter designation.

This usage indicates that "ignorance" does not refer to the absence of actual knowledge but to the absence of habitual knowledge. If someone knows habitually that the capital of Florida is Tallahassee, but he is not now adverting to the fact (because he is thinking of something else), we do not say that he is ignorant concerning the capital of Florida. We might say, rather, that he is ignoring this information; he is not now thinking of it.

Strictly speaking, then, the person who sins from weakness need not be ignorant. He must, however, be ignoring. He might have all that he needs to know habitually, but he does not use it actually. The dictum "those who do evil are always ignorant" might be better translated, "those who do evil always ignore." The person who sins from weakness need not be ignorant, but he must ignore. Sins of ignorance, then, are sins that arise from the lack of habitual knowledge. In contrast, sins of passion arise from ignoring.

What of sins from an evil will? Are they reduced to sins of ignorance?[17] As we have seen, the ignorance involved in these sins concerns which goods are greater; more fundamentally, it concerns which part of oneself is most important. Possibly, this ignorance might sometimes involve only an ignoring. While the person is habitually aware that his rational part is his most important part, under the influence of the desires (of his will) he ignores this priority. It seems reasonable to suppose, however, that often a person in a state of vice has a kind of habitual ignorance. In what way, then, can sins from an evil will be distinguished from sins of

---

16. McCluskey speaks of a "secondary sense" of ignorance, when the person ignores what he knows by habit ("Thomas Aquinas and the Epistemology of Moral Wrongdoing," 110).

17. McCluskey raises the question whether sins of an evil will can be reduced to sins of ignorance ("Willful Wrongdoing," 34–35, 39).

ignorance? In the next section, we will see a text of the *De malo* that suggests a solution to this difficulty.

MIXING KINDS OF SIN

In the *De malo*, Aquinas lists a third manner in which ignorance might be voluntarily caused, and he associates it with the dictum that those who do evil are always ignorant.[18] So far, we have seen two ways in which ignorance might be voluntary. Either the person positively wants to be ignorant, which Thomas calls directly willed ignorance, or he does not want the knowledge badly enough—so that he prefers to do something else rather than gain the knowledge—which Thomas calls indirectly willed ignorance. In the third possibility, which Thomas calls accidentally willed ignorance, the person wills something else from which ignorance follows, for instance, he might drink to excess.

This third possibility may itself be divided into two, for that which causes ignorance might be willed either directly or indirectly. The excessive drinker provides an example of someone who directly wills something from which ignorance follows. The person under the influence of passions provides Aquinas's example of an indirect accidental willing of ignorance. The person wills something from which ignorance follows, namely, to be under the influence of passions, which can obscure the use of reason, but he wills it indirectly: he does not choose to incite his passions; rather, he chooses not to interfere with his passions, thereby allowing them to have sway. As we have seen, the latter case might be better described as a case of ignoring rather than as a case of ignorance. Excessive drinking might likewise often involve ignoring rather than ignorance.

This apparent mixing of the three kinds of sin, such that sins of passion are also described as involving indirectly caused ignorance, is peculiar to the *De malo*. This text, however, suggests that the three kinds of voluntary ignorance (or ignoring) line up with the three kinds of sin. Directly willed ignorance corresponds to sins from an evil will;[19] indirectly willed ignorance corresponds to sins of ignorance; and accidentally willed ignorance corresponds to sins of passion. The first two cases involve ignorance in

---

18. Aquinas, *De malo*, q. 3, a. 8.
19. Hence, McCluskey suggests that sins from an evil will differ from sins of ignorance by a willingness to forsake what is objectively right ("Willful Wrongdoing," 36–38).

the strict sense, that is, the lack of habitual knowledge, but the third case involves ignoring, and only in this third sense (of ignoring), says Thomas, can we say that everyone who does evil is in some manner ignorant.

The division of sins, then, follows upon two different sets of distinctions. First, "ignorance" might refer to habitual ignorance or to ignoring. Second, the cause of ignorance might be directly willed, indirectly willed, or accidentally willed. Habitual ignorance is associated most of all with sins of ignorance, although it can be found in sins from an evil will as well. When the habitual ignorance arises indirectly, then any consequent sin is a sin of ignorance. When the habitual ignorance is directly willed, so that sinning might be performed more comfortably or more easily, then the consequent sin is a sin from an evil will.

Ignoring, as opposed to habitual ignorance, is associated with both sins of passion and sins from an evil will, although the latter can also involve habitual ignorance. A sin of passion might happen to involve habitual ignorance, but this ignorance is not what ultimately causes the sin, for the person, influenced by his passion, does not consult his habitual knowledge. Whether the habitual knowledge is in fact present or absent, the sin follows from the lack of an effort to consult habitual knowledge. The ignoring of the sin of passion arises accidentally, because the person allows his passions to affect what reason considers. In contrast, for sins from an evil will, the ignorance—whether it be habitual ignorance or ignoring—arises directly from the will. The person wants either to be ignorant or to ignore what he knows.

TWO KINDS OF SINS OF IGNORANCE

As we have seen, Thomas identifies two kinds of sins of ignorance. In the first, the person is aware of the sinful nature of this action, but he is unaware of something else that might prevent him from acting, as the thief might be unaware that the owner of the house has a gun. In the second, the person is unaware of the sinful nature of his action. Nevertheless, he is responsible for his sin because his ignorance is itself voluntary. This second kind of sin of ignorance, then, always presupposes some prior sin, namely, the failure to gain information that one should gain. This sin is itself a particular kind of omission, which we will consider in the next chapter.

~? CHAPTER 11

OMISSIONS

Aquinas's treatment of omissions poses several difficulties.[1] Thomas himself seems to have been undecided on certain key points, concerning which he changed his mind at least once and perhaps several times. Most explicitly, he confronted the role of action within omissions, which seem to be the lack of action. Is there any action in an omission or is an omission the complete lack of all action? This difficulty poses another problem: what causes someone to sin by omission? Usually, it turns out, omissions are caused by previous sins, but Thomas seems to allow that even good actions can cause omissions. Most puzzling of all, perhaps, is the question of negligent omissions. How can a person be responsible for failing to do what he does not even consider doing, at least at the time at which he is supposed to do it?[2]

---

1. Parts of this chapter originally appeared in Jensen, "Omissions and Their Causes," *Acta Philosophica* 22 (2013): 117–33.

2. The difficult question of omissions is aggravated by apparent inconsistencies in Aquinas's treatments of the topic. The inconsistencies are found not simply in an early treatment and a late treatment but in two very late treatments, written almost on the heels of one another. In the *De malo* (q. 2, a. 1), Thomas denies a possibility that he seems to affirm in the *Summa theologiae* (I-II, q. 71, a. 5). We cannot directly intend an omission, he asserts in the *De malo*. In the *Summa*, however, he states the exact opposite: "Sometimes the act

ESSENCE AND CAUSE

In all three of Aquinas's treatments of omissions he notes that there are two opinions concerning whether omissions have some action.³ Some claim that every sin must have some action, at least an interior act of will; others claim that omissions need have no act at all, interior or exterior. In the *Sentences*, he simply rejects the first position and comes down firmly in favor of the second. In the *De malo* and *Summa theologiae*, however, he states that both positions have some truth. In these texts, he makes an important distinction between the essence of the omission and the cause of the omission. Regarding the essence, omissions need have no act at all, either an interior act of will or an exterior act.⁴ Regarding the cause, omissions must always have some act as a cause, at least an interior act and sometimes an exterior as well.⁵

[of will] is led directly into the omission itself, for example, when someone wills not to go to church in order to avoid the trouble." Between the two texts, the *Summa* seems to have the better case. Experience confirms that we sometimes directly will not to do something.

Furthermore, the *De malo* claim seems inconsistent with Aquinas's more general view of direct and indirect willing. Indeed, in the *De malo* itself (q. 3, a. 8), Thomas acknowledges only one question later that someone can directly will the nonbeing of ignorance. The *De malo* text is even inconsistent with itself. Most crucial is an inconsistency concerning the meaning of a per se cause and a per accidens cause. Thomas wishes to discover how the will causes an omission, and he begins by defining per se and per accidens causes, as he standardly does, in terms of intention. He proceeds to say that omissions are always outside intention. Given his definition of a per se cause, he should conclude that omissions are never caused per se. Instead, he immediately utilizes a different meaning, never defined, of per se cause. The treatment in the *Summa* again provides a stark contrast. There, Thomas sticks to his standard meaning of per se and per accidens. Consequently, the case of the person who plays, foreseeing that he will miss going to church, is classified differently in the two texts. In the *De malo*, the omission is said to be caused per se; in the *Summa*, it is said to be caused per accidens. The *Summa* conforms not only to Aquinas's more standard usage; it conforms to the initial definition of per se and per accidens causes given in the *De malo*.

3. The three treatments are found in Aquinas, *In Sent.* II, d. 35, q. 1, a. 3; Aquinas, *De malo*, q. 2, a. 1; and Aquinas, *Summa theologiae* I-II, q. 71, a. 5.

4. Kent correctly notes that often sins of omission include no choice ("Aquinas and Weakness," 83).

5. Much discussion of omissions has not focused upon the cause, but has focused upon some expectation that the action will be performed; see Patricia G. Smith, "Contemplating

The essence of missing Mass is precisely the lack of a certain action that the agent is obliged to perform. If someone stays up late the night before and ends up sleeping through Mass, then he sins while he sleeps, performing no action, for it is precisely the failure to perform an action that is the sin. What of the choice to stay up late? Is that not part of the omission? No, says Thomas. This choice does not belong to the essence of the sin. Rather, it is the cause of the sin. Every omission, says Thomas, requires some voluntary action for its cause, but this action is itself not a part of the sin of omission. Every omission needs a cause because an omission is something out of the ordinary, or rather, it is unnatural.[6] An agent naturally performs those operations that are proper to it, and an omission is precisely a failure to perform some proper operation. Some cause, therefore, must prevent an agent from carrying out the proper operation.

Only in the *Summa theologiae* does Aquinas specify that the essence of an omission sometimes has no action and sometimes has only an interior act of will. The other two texts are somewhat ambiguous, but they seem to imply that an omission, in its essence, never has any act at all. This conclusion is reasonable given the supposition (implied in both the *Sentences* and the *De malo*) that no omissions are directly willed, for only such omissions have an interior act belonging to their essence. As Thomas puts it in the *Summa*: "Sometimes the act of will is directly led into the omission itself, for example, when someone wills not to go to church, in order to avoid the work. Such an act of will belongs per se to the omission, for the willing of any sin belongs per se to that sin, since it belongs essentially to a sin to be voluntary."[7]

If someone chooses to skip Mass because he finds Mass unpleasant,

---

Failure: The Importance of Unconscious Omission," *Philosophical Studies* 59 (1990): 159–76. This expectation, for Aquinas, is simply the obligation to perform an action; see Jeffrey Hause, "Voluntariness and Causality: Some Problems for Aquinas' Theory of Responsibility," *Vivarium* 36 (1998): 55–66.

6. Aquinas, *De malo*, q. 2, a. 1.

7. Aquinas, *Summa theologiae* I-II, q. 71, a. 5: "Qui quidem actus quandoque directe fertur in ipsam omissionem, puta cum aliquis vult non ire ad Ecclesiam, vitans laborem. Et tunc talis actus per se pertinet ad omissionem, voluntas enim cuiuscumque peccati per se pertinet ad peccatum illud, eo quod voluntarium est de ratione peccati."

then the choice belongs to the very essence of the omission. The omission still consists of the lack of some action, namely, the lack of the exterior action of going to Mass, but it also includes an action as part of its essence. Interestingly, in this case, the cause of the omission is the choice to miss Mass, and this choice also belongs to the essence of the omission. In all other omissions—which are caused indirectly—the essence will consist in no action at all, interior or exterior, and the cause will be some separate action.

For these latter omissions, it is incidental whether the cause is united to the omission or precedes it. Someone might choose to play at the time of Mass, recognizing that he thereby misses Mass; on the other hand, someone might choose to stay up late, recognizing that he will oversleep and miss Mass. In either case, a chosen action poses an obstacle to the performance of one's duty. The act of playing at the time of Mass is inconsistent with also going to Mass, so the one prevents the other. Likewise, sleeping (at a place other than the church) at the time of Mass is inconsistent with going to Mass, so that which causes one to sleep at the time of Mass (namely, staying up late) causes an obstacle to performing one's duty.

In both these cases—when the cause is simultaneous and when it is prior—the cause is itself not part of the omission. Playing is the cause of missing Mass, for instance, but it is not part of the sin of omission, which consists simply in the lack of action.

CAN AN OMISSION BE CAUSED BY A GOOD ACTION?

Can the cause of the omission be some good action, as is suggested in the following passages of the *De malo*? "A sin can sometimes be caused by some other act, which itself is sometimes a sin (as when one sin is the cause of another sin) and sometimes not a sin."[8] "It is not impossible [for an act done well] to be a per accidens cause of an omission, because the good can be a per accidens cause of evil."[9] Clearly, an indirectly willed

---

8. Aquinas, *De malo*, q. 2, a. 1, ad, s.c. 2 (Editio Leonina, XXIII: 31, ll. 367–69): "Culpam contingit causari ab aliquo actu, qui quandoque est culpa, sicut cum peccatum est causa peccati, quandoque uero non culpa."

9. Ibid., q. 2, a. 1, ad, s.c. 7 (Editio Leonina, XXIII: 31, ll. 394–97): "Si tamen daretur quod aliquis actus non posset male fieri, non esset inconueniens si esset causa per accidens omissionis: quia bonum potest esse per accidens causa mali."

omission might be caused by some evil action, as when someone chooses to commit adultery rather than to go to Mass. It seems plausible, however, that these omissions can also be caused by good actions. As Thomas suggests, someone might pray during the time that he should be honoring his father.[10] He would then knowingly fail to honor his father at the appropriate time, yet he does so on account of the good deed of praying. He indirectly wills the omission; what he directly chooses, however, seems to be a good action.

The most obvious objection to this possibility is that given by Aquinas himself, namely, that what is usually good, such as an act of praying, becomes evil under the circumstances, for the person is praying when he should not. "The very act of praising God in prayer can be done poorly, if it is done when it should not be, namely, when one ought to be doing something else."[11] On this account, then, the action directly willed is itself evil, precisely because it is performed in conjunction with an omission.

In the treatment of the *Sentences*, however, Thomas objects strongly to this account. The two actions—praying and failing to honor one's father (Aquinas consistently asserts that failures are "actions" in the broad sense)—are related accidentally to one another, for the omission is caused *per accidens*. It follows that one cannot belong to the essence of the other. Not only is the cause (praying) not part of the omission (failing to honor one's father), but the omission is also not part of the cause. Consequently, the evil of the omission is not part of the cause, and the cause does not itself become evil by way of the omission. In short, praying remains essentially good, and the evil of the omission that is attached to it does not make the action itself to be evil.

Even if someone wills something that is, considered in itself, an obstacle to the fulfillment of a precept, such as a contrary action, nevertheless he does not sin from the mere fact that he wills it, because the action can be permissible in itself. Still, he sins from the fact that he sets aside that which he ought to do. Never-

---

10. Ibid., q. 2, a. 1, ad 11.

11. Ibid., q. 2, a. 1, ad, s.c. 7 (Editio Leonina, XXIII: 31, ll. 389–92): "Et hoc ipsum quod est laudare Deum ore, potest male fieri si hoc faciat quando non debet, quando scilicet alia facere tenetur."

theless, it remains that the action willed, whether exterior or interior, relates per accidens to the sin of omission, such that the deformity of the omission does not reside in it.[12]

In short, the only sin in such situations is the omission, and it consists in no action at all. The action to which the omission is joined is evil only by association with the omission. In a sense, then, the good action of praying can cause the failure to honor one's parents at the appropriate time.

The same conclusion seems to follow from Aquinas's explanation, in the *De malo*, of why omissions essentially have no action. He says that a sin is most essentially a receding from the proper rule or measure. Since human actions are ruled by both affirmative and negative precepts, it follows that some sins will be actions, namely, those opposed to negative precepts, and some will be the absence of action, namely, those opposed to affirmative precepts.

When someone prays at the time he should be honoring his father, surely the evil and sin is precisely in opposition to the affirmative precept to honor one's father. There is no negative precept, such as, "Do not pray when one should be doing something else." This particular act of praying is in fact opposed to no negative precept. The only precept opposed is affirmative, which means that the only sin is an omission. The cause of the omission, therefore, is in fact good.

The case might be clarified through a distinction between an action being evil in its kind and a concrete action that is good in kind but evil through a connection with some other evil act. Adultery, for instance, is evil in its very kind. In contrast, almsgiving is good in kind but a concrete performance of it can be evil when connected with some other evil action, for instance, when done out of vainglory. Praying when one ought to be honoring one's parents seems to belong to the latter category. It is good

---

12. Aquinas, *In Sent.* II, d. 35, q. 1, a. 3 (Mandonnet v. 2, 906): "Etsi enim aliquid velit quod, quantum est in se, [non] est impedimentum expletionis praecepti, sicut oppositum, constat quod ex hoc quod vult illud, non peccat; quia illud potest esse secundum se licitum; sed peccat in eo quod praetermittit id quod facere debet. Ergo constat quod ille actus vel exterior vel interior per accidens ad peccatum omissionis pertinet; et ita in eo deformitas omissionis non fundatur." I could make sense of this text (especially given the material that appears immediately before the section quoted) only by eliminating the "non" that appears in brackets.

in kind but evil through connection with the omission. Still, the only evil present is in the omission and not in the cause, which is said to be evil only by attachment with the omission. Once again, it seems to follow that a good action can indeed be the cause of an omission.

One further distinction, however, clarifies the manner in which the cause is good. Thomas distinguishes between the exterior action and the interior act of will. We have seen him apply this distinction to the essence of the omission, and we can apply it as well to the cause of the omission. The act of praying is itself twofold. It is a certain exterior activity (not necessarily bodily exterior but exterior to the will, since the person might be praying simply "in his mind"), and it is also the act of will to choose to pray.

As we have seen, the exterior activity of praying is good according to its kind; it may be called evil only by association with the evil of the omission. The same cannot be said for the choice to pray. The two differ because they have different objects.[13] The object of the exterior act of praying is the expression or conveying of certain sentiments to God. The object of the interior act is always a perceived good or evil, for as we have seen, the object of the will is the good.

One might object that the object of the exterior action is also a good; after all, it is good to express the sentiment of praise to God. The point must be granted. Nevertheless, a difference exists between the two cases. The object of the exterior action is indeed some good, but the object of the interior action is a good or evil precisely insofar as it is perceived as good or evil. The object of every power is some good, but only the will has the good as good for its object.[14]

We have seen, however, that any particular good remains good only insofar as it is directed to the chief good. The object of the will, then, must go beyond the immediate good to which the exterior action is directed. The will must aim at this good insofar as it belongs—or does not—to the overall good. In this particular case, the act of praying is not directed to the true concrete realization of the overall good, since it prevents the act of honoring one's father, which at the time is required for the overall good.

13. See Aquinas, *Summa theologiae* I-II, q. 18, a. 6.
14. See ibid., I-II, q. 6, a. 2.

What the will desires, then, is some particular good—found in the act of praying—that is cut off from the true overall good.

The interior act of choosing to pray, then, is not a good action but an evil action. It is evil not on account of the praying, which is good in itself, but on account of the omission, which is attached to the praying. The object of the will, then, is a defective good, that is, a good lacking the order to the chief good.

The cause of the omission is a certain action, but this action is itself composed of two actions, an interior and an exterior action. When we ask whether this action is good or evil, then, we can give three distinct answers. The question might be applied simply to the exterior action, in which case the action (of praying) is good (or at least this action *can* be good). The question might be applied to the interior action, in which case the action (of choosing to pray) is evil. Finally, the question might be applied to the whole action, in which case the action is again evil.

The cause of the omission, then, can be a good action, but if we consider the cause in its completion, then it is not a good action but an evil action. Ultimately, the omission is caused by an evil action. We do not sin by omission simply because we have done what is good; rather, we sin by omission because we have done what is defectively good.

UNFORESEEN OMISSIONS

We have considered two kinds of omissions. First, someone might directly will an omission, as when he chooses to skip Mass because he finds Mass unpleasant. Second, someone might directly will some other action, good or evil, foreseeing that he thereby cannot fulfill his duty; consequently, he wills the omission indirectly. In both cases, the cause of the omission ultimately involves doing some other evil action, at least a defective act of willing.

Indirectly willed omissions, however, may be divided into two kinds. In the first, which we have discussed above, the person foresees the omission. In the second, which is more problematic, the omission is not foreseen.[15] Someone might stay up late, not foreseeing that he will sleep in

---

15. As noted above, Aquinas's usage is anomalous in the *De malo*. In that text, only unforeseen consequences are considered indirect (or per accidens).

past the time of Mass. Again, someone who begins reading might plan to go to Mass but get so engrossed in his reading that he completely forgets about Mass. In the case of staying up late, the cause precedes the omission; in the case of reading through the time of Mass, the cause is conjoined to the omission. Once again, this distinction between conjoined cause and preceding cause appears irrelevant. What matters, it seems, is that in both cases the omission itself is not foreseen.

For indirect unforeseen omissions it may seem that the person is not responsible. In both examples given above, the person plans to go to Mass. In both examples, the person misses Mass because of some oversight. Can he be responsible for such an oversight?

This question can be answered by considering two possibilities. First, the cause of the action might itself be a sin. Perhaps the person drinks to inebriation, and consequently sleeps in past the time of Mass. He did not plan to miss Mass nor did he foresee that he would miss Mass, but his sinful action of getting drunk caused him to miss Mass. Second, the cause of the action might itself not be a sin. Perhaps the person stays up late doing something good, such as comforting someone in need. Once again, he does not plan to miss Mass nor does he foresee that he will miss Mass, but in fact he does. His act of staying up late, which is in itself good, has caused him to fail in his duty.

The first case might appear to be straightforward. After all, the person does commit a sin. It does not seem so troubling, then, to hold him responsible for the unforeseen omission that follows upon the sin. Upon reflection, however, the case is not so straightforward. Consider two people who get drunk and fall fast asleep. The first sleeps through Mass. The second is fortuitously wakened by a loud noise outside his house, so he does not miss Mass.[16] The two have done fundamentally the same thing, but by luck the second does not sin by omission. Is it fitting that the presence or absence of a sin should depend upon luck?[17]

---

16. Aquinas, *Summa theologiae* II-II, q. 79, a. 3, ad 3.

17. M. V. Dougherty has an interesting and enlightening discussion of moral luck in Aquinas, much of which proves helpful for the discussion that follows; see M. V. Dougherty, "Moral Luck and the Capital Vices in *De malo*: Gluttony and Lust," in *Aquinas's Disputed Questions on Evil: A Critical Guide*, ed. M. V. Dougherty (Cambridge: Cambridge University Press, 2016), 222–34.

Thomas argues that the harmful consequences of our sinful actions are not exactly bad luck, at least if they can be reasonably foreseen.[18] Someone who drinks and then drives, consequently killing someone in an accident, is responsible for the homicide, even though another person in a similar situation might have the good luck not to encounter other cars, thereby avoiding the sin of homicide.[19]

The point can be clarified through a distinction between the evil in the will and responsibility for consequences, a distinction that can be elucidated first by way of directly intended evil. Consider two people, Scott and Barb, both of whom intend to poison his or her cousin and both of whom carry out the deed. The upshot of their actions, however, is quite distinct: Scott succeeds, but Barb's cousin accidentally spills his poisoned drink, so that he does not drink enough poison to lead to his death. Both Scott and Barb intend the same evil, and as such the evil in their wills is the same. Nevertheless, Scott is responsible for the death of his cousin, but Barb is not responsible for the death of hers, there being no death for which she can be held responsible. Scott can be tried and convicted for murder; Barb can be tried and convicted only for attempted murder, a much lesser crime.

Next consider indirectly willed but foreseen harm. Joe and Helena are both in a hurry, and both run a red light, recognizing that they might thereby kill someone. Joe does kill someone, but by sheer luck Helena escapes with no accident. Once again, the evil of the will in both cases is the same. Both Joe and Helena are willing to do the action (running a red light) despite recognizing the possible consequences, which indicates, says Thomas, a willingness to accept the risk of the consequences as worthwhile, that is, getting to their destination sooner is worth the risk of killing someone.[20] But once again the two differ in the effects for which they can be held responsible. Joe can be responsible for homicide, while Helena cannot. The offense for which Helena can be convicted is much less significant than the offense for which Joe can be convicted.

Next consider indirectly willed but unforeseen harm that arises from some evil deed. Both Scott and Barb poison their cousins; both succeed.

18. Aquinas, *Summa theologiae* I-II, q. 73, a. 8; I-II, q. 20, a. 5.
19. Ibid., II-II, q. 64, a. 8.
20. Ibid., I-II, q. 73, a. 8.

But Barb's cousin shares his drink with a friend, so that the friend also dies. Once again, the evil in the will is the same, but once again the harm for which each can be held responsible differs. Barb can be held responsible for the death of her cousin's friend, even though she did not foresee it.

How can she be held responsible for a harm that she did not foresee? Thomas says that we are responsible to remove from our actions that which could cause harm.[21] By failing to remove that which could cause harm, we accept the responsibility for the consequent harm. If the harm ensues, then we are indeed responsible for the harm. It follows that we have a responsibility to review our actions, seeing whether they could lead to harm. The failure to make this review might lead to unforeseen harm. More precisely, it leads to the very lack of foresight. We do not foresee the harm because we do not do what we should have done, namely, review our action to try to remove potential harms.

When a person performs an evil action, he is obliged to remove the very evil itself. When Barb chooses to murder, she has already failed to remove that which causes harm—namely, the very evil of murder—even apart from any further bad effects that might result. In this respect, Scott is no different than Barb. He also fails to remove the evil from his action. Both Barb and Scott, then, intend the same evil, and both fail to remove the evil from their actions. Nevertheless, Barb has an additional death for which she can be held responsible.

When discussing homicide, Thomas clearly lays out the responsibility to remove potential harms from our actions, citing two ways in which a person can be responsible for a consequent death:

> Sometimes, that which is neither willed nor intended (in act and per se) can be per accidens willed and intended, insofar as a cause per accidens is said to be that which removes what prohibits. Therefore, he who does not remove that from which homicide follows, if it ought to be removed, will in some manner be guilty of voluntary homicide. This can happen in two ways. First, when killing results from an unlawful deed, which one ought to avoid. Second, when one does not take the required care. Therefore, according to the law, if someone does a lawful deed and he also takes the proper care, but nevertheless someone dies as a result, then he is not guilty of homicide; on the other hand, if he does an unlawful deed,

21. Ibid., II-II, q. 64, a. 8.

or if he does a lawful deed but does not take the proper care, then if death follows upon his action, he does not avoid the guilt of homicide.[22]

Barb falls into the first category, for she has done an evil action from which (an additional) death has followed. Since she ought to have removed the evil from her action but did not, she is responsible for the additional unforeseen death.

Thomas distinguishes two situations in which death (which can readily be extended to other harms) might follow from a good action. Either the person took the proper care to remove the risk of harm, or he did not. Both Beatrice and Max are working with dangerous chemicals for a good purpose. Beatrice properly disposes of her chemicals, but a rat, getting into the disposal, leaves the chemicals strewn about; a passerby touches the chemicals and is blinded. Max carelessly leaves the dangerous chemicals out; a passerby touches the chemicals and is blinded. Neither intends nor foresees the harm. Beatrice is not responsible for the harm, but Max is; for Beatrice took the proper care to remove the possibility of harm, while Max did not. For Beatrice and Max (unlike the previous cases), the evil in the will is not the same. Beatrice has no evil in her will; Max has the evil of negligence, of not taking the proper care to remove the possibility of harm.

The discussion has focused upon harms consequent upon some action. The same reasoning applies, however, when we look not at harmful side effects but at consequent omissions. We have already examined directly willed omissions and foreseen omissions. Someone deliberately avoids Mass because he finds it unpleasant. Someone else stays up late foreseeing that he will miss Mass. Both are responsible for the omission,

---

22. Ibid., II-II, q. 64, a. 8: "Contingit tamen id quod non est actu et per se volitum vel intentum, esse per accidens volitum et intentum, secundum quod causa per accidens dicitur removens prohibens. Unde ille qui non removet ea ex quibus sequitur homicidium, si debeat removere, erit quodammodo homicidium voluntarium. Hoc autem contingit dupliciter, uno modo, quando dans operam rebus illicitis, quas vitare debebat, homicidium incurrit; alio modo, quando non adhibet debitam sollicitudinem. Et ideo secundum iura, si aliquis det operam rei licitae, debitam diligentiam adhibens, et ex hoc homicidium sequatur, non incurrit homicidii reatum, si vero det operam rei illicitae, vel etiam det operam rei licitae non adhibens diligentiam debitam, non evadit homicidii reatum si ex eius opere mors hominis consequatur."

although only the first directly willed it. We have now turned our attention to indirectly willed and unforeseen omissions, which we have divided into two categories: those that are caused by some evil action and those that are caused by some good action.

Someone might get drunk and not foresee that it will cause him to sleep through Mass. The consequent omission is unforeseen, but it follows upon an evil action. He is responsible for the omission, even as Barb was responsible for the additional death. Why? Because he is responsible to remove from his actions that from which an omission could follow. Since we are all responsible to remove the evil from our actions, he is in fact responsible to remove the act of getting drunk, from which the omission might follow. He is responsible whether or not he takes precautions (such as setting an alarm), for he should have removed the evil itself, not just the risk of further evil. His responsibility for the omission, then, does not depend upon the lack of appropriate care; it depends upon the failure to remove the evil action itself, which evil action turns out to be the cause of some omission.

Someone else stays up late doing something good, such as helping a friend study for a test; he then sleeps through Mass. Is he responsible for the omission? That depends. Did he take the proper care to remove the possibility of sleeping through Mass? That proper care might involve a variety of possibilities: setting an alarm, asking a friend to wake him, not staying up quite so late, and so on. If he took proper care, but slept through Mass anyway, then he is not responsible and he does not sin by omission. If he does not take the proper care, then he does sin by omission. In this case, negligence leads to the responsibility for the omission. Consequently, omissions of this type might be described, following Patricia Smith, as negligent omissions.[23]

NEGLIGENT OMISSIONS

Thomas expressly indicates the possibility of these negligent omissions in the *Summa theologiae*. "He who wills one thing that cannot exist simultaneously with a second, wills—as a consequence—to be without

---

23. See Smith, "Contemplating Failure," 160. Barnwell also uses the terminology; see Barnwell, *Problem of Negligent Omissions*.

the second thing, unless perhaps he does not foresee that the deed he wills prevents him from doing what he ought to do, in which case he can still be judged blameworthy through negligence."[24]

According to Barnwell, Aquinas has done the service of identifying negligent omissions, but he has not given an adequate account of them.[25] Barnwell focuses upon those cases in which the cause is simultaneous with the omission, such as the person who gets engrossed with his reading and forgets to go to Mass. Barnwell does not seem to have in mind the person who stays up late, not foreseeing that he will sleep through Mass. At the time of the omission, this latter person is not conscious; Barnwell's analysis, however, focuses upon some limited degree of awareness still retained—at the time the obligation must be fulfilled—by the forgetful person. Would Barnwell classify the case of staying up late as a negligent omission? It is unclear.

Why does Barnwell think that Aquinas's analysis is inadequate? Because Thomas explains negligent omissions in terms of some prior omission, such as the failure to consider the possible consequences of one's actions. This prior omission, presumably, could itself be a negligent omission or not. If it is a negligent omission, then it also must be traced back to some prior omission. To avoid an infinite regress, at some point the prior omission must not be negligent; it must be directly willed or indirectly willed but foreseen. In either case, the negligent omission is ultimately reduced to a non-negligent omission. In short, thinks Barnwell, Aquinas solves the problem by eliminating the reality of negligent omissions and replacing them with some prior non-negligent omission.[26] It is difficult to see, says Barnwell, how the consequent omission can itself be considered voluntary, just because the prior action is voluntary.[27]

Thomas would protest, no doubt, that Barnwell has failed to attend to the difference between the essence of the omission and its cause. Thomas

---

24. Aquinas, *Summa theologiae* I-II, q. 71, a. 5: "qui enim vult aliquid cum quo aliud simul esse non potest, ex consequenti vult illo carere; nisi forte non perpendat quod per hoc quod vult facere, impeditur ab eo quod facere tenetur; in quo casu posset per negligentiam culpabilis iudicari."

25. Barnwell, *Problem of Negligent Omissions*, 97–132.

26. See ibid., 115–22.

27. Ibid., 111–12.

does not *reduce* a negligent omission to some prior omission. Rather, he identifies its cause in some prior omission. The essence of the two omissions is distinct, although the person is responsible for both of them only because of the prior omission.

The cause of a negligent omission is itself another omission, and this prior omission can be described as negligence; it is a failure to consider and to remove those features of an action from which an omission might follow.[28] The consequent omission can be described as a "negligent omission," but it itself is not negligence. Between the two omissions, then, the first is negligence and the second is negligent. Barnwell asks Aquinas to identify the cause of the negligence. If negligence causes a negligent omission, then what causes the negligence?

We might begin by noting that "negligence" can be used in broader and narrower senses. When we perform an action, we should remove from it certain bad features, most especially those features that bring about undesirable consequences. In order to remove these features, we must first consider them. Two things, then, are required: the consideration of the features and the removal of them.

We may well describe something as negligence if it involves only the latter (the failure to remove). If a doctor considers some contraindication for surgery and fails to remove this contraindication (insofar as he is able), then we might describe him as being negligent. In this case he foresaw the negative consequence of his action; he simply failed to remove from his action that which led to the foreseen negative consequence.

Thomas has a narrower meaning of negligence: it always involves the failure *to consider* certain bad features of our actions.[29] Of course, the failure to remove these bad features follows upon the failure to consider them. Aquinas would agree with Barnwell, then, that foreseen omissions

---

28. We should note that the "prior" omission is not necessarily temporally prior; rather, it is prior according to causality. Sometimes, it might happen to be simultaneous with the consequent omission. Someone who is engrossed in reading through the time of Mass, for instance, might fail, at the very time of Mass, to consider whether his act of reading is interfering with some important responsibility. The failure to consider causes a second failure, namely, the failure to go to Mass. The two failures are simultaneous, yet the failure to consider is causally prior.

29. See Aquinas, *Summa theologiae* II-II, q. 54.

are not negligent omissions, although they might arise from the failure to remove some bad features of an action.

Negligence is itself a certain kind of omission, namely, the failure to make certain considerations. Since it is an omission, it requires some cause, which (we have seen) reduces to four possibilities. (1) It might be directly willed, that is, the person might not bother making further considerations concerning his action because it is troublesome. On the other hand, it might be indirectly willed, in which case we have seen three further possibilities. (2) It might be indirectly willed and foreseen. He might not make further considerations because he wants to do something else instead (perhaps simply to go ahead with his action). (3) It might be indirectly willed, unforeseen, and arise from some evil action. He might get drunk, which prevents him from making further considerations on his action. Finally, (4) it might be indirectly willed, unforeseen, and arise through negligence, that is, the negligence itself might arise from some prior negligence, in which case the negligence is itself a negligent omission.

Barnwell does not consider the third possibility, but he finds the other three wanting. The fourth option is certainly realistic, but it only forestalls the ultimate explanation, since we cannot indefinitely explain negligence by way of some prior negligence. That leaves the first and second possibilities. Barnwell finds both wanting because both involve foresight; if they involve foresight, then the omission is not in fact negligent, since it is foreseen.[30]

This argument, however, loses sight of what is foreseen. The person does not foresee the omission; he foresees that he will not consider all that needs to be considered about the action.[31] In the first option, for instance, the person directly wills not to consider, because the consideration is tiresome (or some such thing). He foresees—even directly wills—that he will not consider all that he needs to consider, but he does not foresee

---

30. Barnwell, *Problem of Negligent Omissions*, 120–22.
31. Barnwell seems to consider this possibility, but he narrows the ignorance that is foreseen (ibid., 118–20). On Barnwell's account, the agent foresees that he will not know that he should at some designated time perform some obligatory action. The agent's foresight, however, need not be so specific. He need foresee only that he will not know some important features of his action.

the particular details that he will fail to consider. When he chooses to read, for instance, he also chooses not to consider all the relevant features of this act of reading. He does not thereby know what the relevant features are. If one of those features is that the reading takes place at the time of Mass, he does not foresee that his reading will prevent him from going to Mass. After all, he has not even bothered to consider the time of the reading. He foresees only that he will end up performing an act of reading about which he lacks pertinent information.

In the second case, the person indirectly wills not to consider, because he prefers something else. Perhaps he is so engaged with his reading that he chooses to continue reading, foreseeing that this continuation prevents him from considering relevant features of the act of reading. Once again, he does not foresee the omission; rather, he foresees his lack of consideration with the subsequent lack of knowledge. The details of what knowledge is lacking remain unknown to him (or else the knowledge would not be lacking).

In the end, Aquinas's solution to the problem of negligent omissions is not that different from Barnwell's. In a negligent omission, says Barnwell, the person is aware that he does not know all that he should know, but he is not aware of the details of what is unknown. Concerning the details, he has only what Barnwell calls virtual knowledge, that is, the person has access to the knowledge if he should work to attain it.[32] As we have seen, Thomas would agree with this condition, that is, with the need for access to the knowledge. If the person has no access to it—no way of knowing that his reading will prevent him from going to Mass—then he has invincible ignorance, and he is not responsible for the subsequent sin.[33]

---

32. Ibid., 223–45.

33. Barnwell's account includes a kind of shadowy semi-conscious knowledge of the obligation that must be fulfilled, for instance, the obligation to go to Mass (ibid., 139–55; Stegman similarly speaks of a "vague awareness" that an object is repulsive to reason, see Stegman, "Saint Thomas Aquinas and the Problem of Akrasia," 124). The person is aware of the obligation, says Barnwell, at the periphery of his consciousness. The person is aware that he must do something, but the details of what he must do are not clearly in his mind.

Thomas has no need for this "indistinct intellection," as Barnwell calls it. The person need have no awareness at all that he has an obligation. (He need not be aware, at the moment of choosing to act, that he has an obligation to go to Mass, but he must be aware that he has an obligation to investigate his action further, which investigation would reveal to

Ultimately, then, in his criticism of Aquinas, Barnwell has misidentified what (for Aquinas) the negligent person foresees. He has mistakenly supposed that the negligent person foresees his omission; in fact, he foresees only his ignorance. The content of his ignorance remains unknown to him. He can choose to read, willfully excluding a consideration of the various features of this act of reading, and thereby be ignorant that the reading prevents him from fulfilling his obligation. He is aware, however, that he may well be ignorant of some important (unknown) feature of his act of reading.

---

him the obligation to go to Mass.) He might have *habitual* knowledge of such an obligation, but at the moment of the omission he needs no actual knowledge, however indistinct. Indeed, he might at the moment be asleep. As we have seen, responsibility for the effects of our actions arises from the cause of the effects. If that cause is in some way defective, then responsibility may follow. The cause might be an evil action, or it might be a good action combined with negligence. In either event, the person is responsible for the subsequent harm or omission that follows.

∿ CHAPTER 12

THE FIRST CAUSE OF MORAL EVIL

The cause of moral evil, or at least of certain principal moral evils, is rather mysterious.[1] Thomas notes that some sins can be caused by previous sins. We have seen, for instance, that certain omissions are caused by previous evil deeds. We have also seen that sins of malice presuppose prior sins through which an evil habit has developed in the will. And we

1. Parts of this chapter originally appeared in Jensen, "Aquinas's Original Discovery: A Reply to Barnwell," *American Catholic Philosophical Quarterly* 92 (forthcoming). The extensive discussion on this question includes the following material: Reichberg, "Beyond Privation"; Lawrence Dewan, "St. Thomas and the First Cause of Moral Evil," in *Wisdom, Law, and Virtue: Essays in Thomistic Ethics* (Bronx, N.Y.: Fordham University Press, 2007), 186–96; Steel, "Does Evil Have a Cause?"; W. Matthews Grant, "Aquinas on How God Causes the Act of Sin Without Causing Sin Itself," *The Thomist* 73 (2009): 455–96; Michael D. Torre, "The Sin of Man and the Love of God," in *Jacques Maritain: The Man and His Metaphysics*, ed. John F. X. Knasas (Notre Dame: University of Notre Dame Press, 1988), 203–11; John F. Wippel, "Metaphysical Themes in *De malo*, I," in *Aquinas's Disputed Questions on Evil: A Critical Guide*, ed. M. V. Dougherty (Cambridge: Cambridge University Press, 2016), 25–30; Jacques Maritain, *St. Thomas and the Problem of Evil*, trans. Lewis Galantiere and Gerald B. Phelan (Milwaukee: Marquette University Press, 1942), 20–37; Jacques Maritain, *Existence and the Existent*, trans. Lewis Galantiere and Gerald B. Phelan (New York: Pantheon, 1948), 90–92; Jacques Maritain, *God and the Permission of Evil*, trans. Joseph W. Evans (Milwaukee: The Bruce Publishing Company, 1966), 21–25, 34–38, 44–54; Barnwell, "Problem with Aquinas's Original Discovery."

have seen that ignorance can be caused by sin, which ignorance in turn causes further sin. In many cases, then, the evil of sin finds its cause in some prior sin. Not every sin, however, can be explained in this manner. If we are to avoid an infinite regress, then there must be at least one sin, and perhaps more, that is not caused by some prior sin.

THE PROBLEM OF THE CAUSAL DEFECT

The causal origin of such proto-sins—sins not caused by some prior sin—is problematic. Thomas lays out the difficulty as follows:

> Weakness and ignorance excuse from sin, or at least diminish it. It follows that moral evil is found first and principally in the will alone, which is reasonable since an action is called moral insofar as it is voluntary. Consequently, the root and origin of moral evil must be sought in the act of the will. But it seems that this inquiry faces a difficulty. Since a defective act arises from some defect of the active principle, a defect in the will must precede moral evil. But if this defect were natural, then it would always be found in the will, and when acting, the will would always sin, which is evidently false in light of virtuous acts. On the other hand, if this defect were voluntary, then it would seem to be moral evil, for which we must once again seek the cause, which would then go on to infinity. Consequently, the defect pre-existing in the will cannot be natural, or it would follow that the will would sin in every act; nor can the defect be accidental or by chance, or there would be no moral evil, since what is by chance is without forethought or reason. Therefore, the defect must be voluntary; but it cannot be a moral evil, lest we proceed into infinity.[2]

---

2. Aquinas, *Summa contra Gentiles* III, chap. 10, no. 13–14 (Editio Leonina, XIV: 26, ll. b26–51): "Infirmitas et ignorantia excusant peccatum vel minuunt. Relinquitur igitur quod morale vitium in solo actu voluntatis primo et principaliter inveniatur: et rationabiliter etiam ex hoc actus moralis dicatur, quia voluntarius est. In actu igitur voluntatis quaerenda est radix et origo peccati moralis. Videtur autem hanc inquisitionem consequi difficultas. Cum enim actus deficiens proveniat propter defectum activi principii, oportet praeintelligere defectum in voluntate ante peccatum morale. Qui quidem defectus si sit naturalis, semper inhaeret voluntati: semper igitur voluntas in agendo moraliter peccabit; quod actus virtutum falsum esse ostendunt. Si autem defectus sit voluntarius, iam est peccatum morale, cuius causa iterum inquirenda restabit: et sic ratio in infinitum deducet. Oportet ergo dicere quod defectus in voluntate praeexistens non sit naturalis, ne sequatur voluntatem in quolibet actu peccare; neque etiam casualis et fortuitus, non enim esset in nobis morale

The cause of proto-sins, it turns out, must be a defect of the will. Furthermore, that defect must meet two seemingly conflicting conditions: first, it must be voluntary (not natural); second, it must not be a sin.

Aquinas's solution to this difficulty begins by observing that the will is good insofar as it follows the moral rule as presented to it by reason; it is evil insofar as it diverts from this moral rule. Thomas then identifies the voluntary defect that serves as the cause of moral evil; it is a failure to consider the moral rule. When choosing adultery, for instance, the sinner may not be thinking, "Adultery should be avoided." Does this defect meet the two conditions laid down by Aquinas? Thomas explains,

> There is no need to seek some cause of the failure to consider the rule, for the very liberty of the will suffices for this, by which liberty the will is able to act or not to act. Furthermore, this very failure to consider the rule in act is not evil considered in itself, neither sin nor punishment, because the mind is not obliged, nor is it even able, to consider this rule in act at all times. This failure begins to take on the character of sin when the person proceeds to choose without actually considering the rule. Likewise, a carpenter does not sin by the mere fact that he does not always have his straight edge. Rather, he sins when he does not have the straight edge and he proceeds to make a cut. So it is that the sin of the will is not found in its failure to consider the rule of reason or of the divine law; rather, it is found in not having the rule or measure and *also* proceeding to choose.[3]

The defect is voluntary, says Thomas, because the person can choose to take up the rule. The defect need not be positively voluntary, that is, the person need not make a choice "not to consider." It suffices if he hap-

---

peccatum, casualia enim sunt impraemeditata et extra rationem. Est igitur voluntarius. Non tamen peccatum morale: ne cogamur in infinitum procedere."

3. Aquinas, *De malo*, q. 1, a. 3 (Editio Leonina, XXIII: 16, ll. 268–85): "Huius autem quod est non uti regula predicta non oportet aliquam causam querere, quia ad hoc sufficit ipsa libertas uoluntatis, per quam potest agere uel non agere. Et hoc ipsum quod est non attendere actu ad talem regulam in se consideratum non est malum, nec culpa nec pena, quia anima non tenetur nec potest attendere ad huiusmodi regulam semper in actu; set ex hoc accipit primo rationem culpe quod sine actuali consideratione regule procedit ad huiusmodi electionem, sicut artifex non peccat in eo quod non semper tenet mensuram, set ex hoc quod non tenens mensuram procedit ad incidendum. Et similiter culpa uoluntatis non est in hoc quod non actu attendit ad regulam rationis uel legis diuine, set ex hoc quod non habens regulam uel mensuram huiusmodi procedit ad eligendum."

pens not to be considering the rule but he has the power to consider it.[4] The will may not have brought about the failure, but it can remove the failure. For sins of passion, for example, Thomas thinks that the passions can direct the attention of reason away from the moral evil of an action. When a person is tempted to commit adultery, his passions may direct his attention to the pleasure of his action and exclude from his mind its evil. This focus of his attention was not chosen, since it arose from his passions; nevertheless, Thomas says that it is voluntary.[5] Why? Because the person can still choose to direct his attention upon the moral character of the action.

The absence of the moral rule also meets the other condition laid down by Aquinas, that is, the absence itself is not a sin. We are not always obliged, says Thomas, to keep the rule of behavior in mind. A person, for instance, need not always be thinking that he should avoid adultery. Indeed, he cannot possibly keep this in mind at all times. He must be thinking upon many other things throughout the day. There is no sin, then, in failing to consider the rule. The sin arises, says Thomas, only when the person chooses without the rule, because at that point he is obliged to think upon the rule.

Michael Barnwell and others are dissatisfied with Aquinas's solution.[6] According to Barnwell, Aquinas does identify a voluntary deficiency of the will that is not a sin. Unfortunately, thinks Barnwell, this deficiency cannot possibly serve as the cause of sin; without the rule at hand, the will can hardly be held responsible for what follows. In short, claims Barnwell, Aquinas's solution leaves the will acting out of ignorance, and the person cannot be held responsible for what he does out of ignorance. A more detailed understanding, both of the problem and its solution, is necessary before we proceed to Barnwell's objections.

---

4. Maritain may portray the lack of consideration as positively voluntary; see Maritain, *God and the Permission of Evil*, 45. See also Maritain, *St. Thomas and the Problem of Evil*, 32–33. Stegman asserts a positive move to inattention ("Saint Thomas Aquinas and the Problem of Akrasia," 124).

5. See Aquinas, *De malo*, q. 3, a. 10; Aquinas, *Summa theologiae* I-II, q. 77, a. 7; II-II, q. 156, a. 1, ad 3; II-II, q. 156, a. 2, ad 2.

6. See Barnwell, "Problem with Aquinas's Original Discovery"; Steel, "Does Evil Have a Cause?" Steel thinks that sin ultimately has no explanation.

THE CAUSE OF EVIL IN GENERAL

Aquinas's solution to the difficulty—and indeed, the difficulty itself—is rooted in a broader account of the causes of evil, whether moral or otherwise. Evil can have no per se cause; rather, evil is caused per accidens by what is good.[7] As we have seen, a per se cause intends—or tends into—its effect. In contrast, a per accidens cause tends directly to one effect, which thereby brings about the per accidens effect. Fire per se causes heat; per accidens it causes wax to melt, that is, it first causes heat in the wax and thereby the wax melts.[8]

Evil can have no per se cause, because a per se cause acts from some perfection and then moves out to a like perfection. What a thing has, and what it then gives to another, is always some completion or perfection. A hot item, for instance, heats; by way of the heat it possesses, it moves out to give heat to others. Thomas has previously established, however, that evil is the lack of some perfection, as blindness is the lack of the ability to see.[9] In no way, then, can an agent move out to evil. It always moves out from what it has—which is a perfection—to something similar, which must also be a perfection. What exists can move out to another existence, even as a cat can beget kittens. The lack of existence, however, can have no power to move out to others.

Human beings, of course, can intend evil, but they never intend it precisely as evil. Someone can intend the act of adultery, which is in fact evil, but he intends it, says Thomas, insofar as it is pleasurable, or some such thing. A murderer intends the evil of his victim's death, but he seeks it insofar as it provides vengeance, or insofar as it is useful to gain the inheritance, or some such thing; he does not desire it precisely insofar as it is the evil of his victim.[10]

---

7. Aquinas, *De malo*, q. 1, a. 3; *Summa contra Gentiles* III, chap. 7; chap. 10; *Summa theologiae* I, q. 49, a. 1.

8. One question later in the *De malo*, when discussing the causes of omissions, Thomas uses a slightly modified meaning of per se and per accidens; this modified meaning, as we have seen, is anomalous.

9. Aquinas, *De malo*, q. 1, a. 1; Aquinas, *Summa contra Gentiles* III, chap. 7; see Wippel, "Metaphysical Themes," 16–19.

10. Possibly, in hatred for another person, the hater might indeed desire the evil of his

Evil, then, has no per se cause. Nevertheless, evil must have some cause, for evil steps outside the order of nature.[11] We are forced to conclude, says Thomas, that the good itself causes evil per accidens. Why? Because every agent causes from its own actuality, that is, from its goodness. Whatever causes evil, then, must be doing so by way of the good. Aquinas suggests two ways in which the good might cause evil.

First, the good in the agent might itself be deficient.[12] Thomas gives the example of a birth defect, which is caused on account of some deficiency in the semen. Today we might express the idea by saying that the sperm has a genetic defect and this genetic defect causes the birth defect in the offspring. The sperm is the cause of the offspring, but it is a defective cause. What it causes, it causes by way of its good, but its good is itself lacking, so that the good it effects is also lacking.

A simpler example might be a student who produces a defective paper; he does so by his own defect in knowledge. He produces any paper at all only insofar as he has some good by which he can write down ideas. He has some knowledge of language, and he has some knowledge of the subject matter. Because his knowledge is itself defective, however, the resulting good (the paper) is also defective. The "evil" of the paper is caused by the deficient good found in the student. What is good in the paper is caused by the good in the student; what is lacking in the paper results from an insufficient good in the student's causality.

This first manner of causing evil presupposes that there already is some evil. The semen is defective, and the student's knowledge is deficient. The evil in these agents, then, must itself have a cause. That cause might once again be some deficient agent (for example, the defect in the semen came from a parent with a defect), but then the evil in this prior defective agent must also have a cause. The series cannot continue indefinitely, so there must be some other, more original, cause of evil.[13]

Good can cause evil not only because of some deficiency; it can also

---

enemy precisely as it is his enemy's evil. Still, he perceives his enemy's evil as a certain good, namely, as his own (the hater's) good. See Langan, "Sins of Malice," 196–97; McCluskey, *Thomas Aquinas on Moral Wrongdoing*, 141–43.

11. Aquinas, *De malo*, q. 1, a. 3; Aquinas, *Summa theologiae* I, q. 49, a. 1.
12. Aquinas, *De malo*, q. 1, a. 3; Aquinas, *Summa contra Gentiles* III, chap. 10.
13. Aquinas, *De malo*, q. 1, a. 3.

cause evil from the fullness of its goodness.[14] It can do so, however, only per accidens. By causing one good, it can incidentally cause an evil. Just as the fire per se causes the wax to be hot and by way of the effect of heat causes the wax to be soft, so by causing a good, an agent can incidentally cause some evil. Aquinas has in mind the production of one good that excludes another good. Ultraviolet rays, for instance, might cause a chemical change in the DNA of the sperm. Just insofar as it is a chemical change, this effect is a certain limited good. The change in the DNA, however, excludes the proper and fit ordering of chemicals in the DNA. The lack of this proper ordering, then, is an evil for the animal. Other examples are not difficult to find. Fire heats somebody's finger, and the effect of heat is a certain good. Too much heat, however, causes damage to the finger, which is evil. A tiger makes a deer into food, which is a good thing, but it eliminates the life of the deer, which is evil for the deer.

THE DEFICIENT CAUSE OF MORAL EVIL

When it comes to moral evil, Thomas thinks that both of these causes are present.[15] The per accidens cause, he thinks, is rather evident, for the sinner always intends some good in his sin, as the adulterer intends pleasure. By aiming at some limited good, the person excludes the good of the whole person found in the order to the chief good. Thomas thinks that this per accidens causality, however, is inadequate by itself to account for moral evil; there must also be some deficient agent. Why is this other kind of causality necessary?

His reason is far from clear, but it can be surmised from what we know of sins of ignorance. Full knowledge would prevent the sin, but ignorance removes this obstacle, thereby allowing the sin to follow. Consider the example of adultery. The person knows that the action is pleasurable, and he knows that pleasure belongs to his overall good; consequently, he desires the action. We suppose, however, that he does not have an evil will, since we are dealing with a proto-sin. As such, he will not desire the action if he knows that it is opposed to the true good. His knowledge that the action is adulterous, then, prevents him from choosing it. Although he desires it

---

14. Ibid., q. 1, a. 3; Aquinas, *Summa theologiae* I, q. 49, a. 1.
15. Aquinas, *De malo*, q. 1, a. 3.

insofar as it is pleasurable, he ultimately rejects it insofar as it is opposed to his ultimate good. The sin is possible, then, only if there is some deficiency in knowledge. He must be unaware that the action is adulterous, or if he is aware that it is adulterous, he must be unaware that adultery is opposed to his overall good.

The limited human intellect allows for the possibility of error, because it can fail to consider what needs to be considered:

> The created intellect, because it does not know everything at once, is able to fail insofar as it judges a thing as fitting according to one condition, which it does consider, but the thing is not fitting according to some other condition, which the intellect does not consider. A doctor, for instance, might judge some treatment to be expedient for a sick person because of one ailment, but the treatment is not simply speaking most expedient because of some other ailment, which the doctor does not know about or does not consider.[16]

Thomas is suggesting two causes for sin, one positive and one negative. The positive cause is the desire for some good, such as pleasure. Without this desire, there would be no sin. The negative cause is the failure to consider that the action is opposed to the overall good. Without this defect, there would be no sin. The two causes must combine in order for there to be a choice for what is evil.

For clarity in addressing future issues, we will divide the positive cause into two, giving a total of three elements in the cause of sin. First, there is a desire for the overall good, which is found in the very nature of the will. Second, there is knowledge that this particular good (such as pleasure) belongs in some respect to the overall good (which then leads to a desire for the particular good and the action that realizes it). Third, there is ignorance (or failure to consider) that the action in some manner is opposed to the overall good. A proto-sin is possible only when all three of these conditions are met.

---

16. Aquinas, *In Sent.* II, d. 5, q. 1, a. 1, ad 4 (Mandonnet v. 2, 145): "Intellectus creatus, quia non est omnium simul, potest deficere, ex hoc quod judicat de re quod sit conveniens secundum aliquam conditionem rei consideratam, quod non est conveniens secundum alia quae non considerat: sicut medicus judicans aliquid esse expediens uni aegroto secundum unam infirmitatem ejus consideratam, quod non est sibi simpliciter expediens propter aliam aegritudinem, quam vel non cognoscit, vel non considerat."

Thomas is not much concerned about the first two elements, which he thinks unproblematic. Besides, he is concerned to explain the *evil* of moral evil, which is a privation, and as such is most properly caused by the deficiency in the agent. As we have seen, the deficiency poses the following problem: it must be voluntary (since it cannot be natural or by chance); at the same time it cannot be a sin.

We should note—before proceeding—that, with regard to the cause of sins, only proto-sins require this last condition. The other aspects of the causes of moral evil apply to all sin. For some sins (those that are not proto-sins), however, the voluntary defect is itself a moral evil, that is, the ignorance that causes the sin is itself a sin. On account of negligence, or even on account of an evil will, the person has placed himself in a state of ignorance concerning that which he should know.[17] The original negligence might well be a proto-sin, but the consequent ignorance might itself be a sin (although not a proto-sin), or it might cause other sins, which would not be proto-sins.

We have seen Aquinas's solution to the difficulty. The will is deficient in that it does not have its rule or standard at hand. This deficiency is itself not a sin because we are not required always to be thinking of the moral rule. Without fault we can think about mathematics, about a beautiful sunset, and so on, thereby failing to think about the morality of adultery (or whatever the sin might be). Furthermore, this deficiency is voluntary, at least as long as we are able to turn our thoughts to the moral rule. Perhaps the deficiency did not arise by some choice, but it remains voluntary as long as choice can remove the deficiency. Perhaps the person's passions excluded the rule from his mind. Nevertheless, he must be able to fend off the passions, calling the rule to mind. If he lacks this capacity, then he is not responsible for any subsequent "sin"; indeed, Aquinas classifies him as what we might call temporarily insane.[18] On the other hand, if he retains the ability to fend off the passions and to reconsider the matter in the light of the moral rule, then the absence of the moral rule is still voluntary.

---

17. Aquinas, *Summa theologiae* I-II, q. 6, a. 8; I-II, q. 76, a. 2; Aquinas, *De malo*, q. 3, a. 7.
18. Aquinas, *Summa theologiae* I-II, q. 10, a. 3; I-II, q. 77, a. 7.

CHOOSING WITHOUT THE RULE

Barnwell rightly rejects an interpretation of Aquinas that conflates failing to consider the rule with choosing without consideration of the rule.[19] Thomas draws a stark contrast between a consideration (or the failure to consider) and choice. The person first considers some good, such as pleasurable adultery, and then chooses the good. The initial consideration might lack certain elements, such as a consideration of how the good relates to the ultimate end, and in that sense the person can be said to fail to consider the rule. This failure, however, is distinct from the choice made with this failure.

The lack of consideration is like the carpenter being without his straight edge. Being without his straight edge, however, is not the same as making a cut without his straight edge. Similarly, a person might fail to consider the rule "adultery should be avoided" throughout much of the day, but this failure is not the same as choosing without the rule. The carpenter does no wrong by the mere fact that he lacks his straightedge; he does wrong only when he makes a cut without the straightedge. Similarly, the failure to consider the moral rule, by itself, is not evil. It becomes evil only when the person chooses without the rule.

The two differ as mere negation and evil. Negation is the lack of something, while evil is a particular kind of negation, namely, the absence of something that should be there. The difference might also be expressed as a difference in meaning of the word "privation," which has both a loose meaning and a strict meaning.[20] Privation in the loose sense refers to the lack of some completion. Privation in the strict sense, which is the same as evil, adds the notion that the completion is required for the perfection of the subject. Human beings lack the completion of wings, but this absence is not evil; it is a mere privation, for wings are not necessary for the perfection of human beings.

In what category does the lack of consideration of the moral rule belong? In itself, says Thomas, it is a mere negation; it is the lack of something that is not required.[21] The person is not required, at every moment

---

19. Barnwell, "Problem with Aquinas's Original Discovery," 287–90.

20. Aquinas, *Summa theologiae* I, q. 48, a. 3; *Summa contra Gentiles* III, chap. 6, no. 1.

21. Aquinas, *De malo*, q. 1, a. 3, ad 6 and ad 13; see Dewan, "St. Thomas and the First Cause of Moral Evil," 193; Torre, "Sin of Man," 206.

of the day, to be thinking about the relation of adultery to the ultimate end. At a particular time—namely, at the moment of choice—the lack of consideration changes; it moves from being a mere negation to being an evil.[22] Why? Because at this time the perfection—the consideration of the rule—becomes necessary. When making a choice, our perfection requires that we know in what manner the object relates to the ultimate end. Consequently, choosing without the rule (as opposed to the failure to consider the rule) belongs to the category of evil. It is the lack of some completion required for the perfection of the subject.

In short, the failure to consider the rule is itself not a moral evil, but it is a permitting cause of moral evil. In contrast, choosing without the rule is itself moral evil; it is part of the evil of the proto-sin. The failure to consider the rule is mere ignorance; choosing without the rule is negligence, which, Thomas says, is found in some manner in every sin.[23]

We might also say that the failure to consider the rule is simply the lack of active consideration, while choosing without consideration is error. Someone who fails to consider that four squared is sixteen is not in error, while someone who thinks that four squared is twenty is indeed in error. Likewise, someone who fails to think about the moral rule concerning adultery is not in error. He does not err even if he is actively thinking that sexual activity is good in itself, or even that "This activity is good in itself, just insofar as it is sexual activity." He actively thinks what is true, while he fails to actively consider another truth, namely, that "adultery is wrong," or that "this sexual activity is wrong, insofar as it is adultery." Such active consideration, combined with the failure to consider something else, is no more an error than it is an error to think that the square of five is twenty-five, while failing to think that the square of four is sixteen.[24] The person begins to err only when he chooses without considering the moral rule. He errs by supposing that this action is worth pursuing, even without the knowledge of how it relates to the chief good of the ultimate end.

Barnwell considers an interpretation of Aquinas according to which the failure to consider the rule is simply the failure to use it while choos-

---

22. See Maritain, *God and the Permission of Evil*, 48.
23. Aquinas, *Summa theologiae* II-II, q. 54, a. 1, ad 2.
24. See Caulfield, "Practical Ignorance," 83–87.

ing.²⁵ As Barnwell aptly shows, the collapse of the distinction between the failure to consider and choosing without consideration makes nonsense of the texts of Aquinas.²⁶

Nevertheless, this interpretation has something of the truth. At the moment when choice is possible, the person does not have the rule, just as the carpenter does not have his straight edge. At this very moment, the presence of the rule is not required in one respect, and it is required in another. It is not required if the person does not choose the action; it is required if the person does choose the action. We might say that the rule is conditionally necessary, that is, it is necessary on the condition that the person chooses the action. The voluntary defect is not a sin insofar as the person need not choose to act, in which case the knowledge of the rule was not necessary. The voluntary defect becomes a sin (as an act of negligence that is a part of every sin) if the person chooses to act, for then the knowledge of the rule becomes necessary. The sinful choice is possible only because the rule is absent; the absence of the rule becomes necessary only because the choice is made.

Since we have adequately portrayed the view of Aquinas, we will now turn to objections raised by Barnwell, which may be summarized by four themes, discussed in the next four sections.²⁷ First, since the failure to consider is a kind of ignorance, and since ignorance takes away moral responsibility, the failure to consider does not result (according to Barnwell) in a sin for which the agent is morally responsible. Second, Aquinas's teaching that we must consider the rule whenever making a choice is overly burdensome. Third, it seems to Barnwell that the failure to consider does not explain the sinfulness of the action; rather, the sinfulness is explained through the requirement to consider the rule whenever making a

---

25. The interpretation is suggested by Grant, "Aquinas on How God Causes the Act of Sin," 469, 473–77. Grant himself does not necessarily endorse this interpretation. He also provides an interpretation in line with that presented in this chapter.

26. Barnwell, "Problem with Aquinas's Original Discovery," 287–90. Aquinas's use of "uti" in the *De malo* leads to confusion on this matter. As Barnwell points out, however, the context makes clear that he is referring to a failure to consider the rule, not a failure to use the rule while acting.

27. I speak of "themes" rather than arguments, because it is sometimes difficult to identify distinct arguments within Barnwell's criticism.

choice. Fourth, Barnwell thinks that Aquinas's view (as expressed in the interpretation he calls "U_IP₁") demands a temporal priority between the failure to consider and the sinful choice, but this priority, argues Barnwell, obviates any causality that might arise from the failure to consider. Finally, we will consider a fifth objection that Barnwell might well raise, given the replies to his initial objections.

MORAL RESPONSIBILITY FOR SINS

In a first theme, Barnwell argues that the lack of consideration removes moral responsibility for any consequent "sin." Why? Because if a person chooses in ignorance of the moral rule, then he is not responsible for his sinful action. The person who chooses adultery while being unaware that his action conflicts with the moral law, for instance, cannot be held responsible for breaking the moral law. And if he is not responsible, then the action he performs is not truly a sin. Aquinas's account—according to Barnwell—might explain why somebody can choose adultery, but it cannot explain why that choice is a sinful choice.

Barnwell considers the obvious solution to this difficulty: even in sins of ignorance, the person must be aware of something; he must be aware, for instance, that he is acting without the moral rule. Or, to put the matter in more concrete terms, he must be aware that he has not determined the relation of this action to the ultimate end. He is considering a sexual act, for instance, which he knows to be good in some respect, but he does not know whether some feature of the action might be opposed to the ultimate end. He is aware, however, of this very ignorance. He is aware that if he chooses to act now, then he chooses to act without knowing whether his act can be ordered to the ultimate end. He recognizes, then, that he should consider the rule, in order to determine the order of his action.[28]

Barnwell thinks this solution is inadequate because an awareness that "I should consider the rule" entails that "the agent is somehow aware of the content of the rule."[29] Such an awareness (of the content of the rule),

---

28. In *Summa theologiae* I-II, q. 76, a. 3, Thomas says that the person is responsible for his ignorance if he fails to seek the knowledge that might have restrained him from sinning. Clearly, if Aquinas thinks that the person can seek the knowledge, then the person must be aware that he currently lacks the knowledge. See also ibid., I-II, q. 6, a. 8; Aquinas, *De malo*, q. 3, a. 8.

29. Barnwell, "Problem with Aquinas's Original Discovery," 8n2.

however, is precisely what the voluntary defect excludes. The person, concludes Barnwell, cannot be ignorant of the rule and also aware of his need to consider the rule.

The weak link in Barnwell's reasoning is the supposed entailment. If the agent is aware that he should consider some rule, it follows, thinks Barnwell, that the person must be aware of the content of the rule. Why Barnwell thinks this entailment necessary is unclear. Someone can be aware that he does not know the square root of 169 without thereby being aware of the content of the square root of 169. His awareness concerns his own inadequacy; it is not an awareness about the object in question (the square root of 169), but an awareness concerning himself. If he is taking a math test that requires the square root of 169, then he can be aware not only that he does not know the square root of 169; he can also be aware that he should discover the square root of 169. None of this implies that he already knows what the square root is.

Similarly, an agent might well be unaware of the order an action has in relation to the chief good. At the same time, he can be aware of this failure in his own awareness. Indeed, he can be aware that he should determine what this order is. This latter awareness does not imply that he already knows what the order is. Perhaps the action is ordered to the ultimate end; perhaps not. He is aware of both possibilities, and he is aware that he does not know which it is. Furthermore, he is aware that he should try to find out.

Consider a simple everyday example. Anna is asked to go out to dinner on Friday night with a friend. She does not know whether she has any prior engagements, and she must check her calendar to see whether or not she does. She is aware of her ignorance, and she is aware that she should consider the matter. Does it follow that she knows the answer ahead of time? Certainly not. If she goes ahead and makes the engagement without checking her calendar, and if it turns out that she had a prior engagement, then it seems plausible that she should be held responsible for making these conflicting engagements. She is responsible not because she knew ahead of time that there was a conflict; rather, she is responsible because she was aware that she did not know.

Barnwell may be suggesting that Anna's ignorance is itself culpable, because she is responsible to check her calendar. As noted above, however, she would be responsible to check her calendar only when she actually chooses, which is when her ignorance becomes sinful, as part of her sinful choice. The deficient cause of moral evil is not this ignorance that is part of the sinful choice; it is the ignorance that anticipates the sinful choice and allows it. It is the ignorance that still might be removed, before making the choice. Anna is aware that she should remove this ignorance, *if she goes ahead and makes a choice*. Just as such, however, she has no obligation to remove this ignorance. Only if she chooses must she remove the ignorance. The ignorance allows the choice, but apart from the choice, it itself is not blameworthy.

BURDENSOME DELIBERATION

Barnwell's first attempt to dismiss the obvious solution, then, is unpersuasive, but he has further reasons. Why, asks Barnwell, does the agent know that he should consider the matter? Barnwell considers two possibilities. First, perhaps the sinfulness of the action is already recognizable. Barnwell rightly dismisses this option, since it is just the possibility, considered above, that the person already knows that of which he is ignorant.[30] The second possibility is more plausible: while the agent does not know whether the action is sinful, he does know that for each and every action he performs, he must consider the rule.

For two reasons, thinks Barnwell, this second possibility must be rejected as well.[31] First, the requirement to consider the rule for every single action is simply too burdensome a requirement. Second, and more important in Barnwell's mind, this requirement to consider the rule makes Aquinas's explanation of the cause of sin otiose or meaningless. Barnwell quickly runs past the first difficulty—not developing it in any manner—in order to get to the more important second difficulty. We will follow his lead, providing a brief response to this first objection before we proceed to a more detailed response to the second objection.

It is overly burdensome, thinks Barnwell, to require a person to consult the moral rule for every action he performs, from the largest to the smallest. With this requirement, it seems, we could hardly make it

---

30. Ibid., 285–86.
31. Ibid., 286.

through the day. For each little choice we would have to consult the moral rule.

Thomas, no doubt, does think this requirement applies to all our actions. Ultimately, it is nothing other than the requirement to order our actions to the true chief good. We order our actions to an end, however, only through some awareness of the link between the action and the end. To have the rule is to be aware of this order; to lack the rule is to be unaware of the order of an action to the ultimate end.

Is this requirement overly burdensome? It certainly would be, if for every action, a person had to begin from scratch. To examine each action we perform in order to determine its relation to the ultimate end would be so time consuming that we could get little done in a day. Fortunately, there is no need to begin from scratch. Past reasoning is ready at hand for most of our day-to-day activities.

Consider the act of eating breakfast.[32] If Cordelia has a fairly standard breakfast each day, then she need not reflect on its order to the ultimate end. She has already determined in the past that this action is ordered to the ultimate end and that it provides no obstacle to other ways in which she must order herself to the end. Some days she may have to adjust her behavior. If she has surgery, perhaps she will have to avoid breakfast, for her standard breakfast now poses an obstacle to the manner in which she should be ordering herself to the end. Even these adjustments to unusual circumstances do not pose any great difficulty. Past experience has taught Cordelia what aspects of her day might change matters or what aspects of various actions might prove to be important. She readily recognizes when she needs to make further considerations that do not fit within her past habitual considerations.

The patterns of life, then, remove much of the burden of investigating the relation of our actions to the ultimate end. It becomes second nature to look for certain key features. If the choice concerns an act of sexual intercourse, for instance, then the agent must determine that it is within marriage. If it is indeed within marriage then further considerations must yet be made, but these further considerations (of time, frequency, the state of the spouse, and so on) can also become quite patterned.

32. The example is taken from Butera, "On Reason's Control of the Passions."

Like his first attempt, then, Barnwell's second attempt to dismiss the obvious solution to the problem of moral responsibility is unconvincing. His third attempt, however, has more substance and will require a more detailed response.

A MEANINGLESS EXPLANATION?

According to Barnwell, the requirement to consider the rule for every action makes Aquinas's explanation of the cause of moral evil meaningless. Why? Because, says Barnwell, then the only relevant fact—the only cause of the sin—is the requirement to consider the rule.[33] Why does Thomas bother talking about a voluntary failure to consider the rule? What makes the action a sin is the requirement to consider the rule for every action.

Barnwell has aptly uncovered the need for a further explanation of proto-sins, for a sin requires two kinds of explanation. First, the movement of the will to the action must be explained; second, the responsibility of the agent must be explained. Thomas is concerned with the former explanation; Barnwell with the latter.

The example of Anna reveals the need for both explanations. If we presume that Anna wants to keep all her appointments, then it follows that she will never make conflicting appointments. Yet she does. She makes an appointment on Friday night without checking her calendar, which would have informed her of a prior engagement. What explains this failure on Anna's part? Two elements are needed for an explanation. First, she must desire the proposed engagement on Friday night; second, she must be ignorant of any prior engagement. These two elements correspond to the positive and negative causes of sin discussed above.

While these two causes explain how Anna can make the conflicting appointments, they do not explain in what manner she might be responsible for making the conflicting appointments. This responsibility implies another cause, namely, it implies that she knew she should have checked her calendar. This last cause corresponds to the requirement to consider the rule.

Barnwell thinks that the requirement to consider the rule for every

---

33. Barnwell, "Problem with Aquinas's Original Discovery," 286.

action makes the lack of the rule (that is, the ignorance) otiose. But if we are looking for the causes of Anna's behavior in making conflicting appointments, it is surely insufficient to say that she knew that she should always check her calendar. That alone hardly explains her behavior. If we know that she never wants to make conflicting appointments, then we recognize that another cause is necessary; we recognize that she must have been unaware of the conflict. A full explanation of her behavior requires this additional cause, that is, it requires the ignorance.

The analogy of Anna can be transposed to Aquinas's view of the will simply by changing the overriding desire. Anna desires to make each of her appointments, so that she never desires two conflicting appointments. For the will of the person committing a sin—at least a proto-sin—the overriding desire of the person is for his true chief good; he will never choose anything that excludes his chief good. Yet he does. He chooses to commit adultery. How can this choice be explained? First, the person must be ignorant that adultery is inconsistent with his chief good; were he aware, then he would never choose adultery. Nevertheless, this ignorance alone does not explain why the person is responsible for choosing adultery. His responsibility depends upon something that he knows; it depends upon his awareness that he should consider the rule for every action.

The full explanation of sin, then, requires five elements, all discussed above: (1) The person must have a desire for the overall good; (2) the person must be aware that this action is ordered, at least by itself, to this desired good; (3) the person must be ignorant that the action is opposed to his chief good; (4) the person must be aware that he is ignorant of the order of his action in relation to the chief good; (5) the person must be aware that he should discover the order of his action in relation to the chief good. The first three elements explain how the person can choose to act; the last two elements explain how the person is responsible for acting.

Barnwell thinks the fifth condition of the explanation—the awareness that the rule must be considered—makes the third condition irrelevant. Surely, it does not. The fifth condition explains why the person is responsible for the choice to commit adultery, but it cannot explain—apart from the ignorance—how the person ever makes the choice in the first place.

Barnwell is correct to note that, by itself, the failure to consider the rule does not explain why the person is responsible for the sinful action. This observation, however, does not warrant dismissing Aquinas's explanation as meaningless. Barnwell is also correct to note that this other difficulty—the responsibility for the sinful action—is explained by the awareness that the person should consider the rule. Aquinas's original discovery is meant to explain the possibility of the sinful action. Of course, his discovery does not exclude responsibility. It sets the stage for responsibility, because the ignorance (which allows the possibility of the sinful action) is voluntary precisely insofar as it can be removed. Aquinas's lack of consideration is no mere Socratic ignorance prior to sin. It is ignorance that the agent can choose to remove. Further, he is obliged to remove it, *if he moves forward with choice*. Otherwise, he is not obliged to remove it, which explains why the ignorance is itself not a sin.

In a proto-sin, then, the person acts partly in ignorance and partly in knowledge. He is aware that the action he considers is directed to some good that—considered in itself—is ordered to his overall good, but he is ignorant as to whether the action has additional features by which it might conflict with his chief good. Furthermore, he is aware of two additional things. First, he is aware of his own ignorance, that is, he is aware that he does not know the concrete order of the action (just as Anna is aware that she does not know whether she has a prior engagement on Friday). Second, he is aware that he should try to determine the order of his action (just as Anna is aware that she should check her calendar to determine whether she has a prior engagement). The combination of ignorance and awareness explains both how the choice is possible and how the person is responsible for making the choice.

TEMPORAL PRIORITY

Part of Barnwell's criticism of Aquinas relies upon the notion that the deficient cause of moral evil precedes the actual sin. On Barnwell's reading, the defect in the will, that is, the voluntary failure to consider the rule, occurs at some time prior to the actual sin, perhaps only milliseconds before the actual sin.[34] As Barnwell puts it, the failure to consider occurs at time T_1, while the actual sin occurs at a later moment, time T_2. Barn-

---

34. Ibid., 282.

well does not explain why he thinks Aquinas must maintain this temporal delay, but it seems that many commentators agree with Barnwell on this point.[35]

For the act of choice, it seems plausible that two moments are necessary. First, the will must be presented with some choice-worthy option; second, the will must choose or reject this option. If the person is to choose adultery, for instance, he must first be presented with the act of adultery as in some manner good; second, he must choose this action, or possibly reject it.

As we have seen, however, the choice for adultery is possible only if the presentation involves a lack of consideration of the moral rule, at least for cases of proto-sins in which the agent's desires have not been corrupted by past sins. If the presentation includes the judgment that the action is inconsistent with the chief good, which the person desires, then the person will be unable to choose it.

What difficulty does Barnwell find in this temporal priority? His point is far from clear. At one point, he seems to misunderstand Aquinas, claiming that, "The agent is bound to consider the rule prohibiting adultery when he or she is about to engage in it at T_2."[36] It sounds as if the agent is bound to consider the rule immediately prior to the choice (when he is "about to engage in it"). As we have seen, however, the agent is bound to consider the rule only when actually making the choice. If he were bound to consider the rule in his deliberations leading up to the choice, then the failure to consider the rule at this prior time would be a moral evil rather than simply the absence of some rule.

Setting aside this misunderstanding, Barnwell may still have some argument concerning the temporal priority. The best case that I can make

35. Barnwell, who first brings up the temporal requirement on ibid., page 282, seems to be relying upon Grant, who also provides little justification for the temporal priority ("Aquinas on How God Causes the Act of Sin," 471–72). Others who assert the temporal delay include the following: Reichberg, "Beyond Privation," 768; Torre, "Sin of Man," 208; Maritain, *God and the Permission of Evil*, 51–54; Wippel leaves the question open but favors a temporal priority ("Metaphysical Themes," 28). On the other hand, earlier in his career Maritain seems to have inclined toward an interpretation of temporal simultaneity; see Maritain, *St. Thomas and the Problem of Evil*, 29–33; see also Gallagher, who emphasizes the simultaneity of the acts of the intellect and will ("Free Choice," 276).

36. Barnwell, "Problem with Aquinas's Original Discovery," 286.

of his statements is as follows. Barnwell claims that the temporally prior failure to consider the rule at T_1 is irrelevant if the agent is required to consider the rule at T_2.[37] At T_1 the lack of consideration is not a moral evil, because the agent is not required, at that time, to consider the rule. At T_2, when he makes the choice, he is now required to consider the rule. What matters, thinks Barnwell, is the failure to consider the rule at T_2, because only this failure has led to the sin. The earlier failure did not cause the sin, as is evident if we suppose that at T_2 the agent begins to consider the rule; then the agent would not sin. At best, thinks Barnwell, the failure at T_1 might be a possible cause of the failure at T_2, which is itself the cause of the sin.[38] Even then, it is only one possible cause, so it is not necessary for the explanation of sin.

Barnwell's criticism, it seems, misses the mark. As we have seen, there are two moments (*perhaps* separate in time) required for a sinful choice. First, the good must be presented (at T_1), and it must be presented without the rule. Second, the person must choose the sinful action (at T_2). If the rule were present at the first moment, then the evil choice would not be an option at the second.

Barnwell fails to notice that at T_2 the agent can choose either of two options (or, one might say that he has the options at T_1 but he executes them at T_2). First, he can choose the sinful action. Second, he can choose to reconsider the matter, thereby seeking to discover the moral rule, that is, seeking to determine in what manner the action is ordered to the ultimate end. As Thomas says, "It is within the power of the will that reason should consider a matter actually or that it should cease from consideration, that it should consider this matter or that it should consider that matter."[39] The failure to consider the rule at T_1 is voluntary only if the agent has this second option (of seeking the rule). It is voluntary negatively, not because the agent chooses to set aside the rule, but because the agent can choose to pick it up. At T_2, then, the agent must have the option of looking for the rule. The rule cannot mysteriously appear at T_2,

---

37. Ibid.
38. Ibid., 286–87.
39. Aquinas, *Summa contra Gentiles* III, chap. 10, no. 17 (Editio Leonina, XIV: 27, ll. b16–18): "Itemque est in potestate ipsius quod ratio actu consideret, vel a consideratione desistat; aut quod hoc vel illud consideret."

as Barnwell seems to portray the matter; rather, the rule might appear at some later time (T_3), *if* the agent chooses to look for it. If not, he chooses to act without his rule.[40]

If at T_2 the agent is obliged to seek the rule, then (Barnwell seems to say) the ignorance must itself be sinful at that time (T_2). The obligation to seek the rule, however, is not unconditional. Rather, the agent is obliged to seek the rule, *if he moves forward with choice*. Precisely with this choice, the ignorance itself becomes sinful, as part of the sinful action. At T_2, then, the agent is not necessarily obliged to seek the rule. Only on the condition of choice does the obligation apply. The lack of consideration, then, remains voluntary and yet not necessarily sinful. It becomes sinful only with choice.

INCONSISTENT EXPLANATORY ELEMENTS?

We will consider one further objection that is not made by Barnwell, but he might well raise it, given the analysis we have provided. Perhaps Barnwell would object that the ignorance of the rule (condition 3) by itself might explain how the person makes the choice, but the ignorance combined with the awareness of the ignorance (condition 4) makes the choice once again inexplicable. By supposition, the person desires to choose only that which is ordered to his chief good, or is at least consistent with it. He is aware, however, that the action may not be consistent with his chief good. His desire to choose what is consistent with his chief good, then, should lead him to investigate the matter; it should lead him to seek to overcome his ignorance.

The person is faced with two options: (1) choose the proposed action on account of the good it promises, although it is unclear that the action

---

40. In footnote 22 ("Problem with Aquinas's Original Discovery," 284), Barnwell seems to think that it is perplexing how the agent who has not been thinking about the rule could begin thinking of it at the moment of choice. Barnwell imagines it would require something like a person shouting the rule out to him. Barnwell mistakenly supposes, however, that the agent suddenly begins to think of the rule. Rather, the agent chooses to look for the rule, just as Anna might choose to look for her calendar. At the moment of choice, the rule does not suddenly appear. Instead, the agent must choose between two options: acting without the rule and looking for the rule. If the agent begins to look for the rule, then he may indeed discover it. The absence of the rule, then, is indeed voluntary.

is ordered to the chief good; (2) choose to investigate whether the action is in fact ordered to the chief good. Since the person desires to choose only that which is consistent with his chief good, it is difficult to see how he will ever choose the first option. The person has two motivations. On the one hand, he is motivated to choose the action because it has an order to some good. On the other hand, he is motivated to consider the action further, because he recognizes that it might be opposed to his chief good. Given these conflicting motivations, can the person choose the sin? If he chooses to sin, then he must forgo the further consideration of the action. But it seems that he will not be willing to forgo this further consideration, for he knows that this action *might be* inconsistent with his chief good.

One possibility remains by which he might choose the action: he might decide that the good realized by the action (such as pleasure) is, in fact, his chief good. We have noted that people seek their overall good in diverse objects, some in pleasure, others in power, others in the divine good, and so on. Since we are dealing with a proto-sin, we have presumed that the person desires the true good. He is tempted by some partial good, such as pleasure, which by itself does not realize his overall good, although it can sometimes fit within his overall good. In order to determine whether it does fit within his overall good, he must consider the matter further.

The lack of the rule, however, opens another possibility. If the rule is present, then the person perceives the good as good in relation to other goods, especially in relation to the chief good. That is precisely what the rule is. It is a judgment of how this good can relate to the chief good. As long as the rule is present, then, the person desires the good (or does not desire it) as relating to the chief good. When the rule is absent, however, then the good can be desired in another way. It can be desired as independent, as not subjected to other goods and as possessed solely by the individual as an individual, rather than possessed as shared, rather than possessed by "us." If the person moves forward with choice, that is precisely how he will desire the good. The person knows, however, that he can desire the good in another way, and he knows that if he is to desire it in another way, then he must search for a rule.

If the person chooses, is he responsible for his choice? Previously, we suggested that the person is responsible because of his knowledge that he should consult the rule, which we labeled as condition 5. This condition has now been modified to become conditional. The person knows that he must search for a rule, *if* he is to desire the good as related to other goods. If he desires the good just as such, then he need not search for a rule. Since the person has these two possibilities open to him, then it seems that he is responsible for whichever option he chooses. If he chooses to go ahead without further consideration, then he is responsible for choosing the good as independent. The very rejection of further consideration is a rejection of the good as subordinate. The move forward, then, involves both elements of sin. The person turns away from the true good, and he turns toward some other good as if it were the chief good.

The turning away from the true good is not explicit. The person does not set before himself the true good and the false good and opt for the false. Rather, he has before himself only the false good. He has the option, however, of looking for the true good. By choosing not to look, he rejects the possibility of the true good and sets the good before him as an independent good. He is fully aware that he chooses the good as independent, and he is fully aware that he might have desired the good in another way. This awareness brings with it full responsibility.

The lack of consideration does not explain everything about the sin. It explains how the sin is possible. When the rule is present, then the good is desired as subordinated to the chief good. When the rule is absent, the person *can* desire the good as independent. Nevertheless, he need not. He can search for the rule and desire the good in another way. The lack of knowledge allows the choice; the agent's own desire must complete the choice. If he chooses to search for the rule, then its previous absence was not sinful. If he chooses without the rule, then the absence becomes sinful; now it is needed in order that the good be desired as subordinated to the true good.

A PERMITTING CAUSE

Let us close by examining what we have discovered concerning the deficient cause of moral evil, so that we might determine what manner of cause it is. How can we best summarize Aquinas's original discovery? What are its most salient features, and why is it such an original discovery?

The deficiency, we have seen, must not be natural, or it would apply to all human beings at all times. As a voluntary deficiency, however, it cannot be a moral evil, or it itself would be a sin requiring a cause. Thomas thinks that this deficient cause can be found in the voluntary failure to consider the moral rule. This deficiency need not be voluntary in the sense that the person has chosen not to consider the rule. It suffices if it is voluntary in only a negative sense, in the sense that the person could choose to consider the rule.

We have seen that the desire for some inherent good, such as the desire for pleasure considered in itself, provides the positive cause of moral evil. By itself, this cause is insufficient: if the person is aware that the action is opposed to the chief good, then even with this motivation he will not choose the action. The awareness of the opposition to the chief good, then, poses an obstacle that prevents sin. As long as this knowledge is present, the choice for the evil action cannot ensue. The deficient cause of moral evil is precisely the removal of this obstacle. The ignorance, or ignoring, of the order of the action removes this prohibitive knowledge, thereby allowing the sin.

If the person is to be held responsible for the sin, then this ignorance must itself be voluntary, that is, the person must have the ability to remove the ignorance. Not only must he have the ability; in addition, he must be aware that he should remove the ignorance and that he should examine his action to determine its order to the chief good. The person lacking his moral rule is poised between two options: he can go ahead and choose without the moral rule, or he can examine the action further to determine its relation to the chief good. If he chooses without the rule, then his ignorance becomes negligence, and the inherent good becomes his chief good. As Lawrence Dewan expresses the matter,

> Deliberation may, at any given moment, be a consideration of *only part* of the total situation. To be considering only a part of the situation is not, in itself, a bad thing. In fact, given the sort of beings we are, it must sometimes be the case. However, "not to *have been* thorough in one's consideration" is bad, and "not to have been thorough" can be a reality as soon as one *has pressed ahead*, that is, "made up one's mind." Now, "to make up one's mind" is precisely the act of choice.[41]

---

41. Dewan, "St. Thomas and the First Cause of Moral Evil," 195.

The deficient cause of moral evil, then, causes by way of removing an obstacle that would prevent the sin. What is that obstacle? Knowledge of the moral rule. Sometimes when that which prohibits is removed, then the effect follows of necessity. Aquinas's common example is the rock that sits upon a pillar.[42] Remove the pillar—which prohibits the rock from falling down—and the rock will fall down. The same cannot be said concerning the knowledge of the order of the action; when it is removed, the sin does not follow of necessity. The person can still choose to consider the action further; otherwise, the deficiency would not be voluntary. The final movement to the evil does not follow of necessity but requires the acquiescence of the will. As Michael Torre says, "The voluntary defect is only *rendered causative* by the act of choice or intention."[43]

The ignorance, then, does not cause the sin as some kind of efficient cause that necessitates its effect. Rather, the ignorance causes the sin in the sense of allowing it, making it possible; it is what might be called a necessary condition for sin. With the obstacle removed, the will can now choose evil, but it need not. The will is still free to act or not to act. As Thomas says, "The sufficient cause that completes a sin is the will alone."[44] In short, the deficient cause of moral evil may be characterized by two important features. First, it causes by way of removing that which would prohibit a sin. Second, it does not cause the sin of necessity; rather, it causes as a permitting cause. The will may choose to sin, but it need not; for ultimately the will is free to act or not to act. At the heart of every sin, then, is some kind of fundamental freedom of the will. A complete account of the psychology of sin must have some explanation of this fundamental freedom, to which we will turn in the next chapter.

---

42. For example, Aquinas, *Summa theologiae* I-II, q. 85, a. 5.

43. Torre, "Sin of Man," 207. Patrick Lee also makes this point ("Relation between Intellect and Will," 338). Francisco Marín-Sola, on the other hand, seems to maintain that the sin follows of necessity upon the voluntary defect, but he may be referring to the defect together with a final judgment; see Francisco Marín-Sola, "The Thomist System regarding the Divine Motion," in *Do Not Resist the Spirit's Call: Francisco Marín-Sola on Sufficient Grace*, ed. Michael D. Torre (Washington, D.C.: The Catholic University of America Press, 2013), 47.

44. Aquinas, *Summa theologiae* I-II, q. 75, a. 3. "Sed causa sufficienter complens peccatum est sola voluntas."

CHAPTER 13

COMPATIBILISM OR LIBERTARIANISM

Aquinas's account of the first cause of moral evil requires a fine balance between ignorance and awareness. Ignorance—or lack of consideration—is necessary, for the will naturally moves to what is good, and can move to what is evil only on account of some defect in awareness of the good. Complete ignorance, however, would entirely remove responsibility for sin, so some level of awareness is necessary. The sinner must be aware at least that he does not know all he needs to know in order to proceed to action, and that, consequently, he should consider the matter further (*if* he proceeds to action).

To some thinkers, Aquinas's insistence upon the prior defect of ignorance indicates a kind of intellectualism, on par with the view now called compatibilism, which is often credited to David Hume.[1] Aquinas's account does not allow someone to choose evil when he is fully aware of the evil chosen. Every evil choice, thinks Thomas, presupposes some ignoring in the intellect. This subordination of the will to the intellect, so the argument goes, reveals that Aquinas does not appreciate the freedom of the will, by which the will can move out to that which it knows to be evil.

Thomas himself emphasizes that freedom of will is necessary for any

---

1. See Keenan, "Problem with Thomas Aquinas's Concept of Sin," 401–3.

coherent ethics.² The current objection, however, argues that Thomas does not consistently allow for the freedom of the will. If this objection is correct, then all that we have said concerning sin is irrelevant. The intellect reasons in certain ways and reaches certain conclusions, but the person himself can do nothing about it. He is fixed and determined to follow wherever the intellect leads. Can such determined "sins" truly be sins?

DIVIDED INTERPRETATIONS

According to some interpretations, Aquinas is effectively a compatibilist, that is, his account of free will is compatible with a kind of intellectual determinism.³ The intellect considers what actions are to be done and issues a judgment. The will then follows the lead of the intellect. The whole process is deterministic, from beginning to end. Nevertheless, actions are considered free insofar as they do arise from the person's own beliefs and desires. While an agent is not coerced to act in one way or another, his actions ultimately result from necessity from forces impinging upon him, such as the data presented to reason and the dispositions that affect his judgments of reason.

The contrary interpretation sees Aquinas as a libertarian, as maintaining what is sometimes called the "agency view," according to which free actions are not simply those that arise from an individual's own beliefs and desires.⁴ This condition is necessary but not sufficient. An ac-

---

2. Aquinas, *De malo*, q. 6.

3. See, for instance, Thomas Loughran, "Freedom and Good in the Thomistic Tradition," *Faith and Philosophy* 11 (1994): 414–35. Bowlin seems to think that the correct interpretation of Aquinas is a strong intellectualism, indistinguishable from compatibilism ("Psychology"). He thinks, however, that Thomas maintained a voluntarism for Adam and Eve prior to the fall. Others who interpret Aquinas in a compatibilist fashion include P. S. Eardley, "Thomas Aquinas and Giles of Rome on the Will," *Review of Metaphysics* 56 (2003): 835–62; Robert Pasnau, *Thomas Aquinas on Human Nature: A Philosophical Study of* Summa theologiae Ia 75–89 (Cambridge: Cambridge University Press, 2002), 200–233; Jeffrey Hause, "Aquinas and the Voluntarists," *Medieval Philosophy and Theology* 6 (1997): 167–82; Williams, "Libertarian Foundations," 200–209; and probably Colleen McCluskey, "Intellective Appetite and the Freedom of Human Action," *The Thomist* 66 (2002): 421–56; McCluskey, *Thomas Aquinas on Moral Wrongdoing*, 26–29.

4. Those who promote a libertarian interpretation of Aquinas include Gallagher, "Free Choice"; Eleonore Stump, "Aquinas's Account of Freedom: Intellect and Will," *Monist* 80

tion is free only if it arises from within *and* if it is not determined by the sum total of causes acting upon the person, for a free action is determined by the agent himself. As such, his action is not random or completely uncaused. Rather, it is caused in a very particular way, by an agent that can determine himself. When Christine chooses to eat a piece of chocolate, her choice is not some kind of random occurrence. Rather, she determines herself to eat it; she is the cause of her own actions. As Thomas says, "Free decision is the cause of its own movement, because a man by way of free decision moves himself to act."[5]

In order to avoid anachronism (or perhaps to substitute one anachronism for another), the dispute surrounding Aquinas has often been phrased in terms of two medieval camps or tendencies, namely, intellectualism and voluntarism.[6] Intellectualism tends toward compatibilism, and voluntarism tends toward libertarianism. In its strongest form, intellectualism is equivalent with compatibilism, and the strongest form of voluntarism is in some manner libertarian. The two tendencies, however, allow for intermediate shades.

Both views concede that a free action arises from the interaction of the intellect and the will. They differ concerning which of these two powers plays the primary role. In its purest form, intellectualism maintains that every act of will is preceded by some act of the intellect, such that the will

---

(1997): 576–97; Lee, "Relation between Intellect and Will"; Lawrence Dewan, "St. Thomas and the Causes of Free Choice," *Acta Philosophica* 8 (1999): 87–96; Scott MacDonald, "Aquinas's Libertarian Account of Free Choice," *Revue Internationale de Philosophie* 52 (1998): 309–28; Tobias Hoffmann and Peter Furlong, "Free Choice," in *Aquinas's Disputed Questions on Evil: A Critical Guide*, ed. M. V. Dougherty (Cambridge: Cambridge University Press, 2016); Matthias Perkams, "Aquinas on Choice, Will, and Voluntary Action," in *Aquinas and the Nicomachean Ethics*, ed. Tobias Hoffmann, Jörn Müller, and Matthias Perkams (Cambridge: Cambridge University Press, 2013).

5. Aquinas, *Summa theologiae* I, q. 83, a. 1, ad 3: "Liberum arbitrium est causa sui motus, quia homo per liberum arbitrium seipsum movet ad agendum." Jamie Spiering shows that an agent is not the cause of his own existence but is the cause of his own actions insofar as they arise from himself and move to some end that is distinctly his own ("'Liber est Causa Sui': Thomas Aquinas and the Maxim 'The Free Is the Cause of Itself,'" *The Review of Metaphysics* 65 [2011]: 351–76).

6. For a helpful discussion of the differences between intellectualism and voluntarism, see Bonnie Kent, *Virtues of the Will: The Transformation of Ethics in the Late Thirteenth Century* (Washington, D.C.: The Catholic University of America Press, 1995), 94–149.

follows necessarily upon the intellect. If Christine judges that she should eat the chocolate, then she necessarily chooses to eat the chocolate. Furthermore, she can make no choice unless she first judges that it is best to act in one way rather than another. In contrast, voluntarism (in its purest form) maintains that the will can opt for one option over another with no determination from reason.

No one disputes that Aquinas tends toward intellectualism. There is much dispute, however, over whether he is a strict intellectualist, or whether he has voluntaristic elements in his account of free will. If he is a strict intellectualist, then it seems that he is also a compatibilist. If he has some voluntaristic elements, then perhaps he could maintain the agency view.[7]

AQUINAS'S GENERAL ACCOUNT OF FREE WILL

Before examining the contested question of intellectualism and voluntarism, however, it would be well to review the uncontested elements of Aquinas's teaching on the will and its freedom, which appears in its essentials in the *prima pars* but which can be found most completely in the *prima secundae* and the *De malo*.

Thomas distinguishes two ways in which a potentiality can be moved to act: (1) to this or that action, or (2) to act or not to act.[8] The power of

---

7. In regard to interpreting Aquinas on free will, the waters of discourse have been muddied through much of the twentieth century by Odin Lottin's claim that Aquinas changed his mind on free will, moving from an intellectualist position early in life to a voluntarist position later in life; see Odin Lottin, *Psychologie et morale aux XIIe et XIIIe siècles*, 2nd ed. (Gembloux: J. Ducolot, 1957), 207–16, 225–45. The change was supposedly instigated by the condemnations of 1270, to which Aquinas responded (so the argument goes) with question 6 of the *De malo*, in which he abandoned his intellectualism and asserted a voluntarist view. Ultimately, no convincing case can be made for the change of mind. See, for instance, Lawrence Dewan, "St. Thomas, James Keenan, and the Will," in *Wisdom, Law, and Virtue: Essays in Thomistic Ethics* (Bronx, N.Y.: Fordham University Press, 2007); Daniel Westberg, "Did Aquinas Change His Mind about the Will?" *The Thomist* 58 (1994): 41–60. Indeed, the whole theory of a change seems itself to have been founded upon the fear that Aquinas's intellectualism excludes free will. This fear could be ameliorated, so it was hoped, if Aquinas's intellectualism could be relegated to his "immature" view. A straightforward reading of the later texts, however, reveals an intellectualism alive and well, perhaps more so than in the early texts.

8. Aquinas, *Summa theologiae* I-II, q. 9, a. 1; Aquinas, *De malo*, q. 6; I, q. 82, a. 4.

sight, for instance, might be moved to see blue or to see green, depending upon the object presented to it. On the other hand, the power of sight might be moved to see or not to see, depending upon whether the person opens his eyes or closes his eyes.

Similarly, the will can be moved in two ways: (1) to this or that action, or (2) to act or not to act. On the one hand, the will might be moved to choose chocolate or to choose caramel; on the other hand, the will might choose or not choose. Thomas provides convenient labels for these two manners of being moved. Movement to this or that he calls specification; movement to act or not to act he calls use or exercise.

In general, says Thomas, a power is moved to exercise by the acting subject while a potentiality is moved to specification by its object.[9] The power of sight, for instance, is moved to exercise—to act or not to act—by the subject who sees. It is determined to see green or to see blue, on the other hand, by the object seen. The will is no different. But since the object is presented to the will by the intellect, it follows that the intellect may be said to move the will to specification, to this act or to that act.[10]

While the intellect moves the will according to specification, the will moves the intellect according to exercise, that is, to think or not to think upon some subject. Indeed, the will moves all other powers according to efficient causality, or at least all powers subject to voluntary control.[11] We choose to think about something, we choose to eat, we choose to move our legs, and so on. The will is the ultimate agent cause within the person because the will has the higher end, which then directs the ends of lower powers.

Not only does the will move all other mental powers to their exercise; it even moves itself to its own exercise.[12] Once again, this movement arises because the will has a higher end, so that it can move with regard to some subordinate end. How can the will have a higher end than itself? Because the will has distinct acts. One act, with a higher end, moves to another act, with a lower end. Put another way, the desire for the end

---

9. Aquinas, *Summa theologiae* I-II, q. 9, a. 1; I, q. 82, a. 4.

10. Ibid., I-II, q. 9, a. 1; Aquinas, *De malo*, q. 6.

11. Aquinas, *Summa theologiae* I-II, q. 9, a. 1; Aquinas, *De malo*, q. 6; Aquinas, *Summa theologiae* I, q. 82, a. 4.

12. Aquinas, *Summa theologiae* I-II, q. 9, a. 3.

moves to an act of desiring the means. If Christine desires the end of eating chocolate, she can move herself to desire the means of going to the store and buying chocolate.

The intellect is not absent from the will's self-movement, for the will can move itself only by way of deliberation.[13] If Kenny begins with the desire for health, he cannot immediately move to some means, such as desiring to take medicine. First, he must reflect upon the manner in which health can be attained. Only after concluding, with his intellect, that taking medicine is the best means to attain health, can he then move himself to desire to take the medicine. The desire for the end of health, then, moves to the desire to take medicine, but it does so only by way of deliberation.

Thomas pushes this process backwards until he reaches some first desire of the will. How did Kenny begin to desire health? Presumably as the result of some prior deliberation, which arose from the desire for some higher end. Perhaps he wished to travel to London, which he could do only if healthy. But then what led him to desire to go to London? Again, some prior deliberation based upon some prior higher end. This process cannot go on to infinity, so there must be some first act of the will, before which there is no deliberation. Even this first act of the will, however, must be preceded by some activity of the intellect, if not by deliberation, then by some initial grasp of the good.

The point of tracing this chain of desires is not to find some desire independent of the intellect; rather, it is to find some desire independent of a prior desire. While the will can move itself to act, not every act of the will arises from some prior act of the will. There must be at least some first act independent of prior desires. This first act is none other than the desire for the overall good. This desire arises naturally, simply from the presentation of the object by the intellect.[14]

Within this interplay between intellect and will, do we find any freedom? Thomas finds two ways in which there can be necessity in the will. First, conditional necessity sometimes applies to the will, namely, when the will desires some good for which there is only one possible means, or

13. Aquinas, *De malo*, q. 6; Aquinas, *Summa theologiae* I-II, q. 9, a. 4.

14. Ultimately, Thomas finds the cause of this first act of the will in something external, namely, in God, but God himself moves the will according to its nature.

perhaps one means that is clearly best of all.[15] If you want to cross the sea, says Thomas, then you must get on a ship. This example no longer applies, since we can now travel by airplane or by Chunnel, but it certainly applied in Aquinas's day. This necessity from the end is fairly minimal. It presupposes some desire for the end itself, and even then it arises only when a single means proves necessary for the desired end.

Second, the will is moved necessarily according to what Thomas calls natural necessity, which arises from formal cause.[16] This assertion turns out to be nothing other than the (by now) familiar claim: the will is a certain power with its proper object, which is the overall good of the individual.[17] The will, like any power, must have a certain nature; it must move to some object or other. If it did not, then its activity would be entirely random and meaningless.

Combining these two necessities, we see that the will necessarily desires not only the good in general but all those things that are necessary for the overall good. Thomas says that ordering oneself to God—or belonging to God—is just such a necessary means.[18] It seems to follow that no one could ever desire sin, for sin opposes this order to God. Thomas avoids this conclusion by once again bringing in the intellect. While a particular means (such as belonging to God) might in fact be necessary for the end, the intellect might not perceive the necessity, thereby giving the will the freedom to reject this necessary means.

Even apart from misperception, Thomas finds freedom in the will—or the lack of necessity—for those means that are not necessary in themselves.[19] Thomas provides an interesting analogy. If the power of sight is presented with an object that is in all ways colored, then the object will necessarily be seen, for color is the proper object of sight. But if the power of sight is presented with an object that is partly colored and partly transparent, then the object will not necessarily be seen, for the person might be looking at the transparent part. So also, if the will is presented with an object that is in all ways good—that is, beatitude—then it will

---

15. Aquinas, *Summa theologiae* I, q. 82, a. 1.
16. Ibid., I, q. 82, a. 1.
17. Ibid., I-II, q. 10, a. 1.
18. Ibid., I, q. 82, a. 2.
19. Ibid., I-II, q. 10, a. 2.

necessarily desire this object (if it desires anything at all) but if the will is presented with an object that is partly good and partly not good, then it will not be necessitated to desire this object. Such an object can always be considered as not good, so it can be rejected by the will or accepted by it.

This analysis concerns the freedom of the will with regard to specification. Thomas also says that the will is free from necessity with regard to the exercise of the act.[20] Not only can the will choose chocolate over caramel; the will can also act or not act. Indeed, Thomas makes a very strong statement: with regard to exercise, the will is not determined to desire any object, not even the overall good, for the person need not think about the overall good. In short, then, with regard to exercise, the will is not necessitated at all; with regard to specification, the will is necessitated only for the overall good and for any goods perceived as necessary for the overall good. When reason considers any particular good, it can always find something about it that is not good, which amounts to its being bad.[21] For any matter of choice, then, the intellect can always find some reason to pursue it and some reason to avoid it. Only the overall good, or beatitude, is in all ways good, so that there is no reason to avoid it.

This brief summary of Aquinas's account of the will and its freedom has focused on those points over which there is agreement. It remains to determine whether this account is intellectualist or voluntarist, compatibilist or libertarian. In what follows, we will begin by considering four prominent arguments in favor of a libertarian interpretation. We will see that all of these arguments are either defective or at least inconclusive. We will then turn our attention to two arguments in favor of a compatibilist interpretation, which will also be found to be inconclusive.

FREEDOM OF EXERCISE

One prominent feature of Aquinas's account that seems to favor a libertarian interpretation is Aquinas's repeated claim that the will moves itself with regard to exercise, together with the assertion that this exercise—the determination to act or not to act—is itself not necessary.[22]

---

20. Aquinas, *De malo*, q. 6; Aquinas, *Summa theologiae* I-II, q. 10, a. 2.

21. Aquinas, *Summa theologiae* I-I, q. 13, a. 6.

22. See Kent, *Virtues of the Will*, 120. MacDonald also provides this argument ("Aquinas's Libertarian Account," 315–16).

Most strikingly, it is not necessary even with regard to the overall good, which the will can still fail to desire.

Even this self-movement of the will, however, is open to an intellectualist interpretation.[23] Indeed, Thomas himself provides that interpretation. He states that the will moves itself *by way of deliberation*. By desiring some end, the will is led to desire the means, but that means is determined by way of deliberation.[24] This self-movement of the will, then, still receives its determination from reason. If the will has the freedom to act or not to act, it is only because reason presents acting or not acting as a particular good.

What about the freedom of exercise even with regard to the ultimate end? Unfortunately for the libertarian interpretation, even this seemingly fundamental freedom gets traced back to reason. Thomas says that the will need not desire the ultimate end because the person need not think about the ultimate end. Once again, reason seems to take priority. The person first thinks or does not think about the ultimate end, and then the will desires or does not desire.

Nothing in Aquinas's treatment suggests a fundamental veto power in the face of the ultimate end. The only freedom he presents has to do with the means. The failure to desire the ultimate end, then, is a possibility only because this failure might itself be the means to some end. Aquinas says, in the *De malo*, that even the particular acts of reason and will, such as thinking of the ultimate end or desiring the ultimate end, are particular actions and particular goods. "The will is not necessitated with regard to the exercise of the act [in relation to the ultimate end] because someone is able to will not to think about beatitude, because even the very acts of the intellect and of the will are particular."[25] Consequently, these actions, or their absence, can be viewed as means.

Situations in which we might wish—as a means—not to think about the ultimate end are not difficult to imagine.[26] Anna wants to go to sleep

---

23. MacDonald raises similar concerns regarding this foundation for libertarian freedom ("Aquinas's Libertarian Account," 316).

24. Aquinas, *Summa theologiae* I-II, q. 9, a. 4; Aquinas, *De malo*, q. 6.

25. Aquinas, *De malo*, q. 6 (Editio Leonina, XXIII: 150, ll. 437–40): "Non autem quantum ad exercitium actus, quia potest aliquis non uelle tunc cogitare de beatitudine, quia etiam ipsi actus intellectus et uoluntatis particulares sunt."

26. McCluskey's treatment of choosing not to think about happiness is rather involved,

as a means to health and a clear mind. Sleeping, however, involves the absence of thought, including the absence of thinking about the ultimate end. Anna, then, chooses not to think about the ultimate end in order to attain health. Of course, the ultimate end is always desired virtually, but it need not be desired actually. What Thomas is saying is that the failure in actual desire might be itself quite deliberate. If Brett is taking a test, then he will choose not to think about the ultimate end, because he must concentrate upon the test material. He chooses not to think about the ultimate end in order to attain a good grade, which in turn is desired, ultimately, for the sake of the ultimate end. At the moment of taking the test, however, this desire remains only virtual.

The freedom of exercise with regard to the ultimate end, then, is nothing mysterious.[27] It is no different from any other freedom of exercise with regard to the means.[28] Insofar as exercise with regard to the means can be interpreted in an intellectualist manner, so can the freedom of exercise with regard to the ultimate end. A person chooses not to desire the ultimate end because reason has determined that it is good to do so (at this moment), for the sake of health or a good grade or some such thing.

FREEDOM OF SPECIFICATION

Perhaps the most prominent feature of Aquinas's account that favors a libertarian interpretation is the indetermination of the will with regard to particular goods.[29] The will does necessarily desire the overall good, but any particular good might lack some good, so that it can be rejected as well as accepted.

This argument is certainly suggestive, but it is far from conclusive.

---

given the simplicity and commonplace nature of the case ("Happiness and Freedom in Aquinas's Theory of Action," *Medieval Philosophy and Theology* 9 [2000]: 75–77).

27. Thomas does say, while discussing the necessity with regard to specification for the ultimate end, that when the will is presented with the ultimate end, then it must desire this good, *if it desires anything at all* (*Summa theologiae* I-II, q. 10, a. 2). Here he seems to be saying that even when the person does think about the ultimate end, the will need not desire this good. He does not explicitly say so, however, and it is clear in his other statements that the ability not to will the ultimate end depends upon not thinking about it.

28. Bowlin provides this reading of the freedom of exercise in relation to the ultimate end ("Psychology," 143). See also MacDonald, "Aquinas's Libertarian Account," 319.

29. MacDonald provides this argument ("Aquinas's Libertarian Account," 316–22).

This feature of Aquinas's account can be interpreted in an intellectualist fashion. An inherent lack of determination is not sufficient for the rejection of compatibilism. What matters is the manner in which this lack of determination finally comes to be determined.

When speaking of this lack of determination, Thomas himself uses the example of the power of sight, hardly an instance of libertarian freedom.[30] The power of sight is determined—according to its form—to see color, but it is not determined to see blue or to see green, which are particular objects more limited than the proper object of sight. If the object presented to the power of sight is partly transparent, then the object might not even be seen at all. This lack of determination, however, does not indicate libertarian freedom. The power of sight ultimately receives its specification—necessarily—from its object. Although the power of sight is not determined by its nature to see green, when it is presented with a green object, then it will see green.

Similarly, the indetermination in the will with regard to particular goods is insufficient for libertarian freedom.[31] The indeterminacy found in the will ultimately receives determination from outside, namely, from the intellect. The intellect presents an object as desirable or as not desirable, and the will follows.[32]

Or does it? One interpretation suggests that the intellect does not determine the will to do this or that particular action. Rather, the intellect presents options from which the will can select. If Christine desires to enjoy sweets, for instance, then her reason may present various options, such as eating chocolate, eating caramel, eating ice cream, and so on. With her will, then, she must select between these options. According to this interpretation, reason does not determine to one particular action, but merely lays out possibilities. For Christine, for instance, reason does not direct her will to choose chocolate as opposed to caramel. Rather, reason presents both options, and her will makes the determination between the two.

The role of the intellect that precedes the act of will—according to this interpretation—is not to determine which action is best and to be done; rather, it is to present multiple possibilities. Patrick Lee, for in-

---

30. Aquinas, *Summa theologiae* I-II, q. 10, a. 2.
31. See for example Gallagher, "Free Choice," 267.
32. See MacDonald, "Aquinas's Libertarian Account," 319.

stance, says, "The intellect does not cause the act of will in the sense of specifying or determining that x rather than y be willed."[33] Lee goes so far as to claim that free choice rests upon the absence of any best alternative, an absence that follows upon the irreducible multiplicity of goods.[34]

In what way, according to this interpretation, does reason determine the will according to specification? By providing the act of will with its characterization. When the will acts, choosing some particular option, the act of will is then characterized by the option as presented by reason. When Christine's will moves out to chocolate rather than to caramel, then her choice can be characterized as a choice for chocolate only because reason understands in what way chocolate is good. Reason does not specify, ahead of time, that Christine must choose chocolate, but given that she does choose chocolate, reason provides her act of will with its specification.

In short, what it means to determine by specification, according to this interpretation, is not to determine to some particular action, as if reason determines to choose chocolate over caramel. Rather, to determine by specification is to provide the characterization of an action that receives its existence, and its determination to one action rather than to another, from the self-movement of the will.

What are we to make of this interpretation of Aquinas? Ultimately, it must be rejected. Thomas gives a much stronger role to reason than is suggested by this interpretation. Most fundamentally, Aquinas does not present deliberation as simply providing options; rather, deliberation determines to some one best option. It is true that the will moves itself to act or not to act. Thomas insists, however, that it does so only through the intellectual act of deliberation.[35]

Does that mean that deliberation merely presents multiple options? Or does deliberation determine to one particular option? Thomas himself presents an interesting objection bearing upon this question.[36] The ob-

---

33. Lee, "Relation between Intellect and Will," 340. Similarly, Colleen McCluskey says, "I find no evidence that Aquinas holds the view (often attributed to him) that the intellect must present the best option to the will." See McCluskey, "Intellective Appetite," 434.

34. Lee, "Relation between Intellect and Will," 333.

35. Aquinas, *Summa theologiae* I-II, q. 9, a. 4; Aquinas, *De malo*, q. 6.

36. Aquinas, *Summa theologiae* I-II, q. 13, a. 6, ad 3.

jector argues that sometimes two options appear to be completely equal, such that no choice can be made between the two. Note that the objector presumes that the act of choice does not choose between equals but settles upon that which is best. If Aquinas disagrees with this presumption, then now is the opportunity, in his reply to the objection, to point out this error in the objection. He does no such thing. To the contrary, he gives a very intellectualist response. He says that reason can reconsider the matter in a different light, such that one of the options comes out best.[37] Thomas seems to presume that choice is indeed for that which is best. He further presumes that reason determines which option is best. The freedom of the will is not found in some capacity to select between various options; rather, it is rooted in the flexibility of reason's determination.

These two presumptions—that choice is for that which is best and that reason determines what is best—are not peculiarities of this particular objection and its response. Rather, they form the very characterization of choice and deliberation as presented by Thomas.

Thomas seems to define choice in terms of preference from one thing over another. He says, for instance, "Choice is an act of will insofar as reason proposes to it a good as more useful for the end."[38] And he contrasts choice to consent based upon preference:

> Beyond consent choice adds a certain relation by which one thing is preferred to another; consequently, after consent there yet remains the need for choice. Sometimes deliberation discovers many things that lead to the end, and of these, those that are found satisfactory are also consented to. But from the many things that are found satisfactory, we prefer one by choosing it. But if only one means is found satisfactory, then choice and consent differ only by formality. The act of will is called consent insofar as a means is satisfactory for acting; it is called choice, insofar as the means is preferred to those things that are not satisfactory.[39]

---

37. McCluskey points out that Thomas claims only that, in such situations of seeming equality, nothing prevents us from finding what is better; he does not claim that we *must* find what is better ("Intellective Appetite," 436). Nevertheless, he concedes the presumption of the objection, and in other places he affirms the need to choose what is best.

38. Aquinas, *De veritate*, q. 22, a. 15 (Editio Leonina, XXII.3: 649, ll. 69–71): "Eligere est actus voluntatis, secundum quod ratio proponit ei bonum ut utilius ad finem."

39. Aquinas, *Summa theologiae* I-II, q. 15, a. 3, ad 3: "Electio addit supra consensum quandam relationem respectu eius cui aliquid praeeligitur, et ideo post consensum, adhuc

Choice, like every act of will, must follow upon an act of the intellect. In this case, choice follows upon the judgment of deliberation. According to Aquinas, however, deliberation does not merely present options; rather, through deliberation the intellect judges what option is best and to be preferred. "Choice brings together something on the part of a knowing power and something on the part of a desiring power. On the part of the knowing power, deliberation is required, which judges that one thing is to be preferred to another. On the part of the appetitive power, that which has been judged through deliberation must be received by the appetite."[40]

David Gallagher thinks that the choice for what is judged best follows upon the nature of the will as a rational appetite. As rational, it must follow the judgment of reason concerning what is to be preferred. As an appetite, the standard of what is to be preferred must be the good. Combining the two, it follows that the will must always choose that which is judged best.[41] Gallagher, then, leaves no room for Patrick Lee's interpretation, according to which reason presents multiple options, from which the will selects of its own accord.[42] According to Gallagher, such a selection would have no basis—it must be irrational—if reason does not point out which option is to be preferred.

We must concede that sometimes we do not bother determining which of several options is best, since it seems that the difference between the options is minimal. It matters little to Christine, for instance, whether she takes the chocolate on the right or the chocolate on the left, just so long as she gets a chocolate. Consequently, she does not deliberate

---

remanet electio. Potest enim contingere quod per consilium inveniantur plura ducentia ad finem, quorum dum quodlibet placet, in quodlibet eorum consentitur, sed ex multis quae placent, praeaccipimus unum eligendo. Sed si inveniatur unum solum quod placeat, non differunt re consensus et electio, sed ratione tantum, ut consensus dicatur secundum quod placet ad agendum; electio autem, secundum quod praefertur his quae non placent."

40. Ibid., I, q. 83, a. 3: "Ad electionem autem concurrit aliquid ex parte cognitivae virtutis, et aliquid ex parte appetitivae, ex parte quidem cognitivae, requiritur consilium, per quod diiudicatur quid sit alteri praeferendum; ex parte autem appetitivae, requiritur quod appetendo acceptetur id quod per consilium diiudicatur."

41. Gallagher, "Free Choice," 247–48. See also Williams, "Libertarian Foundations," 206; Bradley, "Thomas Aquinas on Weakness," 102.

42. Lee, "Relation between Intellect and Will," 335–36.

to determine which of the two is better.⁴³ As Thomas says, "Sometimes [there is no cause for doubt] because it matters little whether one does something this way or that way, as happens in small matters, which help or hinder attaining the end very little.... Therefore [we do not deliberate] concerning small matters."⁴⁴ As Alan Donagan says, in such matters, we do not ask what we *must* do in order to attain some end; we ask what we *can* do.⁴⁵

This concession, however, does not undermine the determining role of reason. The very acknowledgment of the exception confirms the rule. We do not deliberate when there is no best, or at any rate when the difference between the options is minimal; it follows that when we do deliberate (or at least deliberate beyond the discovery of some initial means), then we are looking for what is best.

In his response to the objection involving two equal options, Thomas notes that reason can reconsider the matter, discovering something that makes one option better than another. He might have added another possibility: reason could judge that the selection between these options is of little importance, so that it matters little which option is chosen. In either event—whether the matter is reconsidered or whether the matter is deemed unimportant—reason makes the determination.

All that Aquinas says, then, indicates that an individual chooses what he has judged best, and nothing indicates the contrary. Libertarian freedom, then, cannot be grounded in some fundamental capacity of the will to choose between several options.

DIRECTING DELIBERATION

A third feature of Aquinas's general account that favors libertarianism is less obvious. His teaching that the will moves the intellect (with regard to exercise) suggests that the will may have some control over the judgment

---

43. McCluskey argues similarly that in order to eat chocolate someone need not judge that chocolate is the best thing to eat ("Intellective Appetite," 436).

44. Aquinas, *Summa theologiae* I-II, q. 14, a. 4: "Quia non multum refert utrum sic vel sic fiat, et ista sunt minima, quae parum adiuvant vel impediunt respectu finis consequendi; quod autem parum est, quasi nihil accipit ratio. Et ideo de duobus non consiliamur, quamvis ordinentur ad finem, ut philosophus dicit, scilicet de rebus parvis."

45. Donagan, *Choice*, 45.

that reason reaches.[46] The will even moves the intellect to deliberate, and at certain points Thomas indicates that the will can move reason to consider a matter further or it can cut short deliberations. He says, for instance, "It is in the power of the will to will and not to will. Again, it is in the power of the will that reason should consider something in act or should cease from consideration; it is in the power of the will that reason should consider this or that reason should consider that."[47] In the previous chapter, we have suggested that just such a determination—to consider further or to proceed to action—underlies the first cause of evil. In some manner, then, it seems that the will can affect the outcome of deliberations.

Once again, however, this power of the will can be interpreted in an intellectualist fashion. Every act of will follows upon some judgment of reason. It follows that the very act of will by which a person wills to deliberate—or not to deliberate—follows upon some judgment of reason.[48] Reason must first deem that the matter deserves reconsideration before the will can move the intellect to reconsider. As P. S. Eardley expresses the matter, "Even if the will has the ability to control how the object is ultimately regarded by the intellect, nonetheless, any such act has to have been itself determined by a prior judgment of the intellect."[49] Ultimately, then, the will does not determine the content of deliberation; rather, a kind of meta-judgment (a judgment upon the judgments of deliberation) determines the will. In any event, the will is determined by reason.

COMPATIBILISM

Arguments in favor of a compatibilist reading fare no better. Some are suggestive, but none are conclusive. A first argument in favor of a compatibilist reading emphasizes that every act of will must be preceded by an

---

46. See Gallagher, "Free Choice," especially 262–70

47. *Summa contra Gentiles* III, chap. 10, no. 17 (Editio Leonina, XIIII: 27, ll. b14–18): "Nam in potestate ipsius voluntatis est velle et non velle. Itemque est in potestate ipsius quod ratio actu consideret, vel a consideratione desistat; aut quod hoc vel illud consideret."

48. Loughran suggests the need for an additional judgment in order for the will to move to some judgment ("Freedom and Good," 428). See also MacDonald, "Aquinas's Libertarian Account," 321; McCluskey, "Intellective Appetite," 433.

49. Eardley, "Thomas Aquinas and Giles," 845. See also Williams, "Libertarian Foundations," 207.

act of the intellect, while the converse is not true.[50] It seems, then, that there can be no act of will that is independent of the intellect, so that the will must always follow the lead of the intellect.[51]

This feature of Aquinas's view, however, does not place him conclusively among the strict intellectualists. Thomas certainly does think that there is no act of the will that is entirely independent of the intellect; it does not follow that the will must always do only one particular thing that the intellect presents. Thomas might well think, for instance, that the will can reject what the intellect presents, for even a rejection is still following an act of the intellect.[52]

A second argument in favor of a compatibilist reading emphasizes that the will is determined by reason with regard to the object. According to this thinking, the determination to this act or to that act must come from reason; the will itself cannot make this determination.[53] Consequently, when presented with multiple objects of desire, the will must always follow where reason leads.

This second argument, it seems, weighs more forcibly in favor of a compatibilist interpretation. Nevertheless, it does not conclusively require compatibilism. Avenues still remain open for a libertarian interpretation. Perhaps, as has been suggested, the will must follow the determination of the intellect, but the intellect itself is led by the will, since the will moves both itself and the intellect to exercise.

---

50. Aquinas, *Summa theologiae* I, q. 82, a. 4, ad 3.

51. See Pasnau, *Thomas Aquinas on Human Nature*, 222–24; Eardley, "Thomas Aquinas and Giles."

52. This argument in favor of intellectualism suffers, in part, from a misrepresentation of possible libertarian readings of Aquinas. It supposes that any libertarian account must posit some acts of will that are independent of reason. Jeffrey Hause, for instance, characterizes libertarianism (or voluntarism) as claiming that it "is up to the will *alone*, or *independently of the intellect*, to determine its own activity" ("Thomas Aquinas and the Voluntarists," 178). This portrayal of voluntarism does not follow from his earlier portrayal: "An account of human action is voluntarist to the extent that the will, and not any other power, controls its own activity" (168). Hause's reasoning seems to confuse dependence and necessity.

53. See Eardley, "Thomas Aquinas and Giles," 846.

SUPPORT FROM PARTICULAR TEXTS

If the general features of Aquinas's account do not settle the question, one might well seek out particular texts that make strong statements in one direction or the other; for example, the following two texts appear to be forceful statements on either side of the line. First, on the side of a libertarian interpretation, the following text seems to imply that after reason presents a good under diverse considerations, the will then may approve or repudiate it. "Any particular goods, insofar as they fail from some good, may be taken as not good, and under this consideration they may be repudiated or approved by the will, which can be led into the same thing according to diverse considerations."[54] Second, on the side of a compatibilist interpretation, the following text seems to say that the capacity to will diverse things depends entirely upon reason. "Man is able to will or not to will, to act or not to act, to will this or to will that, and to do this or to do that. The reason for this ability arises from the very power of reason, for the will is able to tend into whatever reason is able to grasp as good."[55] This battle of texts tends to suffer the same defect as applies to the general account: the texts are underdetermined, so that they can invariably be included within the opposite reading.

The battle of texts can also attempt to use the absence of texts. Hause, for instance, is impressed with what Aquinas does not say, that is, with his silence, which Hause finds particularly "striking."[56] Aquinas nowhere conclusively states that the will acts independently of reason. Evidently, the opposite silence—Thomas nowhere conclusively states that the will is always in all ways determined by reason—is not so striking. Indeed, when Thomas speaks of the will moving itself to one alternative over an-

---

54. Aquinas, *Summa theologiae* I-II, q. 10, a. 2: "Alia autem quaelibet particularia bona, inquantum deficiunt ab aliquo bono, possunt accipi ut non bona, et secundum hanc considerationem, possunt repudiari vel approbari a voluntate, quae potest in idem ferri secundum diversas considerationes."

55. Ibid., I-II, q. 13, a. 6: "Potest enim homo velle et non velle, agere et non agere, potest etiam velle hoc aut illud, et agere hoc aut illud. Cuius ratio ex ipsa virtute rationis accipitur. Quidquid enim ratio potest apprehendere ut bonum, in hoc voluntas tendere potest."

56. Hause, "Thomas Aquinas and the Voluntarists," 178. This negative argument seems to be Hause's primary argument in favor of an intellectualist interpretation.

other, Hause claims that Aquinas is using a misleading shorthand, by which Aquinas *really* means that the whole person moves himself to one alternative by way of reason.[57] Few arguments can be weaker than an appeal to what an author does not say. This argument is especially weak when the author sometimes seems to say what he is not supposed to say, but then these cases are dismissed as misleading shorthand for what he is supposed to say.

An examination of the *De malo* may reveal that Aquinas's silence is not so silent. In their article on the question, Tobias Hoffmann and Peter Furlong find two texts in the *De malo* that they think conclusive, or nearly so, in favor of a libertarian interpretation.[58] The first text, which we have already seen, appears in question 1, article 3. Thomas is discussing the first cause of moral evil, which he locates in the failure to consider the moral rule. This failure, says Thomas, has no other cause than the liberty of the will: "There is no need to seek some cause of the failure to consider the rule, for the very liberty of the will suffices for this, by which liberty the will is able to act or not to act."[59] Is this text asserting what Hause claims that Aquinas never says, namely, that sometimes the will acts of its own accord with no cause beyond itself?

The second text appears in the question on free choice, question 6, at the very beginning. Thomas lays out a view that appears to be nothing other than compatibilism, which he then categorically rejects.

> Some people have maintained that the human will is moved from necessity to choose something. Nevertheless, they do not maintain that the will is coerced, for being necessary is not the same as being coerced. What is necessary is also coerced only when the principle is outside [the agent]. Some natural movements

---

57. Ibid., 178. Hause is later worried by texts in which Aquinas speaks about reason moving the person to act. These texts seem to eliminate the idea of the whole person acting. He dismisses the worry, however, by noting that the whole person acts by way of his powers. Evidently, when Aquinas speaks of the will moving, he is merely using shorthand for the whole person, but when he speaks of reason moving he is talking about the whole person moving himself by way of his powers; see ibid., 182.

58. Hoffmann and Furlong, "Free Choice," 65–70, 73.

59. Aquinas, *De malo*, q. 1, a. 3 (Editio Leonina, XXIII: 16, ll. 268–71): "Huius autem quod est non uti regula predicta non oportet aliquam causam querere, quia ad hoc sufficit ipsa libertas uoluntatis, per quam potest agere uel non agere."

[although they do not arise from outside] are nevertheless necessary. Violence or coercion is opposed to what is natural as well as to what is voluntary; both natural and voluntary movements arise from within, while the source of violence or coerced movements is from without. This view, however, is heretical.[60]

Hoffman and Furlong are correct: it is difficult to see how this view differs from compatibilism. Thomas proceeds to say that the view is contrary not only to theology but to all sound moral philosophy as well.[61] To maintain that choice is necessary but nevertheless voluntary because it is from within—which is nothing other than compatibilism—is a false philosophical view.

Scott MacDonald provides a similar argument, but it is not based upon a single text; rather, it follows from a general feature of Aquinas's understanding of the will.[62] His approach is particularly helpful, since it focuses upon the causes of freedom, emphasizing an unquestionably intellectualist aspect of Aquinas's thought.

MacDonald's argument is rather involved. Fundamentally, it amounts to the claim that Aquinas's account of animal behavior is a compatibilist account, that is, Thomas explains animal behavior in precisely the way that a compatibilist would explain human behavior.[63] Thomas, however, thinks that human behavior is in some way fundamentally different from animal behavior and that this fundamental difference makes human behavior to be free. Free activity, then, must involve some kind of causal interplay that goes beyond the compatibilist account. Since the only plau-

60. Aquinas, *De malo*, q. 6 (Editio Leonina, XXIII: 147–48, ll. 238–48): "Quidam posuerunt quod uoluntas hominis ex necessitate mouetur ad aliquid eligendum. Nec tamen ponebant quod uoluntas cogeretur: non enim omne necessarium est uiolentum, set solum illud cuius principium est extra. Vnde et motus naturales inueniuntur aliqui necessarii, non tamen uiolenti: uiolentum enim repugnat naturali sicut et uoluntario, quia utriusque principium est intra, uiolenti autem principium est extra. Hec autem opinio est heretica."

61. Hause argues that Aquinas's commitment to the link between free will and morals does not commit him to indeterminism, but Hause does not consider this particular argument that is presented in the *De malo*; see Hause, "Thomas Aquinas and the Voluntarists," 169–70.

62. MacDonald, Aquinas's "Libertarian Account."

63. Gallagher makes a similar claim concerning the difference between human and animal behavior; see David M. Gallagher, "Thomas Aquinas on the Will as Rational Appetite," *Journal of the History of Philosophy* 29 (1991): 564–66.

sible alternative must be some version of libertarian freedom, it follows that Thomas maintained libertarian freedom.

In the *De veritate*, Thomas does indeed describe animal behavior precisely in compatibilist terms:

> Animals have a certain likeness to free choice insofar as they are, concerning one and the same thing, able to act or not to act according to their judgment, so that there is in them a certain conditional liberty, for they are able to act if they judge that they should act, or they are able not to act, if they judge that they should not act. But because their judgment is determined to one outcome, it follows that both the appetite and the action are determined to one.[64]

When a squirrel sees a nut, he may go out to get it or not. Perhaps a dog is nearby, so the squirrel stays safely in the tree. Two different squirrels might exhibit opposite behavior in precisely the same circumstances. One squirrel, with a bolder disposition, risks the danger of the dog and goes out to get the nut; the other, more timid by disposition, stays safely in the tree. The squirrels seem to exhibit precisely the kind of indeterminacy that Aquinas attributes to the will: they may act or not act, they may do this or they may do that.

Such indeterminacy, claims Thomas, is not the same as free choice, for the judgment of the squirrel is determined and his desire follows necessarily upon his judgment, upon which follows his action.

> In animals there is a certain indifference of actions, but it cannot properly be said that in them is found liberty of actions, of acting or of not acting.... If an action is considered in itself, then in animals there is an indifference to act or not to act, but if the action is considered in relation to the judgment from which it derives a determination to one, then even the action itself acquires a certain necessity, so that the character of liberty cannot be found in animals absolutely speaking.[65]

---

64. Aquinas, *De veritate*, q. 24, a. 2 (Editio Leonina, XXII.3: 686, ll. 115–23): "Et similiter est in eis quaedam similitudo liberi arbitrii, in quantum possunt agere vel non agere unum et idem, secundum suum iudicium, ut sic sit in eis quasi quaedam condicionata libertas; possunt enim agere si iudicant esse agendum vel non agere si non iudicant. Sed quia iudicium eorum est determinatum ad unum, per consequens et appetitus et actio ad unum determinatur."

65. Ibid., q. 24, a. 2, ad 3 (Editio Leonina, XXII.3: 686, ll. 152–66): "Quamvis in brutis sit quaedam indifferentia actionum, tamen non potest proprie dici quod sit in eis libertas

In short, the squirrel acts according to compatibilist causality. Whatever free choice is, then, it cannot be simply the same thing as compatibilism.

Robert Pasnau is aware of this difficulty, yet wishes to defend a compatibilist interpretation of Aquinas.[66] He argues that human behavior is different from animal behavior in its complexity. No unique causal principle is found within human behavior, but it involves a much more complex interplay of desire and judgment. We have higher-order desires—the desire for some desire—and we have higher-order judgments—the judgment upon some other judgment. This allows the dispositions of the will to influence the judgments of reason. Freedom, then, is a matter of complexity. Pasnau concedes that such complexity still leaves human beings conditionally necessitated, even as are animals. Nevertheless, the complexity at least gives us the feeling that we are making our own choices. In short, necessary behavior becomes "free" behavior when it arises from within and when it is complex enough to give us a certain feeling of choosing for ourselves.

Thomas himself, of course, does not speak of complexity, but he does locate the difference between human beings and animals, first of all, in the judgment rather than in the appetite. The judgment of animals is determined while the judgment of human beings is free. Whatever is unique to human beings, then, must begin at the level of knowledge. Any libertarian account—which must go beyond the explicit statements of Thomas while yet remaining faithful to his principles—must likewise begin with knowledge.

---

actionum sive agendi vel non agendi.... sit indifferentia ad agere et non agere in bruto considerata ipsa actione secundum seipsam, tamen considerato ordine eius ad iudicium a quo provenit quod est determinatum ad unum, etiam ad ipsas actiones obligatio quaedam derivatur, ut non possit in eis inveniri ratio libertatis absolute."

66. Pasnau, *Thomas Aquinas on Human Nature*, 224–30, 232.

CHAPTER 14

FREE DECISION

If Aquinas is indeed libertarian in his account of the will, he is nevertheless highly intellectualist.[1] He insists that some act of the intellect must precede every act of the will, and he insists that the will is determined by the intellect with regard to specification. In what manner, then, can Aquinas's account be libertarian? Thomas himself does not provide the details of any such account. He provides the general framework, for which we must fill in the details, using clues that Thomas provides.

One prominent clue is Aquinas's repeated insistence that the freedom of the will is rooted in reason. He points to three features of reason that underlie human freedom. First, reason knows in the universal and is consequently indeterminate with regard to particulars. Second, reason bends back upon itself, judging its own acts of judging. Third, reason understands the relation between means and ends. Animal knowledge lacks all of these features and consequently their desires are determined. It is unclear, however, how these three features help to support libertarian freedom. We will begin by examining the universal character of intellectual knowledge.

1. Parts of this chapter originally appeared in Jensen, "Libertarian Free Decision: A Thomistic Account," *The Thomist* 81 (2017): 315–43.

THE INDETERMINATION OF REASON

Thomas attributes free decision to human beings because reason knows in the universal and is able to make comparisons.[2] His treatment of this issue in the *De malo*, although fundamentally the same as his treatment in the *prima pars*, is more helpful because he provides an interesting example, which more clearly illumines what he is trying to convey.

The form of a natural thing is a form individuated through matter, so that the consequent inclination is determined to one, but the form of the intellect is a universal, under which many things may be included. Since action is in singulars, in which there is nothing that exhausts the potential of the universal, it follows that the inclination of the will relates indeterminately to many things. A builder, for instance, may conceive the form of a house in a universal fashion, under which are included diverse shapes of a house; then his will can be inclined to make a rectangular house or a round house, or some other figure.[3]

Thomas has in mind a common feature of our desires, which often have an abstract character. It is not that we desire an abstraction, for we desire what is good, and the good is found in the concrete. Nevertheless, we do desire concrete realities under some abstraction. Kim might begin desiring pizza, for instance, without yet having determined what kind of pizza, such as pepperoni or sausage. Similarly, the builder does not desire an abstract house, which does not exist; he desires a concrete house, but he (initially) desires it abstracted from any particular shape, which will be determined later.

Animals lack this indetermination, but they have another indetermination.

---

2. Gallagher emphasizes this aspect of the will through a contrast with the emotions ("Thomas Aquinas on the Will as Rational Appetite," 579–82).

3. Aquinas, *De malo*, q. 6 (Editio Leonina, XXIII: 148, ll. 284–96): "Forma rei naturalis est forma indiuiduata per materiam, unde et inclinatio ipsam consequens est determinata ad unum, set forma intellecta est uniuersalis, sub qua multa possunt comprehendi. Vnde cum actus sint in singularibus, in quibus nullum est quod adequet potentiam uniuersalis, remanet inclinatio uoluntatis indeterminate se habens ad multa ; sicut si artifex concipiat formam domus in uniuersali, sub qua comprehenduntur diuerse figure domus, potest uoluntas eius inclinari ad hoc quod faciat domum quadratam uel rotundam uel alterius figure."

The active principle in nonhuman animals is midway between the two [reason and nature], for the form apprehended by sense is individual, as is the form of a natural thing; consequently, from this form follows an inclination to one act, as in natural things. Nevertheless, the forms of natural things are always the same (since fire is always hot). In contrast, the form received in the senses is not always the same, but is now one form and at another moment a different form, for example, at one time it might be some pleasurable form and at another time something unpleasant, so that at one time the animal pursues the object and at another time he avoids it. In this respect, [the form upon which animals act] is similar to the active principle of human beings.[4]

Although animals always desire some concrete thing precisely as concrete, nevertheless their desires vary. Given different objects presented to the senses, different desires follow. The animal judgment is necessary and so is the desire that follows the judgment, but the input that gives rise to the judgment changes from one time to the next, just as it might for compatibilist freedom.

Human desire is more expansive than animal desire. We desire objects under an abstraction, under which many different details—often opposing details—might be included. From this general desire more concrete desires might follow, just as probable arguments can reach opposite conclusions (as Aquinas says in the *prima pars*).[5] In contrast, animals have very determinate desires, but what desire arises at any given moment is indeterminate, ultimately receiving determination from the object presented.

The indetermination in human desire does not, by itself, imply libertarian freedom.[6] It might turn out that this original indetermination moves to some particular option through a deterministic process. The

---

4. Ibid. (Editio Leonina, XXIII: 147–48, ll. 296–307): "Principium autem actiuum in brutis animalibus medio modo se habet inter utrumque. Nam forma apprehensa per sensum est indiuidualis sicut et forma rei naturalis, et ideo ex ea sequitur inclinatio ad unum actum sicut in rebus naturalibus. Set tamen non semper eadem forma recipitur in sensu, sicut est in rebus naturalibus, quia ignis est semper calidus, set nunc una nunc alia: puta, nunc forma delectabilis, nunc tristis. Vnde nunc fugit, nunc persequitur. In quo conuenit cum principio actiuo humano."

5. Aquinas, *Summa theologiae* I, q. 83, a. 1.
6. See, for example, Williams, "Libertarian Foundations," 202.

builder begins desiring a house considered abstractly, which desire is indeterminate with regard to particular instances of houses. As he deliberates, however, he settles upon one particular house, which he then desires. If this process of moving from a general desire to a particular desire follows of necessity based upon the input that reason receives, then the initial general desire would not, it seems, give rise to libertarian freedom.[7]

Even if the particular desire is necessitated, Thomas has nevertheless pointed out a real difference between human and animal desires (supposing, at any rate, that his account of animal desire is accurate). Animals never desire some object under a general consideration; they always desire an object considered concretely.[8] As such, they have no desires that can be specified to some more particular desire. In contrast, human beings do desire objects considered abstractly, even as Kim desires pizza without yet having determined what kind of pizza she wants. This desire can be satisfied by diverse particular instances. It is open to many possibilities. Human desire is expansive, including many options under it.[9]

JUDGMENTS HELD TENTATIVELY

A human being and an animal must both reach some particular judgment about some particular action. Seeing a nut, for instance, a squirrel judges that it should go to get the nut. Desiring sweets, Christine judges that she should reach out and take the chocolate. Christine's desire might have begun with a desire for something sweet, leaving aside the particular details, but before she can ever move to action, she must settle upon some particular action, just as does the squirrel.

Nevertheless, Christine's judgment is different from the squirrel's. Both judgments are particular, but Christine's judgment is based upon a universal understanding. As such, she can maintain it in a tentative manner.

Consider two ways in which individuals might agree to the statement that "it will rain tonight." Max thinks that it will rain tonight, but he is

---

7. See ibid., 205.

8. Williams misses this point, when he discusses a dog seeking food in general (ibid., 203).

9. Yves Simon calls this expansive character of human desire "superdetermination" (*Freedom of Choice* [New York: Fordham University Press, 1969], 106).

aware that the evidence is not conclusive, so he does not maintain the proposition firmly but only with a certain probability. As Thomas says, when the evidence for a proposition is not conclusive, reason reaches only opinion or suspicion.[10] Reason maintains the proposition, aware that it might be false and that its contrary might be true. If there are storm clouds on the horizon, then the evidence points to rain. Still, reason can say "it will rain" only with a certain probability or leaning. In such cases, according to Aquinas, reason cannot move to firm assent on its own. The will must intervene.[11]

Unlike Max, Barb firmly maintains that it will rain tonight. If she recognizes that the evidence is indeed inconclusive, then she can maintain this firm assent only through the intervention of the will. With her will, she has moved her reason to assent. The same proposition ("it will rain tonight"), then, is maintained in two different ways by two different individuals. Max maintains it as probable; Barb maintains it with firm conviction.

In a similar manner, the particular judgment of an animal and of a human being might differ. The squirrel judges that it should get the nut with a kind of "certainty," that is, it is unaware of any other possibilities. In contrast, Christine reaches the judgment to eat the chocolate fully aware that the judgment is tentative and that further information might change it. While Christine has settled upon eating the chocolate, she is aware that she could modify her judgment. In contrast, the squirrel is aware of no other possibility.

This difference arises because human beings judge based upon universal knowledge. Christine recognizes that there are many ways of concretely realizing the universal good of eating sweets. Furthermore, she recognizes that no single option fully realizes the universal, if only because it excludes other possibilities. The squirrel is not even aware that there are other possibilities, and he is certainly not aware that the object he desires fails to realize some universal consideration.

Christine is also aware that she might consider more things concerning the object she has judged best. She has considered that the chocolate

---

10. Aquinas, *Summa theologiae* II-II, q. 2, a. 1.
11. Ibid., II-II, q. 2, a. 1, ad 3.

tastes good, but she might also consider whether eating it is rude, whether it is healthy, and so on. This awareness derives from her abstract consideration, for the determinate action that she finally settles upon is still considered at a certain level of abstraction. She can never consider every possible feature of any concrete option, a procedure that would be infinite, or at the very least practically impossible. In contrast, the squirrel is not aware that it might be leaving out details relevant to its action, for it has no notion of considering some features of an action and leaving out others (although, invariably it must do so).

The comparison between probable judgments (such as, "it will rain tonight") and tentative practical judgments comes from Donald Davidson, who distinguishes two kinds of practical judgments: prima facie judgments and all-out judgments.[12] A prima facie judgment considers that an action has certain features, some of which make it desirable and others that make it undesirable. Christine might judge, for instance, that she should eat the chocolate, *insofar as* it is sweet. She does not judge, simply speaking, that she should eat the chocolate; she judges only that in some respect it would be good to eat the chocolate. Other considerations, such as health or rudeness, might indicate otherwise. If Christine were to judge that she should eat the chocolate simply speaking, then she would have moved from a prima facie judgment to an all-out judgment.

Adapting Davidson's terminology to Aquinas, we might say that prima facie judgments depend upon the universal character of human reason. Squirrels make only all-out judgments, because they cannot consider an action under one respect or under another respect, leaving out various considerations. Or, more accurately, squirrels are not aware that they consider an action under one respect or another respect, so they cannot make a judgment with the tentative character of a prima facie judgment.

What Davidson calls all-out judgments, Thomas describes as a consideration of an action in the here and now.[13] Although both judgments give rise to some act of will—some desire or aversion—only the here-and-

---

12. Davidson, "How Is Weakness of Will Possible?" 37–40; Davidson, "Davidson Responds," 197.

13. See Aquinas, *Summa theologiae* I-II, q. 6, a. 6. For a consideration of the different kinds of desire following upon these distinct judgments, see Feingold, *Natural Desire*, 23–25.

now judgment leads to action. This feature of here-and-now judgments corresponds with Davidson's all-out judgments. Prima facie judgments, says Davidson, do not lead to action; only all-out judgments do.[14]

Even when we add a variety of details to our considerations, our judgment usually remains tentative. Should the captain jettison the cargo? That depends upon how bad the storm is. Given the evidence, his judgment to jettison the cargo may well remain tentative. Should Christine eat the chocolate? She may consider factors such as rudeness, weight gain, health, and a variety of other factors, and conclude that she should eat the chocolate. Nevertheless, she still recognizes that further consideration might change her judgment. She cannot say definitively that the action is ordered to the ultimate end. As Perkams expresses it, "[Aquinas's] point seems to be that no single act of practical reason can ever grasp a situation completely."[15]

Even more so, of course, an animal cannot make a definitive judgment given its yet more limited evidence. The human being differs from the animal, however, in recognizing the tentative nature of his judgment. The animal always judges in all-out mode. The human being deliberates in "some respect" mode, that is, he judges actions according to this or that respect, recognizing that these various features of the action do not exhaust all that could be considered concerning it. While deliberating he has not yet chosen, yet his considerations give rise to desires or aversions of a conditional nature. Only when he reaches an all-out judgment does he desire with the completeness of intention that leads to action.

We may summarize the difference between human and animal judgments with the following points. Human beings begin with a general desire, while animals always desire in the concrete. Both humans and animals, however, must ultimately reach some particular judgment. Because of the universal nature of human knowledge however, this particular judgment is maintained in a different way. A human being reaches his particular judgment with the recognition that it is tentative and open to revision. In contrast, the animal has no awareness that its judgment

---

14. Davidson, "How Is Weakness of Will Possible?" 40. Davidson seems to have a parallel distinction of desires ("Intention," 98). We intend, as opposed to merely desire, what we see as worth pursuing given all our current beliefs.

15. Perkams, "Aquinas on Choice," 87–88.

is inconclusive. The troubling upshot, it seems, is that the human judgment does not lead to action, for it is not an all-out judgment. In short, the human judgment is overly indeterminate, so indeterminate as to be practically useless.

Faced with this difficulty, Davidson simply asserts that somehow or other we move to an all-out judgment.[16] This mysterious movement, however, is far from satisfying the human mind. Unveiling the mystery may reveal the heart of free decision.

META-JUDGMENTS

The awareness that a judgment is tentative and can be modified is a kind of awareness of an awareness; it is what Scott MacDonald has called a meta-judgment.[17] It is a judgment that the initial judgment is tentative.[18] Such meta-judgments supply the second feature of reason that Aquinas emphasizes as a foundation for a free choice.[19] Reason can bend back upon itself, judging its own judgments. In the *De veritate* Thomas says,

> If the judgment of the knowing faculty is not in the power of the person but is determined by something else, then neither will the appetite be in his power, and consequently neither the movement nor the activity will be entirely in his power. A judgment is in the power of the one judging, however, insofar as he is able to judge upon his own judgment, for those things that are within our power are those things upon which we can pass judgment. It belongs only to reason, however, to pass judgment upon its own judgment, for the act of reason bends back upon itself, and it knows the relations of the things about which it judges and of those things by which it judges. In short, the entire root of freedom is based in reason. Consequently, something has free decision to the degree that it has reason.[20]

---

16. Davidson, "How Is Weakness of Will Possible?" 39.

17. MacDonald, "Aquinas's Libertarian Account," 327.

18. Dewan thinks that this indeterminacy of deliberation is the root of freedom ("St. Thomas and the Causes of Free Choice," 90).

19. David Gallagher also emphasizes this requirement for free choice; see Gallagher, "Thomas Aquinas on the Will as Rational Appetite," 571–74.

20. Aquinas, *De veritate*, q. 24, a. 2 (Editio Leonina, XXII.3: 685–86, ll. 88–102): "Si iudicium cognitivae non sit in potestate alicuius, sed sit aliunde determinatum, nec appetitus erit in potestate eius, et per consequens nec motus vel operatio absolute. Iudicium autem

The essential difference between human judgments and animal judgments, then, is that human beings pass judgment upon their judgments. Christine judges, for instance, that her judgment is tentative and can be revised. Only as such, thinks Thomas, can human beings have free choice. As Pasnau says, "To be free from determinism and necessity is to be capable of inspecting the reasons behind our judgments, and to change our mind should circumstances warrant."[21]

Unfortunately, it is far from clear how these meta-judgments can extricate Aquinas from intellectual determinism. Suppose Christine passes judgment upon her judgment. She has judged that she should eat the chocolate, but she recognizes that she might consider the matter further and reach a different conclusion. Will she in fact reconsider the matter? That depends upon her will. She can either move or not move her intellect to reconsider. As we have seen, however, every act of the will is preceded by some act of the intellect. In other words, if she wills to reconsider, she must first judge that it is best to reconsider. Whether or not she reconsiders the matter, then, is determined by some prior judgment.

It does no good to seek some meta-judgment upon this prior meta-judgment. Presumably, if Christine judges that she should reconsider the matter, she is aware that even this prior judgment is open to reevaluation. She might want to reconsider whether or not she should reconsider. Such meta-meta-judgments do not solve the problem but lead to an infinite regress. However deep the layers of judgments upon judgments, the will must still follow reason.[22]

---

est in potestate iudicantis secundum quod potest de suo iudicio iudicare; de eo enim quod est in nostra potestate, possumus iudicare. Iudicare autem de iudicio suo est solius rationis quae super actum suum reflectitur, et cognoscit habitudines rerum de quibus iudicat, et per quas iudicat; unde totius libertatis radix est in ratione constituta. Unde secundum quod aliquid se habet ad rationem, sic se habet ad liberum arbitrium." See also Aquinas, *Summa contra Gentiles* II, chap. 48, no. 3.

21. Pasnau, *Thomas Aquinas on Human Nature*, 219.

22. MacDonald worries that the choice to continue deliberating requires some prior judgment of reason, which then might determine the will to continue deliberating ("Aquinas's Libertarian Account," 321). Gallagher tries to avoid the infinite regress by making the acts of intellect and will simultaneous ("Free Choice," 276). There still seems to be an infinite causal series, whether simultaneous or not, as Dewan points out ("St. Thomas and the Causes of Free Choice," 88).

The above argument in defense of intellectual determinism, however, has misunderstood the nature of meta-judgments. One might suppose that a meta-judgment is a practical judgment to reconsider or not to reconsider some prior judgment. Christine has two judgments: a judgment to eat the chocolate, and a judgment to reconsider this first judgment. The above argument has treated the second judgment as a kind of meta-judgment. In contrast, the meta-judgments we have been examining are not judgments to reconsider or not to reconsider. Rather, they are judgments that a judgment is itself tentative and is open to reconsideration. They are a kind of awareness that the current judgment is not conclusive and that further information might change it. Ultimately, they are an awareness of the person that his current judgment is not sufficient to move him to act; it provides reason to act, but not decisive reason. The intellect cannot yet determine the will to act, for it has not yet judged that the action is good; it has simply judged that the action is good in some respect, or that it is probably good.

THE BEGINNINGS OF DELIBERATION

The third feature of reason that underlies free choice is its ability to recognize the relation between means and ends. Christine recognizes, for instance, that eating this chocolate is a means of eating something sweet, which was her initial desire. Only through this ability of reason, says Thomas, can the will move itself to exercise, since the will moves itself to exercise only by way of deliberation, which is the process by which we examine the means to achieve a desired end. As Thomas notes, "The will moves itself insofar as it wills the end and reduces itself to willing those things that are ordered to the end. It can do this, however, only by way of deliberation."[23]

Christine begins by considering that eating sweets is good. She then desires to eat sweets, generally considered. Next, or so it would seem, she moves herself to deliberate concerning how to eat sweets. This most recent step, however, faces a difficulty.[24] If the will moves the intellect

23. Aquinas, *Summa theologiae* I-II, q. 9, a. 4: "Et quidem, sicut dictum est, ipsa movet seipsam, inquantum per hoc quod vult finem, reducit seipsam ad volendum ea quae sunt ad finem. Hoc autem non potest facere nisi consilio mediante."

24. Ibid., I, q. 82, a. 4, obj. 3.

to deliberate, then it does so only by some prior judgment of the intellect (that deliberation is good), which judgment must have been reached by some prior deliberation. But where did this prior judgment and prior deliberation come from? Presumably, the will moved the intellect to deliberate about whether to deliberate. But this movement of the will presupposes yet another judgment of reason (that it is good to deliberate about whether to deliberate), which must have been reached by yet another deliberation, etc., etc.

In his reply to this objection, Thomas dissolves the infinite regress by noting that every act of will must always be preceded by some act of understanding of the intellect, but the converse is not true.[25] Not every act of the intellect must be moved to exercise by the will. The initial movement to deliberation, then, sometimes arises from the intellect with no instigation from the will.

When presented with certain objects, the intellect naturally moves to understand. Sometimes, the intellect moves to deliberation by its very nature, without the instigation of the will. How does the intellect move to deliberation by its nature? The process begins with the intellect presenting some good. This very first presentation cannot arise from the instigation of the will; rather, it must arise simply because the intellect was thinking upon an object that is good. Suppose, for instance, that a plate of sweets is presented to Christine. It takes no special movement of the will for Christine to begin thinking about sweets, for that is the object before her, and it takes no special movement of the will for her intellect to recognize that the sweets are good. Upon this recognition, a desire of the will follows.

The intellect then recognizes (again, with no push from the will) that it is good to attain the sweets. Two further recognitions on the part of the intellect will lead to deliberation. First, the intellect must recognize that the sweets can be attained only if it (the intellect) is aware of how to attain the sweets (in this case, by settling upon one particular kind of sweet). Second, the intellect must recognize that currently it is not aware how to attain the sweets (it is not aware which sweet is best to take). Given these two, the intellect will readily recognize a third thing: it is good to discover

---

25. Ibid., I, q. 82, a. 4, ad 3.

how to attain the sweets, that is, deliberation is good. Indeed, the intellect will often reach a stronger conclusion: deliberation is necessary to attain the desired goal.

From such a judgment of necessity, a conditional necessity follows in the will, for Thomas says that the will can have conditional necessity when one means is necessary for a desired goal.[26] As long as she desires sweets, for instance, Christine necessarily desires, with her will, to deliberate. In short, the conclusion (that she must deliberate) is not tentative; it is not a prima facie judgment but an all-out judgment. From her desire for the sweets, then, Christine will move to the desire for the means of attaining the sweets, which is deliberation. At this point, for the first time, the will moves the intellect to exercise. The intellect has judged (with no instigation from the will) that deliberation is necessary, and the will (of necessity) then moves the intellect to deliberate.[27]

So far the movement is as follows: (1) with no instigation from the will, the intellect has reflected upon sweets and perceived that they are good; (2) the will has desired sweets; (3) the intellect has judged (again, not moved by the will) that deliberation is necessary to attain the sweets; (4) the will has moved itself to desire the means of attaining sweets, which is deliberation; then (5) the will has moved the intellect to exercise, that is, to deliberate.

In this scenario, attaining the sweets is the end, and deliberation is the first means; the end can be attained only by way of deliberation. In order to arrive at this point, reason has already used its capacity—not shared with the animals—of grasping the relation between the means and the end. Animals might judge concerning certain means by way of instinct,

26. Ibid., I, q. 82, a. 1.

27. We should make an important note about deliberation. Thomas says that deliberation is not always necessary (ibid., I-II, q. 14, a. 4). Judgment can be reached without deliberation in two situations. First, deliberation is not necessary when there is some standard means to attain the end. If Anna is going to the grocery store and she has driven there many times before, then she need not deliberate about the route. Note that the lack of necessity of deliberation, in this case, arises only because of past instances in which there was deliberation. Second, deliberation is not necessary when the difference between the options is insignificant. This second instance seems to be more a case where *further* deliberation is not needed, for presumably the person has arrived at the point of recognizing multiple options (between which there is no significant difference) only by way of deliberation.

not recognizing that they are means. In contrast, human beings recognize the causal relation between the means and the end, and they recognize that the means themselves become a certain good on the way to the goal.

Deliberation is the first means recognized by reason, and it is typically a necessary means, giving rise to conditional necessity in the will. This first means (of deliberation), however, will not remain necessary. After deliberation has proceeded and reached a conclusion, then it is no longer necessary. Indeed, at some point further deliberation becomes a hindrance. Christine will never attain the sweets if she deliberates indefinitely.

THE WILL AT AN IMPASSE

We have identified three features of reason that underlie free decision. First, reason understands in the universal. It follows that the will can desire an object under a general consideration. This desire, then, is open to many particular realizations. Second, reason bends back upon itself, judging its own judgments. In particular, in deliberation reason is aware that its conclusions are tentative, that further evidence might indicate a different conclusion. Third, reason recognizes the relation between means and ends. Only as such, can reason present deliberation, which is the first means, as good to the will. Only as such, does deliberation itself make sense.

How do these three features of reason support free decision? Thomas never provides a detailed account. The first feature provides an indeterminacy in the desires of the will, such that a general desire might be satisfied by diverse particular instances. This indeterminacy, however, is insufficient for free will. What matters is the manner in which the determination is reached. If the general desire is determined to some specific desire of necessity, then there will be no freedom in the will.

The second feature reveals that at least sometimes the manner of determination is not necessary. More importantly, the person recognizes that it is not necessary. The conclusions of deliberation are held tentatively. Does this second feature, then, indicate that general desires of the will reach determination free from necessity? It would seem not. Rather, the second feature indicates that deliberation, at least when it is known to be tentative, reaches no determination at all. Or rather, it reaches a tentative determination, which is not sufficient to move the will to some specification. In other words, the second feature does not leave us with a self-determined will; it leaves us with the will undetermined and with no evident means of reaching determination.

The third feature reveals that deliberation, as the first means to the goal, initially arises with sufficient determination, that is, reason presents deliberation as conditionally necessary in order to attain the end. By its nature, however, this sufficiency must eventually cease. Deliberation cannot always remain a necessary means to the end, for an indefinite deliberation will never attain the end. The initial judgment that deliberation is necessary will eventually cede to a tentative judgment that further deliberation is good (or, alternately, a tentative judgment that further deliberation is bad).

When deliberation reaches a conclusion, the person is in a difficult situation. The conclusion itself is held tentatively, so that it is not sufficient to specify the will. Once the conclusion has been reached, however, then the very deliberation itself is good only with a certain probability. Deliberation is indeed good to attain the end, but it may no longer be good, since continued deliberation will interfere with the means. When Christine has tentatively concluded that taking the chocolate is a good means to enjoy sweets, then continued deliberation is no longer a necessary means. It might prove helpful, since more information might indicate a different course of action, but it might prove a hindrance, since indefinite deliberation will prevent the sweets from ever being enjoyed.

If Christine's desire for the end of sweets is strong enough, she may wish to forgo further deliberation, that is, she may cease willing deliberation as a means; after all, it poses an obstacle to attaining the chocolate now. As Scott McDonald expresses the point:

> Considerations of optimality can be brought to bear on reasoning about the desirability of deliberation itself, and optimific necessity can enter into practical reasoning at what might be called the meta-level. We sometimes choose a particular course of action not because we take it to be, in itself, the best way of attaining our goal but because we judge that there is no overall utility in searching for or evaluating alternatives to the course of action that has presented itself.[28]

---

28. MacDonald, "Practical Reasoning," 143.

Christine is left with two means: (1) deliberation itself, and (2) taking the chocolate. For the sake of clarity, we will refer to deliberation as means1 and the conclusion of deliberation (for example, taking the chocolate) as means2. Both means are presented as good only tentatively. The three features of reason have left the will undetermined in multiple ways with no evident manner of reaching determination.

In the next three sections, we will see how the impasse might be broken and how the will itself might break the impasse by bending back upon itself. The will, like the intellect, bends back upon itself, willing its own acts of will. While Aquinas unquestionably affirms this feature of the will, he does not connect it with the freedom of the will. Precisely this feature of the will, however, will prove necessary to move beyond the impasse that reason presents.

FALLING DOMINOES

How can the agent break the impasse? How can the agent cease judging tentatively and move to an all-out or conclusive judgment? How can Christine cease judging that it is *probably* good to take the chocolate and begin judging, instead, that it is good, simply speaking, to take the chocolate?

Previously, we have seen that when the evidence is inconclusive, reason itself is unable to reach firm assent; it must judge tentatively or with probability. In such situations, the move to firm assent requires the intervention of the will. Reason by itself will judge the case by the evidence, which is inconclusive. It seems, then, that the impasse can be broken only with some special act of will, moving the intellect to an all-out judgment. Unfortunately, every act of will must be preceded by some act of the intellect, and in this situation the intellect is not firm but tentative. The needed act of will, then, lacks the necessary precondition in the intellect.

I wish to suggest that the impasse is not broken by some new act of will. Rather, the impasse is broken by the cessation of an ongoing act of will. At the moment of the impasse, the agent is in fact firmly intending means1 (to deliberate). At the moment of the impasse, she has reached a tentative conclusion concerning means2 (for example, to eat the chocolate), which is not yet intended. If the ongoing intention of means1 (to deliberate) continues, then the deliberation will also continue and the agent will not choose the proposed means2.[29] If her current intention ceases, however, then she will cease to deliberate. And if she ceases to deliberate, then she will accept her current conclusion as definitive.

Alan Donagan makes a similar suggestion: "Given that you have elected to gratify a certain wish, [and that] you can gratify it in such and such a way, [then,] if you do not wish to inquire whether there is a better way, your practical question is answered."[30] Indeed, he goes so far as to say that if you have found some means that satisfies your goals, and if you judge that there is no need to inquire further, that is, if there is no further need for deliberation, then you cannot consistently reject the proposed means.[31]

What is key, then, is the cessation of deliberation. Or rather, prior yet is the cessation of the ongoing intention to deliberate. When this intention ceases, a series of events follows, like a series of falling dominoes. The cessation of the intention to deliberate effectively dismisses the importance of anything that further deliberation might discover. The current judgment is tentative because more evidence might suggest an alternate conclusion. If that (potential) further evidence is set aside as irrelevant, then the current judgment can be maintained firmly, without worry concerning some contrary conclusion. The potential evidence is indeed deemed irrelevant by the very cessation of the intention to deliberate. By this cessation, then, the means2 changes from being proposed tentatively and now comes to be proposed conclusively.

Christine has reached the tentative judgment that she can satisfy her desire to enjoy sweets by taking this chocolate before her and eating it. Within this same judgment, she recognizes that further deliberation might reveal a different and better means2, or it might reveal that this means2 is in fact defective. If she ceases her current intention for means1 (to deliberate), then she dismisses these possible alternatives as irrelevant for her goal. Once these alternatives have been dismissed, then the current judgment ceases to be tentative; that which made it tentative is no longer relevant.

This change in judgment, from a tentative judgment to an all-out judg-

---

29. As Perkams says, if the will does not intervene, then it leaves the infinite process of deliberation to continue unattended ("Aquinas on Choice," 88).

30. Donagan, *Choice*, 94.

31. Ibid., 136.

ment, leads to further changes in the will. Since the conclusion of the deliberation is no longer "in some respect," the will moves itself to will the means2. Christine, for instance, by willing the end of enjoying sweets, moves herself—by way of the now conclusive deliberation—to will the means of picking up the chocolate (rather than the caramel). Finally, the will moves the body to execute, that is, Christine actually picks up the chocolate.

The analogy with the dominoes is not quite accurate. In a series of dominoes, each by itself stands on its own, and some external force pushes it over. The first domino is pushed by a finger, or some such thing, and subsequent dominoes are pushed by prior dominoes. In the case of the impasse, what we have is more like a domino that is tending to fall but is propped up by some object. When that object is removed, then the domino falls.

The domino that is ready to fall (but prevented by some obstacle) is the judgment of the proposed means2. It is tending to an all-out judgment, but an obstacle prevents it from becoming all-out. The obstacle is the possibility of contra-indicating evidence. Further evidence might reveal that the proposed means2 is inadequate. This potential further evidence, then, prevents the judgment from becoming all-out. If the potential further evidence can be removed, then the judgment will follow its tendency and become an all-out judgment. This potential further evidence itself, however, is kept in place by the intention for means1 (to deliberate), which is precisely the intention to examine potential evidence concerning the goal. If the intention ceases, then the potential further evidence is removed—being dismissed as irrelevant—and the judgment can become all-out.

HOW TO CEASE DELIBERATING

The impasse will be broken, then, when the intention to deliberate ceases. But when will this intention cease? One obvious possibility is that the person judges that he should cease deliberating. We certainly do make such judgments. After thinking over some choice, looking at it from various angles, considering the pros and cons, we come to the judgment that we need think no further on the matter; we have covered all that is likely to prove relevant. We make what Davidson calls an "all things considered" judgment.

For two reasons, however, all-things-considered judgments appear inadequate to resolve the impasse. First, we do not pass such judgments for every choice we make; we do not always consider whether we have considered all the relevant evidence. More importantly, these judgments themselves are tentative. As Davidson says, all-things-considered judgments are still prima facie judgments; they are not all-out.[32] When we judge that we have considered the matter well enough, we recognize (with a meta-judgment) that we remain uncertain: we may not have considered the matter sufficiently. Reason is left unable to bring closure to its own deliberations. Even when it attains a high measure of certainty, some doubt remains.

Reason is unable to break the impasse on its own, and it seems that the will must intervene. As Perkams notes, practical reason is incomplete, such that it cannot issue all-things-considered judgments (Davidson's all-out judgments) that leave no room for the will.[33] Whatever reason may do, the will must make the final movement. Thomas leaves little doubt on the matter.

Choice is the final acceptance by which something is to be pursued, which acceptance does not belong to reason but to the will. For however much reason prefers one thing to another, it is not accepted for action until the will is inclined into one more than into the other, for the will does not follow of necessity upon reason. Nevertheless, choice is not an act of the will separated from reason but together with the order to reason, for within choice is found that which is proper to reason, namely, to relate one to another, or to prefer.[34]

The cessation of the will's ongoing intention, then, must ultimately depend upon the will itself. Unfortunately, it is unclear how Aquinas's own principles allow for such independence of the will. As we have seen, the will itself has no movement except following upon the judgment of reason.

32. Davidson, "How Is Weakness of Will Possible?" 40.
33. Perkams, "Aquinas on Choice," 87.
34. Aquinas, De veritate, q. 22, a. 15 (Editio Leonina, XXII.3: 649, ll. 49–59): "Electio enim est ultima acceptio qua aliquid accipitur ad prosequendum; quod quidem non est rationis sed voluntatis, nam quantumcumque ratio unum alteri praefert, nondum est unum alteri praeacceptatum ad operandum, quousque voluntas inclinetur in unum magis quam in aliud; non enim voluntas de necessitate sequitur rationem. Est tamen electio actus voluntatis non absolute sed in ordine ad rationem, eo quod in electione apparet id quod est proprium rationis, scilicet conferre unum alteri vel praeferre."

If reason does not cause the cessation of intention, then what does? How can the will be sufficient to terminate its own intention? We will turn our attention from judgment, which is an act of reason, to satisfaction (or enjoyment), which is an act of the will. When the will is satisfied, then the intention will cease. An intention ceases when its goal is achieved (or when the achievement is deemed impossible). Christine's intention to go to the grocery store (to buy some chocolate) ceases when she actually gets to the grocery store. Likewise, the intention to deliberate will cease when its goal is achieved, or at least when the will is satisfied that it has been achieved.

What is the goal of this deliberation? The goal that initially gives rise to the deliberation is some desired good. Christine, for instance, desires to enjoy sweets, so she then deliberates in order to achieve this goal. We should not get distracted by this initial goal, however, for it is not the immediate goal of deliberation itself. Christine first wants to enjoy sweets. She then recognizes that she must become aware of how to enjoy sweets. She then recognizes that she must deliberate in order to attain this crucial awareness. The immediate goal of her deliberation, then, is not the enjoyment of sweets (although this is the remote goal); rather, the immediate goal is the attainment of knowledge concerning how to enjoy sweets. When this knowledge is attained, then her intention to deliberate will cease. To avoid confusion we will adopt the convention of labeling the first goal (that gives rise to deliberation, for example, the desire for sweets) as $goal_1$ and labeling the second goal (of gaining knowledge about how to achieve $goal_1$) as $goal_2$.

At the moment of the impasse, the agent has several simultaneous goals. Christine, for instance, desires to enjoy sweets ($goal_1$); she further intends to gain knowledge about how to enjoy sweets ($goal_2$); then she yet further intends to deliberate, for deliberation is the means by which she will gain $goal_2$. Most precisely, she intends to gain knowledge ($goal_2$) by way of deliberation, for intention—by its nature—is for some goal by way of a means.[35] $Goal_2$ is the gaining of knowledge; the means is deliberation.

$Goal_2$ is a universal goal, that is, it is like the house with no determinate shape. What is sought is knowledge, but the determinate contours

---

35. Aquinas, *Summa theologiae* I-II, q. 12, a. 4, ad 3.

of that knowledge are left open. Consequently, the resulting desire can be called a general desire. Just as Christine can have a general desire for sweets, without yet determining what kind of sweets, so she can have a general desire to gain knowledge about how to enjoy sweets, without yet determining the precise nature of that knowledge. And just as chocolates and caramels are particular instances of sweets, each of which partially realizes Christine's general desire, so any knowledge of diverse means (means2) to the enjoyment of sweets—such as eating chocolate, eating caramel, and so on—is a particular instance of the universal goal2 (to gain knowledge), each of which partially realizes the general desire.

The intention to gain knowledge ceases when that knowledge is in fact gained. Awareness of some particular means (for example, eating chocolate) is itself a partial realization of goal2. As we have seen, however, reason is inadequate to determine whether this partial realization is sufficient. Its judgment remains tentative. More information might reveal that the universal good of goal2 (to gain knowledge about how to enjoy sweets) is better realized in some other conclusion.

In short, the intention to gain knowledge has some grounds for ceasing but not decisive grounds. The general goal (knowing the means) has been reached tentatively and to some extent. As such, the intention to deliberate might cease but it might also continue. The tentative nature of the judgments of reason leave the will in the following state. It is actively intending to deliberate, for, previously, reason has judged that deliberation is needed for the goal. While it actively intends to deliberate, it is also partially satisfied that goal2 (of attaining knowledge) has been achieved. While it intends to deliberate, then, it also has some reason to cease deliberating.

The movement of the will, or the cessation of movement, depends upon whether or not the person is satisfied that goal2 has been reached. If he is not sufficiently satisfied, then he will continue to intend to deliberate. If he is sufficiently satisfied, then he will cease to intend to deliberate, for when goal2 has been achieved, intention ceases.

The agent will have some degree of satisfaction, for goal2 has been attained to some degree, that is, the agent has obtained some awareness about how to achieve goal1. Is this measure of satisfaction sufficient? Christine, for instance, has attained some knowledge about how to enjoy sweets, and she is somewhat satisfied with this knowledge. Is her desire for knowledge (goal2) fully satisfied, such that she can cease deliberation? Reason cannot say. Only her desire can determine the matter.

The standard has shifted. Deliberation is concerned with truth, with answering the following question: Is this action truly a means to goal1? Consequently, deliberation is also concerned with certainty. How certain is this judgment concerning the means? In contrast, the will is not a knowing power. It does not judge truth or certainty. Rather, it desires the good. Reason queries how *certain* is the conclusion of deliberation. The will seeks the *good* of the conclusion of deliberation. Is it good enough to satisfy the desire for knowledge?

The will can be satisfied with the conclusions of deliberation in diverse ways. The will seeks knowledge, and the good of knowledge is truth, so it can be more or less satisfied depending upon the measure of truth or certainty. If reason is quite certain of the conclusion of deliberation, then the will can be more satisfied in this truth.

Truth, however, is not the only good by which the will may be satisfied. The immediate goal2 of deliberation is the truth concerning the means, but the remote goal1 is the further end that gave rise to the deliberation. The conclusion of deliberation, then, might be good not only insofar as it is true; it might be good insofar as it achieves goal1. Christine might find satisfaction in the conclusion because it gets her closer to the enjoyment of sweets. This good can apply to the conclusion even if it has doubtful truth.

Other goals might come into play as well. If Christine is worried that the chocolate belongs to someone else, then she might find the conclusion of her deliberation—that is, "pick up the chocolate"—unsatisfactory because of her goal of respecting others.

On top of all this, we must keep in mind that the deliberation itself can be perceived as an obstacle, since continued deliberation will prevent the timely acquisition of the good (goal1). If Christine wants to enjoy the chocolate *now*, then continued deliberation will be averse to her. Consequently, the current conclusion of deliberation will be that much more satisfying to her. The more urgent her desire to enjoy the chocolate, the more satisfying her current conclusion becomes.[36] As Joseph Caulfield

---

36. Caulfield, "Practical Ignorance," 75.

says, "If this goodness, however limited, actually pleases the will, the latter [that is, the pleasing] will bring the reason to limit its consideration to [this limited goodness], and to ignore the other aspects of the thing."[37]

Depending upon all of these factors, Christine will have some measure of satisfaction with the conclusions of her deliberation. This satisfaction gives some warrant for ceasing her intention to deliberate. As we have seen, however, reason cannot determine whether the warrant is sufficient. With her will, Christine must accept the conclusion as satisfactory or reject it and continue deliberating.

But from where can this act of will arise? From some prior judgment of reason (such as, "this conclusion is sufficiently satisfactory")? If this prior judgment is itself tentative (as is typically the case), then the act of will does not follow. If this prior judgment is conclusive, then in fact the cessation of the intention to deliberate does not depend upon the will but depends upon the conclusive judgment of reason. Unfortunately, reason does not typically have the evidence to reach this conclusive judgment. Apparently, the impasse remains.

THE WILL BENDS BACK UPON ITSELF

We can break the impasse by using a doctrine that Thomas himself does not explicitly apply to free decision. The will shares reason's capacity to bend back upon itself. Just as a single act of reason can know the conclusion of deliberation, can know that it is tentative, and can know that the conclusion is a means to the end, so a single act of will can have diverse movements corresponding to the diversity in the judgment of reason.

Thomas clearly affirms the capacity of the will to bend back upon its own actions. He says, for instance, "Because the acts of the will bend back upon themselves, in a single act of will may be found consent, choice, and use, so that we may say that the will consents to choose, and that it consents to consent, and that it uses itself to consent and to choose."[38] Elsewhere, he draws a clear parallel with reason knowing that it knows, indicating that

37. Ibid.
38. Aquinas, *Summa theologiae* I-II, q. 16, a. 4, ad 3: "Quia actus voluntatis reflectuntur supra seipsos, in quolibet actu voluntatis potest accipi et consensus, et electio, et usus, ut si dicatur quod voluntas consentit se eligere, et consentit se consentire, et utitur se ad consentiendum et eligendum."

the will enjoys that it enjoys: "Just as there are not two ends, God and the enjoyment of God, by the same reasoning, it is the same act of enjoyment by which we enjoy God and by which we enjoy our enjoyment of God."[39]

These texts leave no doubt that the will bends back upon itself. Furthermore, in a single act of will, Thomas affirms diverse kinds of actions. He says that in a single action the will consents to choose or that it uses itself to consent. This diversity was evident in the previous discussion concerning the partial satisfaction of the goal2 intended. The agent intends to gain knowledge concerning the means, and has reached a partial realization of this goal2. At the same time as he intends this goal2, then, he is partially satisfied in goal2 (or takes enjoyment). By a single action, reason presents both goal2 (gaining knowledge) and a partial realization of this goal2 (this particular instance of knowledge); in the same action, then, the goal is presented as something to be attained and as something partially attained. The will can respond to this dual presentation—in a single action—with the continued intention to gain knowledge and with partial enjoyment in that which has already been realized.

If intention and satisfaction can coexist in a single action, then also intention and intention can coexist. The will can intend to intend, even as Aquinas affirms that the will can consent to consent. So long as the realization of the goal is only partly satisfactory, the agent intends to intend to deliberate, which is not an action distinct from intending to deliberate.

How can this capacity of the will to bend back upon itself break the impasse? By eliminating the need for a new act of will. The will can intend to deliberate and can intend to intend to deliberate in a single action. With no additional action, the will can cease this intention. Someone who drives to the grocery store does not, when he arrives at the store, perform a new act of "ceasing to drive." Rather, the action ceases because it is complete. Similarly, intention ceases when its object is achieved, and its object is achieved when the will is satisfied with the object. At that point, the intention ceases, with no new action needed. As we have already seen, once the intention ceases, the impasse is broken. The will (by the cessation of its activity) effectively moves the intellect to disregard possible further evidence, thereby leading the intellect to judge conclusively that the proposed

---

39. Ibid., I-II, q. 11, a. 3, ad 3: "Sicut igitur non est alius finis Deus, et fruitio Dei; ita eadem ratio fruitionis est qua fruimur Deo, et qua fruimur divina fruitione."

means should be pursued. Upon this all-out judgment follows a new act of will, namely, choice. The will has begun by desiring some end, has moved the intellect to deliberate, and now moves itself to choose the means.

Every new act of will follows upon an act of the intellect, and that new act of will receives its character from the judgment of the intellect. The cessation of an act of will, however, is not a new act of will. It requires no prior conclusive judgment of reason. The will bends back upon itself to cease its own action. The intellect begins the action by judging that deliberation is necessary to attain the goal. The will then begins to intend to deliberate and moves reason to the act of deliberation. When deliberation reaches a conclusion, then reason is aware that the deliberation itself is not strictly necessary. As such, the will, bending back upon itself, can cease to intend to deliberate, thereby adding no new act of will. The will ceases deliberation when it is sufficiently satisfied with the achievement of goal$_2$ (that is, knowledge of the means). This satisfaction is not a distinct act of the will, but coincides with the intention to attain the goal.

The will, then, does not move itself to some new act independent of reason. Nevertheless, the will has a certain independence from reason. It can continue its own action or cease its action of its own accord, requiring no new action. Whichever it does (continue deliberation or cease to intend to deliberate), it does for some reason. It may continue its intention to deliberate on account of a desire for a more satisfactory knowledge of the means, or it may cease to intend to deliberate on account of the satisfaction in the means$_2$ presented. The continuation or cessation of intention, then, is not a random uncaused event; it is not inexplicable but is grounded in solid reasons. Nevertheless, it is not determined by reason. The intention ceases because the act of intention bends back upon itself for its cessation.

What reason presents to the will is ultimately inconclusive, not necessitating the will. It becomes conclusive only when the will itself accepts the means presented as sufficiently satisfying. As Thomas expresses the matter, "Choice brings together something on the part of a knowing power and something on the part of a desiring power. On the part of the knowing power, deliberation is required, through which it is judged that one thing is to be preferred to another. On the part of the appetitive power, that which has been judged through deliberation must be received by the appetite."[40]

40. Ibid., I, q. 83, a. 3: "Ad electionem autem concurrit aliquid ex parte cognitivae vir-

If the person rejects the proposed means and continues to deliberate, then reason may discover some alternate means2, which in its turn must be accepted or rejected. If the alternate means2 is rejected, then deliberation continues, perhaps suggesting yet another means2 or perhaps returning to the first proposed means2. So it must continue until the will is satisfied with the knowledge gained, such that it ceases to intend to deliberate.

Free decision, then, always operates with the binary options of continuing deliberation or ceasing deliberation, but the continuation of deliberation offers more than binary choices.[41] As MacDonald expresses the matter: "Free choice is grounded not so much in an irreducible ability to *choose* between alternatives ... as in an irreducible ability to give oneself alternative reasons for acting."[42]

Free choice, then, is located most precisely in the ability of the will to continue deliberation or cease deliberation.[43] By continuing deliberation, the proposed means is rejected, at least temporarily. By ceasing deliberation, the proposed means is accepted.

For this reason, medieval thinkers called free will *liberum arbitrium*, which might be rendered "free decision," or even "free judgment." The emphasis does not lie with the will but with judgment. Everything hangs upon this judgment. Will it be accepted as satisfactory or not? It is free because the satisfaction cannot be reached conclusively, so that the will can continue deliberating or cease deliberating, depending upon how pleased the person is with the judgment.

---

tutis, et aliquid ex parte appetitivae, ex parte quidem cognitivae, requiritur consilium, per quod diiudicatur quid sit alteri praeferendum; ex parte autem appetitivae, requiritur quod appetendo acceptetur id quod per consilium diiudicatur."

41. The free decision advocated by Aquinas, then, is not the limited freedom of the power to veto reason that Hause criticizes; see Hause, "Thomas Aquinas and the Voluntarists," 171–76.

42. MacDonald, "Practical Reasoning," 158.

43. Loughran suggests that the freedom of exercise is a freedom to continue considering or to will the means ("Freedom and Good," 426). Gallagher suggests that the freedom of the will lies in the freedom to decide about one's decisions or judgments ("Thomas Aquinas on the Will as Rational Appetite," 573). Likewise, MacDonald suggests the possibility that the will controls its own choices by controlling whether or not to deliberate further ("Aquinas's Libertarian Account," 321). Pasnau says, "To have a free decision is to be capable of second-guessing, to be able to contemplate whether our first inclination is really right, or whether we might be better off doing things in another way" (*Thomas Aquinas on Human Nature*, 218).

CHAPTER 15

CHOOSE LIFE

In every sin is found some ignorance. The human heart is not made for evil. It has no capacity to turn toward evil. In all that it does, it strives after the good. When it seeks evil, it seeks what in fact is evil but under some apprehension of good. The adulterer chooses an evil action, but he perceives it as good insofar as it is pleasurable. His misperception—his ignorance or ignoring—is not without blame. He is ignorant because he wants to be ignorant. At the very least, he does not want knowledge of the true good badly enough. He prefers to act without the knowledge.

Even someone with a good will still might be enticed toward evil. Because he has a good will, he does not choose to be ignorant, but his limited mind places him in situations where he does not know—or at least he does not think upon—all that he needs to know. He is faced with the option of choosing the present good, with his limited knowledge, or pursuing a deeper understanding of the good. If he chooses without knowledge, then his lack of thought becomes ignoring, or deliberate lack of thought. What was ignorance arising from the limitation of his mind becomes ignorance arising from the impulse of his will.

The presence of ignorance in every sin is demanded by Aquinas's insistence that the will is a single nature with a single object, namely, the overall good of the individual. If the will has multiple natures, or multiple autonomous desires, then ignorance becomes unnecessary. If the will has a desire for justice that is entirely independent from its desire for what is advantageous, then a person might choose what is advantageous at the sacrifice of what is just, fully aware in all respects of what he is doing. Or if the will has an independent desire for each separate inherent good, with no overarching good that unites them all, then one desire might happen to trump another desire. Someone might sacrifice the good of religion, for which he has an independent desire, while choosing the good of play, for which he has another independent desire. This facile explanation of the choice for evil comes at great expense. The person has lost his unity, and one disjointed part of him is at odds with another. One natural desire is evil in relation to another natural desire.

If human beings truly have a single nature with its corresponding single good and its single desire for the good, then sin becomes much more perplexing. There must be some defect in the person, such that he can move out to what is evil for him. This defect is none other than the ignorance that is present in all sins.

THREE SOURCES OF IGNORANCE

This ignorance has three sources. It might arise from passion, from an evil will, or from a negligence in informing ourselves. First, the focus of our minds might become limited because of our passions. We are complex beings with a rational mind that grasps universal truths and an imagination that we use to apply these truths to concrete situations. Corresponding to reason we have desires of the will; corresponding to our imagination and senses we have desires of the emotions or passions. These passions can drag our imagination along, focusing our attention on this or that particular feature in the concrete situation. Reason is hindered, then, in applying its universal knowledge to the concrete situation. A person might know that he should not commit adultery, but he might fail to apply this knowledge to this particular act of adultery because his passions draw his attention simply to the pleasure of the action, ignoring those features that make it evil.

Despite this weakness of his mind, the person is not a slave to his passions. He can choose to examine the action more thoroughly. Perhaps if the passion is too violent, his reason may not be able to focus upon anything else. Short of such temporary insanity, however, if the person chooses to think further, then his reason can focus on other relevant features of the action, however difficult it sometimes might be. If he chooses to act without such further examination, then the limitation of his mind becomes voluntary. He has moved from a lack of awareness to ignoring. He has chosen to act without knowledge.

These sins can occur even with a will properly disposed to the true ultimate end. The person does want the divine good above all. How does he choose against the divine good? Because he is not aware, on account of the focus from his passions, that his action is opposed to the divine good. Then why is he responsible for his sin? Because he chose to act without determining the order of his act, an option that was available to him.

The defect of ignorance leading to sin can arise in a second way, from an evil habit of the will. Those who have developed a habit for evil, by repeatedly sinning, now no longer seek the true concrete end. Some other good serves as their chief good, even on a habitual basis. They can now choose an action that they clearly understand to be opposed to the divine good. They may lament this fact about the action, but ultimately they judge that it is worth pursuing nevertheless. Although the divine good is lost, they attain some other good that they prize more highly than the divine good. A person might choose adultery, for instance, recognizing that it separates him from God. He does not desire the separation in itself, any more than someone who needs an amputation desires the loss of his arm. Still, he does desire it. This loss is worth the gain of some other good.

This person who sins from an evil will has misperceived what is most central to himself. He recognizes that he is a being that can be ordered to God, but this feature, he thinks, is not most essential. Rather, he is most of all, so he thinks, an animal that can gain pleasure, or some such thing. This confusion follows upon his own evil will. He chooses to evaluate himself based upon his own predilections, rather than based upon his true nature.

Both the person who sins from passion and the person who sins from an evil will choose not to think about some inconvenient truth, but they do so in different ways. The one who sins from an evil will chooses not to think about his good; the one who sins from passion does not choose to think about his action. With an evil will, the person chooses not to think;

with passion, the person does not choose to think. The two differ as direct and indirect. With an evil will, a person directly chooses his ignorance or error; with passion, a person indirectly chooses his ignorance.

More precisely, with passion the indirect choice is also accidental, that is, the person chooses one thing upon which ignorance follows. He chooses to remain under the sway of his passions. The passion is itself the original source of the ignorance. The person merely chooses to live with this ignorance.

In this manner, a sin of passion differs from the third way in which the defect of ignorance can arise. In a sin of ignorance, the ignorance is indeed most properly indirect, with no accidental accompaniment. The person has failed to think about some matter because he prefers something else to the act of informing himself. Between the options of informing himself and doing what he likes to do, he chooses his preference, recognizing that the ignorance will follow. It was not passion that first removed the awareness from his mind; it was simply his lack of effort to think upon the matter.

In every sin, then, is found some ignorance. Indeed, in every sin is found some voluntary ignorance. What is made for good—the human will—chooses a defective good. It chooses without full knowledge of the true good.

INCONSTANCY AND NEGLIGENCE

The virtue of prudence assures properly ordered practical reason. It presupposes a desire for the true good, which serves as the principle of all further reasoning, which reasoning seeks the way to achieve this good. The process of deliberating involves three actions.[1] In the act of counsel, the person must consider his alternatives. What possible options will bring him to the true good? In the act of judgment, the person must determine which of these options is to be pursued. In the act of command, he must order himself to execute this judgment. Hamlet begins by seeking justice. He considers options, such as inaction or killing his usurping uncle. Next, he judges that he must kill his usurping uncle. Finally, he proceeds to command himself to execute the deed. The whole of practical reasoning is moving toward command as its culmination. The act of

---

1. Aquinas, *Summa theologiae* II-II, q. 47, a. 8.

command, then, is the completion of practical reasoning, and the failure in this command is the ultimate failure of practical reasoning.

Several things go wrong with Hamlet's practical reasoning. He may begin by insufficiently considering his options, which then perhaps leads to a faulty judgment. He certainly fails to proceed to command, at least until no more time remains. He hesitates, he reconsiders, he delays, and so on. These three successive acts—counsel, judging, and command—build one upon another. If the person fails to take good counsel, then his judgment will likewise be inadequate, and if he fails to make good judgment, then he will fail in command. Even if he reasons well in the first two steps, he still might fail in command.

This failure of command might take the form of one of two opposite extremes. On the one hand, the person might, like Hamlet, fail to keep to his command. On the other hand, the person might command when he should not. The first failure Aquinas calls inconstancy; the second, negligence. In inconstancy, a person makes the appropriate command, but does not stick by it; rather, he goes back and reconsiders the matter.[2] In negligence, a person fails to take the due care necessary to make an appropriate command to do what is right.[3] Instead, he commands himself to some defective deed. The two failures fit within the pattern of Aristotelian opposing vices: inconstancy involves reasoning too much; negligence involves reasoning too little. Inconstancy leads to the failure to do what is right; negligence leads to doing what is wrong (although we have seen that negligence can subsequently issue in a separate omission). On the other hand, the excessive deliberations of inconstancy might eventually issue a command lacking in consideration, that is, inconstancy might ultimately lead to negligence and an evil deed.

Given our analysis of free decision, it should be little surprise that there are two fundamentally different ways to sin. If every choice follows upon the cessation of the will to deliberate, then a person might cease deliberating when he should have deliberated further or he might continue deliberating when he should have ceased.[4] To cease deliberating pre-

---

2. Ibid., II-II, q. 53, a. 5.
3. Ibid., II-II, q. 54.
4. Dewan suggests that sin is at least sometimes pressing forward without sufficient consideration ("St. Thomas and the First Cause of Moral Evil," 195).

maturely is negligence; to deliberate unnecessarily is inconstancy, at least in tendency. As we have seen, if the person does not take the appropriate steps in deliberation, then he will not reach the correct judgment; and if he does not take care with his judgment, then he will not reach the right command. Any failure to take the appropriate care at any of the earlier stages, then, ultimately leads to negligence, a failure of the appropriate care for the act of command.

Inconstancy is a little different. Strictly speaking, inconstancy occurs when a person makes the appropriate command but does not stick by it; some temptation or concern leads him to reconsider the matter. A tendency to reconsider (or to consider what one should not consider) that occurs in the earlier stages of prudence, then, does not necessarily issue in an act of inconstancy. Rather, this over-consideration may not issue an act of command at all, or at least not the appropriate act of command. Nevertheless, we might say that these failures of over-consideration at earlier stages of deliberation reduce to the vice of inconstancy at least by similarity.

The three kinds of sin—passion, evil will, and ignorance—exhibit these two fundamental failures. Sins of ignorance always involve the failure to consider what should be considered. As such, they are prototypical instances of negligence. The negligence might result from habitual ignorance concerning relevant features of the situation.

In a sin of passion, the individual fails to consider all that he need consider concerning the action. As such, he is negligent. His passions urge him to choose, and consequently he ceases deliberating when he should continue. Sins of passion, however, can also exhibit inconstancy. If the individual does indeed reason appropriately and issue the appropriate command, then he is led, by his emotions, to reconsider his reasoning. His attention is drawn away from what is relevant toward what is pleasing to the passions. Someone might correctly judge that he should not engage in this adulterous action. Led on by his passions, however, he hesitates and reconsiders the question, this time concluding that he should do this pleasurable act.

In sins from an evil will, a person fails from prudence entirely, not even deliberating at all concerning the true ultimate end, for he has set up a false end, concerning which he deliberates. Consequently, he has the greatest negligence of all. At the same time, he has the greatest "inconstancy" in the sense described above, in that he considers matters that he should not consider; for example, he considers how he might accumulate wealth for himself. Insofar as he deliberates concerning the false end, he has something that might look like prudence, a kind of cleverness or craftiness in achieving his evil goals, but he has no true prudence at all.[5]

REACHING TOWARD THE END

Since prudence seeks to discover the proper order of one's actions to the ultimate end, a failure in prudence results in a failure of this proper order. If an individual sets aside prudence, or terminates its activity too soon, then he also sets aside the order to the ultimate end. When the ultimate end is a shared good, then a failure in prudence results in a failure of the order to the good of others. Some other good, besides the good shared with others, must take precedence. The individual sets himself up as higher or more important than the others to whom he should be united.

Only by submitting ourselves to the good shared with others, only by recognizing that we are limited parts who must contribute to the whole, can we realize that goal for which we were made. Our completion is found beyond ourselves, in a good to which we must direct our actions and our very being. That good is the divine good, in which all other goods share. Only by recognizing that our very existence is for God can we come to completion, attaining that end for which we were made.

We must order ourselves to God through our actions. First, we direct our very selves and our good to God; we belong to him. With this initial direction, all of our actions become habitually directed to God, insofar as the one who performs the action is directed to God. We must do more yet. We must direct our actions at least virtually to God. We must see how each of our good actions holds within itself a link to the divine. Further yet, we must strive, when possible, to order our actions actually to God, recognizing, at the moment of choice, a link to the divine. Sin severs us from the divine. Venial sin cuts off the virtual order to God. By mortal sin, we choose to set up another good in place of God, thereby losing even our habitual order to God.

---

5. Aquinas, *Summa theologiae* II-II, q. 55.

When we fall, cutting ourselves off from the shared good, we must turn back. We have set our eyes upon a false good; we must turn away from this false good and return to the one true good, without which nothing can be good. We must strive to direct ourselves, and everything in our lives, to this good beyond ourselves.

Moses speaks to the Israelite people, setting before them the most fundamental choice between good and evil.

> See, I have set before you this day life and good, death and evil. If you obey the commandments of the Lord your God which I command you this day, by loving the Lord your God, by walking in his ways, and by keeping his commandments and his statutes and his ordinances, then you shall live and multiply, and the Lord your God will bless you in the land which you are entering to take possession of it. But if your heart turns away, and you will not hear, but are drawn away to worship other gods and serve them, I declare to you this day, that you shall perish.... I call heaven and earth to witness against you this day, that I have set before you life and death, blessing and curse; therefore choose life, that you and your descendants may live, loving the Lord your God, obeying his voice, and cleaving to him. (Deut 30:15–20 RSV)

We must either choose for God or against God. Sin turns one from God; it sets the soul at enmity with God. It sets the creature against his creator. Sin treats the divine gifts—whether within ourselves or within others—as obstacles to be cast aside in our pursuit of self-constructed goods. God and his good cease to be the end to which we strive; they become the evil we flee. We cry, with Milton's Satan, "Evil, be thou my good."

The choice for death and evil is not only a choice against God; it is a choice against our own good. We prefer what we know to be evil so that we can gain a fleeting appearance of good. While sinning, we strain to grasp our own fulfillment, yet we know, at heart, that our action is ultimately self-destructive.

Choose life or choose death. There is no middle ground. Where do our hearts lie? With God or with creatures? We must set ourselves either toward God or toward some faint substitute. By turning toward one, we turn away from the other. We are offered no compromise, by which we might have a little bit of God and a little bit of creaturely good. Our entire being must strive, in all its goods, to the one, true, divine good.

BIBLIOGRAPHY

PRIMARY SOURCES

Aristotle. *Nicomachean Ethics*. Translated by Terence Irwin. Indianapolis, Ind.: Hackett, 1985.

Thomas Aquinas. *In Duodecim libros Metaphysicorum Aristotelis exposition*. Taurini-Rome: Marietti, 1950.

———. *Opera omnia iussu Leonis XIII P. M.* 50 vols. Rome: Editori di San Tommaso, 1982–2014.

———. *Quaestiones disputatae*. Vol. 3. Taurini-Rome: Marietti, 1925.

———. *Scriptum super Sententiis magistri Petri Lombardi*. 3 vols. Edited by P. Mandonnet and M. F. Moos. Paris: P. Lethielleux, 1929–47.

———. *Super epistolas S. Pauli lectura*. Vol. 1. Taurini-Rome: Marietti, 1953.

SECONDARY SOURCES

Anscombe, G. E. M. *Intention*. 2nd ed. Ithaca, N.Y.: Cornell University Press, 1963.

Ardagh, David W. "Aquinas on Happiness: A Defense." *New Scholasticism* 53 (1979): 428–59.

Augustine. *Confessions*. Translated by Henry Chadwick. New York: Oxford University Press, 1991.

Barnwell, Michael. "Aquinas's Two Different Accounts of Akrasia." *American Catholic Philosophical Quarterly* 84 (2010): 49–67.

———. *The Problem of Negligent Omissions: Medieval Action Theories to the Rescue*. Leiden: Brill, 2010.

———. "The Problem with Aquinas's Original Discovery." *American Catholic Philosophical Quarterly* 89 (2015): 277–91.

Bowlin, John R. "Psychology and Theodicy in Aquinas." *Medieval Philosophy and Theology* 7 (1998): 129–56.

Bradley, Denis J. M. "Thomas Aquinas on Weakness of Will." In *Weakness of Will from Plato to the Present*, edited by Tobias Hoffmann, 82–114. Washington, D.C.: The Catholic University of America Press, 2008.

Bratman, Michael E. *Intentions, Plans, and Practical Reason*. Cambridge, Mass.: Harvard University Press, 1987.

Brickhouse, Thomas C. "Does Aristotle Have a Consistent Account of Vice?" *Review of Metaphysics* 57 (2003): 3–23.

Brock, Stephen L. "Realistic Practical Truth." *Doctor Communis* (2008): 62–75.

Butera, Giuseppe. "On Reason's Control of the Passions in Aquinas's Theory of Temperance." *Medieval Studies* 68 (2006): 133–60.

Cajetan, Thomas De Vio. *Commentaria in Summam Theologicam S. Thomas Aquinatis*. Rome: Editori di San Tommaso, 1892.

Caulfield, Joseph. "Practical Ignorance in Moral Actions." *Laval théologique et philosophique* 7 (1951): 69–122.

Celano, Anthony J. "The Concept of Worldly Beatitude in the Writings of Thomas Aquinas." *Journal of the History of Philosophy* 25 (1987): 215–26.

Colvert, Gavin T. "Aquinas on Raising Cain: Vice, Incontinence and Responsibility." *Proceedings of the American Catholic Philosophical Association* 71 (1997): 203–20.

Dahm, Brandon. "Distinguishing Desire and Parts of Happiness: A Response to Germain Grisez." *American Catholic Philosophical Quarterly* 89 (2015): 97–114.

Davidson, Donald. "How Is Weakness of Will Possible?" In *Essays on Actions and Events*, 21–42. Oxford: Clarendon Press, 1980.

———. "Intention." In *Essays on Actions and Events*, 84–102. Oxford: Clarendon Press, 1980.

———. "Davidson Responds: Intention and Action/Event and Cause." In *Essays on Davidson: Actions and Events*, edited by Bruce Vermazen and Merrill B. Hintikka, 195–229. Oxford: Clarendon Press, 1985.

De Koninck, Charles. *De la primauté du bien commun contre les personnalistes*. Montreal: Fides, 1943.

De Kirchner, Beatriz Bossi. "Aquinas as an Interpreter of Aristotle on the End of Human Life." *The Review of Metaphysics* 40 (1986): 41–54.

De Letter, P. "Venial Sin and Its Final Goal." *The Thomist* 16 (1953): 32–70.

Decosimo, David. *Ethics as a Work of Charity*. Stanford, Calif.: Stanford University Press, 2016.

Dewan, Lawrence. "St. Thomas and the Causes of Free Choice." *Acta Philosophica* 8 (1999): 87–96.

———. "Natural Law in the First Act of Freedom: Maritain Revisited." In *Wisdom, Law, and Virtue: Essays in Thomistic Ethics*, 221–41. Bronx, N.Y.: Fordham University Press, 2007.

———. "St. Thomas, James Keenan, and the Will." In *Wisdom, Law, and Virtue: Essays in Thomistic Ethics*, 151–74. Bronx, N.Y.: Fordham University Press, 2007.

———. "St. Thomas and the First Cause of Moral Evil." In *Wisdom, Law, and Vir-*

tue: Essays in Thomistic Ethics, 186–96. Bronx, N.Y.: Fordham University Press, 2007.

DeYoung, Rebecca Konyndyk. "The Roots of Despair." *Res Philosophica* 92 (2015): 829–54.

Di Blasi, Fulvio. "Ultimate End, Human Freedom, and Beatitude: A Critique of Germain Grisez." *American Journal of Jurisprudence* 46 (2001): 113–35.

Donagan, Alan. *Choice: The Essential Element in Human Action*. New York: Routledge and Kegan Paul, 1987.

Dougherty, M. V. "Moral luck and the Capital Vices in *De malo*: Gluttony and Lust." In *Aquinas's Disputed Questions on Evil: A Critical Guide*, edited by M. V. Dougherty, 222–34. Cambridge: Cambridge University Press, 2016.

Eardley, P. S. "Thomas Aquinas and Giles of Rome on the Will." *Review of Metaphysics* 56 (2003): 835–62.

Feingold, Lawrence. *The Natural Desire to See God According to St. Thomas Aquinas and His Interpreters*. Ave Maria, Fla.: Sapientia Press of Ave Maria University, 2010.

Froelich, Gregory. "Ultimate End and Common Good." *The Thomist* 57 (1993): 609–19.

Gagnebet, M. R. "L'amour naturel de Dieu chez saint Thomas et ses contemporains." *Revue Thomiste* 48 (1948): 394–446.

Gallagher, David M. "Thomas Aquinas on the Will as Rational Appetite." *Journal of the History of Philosophy* 29 (1991): 559–84.

———. "Free Choice and Free Judgment in Thomas Aquinas." *Archiv für Geschichte der Philosophie* 76 (1994): 247–77.

———. "Thomas Aquinas on Self-Love as the Basis for Love of Others." *Acta Philosophica* 8 (1999): 23–44.

Gardner, Patrick M. "Thomas and Dante on the *Duo Ultima Hominis*." *The Thomist* 75 (2011): 415–59.

Garrigou-Lagrange, Reginald. "La fin ultime du péché veniél." *Revue Thomiste* 29 (1924): 313–17.

Grant, W. Matthews. "Aquinas on How God Causes the Act of Sin Without Causing Sin Itself." *The Thomist* 73 (2009): 455–96.

Grice, Paul, and Judith Baker. "Davidson on 'Weakness of the Will.'" In *Essays on Davidson: Actions and Events*, edited by Bruce Vermazen and Merrill B. Hintikka, 27–49. Oxford: Clarendon Press, 1985.

Grisez, Germain. *The Way of the Lord Jesus*. Vol. 1, *Christian Moral Principles*. Chicago, Ill.: Franciscan Herald Press, 1983.

———. "Natural Law, God, Religion, and Human Fulfillment." *American Journal of Jurisprudence* 46 (2001): 3–36.

———. "The True Ultimate End of Human Beings: The Kingdom, Not God Alone." *Theological Studies* 69 (2008): 38–61.

Grisez, Germain, John Finnis, and Joseph M. Boyle. "Practical Principles, Moral Truth, and Ultimate Ends." *American Journal of Jurisprudence* 32 (1987): 99–151.

Guevara, Daniel. "The Will as Practical Reason and the Problem of Akrasia." *Review of Metaphysics* 62 (2009): 525–50.

Hardie, W. F. R. "The Final Good in Aristotle's Ethics." *Philosophy* 40 (1965): 277–95.

Hause, Jeffrey. "Thomas Aquinas and the Voluntarists." *Medieval Philosophy and Theology* 6 (1997): 167–82.

———. "Voluntariness and Causality: Some Problems for Aquinas' Theory of Responsibility." *Vivarium* 36 (1998): 55–66.

Hoffmann, Tobias, and Peter Furlong. "Free Choice." In *Aquinas's Disputed Questions on Evil: A Critical Guide*, edited by M. V. Dougherty, 56–74. Cambridge: Cambridge University Press, 2016.

Irwin, Terence. "Vice and Reason." *Journal of Ethics* 5 (2001): 73–97.

Janssens, Louis. "Ontic Evil and Moral Evil." *Louvain Studies* 4 (1972): 115–56.

Jensen, Steven J. "The Error of the Passions." *The Thomist* 73 (2009): 349–79.

———. "Omissions and Their Causes." *Acta Philosophica* 22 (2013): 117–33.

———. "Venial Sin and the Ultimate End." In *Aquinas's Disputed Questions on Evil: A Critical Guide*, edited by M. V. Dougherty, 75–100. Cambridge: Cambridge University Press, 2016.

———. "Aquinas's Original Discovery: A Reply to Barnwell." *American Catholic Philosophical Quarterly* 92 (forthcoming).

———. "Libertarian Free Decision: A Thomistic Account," *The Thomist* 81 (2017): 315–43.

Keenan, James F. "The Problem with Thomas Aquinas's Concept of Sin." *Heythrop Journal* 35 (1994): 401–20.

Kenny, Anthony. *The Aristotelian Ethics: A Study of the Relationship Between the Eudemian and Nicomachean Ethics of Aristotle*. Oxford: Clarendon Press, 1978.

Kent, Bonnie. "Transitory Vice: Thomas Aquinas on Incontinence." *Journal of the History of Philosophy* 27 (1989): 199–223.

———. *Virtues of the Will: The Transformation of Ethics in the Late Thirteenth Century*. Washington, D.C.: The Catholic University of America Press, 1995.

———. "Aquinas and Weakness of Will." *Philosophy and Phenomenological Research* 75 (2007): 70–91.

Kent, Bonnie, and Ashley Dressel. "Weakness and Willful Wrongdoing in Aquinas's *De malo*." In *Aquinas's Disputed Questions on Evil: A Critical Guide*, edited by M. V. Dougherty, 34–55. Cambridge: Cambridge University Press, 2016.

Knobel, Angela McKay. "Aquinas and the Pagan Virtues." *International Philosophical Quarterly* 51 (2011): 339–54.

Langan, John. "Sins of Malice in the Moral Psychology of Thomas Aquinas." In *The Annual of the Society of Christian Ethics*, edited by D. M. Yeager, 179–98. Washington, D.C.: Georgetown University Press, 1987.

Lee, Patrick. "The Relation between Intellect and Will in Free Choice According to Aquinas and Scotus." *The Thomist* 49 (1985): 321–42.

Lottin, Odin. *Psychologie et morale aux XIIe et XIIIe siècles*. 2nd ed. Gembloux: J. Ducolot, 1957.

Loughran, Thomas. "Freedom and Good in the Thomistic Tradition." *Faith and Philosophy* 11 (1994): 414–35.

MacDonald, Scott. "Ultimate Ends in Practical Reasoning: Aquinas's Aristotelian Moral Psychology and Anscombe's Fallacy." *The Philosophical Review* 100 (1991): 31–66.

———. "Aquinas's Libertarian Account of Free Choice." *Revue Internationale de Philosophie* 52 (1998): 309–28.

———. "Practical Reasoning and Reasons-Explanations: Aquinas's Account of Reason's Role in Action." In *Aquinas's Moral Theory: Essays in Honor of Norman Kretzmann*, edited by Scott MacDonald and Eleonore Stump, 133–60. Ithaca, N.Y.: Cornell University Press, 1998.

———. "Aquinas's Ultimate Ends: A Reply to Grisez." *American Journal of Jurisprudence* 46 (2001): 37–49.

Mansini, G. "Duplex Amor and the Structure of Love in Aquinas." In *Thomistica*, edited by E. Manning, 137–96. Leuven: Peeters, 1995.

Marín-Sola, Francisco. "The Thomist System regarding the Divine Motion." In *Do Not Resist the Spirit's Call: Francisco Marín-Sola on Sufficient Grace*, edited by Michael D. Torre, 1–55. Washington, D.C.: The Catholic University of America Press, 2013.

Maritain, Jacques. *St. Thomas and the Problem of Evil*. Translated by Lewis Galantiere and Gerald B. Phelan. Milwaukee, WI: Marquette University Press, 1942.

———. *Existence and the Existent*. Translated by Lewis Galantiere and Gerald B. Phelan. New York: Pantheon, 1948.

———. *The Range of Reason*. New York: Scribners, 1952.

———. *God and the Permission of Evil*. Translated by Joseph W. Evans. Milwaukee: The Bruce Publishing Company, 1966.

McCluskey, Colleen. "Happiness and Freedom in Aquinas's Theory of Action." *Medieval Philosophy and Theology* 9 (2000): 69–90.

———. "Intellective Appetite and the Freedom of Human Action." *The Thomist* 66 (2002): 421–56.

———. "Willful Wrongdoing: Thomas Aquinas on *certa malitia*." *Studies in the History of Ethics* 6 (2005): 1–54.

———. "Thomas Aquinas and the Epistemology of Moral Wrongdoing." In *Handlung und Wissenschaft: die Epistemologie der praktischen Wissenschaften im 13. Und 14. Jahrhundert (Action and Science: The Epistemology of the Practical Sciences in the 13th and 14th Centuries)*, edited by Matthias Lutz-Bachmann and Alexander Fidora, 107–22. Berlin: Akademie Verlag, 2008.

———. *Thomas Aquinas on Moral Wrongdoing*. Cambridge: Cambridge University Press, 2017.

McCormick, Richard A. *Ambiguity in Moral Choice*. Milwaukee: Marquette University Press, 1973.

McInerny, Ralph. *Aquinas on Human Action: A Theory of Practice*. Washington, D.C.: The Catholic University of America Press, 1992.

Müller, Jozef. "Aristotle on Vice." *British Journal for the History of Philosophy* 23 (2015): 459–77.

Murphy, Claudia Eisen. "Aquinas on Our Responsibility for Our Emotions." *Medieval Philosophy and Theology* 8 (1999): 163–205.

Osborne, Thomas M. *Love of Self and Love of God in Thirteenth-Century Ethics*. Notre Dame, Ind.: University of Notre Dame Press, 2005.

———. "Perfect and Imperfect Virtues in Aquinas." *The Thomist* 71 (2007): 39–64.

———. "The Threefold Referral of Acts to the Ultimate End in Thomas Aquinas and His Commentators." *Angelicum* 85 (2008): 715–36.

Pasnau, Robert. *Thomas Aquinas on Human Nature: A Philosophical Study of* Summa theologiae Ia 75-89. Cambridge: Cambridge University Press, 2002.

Penner, Terrence M. "Plato and Davidson: Parts of the Soul and Weakness of Will." *Canadian Journal of Philosophy* 16 (1990): 35–74.

Perkams, Matthias. "Aquinas on Choice, Will, and Voluntary Action." In *Aquinas and the Nicomachean Ethics*, edited by Tobias Hoffmann, Jörn Müller, and Matthias Perkams, 72–90. Cambridge: Cambridge University Press, 2013.

Reichberg, Gregory M. "Beyond Privation: Moral Evil in Aquinas's *De Malo*." *Review of Metaphysics* 55 (2002): 751–84.

Roochnik, David. "Aristotle's Account of the Vicious: A Forgivable Inconsistency." *History of Philosophy Quarterly* 24 (2007): 207–20.

Rousselot, Pierre. *Pour l'histoire du problème de l'amour au moyen age*. Munster: Aschendorffsche Buchhandlung, 1908.

Ryan, Peter F. "Must the Acting Person Have a Single Ultimate End?" *Gregorianum* 82 (2001): 325–56.

Schüller, Bruno. "Direct Killing/Indirect Killing." In *Moral Norms and Catholic*

Tradition, edited by Charles E. Curran and Richard A. McCormick, 138–57. Readings in Moral Theology 1. New York: Paulist Press, 1979.

Shanley, Brian J. "Aquinas on Pagan Virtue." *The Thomist* 63 (1999): 553–77.

Simon, Yves R. *Freedom of Choice*. New York: Fordham University Press, 1969.

Skrzypczak, Edmund R. "Actual, Virtual, and Habitual Intention in St. Thomas Aquinas." Master's thesis, University of Chicago, 1958.

Smith, Patricia G. "Contemplating Failure: The Importance of Unconscious Omission." *Philosophical Studies* 59 (1990): 159–76.

Spiering, Jamie Anne. "'Liber est Causa Sui': Thomas Aquinas and the Maxim 'The Free Is the Cause of Itself.'" *The Review of Metaphysics* 65 (2011): 351–76.

Steel, Carlos. "Does Evil Have a Cause? Augustine's Perplexity and Thomas's Answer." *Review of Metaphysics* 48 (1994): 275–98.

Stegman, Thomas D. "Saint Thomas Aquinas and the Problem of Akrasia." *Modern Schoolman* 66 (1989): 117–28.

Stevens, Gregory. "The Disinterested Love of God According to Saint Thomas and Some of His Modern Interpreters." *The Thomist* 16 (1953): 307–33, 497–541.

Stump, Eleonore. "Aquinas's Account of Freedom: Intellect and Will." *Monist* 80 (1997): 576–97.

Sullivan, Ezra. "Seek First the Kingdom: A Reply to Germain Grisez's Account of Man's Ultimate End." *Nova et Vetera* (English) 8 (2010): 959–95.

———. "Natural Self-Transcending Love According to Thomas Aquinas." *Nova et Vetera* (English) 12 (2014): 913–46.

Toner, Christopher. "Angelic Sin in Aquinas and Scotus and the Genesis of Some Central Objections to Contemporary Virtue Ethics." *The Thomist* 69 (2005): 79–125.

Torre, Michael D. "The Sin of Man and the Love of God." In *Jacques Maritain: The Man and His Metaphysics*, edited by John F. X. Knasas, 203–11. Notre Dame, Ind.: University of Notre Dame Press, 1988.

Westberg, Daniel. "Did Aquinas Change His Mind about the Will?" *The Thomist* 58 (1994): 41–60.

———. *Right Practical Reason: Aristotle, Action, and Prudence in Aquinas*. Oxford: Clarendon Press, 1994.

White, Thomas Joseph. "Imperfect Happiness and the Final End of Man: Thomas Aquinas and the Paradigm of Nature-Grace Orthodoxy." *The Thomist* 78 (2004): 247–89.

Williams, Thomas. "The Libertarian Foundations of Scotus's Moral Philosophy." *The Thomist* 62 (1998): 193–215.

Wippel, John F. "Metaphysical Themes in *De malo*, I." In *Aquinas's Disputed Questions on Evil: A Critical Guide*, edited by M. V. Dougherty, 12–33. Cambridge: Cambridge University Press, 2016.

INDEX

abstract consideration, 29, 135–36, 263, 265
abstraction, 9, 11–12, 17, 29, 56, 61, 104, 135–36, 139, 181, 261–63, 265
action: considered in itself, 135, 138–40, 147, 162–64, 166–68, 176, 181–82, 198, 258; exterior and interior, 195–201
adultery, 64, 122, 126–27, 129, 133, 136n27, 137, 139–40, 146–49, 153, 156–57, 159–68, 174, 179, 181–82, 188, 191, 198–99, 214–24, 229, 231, 285–87, 290
aggregate view, 14, 45–50, 53, 75, 77, 79–80, 161
Anscombe, G. E. M., 8, 11n39, 133
appetite, 33, 129, 143–44, 170, 251, 258–59, 267, 283
Ardagh, David W., 31n35, 34n45, 49n18
argument of the passions, 126–27, 130, 141, 150n29, 176
Aristophanes, 107
Aristotle, 8, 35, 42n8, 61, 63–64, 129n13, 147–48, 156, 168, 173, 183, 289
assortment view, 14, 43–46, 49, 52–54, 75, 77, 79, 161
Augustine, 1, 119
aversion, 64, 69–70, 159, 163–64, 183, 265–66

Baker, Judith, 131n15
Barnwell, Michael, 3n7, 3n10, 20n17, 136n27, 140n34, 147n19, 206n23, 207–11, 212n1, 215, 221–26, 228–33

beatific vision, 12–13, 15–16, 39, 41–42, 49, 54–56, 58–61, 64–65, 74–76, 78, 101, 103, 109–11, 113–14, 178–79
beatitude, 4, 9n35, 96n32, 244–46. *See also* happiness
belief, 145–46, 239, 266n14
Bowlin, John R., 62n44, 144n10, 239n3, 247n28
Boyle, Joseph, 42n8, 44nn11–12; 47n16, 128n11
Bradley, Denis J. M., 124n1, 129n13, 142n8, 144n10, 147n17, 149n23, 167n17, 251n41
Bratman, Michael E., 11n39, 20n16
Brickhouse, Thomas C., 173n26
Brock, Stephen L., 187n5
Butera, Giuseppe, 174n30, 227n32

Cajetan, Thomas De Vio, 88–91, 95–96
Caulfield, Joseph, 124n1, 129n13, 158n1, 161n10, 162n13, 169n19, 172n24, 188n9, 190n15, 222n24, 280
cause, 56, 60, 82, 90, 93, 97, 100, 106–7, 123, 125, 128, 140, 149, 151, 154, 169, 186–90, 192–202, 204, 206–9, 210n23, 213–14, 216–18, 220, 222, 228–29, 235–37, 240, 243n14, 249, 252, 256–57, 278, 283; dispositive, 154, 157; efficient, 151, 154, 157, 242; final, 52, 154–57; formal, 52, 154, 244, 261–62; perfective, 154, 157
Celano, Anthony J., 56n25, 60n37
choice, 1–2, 5, 7, 14, 23, 81–82, 84–85, 93,

choice (cont.)
    96, 99, 101, 109, 119, 121, 123, 126, 129,
    133, 139, 142n3, 147–48, 150, 153, 159, 161,
    164, 169–70, 175–76, 195n4, 196–97,
    200, 214, 219–24, 226–27, 229–38,
    240–41, 245, 249–51, 256–59, 267–69,
    276–77, 281, 283–84, 286, 288–89,
    291–92
Colvert, Gavin T., 149n23
compatibilism, 238–41, 245, 248, 253–59, 262
compulsive behavior, 182–84
continence, 150–53, 155–57
conversion, 69, 96n32
creature, 4–6, 12–13, 38–39, 60, 66, 69,
    85, 91–93, 105, 113–14, 219, 292

Dahm, Brandon, 15n1, 41n3, 59, 113–14
Davidson, Donald, 125n3, 127–32,
    134–35, 138, 141–43, 147, 265–67,
    276–77
Decosimo, David, 111n5
de Kirchner, Beatriz Bossi, 49n18
de Koninck, Charles, 105n1, 115n11, 117
De Letter, P., 11n41
deliberation, 8–9, 11, 20, 29, 36–37, 44,
    46, 72, 86–89, 92, 94, 97–98, 101,
    133–34, 146, 150n29, 154, 226, 231, 236,
    243, 246, 249–53, 263, 266, 267n18,
    268n22, 269–84, 288–91
desire: abstract, 29, 135, 261–63, 265;
    concrete, 29, 61, 134, 261–63, 266;
    full-fledged, 62–65, 78, 94, 96, 135, 181,
    184; natural, 5, 12, 28, 31, 53, 61–65,
    94, 118, 160, 163, 243, 286; perfect and
    imperfect, 61–64, 94, 154–56, 163, 173,
    180–81; for something in itself, 61–63,
    134, 164, 236
Dewan, Lawrence, 90–95, 97–98, 101,
    109, 212n1, 221n21, 236, 239n4, 241n7,
    267n18, 268n22, 289n4
DeYoung, Rebecca Konyndyk, 180n46

Di Blasi, Fulvio, 31n35, 46n15, 57n28,
    76n17, 82n21
direction to an end. *See* order to an end
discretion, age of, 84, 86–87, 97–98, 100
disposition, 82, 143, 150–57, 164, 170,
    172–73, 177, 182, 239, 258–59. *See also* habit
divine good. *See* good
Donagan, Alan, 75n16, 137, 142n3, 252, 275
doubt, 145, 252, 277, 280
Dougherty, M. V., 202n17
Dressel, Ashley, 142n3, 158n1, 161n10,
    173n27, 174n29, 175n32, 177n36, 178n39

Eardly, P. S., 239n3, 253, 254n51, 254n53
egoism, 100, 115–19
emotion, 125, 139–40, 156, 158, 174–75,
    261n2, 286, 290
enjoyment, 52, 55–57, 59, 71, 74, 106, 108,
    248, 273, 275–76, 278–80, 282. *See also* satisfaction

Feingold, Lawrence, 61n39, 64n47, 265n13
Finnis, John, 42n8, 44n11, 44n12, 47n16, 128n11
first moral act, 2, 5, 84–102
free decision, 240, 260–84, 289
freedom, 7, 80, 123–24, 237–39, 241,
    243–50, 252, 257–60, 262–63, 267, 272,
    274, 284n41, 284n43
Froelich, Gregory, 121n20
Furlong, Peter, 239n4, 256–57

Gagnebet, M. R., 91n19
Gallagher, David M., 91n19, 146n15,
    231n35, 239n4, 248n31, 251, 253n46,
    257n63, 261n2, 267n19, 268n22, 284n33
Gardner, Patrick M., 56n25
Garrigou-Lagrange, Reginald, 11n41
gluttony, 6

good: chief, 13, 36–37, 42–44, 47–54, 56–58, 64–65, 75–79, 81–83, 97, 110–12, 115, 122, 156, 170, 174, 181–82, 184, 200–201, 218, 222, 225, 227, 229–31, 233–36, 287; divine, 5–7, 13, 21n19, 22, 26, 32, 35, 37–39, 55, 57n28, 67–69, 74–76, 97, 99, 102–3, 105, 108, 111, 114, 121–22, 161–64, 169–70, 179–82, 234, 287, 291–92; false (or apparent), 1, 5, 13, 15, 38, 49, 52, 109, 122–23, 153, 155–56, 159, 161n11, 173, 177, 235, 290–92; in general, 9–10, 244; inherent, 14, 43–45, 48–58, 62–65, 77, 79, 109–10, 163, 236, 286; instrumental, 44, 46; in itself, 43, 45–46, 48–50, 104, 201, 222; overall, 5–6, 9–14, 24, 27–40, 42, 45–54, 56, 59–69, 74, 76–79, 81–83, 86, 94, 109, 118, 121–22, 159, 200–201, 218–19, 229–30, 234, 243–47, 285; perfect, 34, 117; shared, 14, 55–57, 59–60, 92–93, 95, 97–101, 103–23, 171, 179, 181, 234, 291–92; subject of, 45, 47, 79–80, 89, 93, 95, 102–6, 109, 113, 120, 122, 166–69, 221–22

grace, 22, 26, 37–39, 61, 65, 67, 69, 75–75, 84, 87, 94–95, 111–12, 159, 179–80

Grant, W. Matthews, 212n1, 223n25, 231n35

Grice, Paul, 131n15

Grisez, Germain, 2n5, 4n14, 15n1, 16n2, 16n5, 28, 30–32, 41–42, 43n9, 44nn11–13, 47n16, 55n23, 60n34, 64n48, 66n1, 67nn3–4, 79n18, 128n11

Guevara, Daniel, 2n6, 125n3, 148n22, 182n47

habit, 20, 21n19, 26, 126, 150, 161, 164, 174, 177–81, 212, 287

Hamlet, 288–89

happiness, 8–9, 12, 34–35, 55, 58–60, 79, 246n26; imperfect, 56–58, 60–61, 63; perfect, 28, 56, 58, 61

Hardie, W. F. R., 42n8

Hause, Jeffrey, 144n11, 195n5, 239n3, 254n52, 255–56, 257n61, 284n41

heaven, 13, 41–42, 54–55, 59–60, 63, 76n17, 112–14, 178; desire to have bodies back, 41, 54–55, 112

Hoffmann, Tobias, 239n4, 256–57

Hume, David, 238

identity, 6, 79, 81, 86, 164, 166

ignorance, 1, 3, 5, 7, 13–14, 65, 71, 125, 146–48, 159, 162, 164, 172, 185–93, 194n2, 209n31, 211, 213, 215, 218–20, 222–26, 228–30, 233, 236–38, 285–88, 290; affected, 188, 190; antecedent, 188; concomitant, 190; consequent, 149n23, 220; direct and indirect, 189, 193; invincible, 187–88, 210; voluntary and involuntary, 187–89, 192–93. *See also* sin

ill-consideration, 139–40

immortality, 61, 63, 181

inconstancy, 288–291

incontinence, 129n13, 144, 150–53, 156–57, 174, 183

intellect, 4, 11, 31, 48–49, 51, 55–59, 82, 93, 105, 120, 145–46, 159, 169, 181, 219, 237n43, 238–46, 248–49, 251–54, 260–61, 268–71, 274, 282–83

intellectualism, 238–41, 245, 247–48, 250, 253–54, 255n56, 257, 260

intention, 18n11, 19, 75n16, 87, 125, 160, 194n2, 195, 203–5, 216, 218, 237, 266, 274–79, 281–84

Irwin, Terence, 157n1, 170n21, 173n26

Janssens, Louis, 45n14

Jensen, Steven J., 17n1, 41n3, 67n2, 124n1, 143n5, 194n1, 212n1, 260n1

judgment: all-out, 135–36, 138–39, 145–46, 265–67, 271, 274–77, 283; all-things-considered, 131, 134, 137, 141, 276–77; of the passions, 126–31, judgment: of the passions (*cont.*) 140–41, 144, 146, 157; prima facie, 131, 133–35, 265–66, 271, 277; of reason, 3, 5, 126, 131–33, 137, 147–48, 157, 174, 239, 251, 253, 259, 268n22, 270, 277, 279, 281, 283; restricted, 163

Keenan, James F., 3n10, 238n1, 241n7
Kenny, Anthony, 42n8
Kent, Bonnie, 124n1, 129n13, 139n32, 142–43, 144n10, 147n19, 149–52, 154, 158n1, 161n10, 173n27, 174n29, 175n32, 177n36, 178n39, 195n4, 240n6, 245n22
Knobel, Angela McKay, 111n5
knowledge: actual and habitual, 126, 144, 147, 162, 191, 193, 210n33

Langan, John, 2n4, 158n1, 161n11, 174n28, 216n10
Lee, Patrick, 3n10, 49n19, 237n43, 239n4, 248–49, 251
libertarianism, 238–40, 245–48, 252, 254–56, 258–60, 263
Limbo, 42, 60n34, 64n48
Lottin, Odin, 241n7
Loughran, Thomas, 239n3, 253n48, 284n43
love: of concupiscence, 88–89, 107; of friendship, 88–89, 91, 107; natural, 91, 93–96, 105, 118–19, 161, 173; perfect and imperfect, 94–95, 119, 173

MacDonald, Scott, 11n39, 29n32, 31n35, 34, 38n46, 42n8, 45n14, 63n46, 138nn30–31, 239n4, 245n22, 246n23, 247nn28–29, 248n32, 253n48, 257, 267, 268n22, 273n28, 284
malice, 148n22, 158n1, 185, 212. *See also* sin, from an evil will
Mansini, G., 88n12
Marín-Sola, Francisco, 237n43

Maritain, Jacques, 85–86, 89n13, 98n34, 212n1, 215n4, 222n22, 231n35
McCluskey, Colleen, 158n1, 161nn10–11, 169n20, 172n25, 174n29, 177n36, 179n45, 191nn16–17, 192n19, 216n10, 239n3, 246n26, 249n33, 250n37, 252n43, 253n48
McCormick, Richard A., 45n14
McInerny, Ralph, 31n35, 34n45, 47n17, 49n18, 56n25
meta-judgment, 253, 267–69, 277
moral evil, 3, 5, 149, 212–15, 218, 220, 222, 226, 228, 230–32, 235–38, 256. *See also* sin
moral rule, 3, 214–15, 220–22, 224, 226, 231–32, 236–37
Moses, 292
Müller, Jozef, 173n26
Murphy, Claudia Eisen, 174n31

necessity: absolute, 133, 241; conditional, 56–58, 80, 133, 137n29, 222–23, 243–46, 271–73, 283; natural, 4, 221, 244, 247
negligence, 139n32, 144, 189, 205–9, 211, 220, 222–23, 236, 286, 288–91

object, 4–9, 11, 42, 53, 56, 61–62, 91–96, 103, 107, 113, 155, 170, 177, 200–201, 222, 225, 234, 242–45, 248, 253–54, 262–64, 270, 272, 280, 285
Oedipus, 186
omissions, 2, 5, 87, 121, 123, 150, 193–212, 216n8, 289; negligent, 20n17, 194, 206–10
opinion, 145–46, 264
order to an end, 2, 6, 8, 10, 12–14, 25, 42–46, 48–51, 53, 57, 64, 71, 73–74, 76, 79, 82, 85, 87–93, 95–100, 102–5, 108–11, 115, 119, 121–23, 137, 181, 200–201, 218, 227, 230, 234, 236, 242, 244, 252, 291–92; actual, 14, 17–24, 26, 35, 37–38, 50, 67–68, 71, 102, 104, 121,

247, 291; conscious and nonconscious, 17–20, 22–23, 50–52; explicit and implicit, 85, 90; habitual, 14, 17–24, 26, 35, 37–39, 50, 66, 68, 71, 75, 82–83, 102, 104, 121–22, 126, 287, 291; virtual, 14, 17–28, 30, 35, 37–39, 50–51, 66–69, 71, 74, 76, 82–83, 102–4, 122, 247, 291

original sin. See sin

Osborne, Thomas M., 18n11, 26n27, 91n19, 92n20, 111n5, 117, 118n16

overall good. See good

Pasnau, Robert, 239n3, 254n51, 259, 268, 284n43

passions, 5, 36, 80, 123, 126–28, 130, 139–44, 147–54, 156, 158–60, 163–64, 169, 173–74, 176–77, 182–83, 190–93, 215, 220, 286–88, 290. See also emotions

Paul, St., 90

Penner, Terrence M., 146n16

perfection, 10, 12, 58, 60, 104, 118–20, 216, 221–22

Perkams, Matthias, 239n4, 266, 275n29, 277

pleasure, 6, 9–10, 12–13, 16, 23, 31–32, 34–37, 45–46, 49, 59, 64, 68, 74–78, 81, 83, 100, 105, 109, 126–133, 139–40, 147–48, 153–57, 160–64, 169–70, 172–73, 175–76, 182–83, 215, 218–19, 234, 236, 286–87

possession of the good, 55–61, 93, 104–9, 111–17, 119–20, 167, 173, 176–77, 234, 292

practical reason, 44, 46, 79, 133, 139, 191, 266, 288–89

privation, 220–21

proposition, 130–35, 136n27, 137n29, 138, 141, 145, 168, 264

proto-sin. See sin

reason, 3, 5, 25, 56, 72, 85, 87, 94, 97, 125–33, 137, 140–58, 160, 162–63, 165–67,

169–70, 172–76, 190, 192–93, 210n33, 214–15, 232, 239, 241, 245–56, 259–65, 267–74, 277–84, 286–87, 290

Reichberg, Gregory M., 158n1, 212n1, 231n35

responsibility, 3, 5, 14, 65, 123, 127, 142–43, 146, 148–50, 152, 174, 185–89, 193–94, 202–6, 208, 210, 215, 220, 223–26, 228–30, 234–36, 238, 287

restricted consideration, 130–36, 141, 163

Roochnik, David, 173n26

Rousselot, Pierre, 91n19

Ryan, Peter F., 2n5, 4n14, 16nn2–3, 17–18, 20n14, 24, 28–32, 35, 38–39, 66n1, 67nn3–4, 73n15

Satan, 292

satisfaction. 14, 16, 41–65, 74–75, 78, 112–14, 173, 278–84

Schüller, Bruno, 45n14

Scotus, John Duns, 6n28

Shanley, Brian J., 111n5

Simon, Yves R., 263n9

sin: from an evil will, 123, 125, 129n13, 150, 158–184, 189–93, 286–88, 290; first cause of, 3, 5, 149, 212–37, 253, 256; of the heart, 174–77; of ignorance, 123, 125, 164, 174n29, 182, 185–193, 218, 288, 290; mortal, 2, 4–6, 22, 25–26, 39, 65, 68–76, 83–87, 91, 93, 100–104, 111–12, 122, 137–38, 179–81, 291; original sin, 17, 84, 87, 95, 112; of passion, 124–43, 148–50, 152–53, 158–59, 162–63, 169, 174, 176, 182, 190–93, 215, 287–88, 290; proto-sin, 213–14, 218–20, 222, 228–31, 234; venial, 3–7, 14, 16–17, 25–26, 37–39, 41n3, 65–84, 86–87, 91, 99, 101, 104, 122, 137, 177, 291; of weakness, 2, 5, 125, 139n32, 142, 146, 148n22, 150n29, 173, 176, 182, 185, 190–91

Skrzypczak, Edmund R., 18n11

Smith, Patricia G., 195n5, 206

Socrates, 1, 2n3, 7
soul, 55–56, 59, 63, 142, 148–49, 155, 165, 168, 292
Spiering, Jamie Anne, 240n5
Steel, Carlos, 2n4, 3n10, 212n1, 215n6
Stegman, Thomas D., 146n16, 149n23, 210n33, 215n4
Stevens, Gregory, 91n19
strong-set view, 14, 47–51, 53, 65, 76–81, 109–12, 122, 160, 168
Stump, Eleonore, 138n30, 239n4
Sullivan, Ezra, 15n1, 55n23, 92n20, 94n29
suspicion, 145–46, 264
syllogism, 87, 98, 136, 139, 141, 150n29, 162–63, 166–69, 180–81, 188

temporary insanity, 144, 146, 287
Toner, Christopher, 6n28
Torre, Michael D., 212n1, 221n21, 231n35, 237

ultimate end, 4–18, 21n19, 22–35, 37–38, 40–42, 52, 54, 55n23, 62, 64, 66, 69–78, 86, 101–2, 105, 112, 120–23, 138, 181, 221–22, 224–25, 227, 232, 246–47, 266, 287, 290–91; concrete realization of, 10–13, 15, 24–35, 39–40, 42, 47, 51, 53–54, 56, 58–61, 63–69, 74–75, 77–79, 82–83, 86, 91, 105, 109, 122, 151, 200

unbaptized youth, 2, 5, 84, 86, 93, 95–96, 101, 109, 112, 118–19, 121
union with others, 57, 60, 94, 106–8, 110, 117, 120–21

velleity, 62
vice, 156, 162–64, 166–74, 176–77, 179–83, 191, 289–90
vision of God. *See* beatific vision
voluntarism, 239n3, 240–41, 245, 254n52

weakness, 17, 82, 124–28, 129n13, 140–43, 144n10, 147–49, 177, 183–84, 213, 286
weakness of will, 128, 131, 137, 141–57
weak-set view, 14, 76–79, 81, 109–12, 180
Westberg, Daniel, 128n11, 241n7
White, Thomas Joseph, 56n25, 64n47
will, 1, 3–9, 12, 14, 20, 28n29, 31–32, 35, 50, 52–53, 61–62, 65, 89, 91, 96n32, 103–4, 108, 111, 118–19, 123–25, 127, 129n13, 131–32, 137, 141, 159–61, 163–66, 169–73, 175, 177–78, 182, 186, 188–93, 195–98, 200–201, 203–7, 209, 211–15, 218–20, 228–32, 234, 237–38, 285–90; free will, 3, 146, 214, 238–84
Williams, Thomas, 239n3, 251n41, 253n49, 262n6, 263n8
Wippel, John F., 212n1, 216n9, 231n35

Zechariah, 87, 95

꙳ *Sin: A Thomistic Psychology* was designed in Adobe Jenson and composed by Kachergis Book Design of Pittsboro, North Carolina. It was printed on 60-pound Natural Eggshell and bound by McNaughton & Gunn of Saline, Michigan.

www.ingramcontent.com/pod-product-compliance
Lightning Source LLC
Chambersburg PA
CBHW031407290426
44110CB00011B/293